THREE MASTER BUILDERS AND ANOTHER

Solness : . . . I am building a new home for myself—just opposite here. . . . It is almost finished. And on that there is a tower.

Hilda : A high tower ? . . .

Solness : No doubt people will say it is too high—too high for a dwelling-house.

IBSEN—*The Master Builder*, Act i

THREE MASTER BUILDERS AND ANOTHER

STUDIES IN MODERN REVOLUTIONARY AND LIBERAL STATESMANSHIP

BY

PELHAM H. BOX

ASSISTANT LECTURER IN MODERN HISTORY AT THE UNIVERSITY OF ST ANDREWS

WITH AN INTRODUCTION BY

ERNEST BARKER

PRINCIPAL OF KING'S COLLEGE, LONDON

Essay Index Reprint Series

BOOKS FOR LIBRARIES PRESS
FREEPORT, NEW YORK

First Published 1925
Reprinted 1968

LIBRARY OF CONGRESS CATALOG CARD NUMBER:
68-22904
PRINTED IN THE UNITED STATES OF AMERICA

TO MY FATHER

PREFACE

I OWE some words of explanation why I have selected these four political figures for study, and not others. The choice was not fortuitous. I had in mind the presentation of two protagonists on either side of the present great debate of liberalism and anti-liberalism, democracy and anti-democracy.

President Wilson may be regarded as a representative of liberalism and the liberal tradition which in its international aspect created the League of Nations. Venizelos is the type of liberalism operating on a national stage and for national ends. Mr Bagger has called him of the house and lineage of the nineteenth-century National Liberals. This may be true; not however the inference that Venizelos is a statesman born out of due time. A problem was presented to him such as faced Cavour: the achievement of national unity as the supreme issue before the nation. President Masaryk is such another.

Lenin similarly may be regarded as the head and forefront of the anti-liberal and anti-democratic reaction working on an international scale. Though he proclaimed "the dictatorship of the proletariat" as the forerunner of a new democracy, yet the democracy of the liberal tradition he was never tired of denouncing as the last of hypocrisies, and its international manifestation, the League of Nations, as a predatory alliance of imperialists. Of course, this is not the only aspect from which the great Russian can be regarded. As I have endeavoured to show, he was more national than he suspected. But that he was the embodiment of an international anti-liberal reaction is not the less certain.

Mussolini, on the other hand, is, in a very different way, the personification of the anti-liberal reaction operating on a national scale. Fascismo is in origin the desperate reaction of national feeling denied and insulted by the revolution directed from Moscow. The triumph of Fascist over Communist violence in Italy converted this nationalism into a vehement anti-Liberal reaction. Mussolini would at least join Lenin in the assertion that the liberal tradition is now a sham, whatever it may once have been. He has labelled it "Nineteenth Century." That apparently is enough to condemn it.

These antitheses may be felt to be incomplete, since Venizelos can also be regarded as a revolutionary. Indeed, Mr Lansing has testified that the only cloud that ever came between him and a thorough appreciation of Venizelos was his occasional recollection that the great Cretan had been in continual rebellion against constituted authority—even against that of the Sultan Abdul Hamid. This observation tells us more about Mr Lansing than it does about Venizelos; but it raises conveniently the question when and how a revolutionary can also be a constructive statesman.

Can Lenin and Mussolini be regarded as builders of substantial political edifices in the same way in which Wilson and Venizelos can be so regarded? Although there can be no final judgment, a provisional answer may be attempted.

In the case of Russia, the traditional Government, as the result of a disastrous war and of its own superhuman incompetence and corruption, collapsed suddenly; and with its fall, the whole fabric of constituted authority began to crumble away. The efforts of the Russian Liberals to arrest the disintegration failed lamentably, for psychological reasons that I have endeavoured to emphasize. The advent of Lenin was the success of a man who has known how to shoot the rapids of a revolution that he did not make. He had at first no desire to calm the tumult that was raging in the land, rather he tended in a characteristically Russian way to regard the work of destruction as in itself of positive significance, a holy work, and a casting down of idols, implying the simultaneous triumph of his faith. This attitude of mind—which may be called apocalyptic—was his strength; because without it he would never have made his voice heard above the clamour. His belief in revolution, and world-revolution, as in itself creative, proves him to have been sufficiently far removed from Marxian thought: because he chose to use a certain terminology and had a gift for polemics, he does not thereby qualify to be regarded as a scientific thinker.

But the essential point is that he and his party found themselves, as the result of an unparalleled convulsion, and of their own sublime self-confidence, the sole possible centre of authority and reconstruction in Russia. Their opponents, whom they so ruthlessly cut off, had had their day of power, and had not known how to use it; Russia was in ruins; whatever then the Bolsheviks did that has given the State some semblance of a new existence will probably pass into the fabric of the future Russia. The system of Soviets, a spontaneous creation of the revolution, has been organized by the Bolsheviks who work the machine they have created. But the machine would work without them. This possibility

Lenin divined, and he regarded it frankly as a danger. "The Communist Party," he declared, "must refuse to allow itself to be Sovietized." But in view of what Mr Farbman has called "the transformation of the Communist Party," can it avoid the fate of being absorbed into its own system? Sooner or later the vast moral energy of the Russian Communists must expend itself; their successors will probably have to accept not only the result of their destructions, but also of their creative efforts.

With Mussolini the case is different. As I have endeavoured to show, he has exploited a reactionary movement of which he and his party were not the inspiration. Revolutionary communism was already defeated by the good sense of the Italian people before the triumphant Fascists fell on its disordered forces. Their claims grew with their successes, and they seized the government of Italy. It needed renovating and strengthening, or rather the men who worked it stood in that need. It is easy enough for the clumsy workman to blame his tools. But the rôle of the restorer of the Commonwealth has not appealed to Mussolini as it appealed to Venizelos. He seems resolved to retain power until he has translated his hatred of liberalism into a system. Like Lenin, Mussolini seems to be a mystic in his political conception, but he has not had Lenin's opportunity. Mussolini has not razed to the foundations the work of Charles Albert and of Cavour, nor has that work fallen into ruins. His refusal to confine himself to the only task he has had the full opportunity of carrying out—the task of restoring and vindicating the constitution—has led to a deadlock. The liberal tradition in Italy is strong, and is becoming stronger. Mussolini is in power, and intends to maintain himself in power, if necessary by force.

But the constitution of 1848 hangs round his neck like a millstone; nor is it difficult to foresee his failure, which already seems to define itself as the failure of one who is not a revolutionary on occasion, for clearly envisaged and swiftly realised ends, but a permanent revolutionary, who believes that the unravelling of political tangles is an unworthy pastime, and who is ever ready with a high gesture to cut the Gordian knot. On the lips of such a man, what can "normalization" mean but the recognition of the unchallenged supremacy of Fascismo? After all, there is some difference in political maturity between a Russian moujik and an Italian peasant; between the victim of successive despotisms and of his own lack of self-control, and the heir of that new birth of liberty, the Risorgimento. A revolutionary reconstruction was possible in Russia, because the collapse was so overwhelming: that prerequisite, fortunately for the happiness and peace of the Italian people, was absent in Italy. Adjustment and rehabilitation, not destruction and revolution, are her needs. But the master of force stands true to his past in this, that he remains bent on re-making the political life and institutions of his country, instead of strengthening them—in a word, he remains a revolutionary, but without that "revolutionary situation" which would afford him elbow-room to create a new polity.

I do not claim this book to be a work of historical research. It is simply a sincere attempt to reconstruct a coherent narrative of the lives of these four political leaders, from what material lies more immediately to hand, and such as my opportunities and limitations allowed me to utilize. From the form of essay adopted I fear I have sometimes been led to take up a dogmatic attitude at points where the facts are far from certain, and where a discussion would have been more in place. For this, for the inevitable mistakes of any attempt to tell the story of lives lived so near us in time, and for the disproportions of which I am conscious, I desire to apologize in advance. My hope is that these biographical studies may be interesting, and perhaps even useful to some readers, since I have tried in every case to indicate my sources.

I wish to thank with a deep sense of my obligation to their kindness, Mr N. Eumorfopoulos, Mr John Mavrogordato, and Mr E. C. W. Hannan, who placed at my disposal material, some of it unpublished, to which I could not otherwise have gained access. To the Baron Meyendorff, who was good enough to give me valuable time in answering my questions; to my brother, Mr Herbert Box, who read my work both in manuscript and in proof; to Lieutenant-Colonel W. H. Salmon, and to Mr J. D. Mackie, who lent me newspapers and books; and to Mr A. O. Anderson, for his unfailing encouragement and valuable criticism, my cordial thanks are also due.

Needless to say, I am wholly responsible for all opinions expressed in these essays.

PELHAM H. BOX

THE UNIVERSITY
ST ANDREWS, *December* 1924

CONTENTS

INTRODUCTION

I HAVE been asked by the author of this book to write some words by way of an introduction. The reader who begins the book by reading the preface (as I would advise every reader to do) may very well murmur, as he comes to this introduction, "But what need was there for you?" If such a writ of *Certiorari* is issued against me, I must at once return an *Ignoramus*. I really do not know. I will only say that I was asked to write an introduction; and since he who asked me was the son of a colleague at King's College, and had himself at one time been a student of the College, and since, again, this was his first book, and I thought it a live and stimulating book, I consented to do a work of supererogation.

"Three Master Builders and Another." Who is the other? I can only join the reader in trying to guess. Those who see red when they hear or read of anything Red (and I have met such) will at once suggest that he is Lenin. The difficulty is that Lenin after all did build, however grim and even ghastly (as of some edifice in Mars) the beams and pillars of his building may be. Nor has the system which he originally built, even if he himself subsequently altered it in a drastic way, as yet collapsed. Was the other, then, Wilson? After all, he did not build any particularly new structure in his own country; and if he may be said to have sketched a dim adumbration of the League of Nations, he was hardly its "builder." But I should fancy, from my reading of his essay on Wilson, that Mr Box intends to include the President in the circle of the Three, and that he is not meant to be left outside the circumference

Alone and palely loitering

as merely "another." For myself, I do not know whether I should really admit Mr Wilson among the elect, or, indeed, whether I should subscribe to the version which Mr Box gives of some portions of his career—as, for example, of his struggles at Princeton, or of the causes which led to his becoming the Governor of New Jersey. There are things in contemporary history which do not get into books or articles; and what one hears in talk from those who were themselves concerned in events is part of the evidence in the case. All the same, a man who stamps himself on the hot wax of affairs leaves a pretty clear impression which a student can record and describe; and whatever else Mr Wilson did, he certainly impressed a clear-cut character on everything with which he was concerned.

But who then is "another"? He is not, I should guess, Lenin; he is not, I believe, Mr Wilson. He is neither of the two who are dead; he must be one of the two who are living. He cannot be Venizelos, for he is obviously a master builder after the author's heart. There remains Mussolini. He has built at any rate a new militia; and one sometimes hears of a Fascist organization in England which appears to be a subdued Northern copy of his glowing Roman Legions. He has even sketched plans of a new political and economic organization of Italy; but they appear to remain in the category of sketch plans, which need some definite specifications and elevations before much building can be begun. It would seem that he is the other—at any rate for the time being. But he has this advantage over the rest, of whom two have ceased to be, and one has left the practice of politics, that he is still in power, and that he is only forty-one years of age. Time will tell; and office, if it endures, will show the man.

Mr Box has selected the three master builders of his choice. Each has had his programme and his principles: each has wrought greatly, if not always well or wisely, on a great stage. Few of his readers would dispute that Mr Box has hit upon the very figures which general consent would agree to be the most striking of their time in their appeal to popular imagination. There are, of course, others. There is, for example, as Mr Box mentions in his preface, President Masaryk, a thinker, a statesman, the father of his people. There is, again, General Smuts, who must also be counted among the builders of the League of Nations. But we should most of us allow that Mr

Box's choice may stand; and on that basis we may ask, What is a master builder? and, if we are curious enough to ask still another question, which, as we shall see, springs naturally from the answer to the first, we may also ask, Why do the older countries of Western Europe provide no name for inclusion in the list of those who fit the definition?

I take it that a master builder, in the world of politics, is a man who, on a troubled and revolutionary scene, out-tops his fellows, in power of mind or energy of will, or both: a man of ideas—whether they be his own, or, like those of Lenin, borrowed from another—who seeks to bend and hammer into the shape of those ideas the facts of contemporary life when they are heated and made malleable by the fire of turmoil and the glow of his own personality. Of such sort was Napoleon in France, or Bismarck in Germany, or again, if we go far enough back (and it is significant that we have to go so far back), Oliver Cromwell in England. Perhaps the greatest of all was Julius Cæsar: perhaps the purest was Abraham Lincoln. Of such we may say, in the words of an old Greek thinker, "One man is to me as ten thousand," or again, in the words of Homer,

οἶος πέπνυται, τοὶ δὲ σκιαὶ ἀΐσσουσιν.

"He alone is wise, and they like shadows flit." That is a large thing to say of any man, and a still larger thing for a man to say of himself. Yet some, at any rate, of the men described in this book have had the feeling, "I alone can save this country." A would-be master builder must often have a conceit of his powers, and a power to eliminate others when it comes to the last decision, which are based on a proud and confident self-regard that is never prouder or more confident than when it is a regard for principles which are, perhaps unconsciously, assumed to be enshrined in the self. Lenin and Wilson seem to me to be of this order; with Mussolini there may be more regard for self than for any principles which it enshrines—and yet he too has a principle of ardent nationalism: in Venizelos alone I do not see this austere self-concentration, but more of that power of action by consultation and persuasion of others which is perhaps the highest power of statesmanship.

In what has just been said a reason may already appear for the absence of British names from any list of master builders. We have, perhaps, passed beyond that stage of affairs and that conjunction of events which permit of a master builder. For one thing, such a figure belongs to a time of troubles, when a saviour of society is needed to reconcile or to end grave social conflicts or to achieve an unrealized but ardently desired ideal of national unification. For another thing (and this goes deeper), such a figure belongs to a society which has not yet attained to the stage of organized management of collective thinking. Such organized management of collective thinking is the postulate, as it is the essence, of a safe and sure democracy. It means that every citizen, to the best of his ability, contributes to the common stock of ideas and opinions; it means that by discussion—the sovereign method of collective thought—that common stock is distilled and clarified until there emerges a genuine public opinion and a general will. It means, again, that parties are formed for the conduct of discussion by the formulation of programmes, the defence of programmes by argument, and the realization of programmes (once they are endorsed by public opinion) through the concerted action of their leaders. In a system based on discussion between parties at the bar of public opinion—and that is the system on which we have worked, with an ever-increasing scope of the area of discussion, since the Revolution of 1688—there is little room for any dominant and outstanding master of the event. Collegiate thinking and action takes the place of individual pronunciamentos and *coups de main.* The highest form of such collegiate thinking and action is a good and harmonious cabinet; and it is a common observation that cabinets are most successful when there is no dominant personality, and a general spirit of loyal team-work is the driving force. The conduct of affairs on this basis means a greyer and less strongly coloured record in the pages of history. Events which are dominated by a great personality glow with a dramatic vigour; and indeed there is always a passion among men to personalize politics and to find "the man who did it." But the greatest things are perhaps those which are done by no single man; and the most successful college or school, just as much as the most successful State, may owe its success to the collective thinking of all the best members of its governing body. There is a charm and a drive in the single human personality; there is a wisdom and a sanity in a group of persons resolved to act loyally together. When once a community is prepared for collegiate guidance, it is a mistake for any person to draw affairs exclusively into the orbit of his own personality. It was this mistake which led to the eventual shipwreck of Mr Wilson, for all his high thinking and all the earnestness of his moral purpose.

There is a passage in Mr Box's essay on Mussolini (pp. 159-160) which states admirably the argument for a sound democracy soundly based on collective thought. I will end by quoting some sentences from that passage. "Leadership is required, but leadership is not, as some imagine, incompatible with truly representative government. The leader to be efficient should not be elevated so far above criticism that he hears it merely as 'the winding of a shell on the far-off sea-shore.' Rather his place is in the thick of the wordy battle from which emerge measures of national policy tested by criticism." These are good and true sayings.

ERNEST BARKER

November 17, 1924

NIKOLAI LENIN

ὁ θαυμάσας βασιλεύσει.

Logion, from CLEMENT OF ALEXANDRIA.

"If a Russian does not believe in God, that means simply that he believes in something else."

TCHEKOV.

NIKOLAI LENIN.

NIKOLAI LENIN

ONE afternoon in the summer of 1909, M. Berendson, a Danish business man interested in the European revolutionary movement, was introduced to a group of Russian exiles at a tea-party at Vevey. Among those he met was a certain M. Ulyanov, for whom the other members of the little gathering appeared to entertain the deepest respect, hanging on every word he uttered and solemnly repeating his generalizations almost as though they were attempting to commit them all to memory.

" There was something in the physique of the man—was it his dome-like head or his deep-set, cruel, steel-grey eyes ? —which arrested attention. Even before he had begun to speak, he made himself felt as a person with a certain magnetic force about him ; but when he began to talk, his superiority to the common herd of Russian revolutionary exiles became manifest. His converse was quiet, confident, singularly devoid of cloudy denunciation. He abused no individuals ; he did not even mention the Tsar. He just explained to a submissive audience of compatriots the measures which he proposed to take when he assumed power in Russia. Nobody among his hearers appeared to challenge his authority or to doubt his success. . . . Even the Danish stranger, a hard-headed business man, found himself insensibly sharing the common assumption that somehow or other M. Ulyanov would have his day. 'I notice,' he said in parting, 'that you make no mention of the Tsar.' 'Oh,' replied the Russian, 'personalities do not concern me. If the Tsar does not accommodate himself to my system, he must find some nail from which to hang himself.' The Dane returned to his hotel in Lausanne and noted in his diary : 'I met a M. Ulyanov at Vevey—a terrible man who intends to be master of Russia.' "[1]

At the moment when M. Berendson met him, Vladimir Ilyitch Ulyanov—the " Nikolai Lenin " of the innumerable pamphlets and articles by which he had established an intellectual ascendancy in the revolutionary underworld—was already the acknowledged and autocratic leader of the most highly disciplined of Russian revolutionary parties. In the five years that remained before the outbreak of the world war that he had long foreseen, and that was to open to him the gates of supreme power, he consolidated his commanding position yet further. But before attempting to present in sequence the chief events in the history of this tremendous

[1] " Lenin," article by H. A. L. Fisher, *The Cornhill Magazine*, March 1924.

personality who was to subdue and fascinate first a small band of devoted adherents and then one of the greatest, if most enigmatic, of nations, we must endeavour to sketch in roughly the Russian background before which the uniquely Russian figure of Lenin stands out most clearly. For Lenin was a Russian before he was an internationalist—Russian in the fixity of his purpose, Russian in the Messianic passion he brought to the service of his ideal.

The history of modern Russia has been the history of arrested development followed by the perversion of all the life-forces of the State. A great hope was born when the autocracy, shaken by the disasters of the Crimean War, decreed the emancipation of the serfs in 1861. But the Russian peasant, though he ceased to be the private property of his lord and became the owner of his own soul, yet passed rapidly into an economic in place of a legal serfdom. Briefly, the terms of redemption were so high that the peasants (who constitute practically the Russian nation), while they secured their land, could not secure their economic independence, and were forced back into the service of their former lords as hired labourers. Often they paid for their land, now their own, in labour services to the former owner—services which were demanded by the lords not only for the lands held by the peasants, but for the redemption of their persons. Since the serfs and their lands had once been equally the property of the lords, the serfs, when they were emancipated, must pay not only for their land but for their souls!

The solution of the agrarian problem was further complicated by the fact that the emancipated peasants still remained members of the primitive communal village unit of Russia—the "Mir," which they could not leave. In a rapidly changing industrial age, the Mir became a clog to all agricultural progress. Land was held in common and repartitioned among the members of the Mir every year. Each holding consisted of many widely scattered strips (a device that ensured that each member of the Mir should have his just share of good and bad land), the cultivation of which involved unnecessary waste of time. In addition, the Mir was the unit of State taxation, and members had to bear the burden of any individual bankruptcy or other failure to pay.[1] The continued

[1] It will scarcely be credited that the liberty of the peasant was so restricted that he required a passport to move from one village to another. But such was the case.

existence of the Mir was the chief cause of the comparative failure of the Zemstvos, or county councils, instituted in 1864, and elected from all classes. The circumstances favourable to their development were absent.

The agrarian position after 1861 gave rise to a two-fold movement among the peasants. In the first place the ecomonic consequences of the Emancipation of 1861, whereby they were forced back into dependence on their former lords, gave rise to the intense land-hunger that added the immense momentum of the peasantry to the revolutionary movement of 1917. Then the idea of personal emancipation from the lords gave rise to a movement, weak at first, but steadily increasing in strength, for personal emancipation from the Mir. The traditional Communism of the village was felt as a shackle to individual initiative. Not until after the revolution of 1905 was the agrarian problem squarely and constructively faced by Stolypin. By enabling any peasant who desired to embark on individual farming to leave his Mir, Stolypin began a process which, had it been undertaken immediately after the Emancipation, would gradually and steadily have broken up the mediæval organization of the Russian village; facilitated the acquisition of land by the peasant, and developed a powerful class of small farmers independent alike of lord and Mir. Stolypin's ideal was to set in motion forces which in due course must have destroyed the Mir, and equally have extinguished all large landed proprietors who were not willing to embark on intensive and scientific farming.

But reforms which required a long period of peaceful work were fatally interrupted by the outbreak of the European War and the convulsions to which it gave rise in the weak and loosely knit fabric of the Russian State. Stolypin was too late to remedy the consequences of the disastrous reaction that gripped Russia after the reforming effort of the 'sixties. The autocracy, terrified by the extravagant hopes of the Liberals, embarked on a system of repression. Repression led to the counter-offensive of the Terrorists, whose activities culminated in the assassination of the Tsar Alexander II. in 1881. Terrorism itself led to intensified reaction. The vicious circle was broken only after the Revolution of 1905, and then, as we have seen, it was too late.

The other great factor in the complex of influences making for revolution in Russia was the industrial transformation. Russian industry may be said to date from the 'sixties, although the textile trade had been strongly established round Petrograd and Moscow in the 'forties and 'fifties. The speed of industrial development was astonishing. To take one example, there was a 600 per cent. increase in the production of cast-iron during the years between 1888 and 1900. Between 1885 and 1897 there was an increase in the town population of 33 per cent. The significance of this remarkable advance becomes obvious when it is realized that this is a rate of increase over twice as high as that of the entire population of Russia, which in the same period advanced at the rate of only 15·2 per cent.[1]

This sudden and catastrophic development of capitalism in Russia was deliberately favoured by the Imperial government, which exerted itself to make the Empire the paradise of industrial adventurers by protecting new enterprises by high tariffs. More than half of the capital on which the new Russian industries depended was foreign. One consequence of the unlimited favours lavished on foreign enterprises in Russia was that the capitalists, while attaining enormous economic, never aspired to corresponding political, power. By a sort of *quid pro quo* the Imperial government was left uninfluenced politically, whether for good or evil, by the new industrial forces. The economic bourgeoisie was, as a result, singularly timid and unenterprising in its attitude to the autocracy.

Another consequence of the headlong development of Russian industry was the creation of stupendous factories where vast aggregates of men, women and children worked under conditions resembling those of the earlier phase of capitalism in Great Britain, and characterized by ruthless exploitation of the workers. In the words of the report of Lord Emmott's "Committee to collect information on Russia (political and economic)," "a study of industrial conditions in Russia discloses a disregard on the part of employers for the dignity of human life and for the social dangers proceeding from the physical and psychological results of sweated labour often performed amid surroundings of a degrading and dehumanizing character." [2] In Petrograd alone there were more factories containing over 5000 workers each than in the whole of capitalist Germany.[3] Of the industrial workers of Russia

[1] Farbman, "Bolshevism in Retreat," pp. 15-16.
[2] Report : Russia No. 1 (1921), Cmd. 1240, para. 17.
[3] Farbman, "Bolshevism in Retreat," p. 20.

43·8 per cent. worked in factories of over 1000 hands, while only 20·5 per cent. of the industrial population of U.S.A. worked in factories of like size.[1]

Obviously, such vast aggregations of labour under conditions so retrograde afforded a fruitful soil for the propagation of revolutionary theories. The proletariat became intensely and justly self-conscious in the great factories. There it learned vividly a sense of its own solidarity, and there it rapidly passed from a state of economic hostility to the employer to that of fierce political opposition to the régime on which the capitalists had to lean more and more for the necessary support against the exploited masses. As a result, at the head and forefront of the attack on the autocracy stood the industrial proletariat, largely recruited as it was from the floating population of the villages. The occupational and social stratification which prevented co-operation to so marked a degree among Russian classes had affected least the peasants and the industrial proletariat who still retained contact.[2]

This notable feature of Russian conditions, that not the bourgeoisie but the proletariat constituted the true opposition to the autocracy, cannot be over-emphasized. The supine timidity of the Russian capitalists and the small middle class was notorious. It justified Plekhanov's prophecy, made in the early 'nineties, that " the Russian Revolution will succeed as a proletarian Revolution, or never succeed at all." [3]

It was during the 'nineties and among the industrial workers of the capital city that was afterwards to bear the name by which he will be known to history,[4] that Lenin began his great work.

Vladimir Ilyitch Ulyanov was born 10th April 1870, at the town of Simbirsk on the Volga. His father, a man of wide local popularity, was an official of the Ministry of Education and eventually rose to the rank of State Councillor. Under the Imperial system, the elder Ulyanov as a State Councillor automatically entered the lower ranks of the nobility, and so Vladimir Ilyitch was in due course registered at the local police office as an hereditary noble. His mother possessed a small estate in the province of Kazan and after her husband's death received a State pension.

[1] Farbman, p. 20.
[2] Kurt Wiedenfeld, " The Remaking of Russia," pp. 5-10.
[3] Quoted Farbman, p. 14.
[4] Petrograd was renamed Leningrad in February 1924.

The five children of the marriage—Alexander, Vladimir Ilyitch, Dmitri, Maria, and Anna—were thus brought up in comfortable circumstances, enjoying the general regard in which the family was held by the townspeople of Simbirsk. Vladimir Ilyitch began his education at the local "gymnasium," where the father of Alexander Kerensky, later the "prima donna," as Mr Farbman so well calls him, of the revolution of March 1917, whom Lenin was to displace in the government of Russia, was his headmaster. In 1887, he left the Simbirsk Gymnasium at the age of seventeen after a brilliant scholastic career. This is the "character" given him on leaving school by his headmaster, Mr F. M. Kerensky: "Extremely talented, always industrious and accurate, Ulyanov has been top of every class, and at the conclusion of his course has been awarded a gold medal as the most deserving scholar in achievement, development, and conduct. Neither in the Gymnasium nor outside it has anything taken place whereby Ulyanov, by speech or action, could give the directors and controllers of the Gymnasium a bad opinion of him." Mr Kerensky had only one fault to find: Vladimir Ilyitch was "too reserved, shunning the company even of his acquaintances, and out of school and with his friends generally unamiable."[1] His elder brother, Alexander, had preceded him at the same secondary school.

Alexander seems to have been a noble-minded youth of ardent and idealistic, if ill-balanced, temperament. On leaving Simbirsk, he flung himself into the revolutionary movement against the autocracy—a movement which in the 'eighties was still dominated by the Terrorists. As a member of a Secret Terrorist society he was implicated in a student bomb-plot in 1887 against the reactionary Tsar Alexander III. The plot was discovered by the secret police, and Alexander Ulyanov was arrested with other young conspirators. The panic that animated the autocracy during these years is clearly shown by the fact that Alexander Ulyanov, although guilty of no overt criminal act, was sentenced to death and executed.

M. Alexander Kerensky has stated that he well remembers, although he was only five years old at the time, how he vibrated to the feeling of horror and dismay that swept through Simbirsk when the dreadful news came that Alexander Ulyanov had been hanged.[2] This tragedy that burst upon him at the

[1] Quoted, B. Myakotin in article "Lenin"—*Slavonic Review*, March 1924.
[2] Ross, "The Russian Bolshevik Revolution."

age of seventeen has been regarded as the decisive moment in the life of Lenin which launched him on his unique revolutionary career. This may or may not be so, but it is certain that his two sisters and his brother Dmitri all became active members of various extreme revolutionary parties. Madame Ulyanov from the moment that she lost her eldest child concentrated her affection on Vladimir Ilyitch, who was a most devoted son. She withdrew from Russia in later years and settled in Stockholm, where she died in 1913, and it was to Stockholm that Lenin would pay his flying visits to his mother any time he could tear himself away from his work during the long years that he was forging the Bolshevik party into the tempered sword of the Russian Revolution. It is legitimate to guess that Mme. Ulyanov shared her son's ideals and also, like M. Berendson, experienced the force of his strange and compelling conviction of destiny.

In 1889, Lenin entered the University of Kazan, but, as the brother of an executed terrorist, he was suspect from the first, and within a month he was expelled for taking part in a students' political riot. Though at first he was debarred from entering the university of either of the capital cities, he was eventually successful in enrolling himself as an external student at Petrograd in 1891 and taking his degree in Law in 1893. In later life he often referred with amusement to his few days' "practice" at the bar.[1] He had already chosen another and even more arduous profession.

Through his brother Alexander he was in touch with the older school of Terrorist revolutionaries, but he never became a member of their organizations. He often referred to these "Populists" with respect, but he regarded them always as the heroic pioneers. His scientific, almost academic, type of mind inevitably drove him to condemn the mystic Utopianism and spasmodic activities of these apostles of a bloodstained righteousness. After all, however effective in rousing "the insulted and injured" might be some high gesture by an isolated devotee prepared to sacrifice his life in taking that of a tyrant, a bomb was no substitute for a gospel—an articulated and profoundly pondered system of thought, patient organization on a national scale for ultimate revolutionary action—in a word—discipline.

Very soon he was crossing swords with the idealists of the old revolutionary school—a school purely Russian in character

[1] Zinoviev, "N. Lenin: His Life and Work," p. 5.

and as yet uninfluenced by Marx and the scientific Germans. After his expulsion from Kazan, while at Samara, Lenin became acquainted with the work of Karl Marx. He followed up what was a new way of revelation to his profoundly practical and realistic temperament by a study of the works of that heroic Russian pioneer of scientific Marxism in Russia, Plekhanov, whom he met in Germany in 1895 on the occasion of his first journey abroad. Lenin used to relate in later years how on his first coming to Petrograd he had walked about the city in search of a Marxian.[1]

Here it may not be out of place to ask the question : " What doctrines characterize a Marxian ? " It will be as well to indicate some essential doctrines in the great fabric of thought built up by Karl Marx, the indefatigable genius whose word has been a consuming fire, and whose spirit presides over the Russian Revolution.

The two chief literary sources in which this body of teaching can be found are the Communist Manifesto of 1848, drawn up by Marx and Engels, and the three volumes of Marx's "Capital," the first of which only Marx saw through the press himself, his friend Engels issuing the second and third after the death of the great socialist and revolutionary. The Communist Manifesto, which appeared shortly before the outbreak of the revolution of 1848, is the bold spirit-stirring formulation of the position afterwards expanded, elucidated, and buttressed throughout the work on "Capital." In the words of the distinguished historian of British Socialism, "From the standpoint of social philosophy, the Manifesto, a document reflecting its time, is almost perfect. Strong emotion and extraordinary intellectual power are united in it. Years of study of one of the boldest and most fertile minds are here welded together in the glowing heat of one of the most active of intellectual workshops." [2]

At the root of the Marxian theory lies a conception of historical development in part derivable from the conservative philosopher Hegel. On the one hand, it is asserted that any given state of Society must eventually in the course of its self-expression give rise to its social opposite. The thesis gives rise to the antithesis ; the old Society gives birth to that which must ultimately destroy it. The clash of these opposites produces that which is neither the one nor the other, but the

[1] Zinoviev, " N. Lenin : His Life and Work," p. 8.
[2] M. Beer, " The Life and Teaching of Karl Marx," p. 47.

synthesis of both. Thus capitalism and modern civilization give birth to the proletariat which feels itself the victim of exploitation at the hands of the masters of economic power. A conflict is inevitable. The self-evident decay of capitalism means the conquest of economic and political power by the proletariat, in other words, a dictatorship of one class over another. But this is only the transition period. The proletariat, the victim of class oppression and private property, is driven to seek the extinction of both. This work accomplished, the dictatorship of the proletariat will pass away, and the synthesis of the whole historical conflict will be the Communist Society.

Another root assumption of Marx was that all the mass movements of history, wars, conflicts of classes, social institutions, have their origins in the material conditions of life. This " materialistic conception of history " is quite distinct from philosophical materialism, or the assertion that all knowledge and all mental processes arise from purely physical causes. To accept the one does not necessarily involve acceptance of the other. There are, as Mr Bertrand Russell has pointed out, innumerable ways of viewing history which are materialistic in the philosophic sense (such as Buckle's assertion that climate is a decisive factor in human politics, or Freud's theory of sex as the ultimate motive from which all individual actions and thoughts are derivable) without being economic.[1] In point of fact, most Marxians accept both the materialistic conception of history and philosophic materialism, but the two should be kept apart in discussing the " materialistic conception of history." " Just as men produce various material goods out of the materials and forces made available to them by nature, so they create out of the reactions of the productive forces upon the mind definite social, political and legal institutions, as well as systems of religion, morals and philosophy." [2] In the words of the Communist Manifesto, " With the dissolution of primeval communities, society begins to be divided into separate and finally antagonistic classes : Freeman and slave, patrician and plebeian, baron and serf, guild-master and journeyman, in one word, oppressor and oppressed, standing constantly in opposition to each other, carried on an uninterrupted warfare, now open, now concealed ; a warfare which always ended either in a revolu-

[1] Bertrand Russell, " The Practice and Theory of Bolshevism."
[2] Beer, " The Life and Teaching of Karl Marx," p. 67.

tionary transformation of society or in the common ruin of the contending classes."

The contending classes are supporters of conflicting economic interests and ideals. The bourgeois tradesman or citizen fought against the feudal lords for the right of self-expression, freedom of person and trade. With the victory of the middle class, property has steadily become concentrated ; co-operation of great interests sets in, and the proletariat is recruited from the expropriated members of all classes—small shopkeepers, peasant proprietors, handicraftsmen. The proletariat cannot fight for the right of individual property, but it must push co-operation to its logical conclusion and aim at " the socially conducted utilization of the means of production belonging to the community and of the goods produced." [1]

Obviously, the proletariat cannot have any nationality; the class struggle that consumes its energies tends to unite all workers throughout the world in their struggle against the bourgeoisies. The pivot of the struggle is the State, which is the organ of class-domination and came into existence simply to hold Society together, not to harmonize its various elements. The proletariat must capture the State before it can achieve that transformation of Society involved in the abolition of economic classes and private property and ultimately the State itself, thus rendered unnecessary. In the last superb challenge of the Manifesto, " The Communists everywhere support every revolutionary movement against the existing social and political order of things. In all these movements they bring to the front as the leading question in each, the property question, no matter what its degree of development at the time. . . . The Communists disdain to conceal their views and aims; they openly declare that their ends can be attained only by the forcible overthrow of all existing social conditions. Let the ruling classes tremble at a Communistic revolution ; the proletarians have nothing to lose but their chains. They have a world to win. Working men of all countries, unite ! " [2] Without going further into the economic ideas of Marx, developed at great length and with astounding erudition in " Capital," or even touching upon the famous foundation-theory of " surplus value," whereby Marx endeavours to show that all profit is robbery and that

[1] Beer, " The Life and Teaching of Karl Marx," p. 46.
[2] " Manifesto of the Communist Party," by Karl Marx and Friedrich Engels, authorised English translation, 1888.

labour is the sole determinant of value, one can appreciate that Marxianism as expressed in the Communist Manifesto is a uniquely revolutionary and crusading creed. Perhaps the most notable feature about it is its economic determinism. Marx did not consider that he was "making" a revolution; he was but conforming to the structure of events, and urging others to see that development had set with a strong tide in a certain direction. Swim with the current rather than against it. In any case, the necessity of things will carry Society to the goal. To talk of "great men" directing events or having any particular influence on them would have seemed to him hopelessly unscientific.

In other words, Marxian Communism claims to have discovered the world-pattern. The main outlines of past, present and future are established; all that remains is to convert humanity to the duty of conforming. That there is something religious in this attitude is obvious. The Marxians are Puritans expounding an economic Calvinism. They are proof against all failures and all disappointments, since on their side they feel are all the ultimate life-forces of the world, and after many days their war against the disease of capitalism must be crowned with a supreme victory. In a violent metaphor Lenin has revealed this attitude of mind when, referring to the mistakes and miscalculations of the Bolshevik government, he reminds his readers that a Japanese scientist compounded 605 preparations in his search for a cure of syphilis before he found the 606th, which was successful.[1]

Lenin's complex character, at once visionary and practical, was satisfied by the clear-cut lines of the Marxian thesis. Here was a philosophy as definitive as a deed or piece of propaganda, and it was in the practical sphere of control and organization that Lenin's unique genius showed itself. As a thinker he was always a disciple, but endowed with that minute textual knowledge of his master that gives the devotee an advantage over all comers. As an exponent of a difficult piece of theory he was unrivalled for lucidity—his pamphlets are always telling, vivid, and admirably arranged. He is never tired of presenting his readers with the same idea again and again from a slightly different angle. He dissects the problem and then compels one to look at each fragment carefully before he regroups the argument and draws it to a

[1] Lenin, "The Great Initiative, being the story of Communist Saturdays."

conclusion. He is, in a word, academic but with this difference, through all his writings and speeches runs an undefinable impression of vigour, almost physical force. Maxim Gorky has noted this sense of abounding, even menacing, vitality.

With a little group of devoted followers (among the most notable was Ivan Vasilyevitch Babushkin), he founded the first working-class organization in Petrograd and organized the first strikes. From an economic he moved swiftly towards a political objective. In fact, from the first Lenin kept steadily before his eyes the speedy conversion of all purely economic struggles into revolutionary movements. For this purpose he founded a Marxian Society, the " Union for the Struggle for the Emancipation of Labour."

His journalistic activity was immense, and he began to attract attention by his brilliant articles directed against N. K. Mikhailovsky, the protagonist of the older Populist school of revolutionaries. Soon he was noted by the police, and after his first illegal pamphlet " On Fines," he had to go into hiding in the working-class quarter of Petrograd. There he was arrested in 1897 on a charge of revolutionary activities and exiled for three years to Siberia after a term of imprisonment in Russia. The last part of his exile he spent at the little village of Sushenskoe on the confines of the remote Yenisei Government.

During his exile he had not been idle. He devoted himself to reading and the writing of pamphlets, and began his most important lasting work, " The Development of Capitalism in Russia," which he completed in France after his return from Siberia. His enforced leisure enabled him to devote himself to his favourite studies, economics and political science. His capacity for continuous intellectual work was phenomenal, truly Marxian. Always an ardent lover of books, he thought little of twelve to fifteen hours' reading, once he had embarked on a line of research. To this day, " The Development of Capitalism in Russia " remains a veritable treasure-house of splendidly organized erudition. Zinoviev relates how in 1902, when he was still a student at the " School of Social Sciences," Professor Maxim Kovalevsky, its founder, exclaimed, " What a fine professor might have been made out of Lenin ! " [1]

After his return from Siberia to Western Europe, since, on

[1] Zinoviev, " N. Lenin : His Life and Work," p. 12.

the expiry of his sentence, he had been forbidden to reside in any of the important cities or factory centres of Russia, he did two most decisive things. In 1900, he joined the "The Unified Russian Social Democrat Party," founded in 1898 by Plekhanov, the father of Russian Social Democracy, and he married Nadiejda Konstatinovna Krupskaia.

Madame Lenin shared her husband's ideas and was a revolutionary before he married her. In the words of Mr Bruce Lockhart, they seem to have lived together "in a state of ascetic happiness." She was with him when they moved incessantly from one garret to another in Paris, Berne, Zurich, or Cracow, and when the furniture in their room in Paris was sold for 45 francs; she was with him at the end when she watched beside the deathbed of the ruler of Russia. Her industry was as indefatigable as his own, and she conducted practically the whole of his vast correspondence with Russian revolutionaries who held Nadiejda Konstantinovna in the highest respect. Without family or home life, absorbed in relentless devotion to the revolutionary idea, they are a strange and austere couple. The good son was also the good husband, and the despiser of bourgeois morality lived a blameless and devoted life.

To the new party Lenin brought not only his inexhaustible energy but his implacable vendettas and his unswerving, though unformulated, claim to be the sole interpreter of Marxism. Already before his exile he had embarked upon yet another polemic. In addition to the paper war he waged on the Populists, the followers of Mikhailovsky, "fantasists" and Utopians, as he called them, who dreamed not only of the abolition of capitalists but of escaping any capitalist phase of society in Russia, he had embarked on a struggle with the "legal" Marxians headed by Peter Struve. Struve published a book directed against Mikhailovsky and entitled "Critical Remarks," which concluded with the following words: "Let us acknowledge our want of culture and place ourselves as apprentices under capitalism." Both Plekhanov and Lenin published replies to Struve. Lenin took the line that the book betrayed a willingness on the part of Struve to compromise with the bourgeoisie, in other words, to become an apprentice not so much to capitalism as to capitalists. Though Struve had been an invaluable fellow-worker in the Socialist cause, that he should show signs of becoming a "reformist" was enough in Lenin's opinion to justify a ruthless polemic against him, which he began in a series of articles written over the pseudonym of Tulin. For Lenin, now, as always, its revolutionary programme was the essence of true Marxism. Power could be attained by the proletariat only through revolution. And yet, on this question the prophet spoke with a double voice. In the 1872 preface to the Manifesto signed by Marx and Engels occurs the passage: "The practical application of the principles will depend, as the Manifesto itself states, everywhere and at all times, on the historical conditions for the time being existing, and for that reason no special stress is laid on the revolutionary measures proposed at the end of Section II. That passage would, in many respects, be very differently worded to-day."

When we turn to the end of Section II. of the Manifesto we find that after the proletariat has wrested political power from the bourgeoisie it must use it "to wrest by degrees all capital from the bourgeoisie, to centralise all instruments of production in the hands of the State. . . . This naturally cannot be accomplished at first except by despotic inroads on the rights of property and on the bourgeois conditions of production; by measures, therefore, which appear economically insufficient and untenable, but which . . . are indispensable as means of revolutionising the whole mode of production." These suggested measures are worth quoting in view of the programme carried out by the Bolsheviks when they finally decided, after the November revolution of 1917, to take what many of them had up to then regarded as the risk of a wholesale and immediate application of Communist principles:—

1. Abolition of property in land and confiscation of ground rents to the State.
2. A heavily progressive income tax.
3. Abolition of inheritance . . .
4. Centralization of credit in the hands of the State by means of a national bank with State capital and an exclusive monopoly.
5. Centralization of the means of transport in the hands of the State.
6. Extension of national factories and instruments of production . . . in accordance with a general social plan.

7. Obligation of all to labour; organization of industrial armies, especially for agriculture.[1]

Marx in his later phase was perfectly willing to admit that in England, Holland and other Parliamentary States revolution was unlikely and undesirable. His ideas, or rather the future phase of society which he announced, could be attained by normal political evolution. This view is sufficiently far removed from the semi-mystical belief in "world revolution" of the Manifesto. But it is to the Marx of the Communist Manifesto that the Bolsheviks offer incense.

For Lenin, armed seizure of power by the proletariat was the sole possible beginning of the Socialist State. He held this to be of the essence of Marxism, all modifications or denials of this thesis are "reformism" and indicate a bourgeois mentality. Years later, he developed this unchanging theme in his brilliant brochure, "The State and Revolution," when, by means of copious extracts from Marx and Engels, he endeavours to show that the "dictatorship of the proletariat" inhered in all the work of the two founders of scientific socialism. Wherein Lenin did admit of "reformism" in a special sense was in the question of the exact extent to which Communist principles should be put into force immediately *after* the seizure of power. We shall see how vital this question becomes when he found himself master of Russia in November 1917. At the period we have now reached, it may be as well to indicate his position, developed in the leaflet, "The Two Tactics," published at Geneva in 1905. In this work he still thinks that Russia must go through a period of political democracy to prepare the masses for the application of Socialism: "Whoever wants to try any path to Socialism other than political Democracy, he will inevitably come to absurd and reactionary conclusions both in an economical and a political sense. If some workmen ask us, 'Why not achieve the maximum programme?' we shall answer them by pointing out just how alien to Socialism the democratic masses are, how undeveloped the class contradictions, how unorganized the proletarians. Just try to organize hundreds of thousands of workmen all over Russia! Try to teach millions to sympathize with your programme! Try to do that without limiting yourself to sonorous but empty anarchical phrases, and you will see at once that the largest

[1] "The Manifesto of the Communist Party," by Karl Marx and Friederich Engels; translated for Socialist Labour Party by L. G. Aitken and F. G. Budgen.

possible realization of democratic reforms is necessary and requisite for the spreading of Socialistic enlightenment, *and for introducing appropriate organization.*" [1]

Lenin, then, by 1901 is waging a paper war on three fronts, against the Tsar, against the idealist Utopians, the Populists, and against the "legal" preachers of an emasculated Marxism, headed by Peter Struve, a "Marxism" bound to lead him, so Lenin contended, into the camp of the Liberal bourgeoisie. The organ of his polemics was the paper *Iskra* (The Spark), published in Switzerland and founded by him and Martov, afterwards his bitter Menshevik enemy.

In his first important article in what was uniquely his paper, Lenin tackles the question of tactics in his famous article "Where to Begin." In this article he lays down what his iron resolution was later to make into the practical programme of the as yet non-existent Bolshevik party. He followed it up by a book, "What to Do," which became the pivot of the controversy that was to split the newly formed "Russian Socialist Democrat Labour Party" into two wings. The very titles of these publications, arresting in their challenging decisiveness, bring the man vividly before us—above all things he was positive, definite. If he indulged in dreams, he usually said so. At any moment, he knew how to say decisively and with no element of hesitation exactly what he proposed to do next.

In a short time the *Iskra* was engaged in polemics against the newly-founded Social Revolutionary party which represented the revolutionary peasantry rather than the town workers. At this time it prided itself on being more advanced than any other party in Russia. Lenin at once detected the political irresponsibility of a party that considered it had done something quite important by blowing up a Grand Duke; its peasant roots gave him a hint of its future, and he came out decisively and characteristically with the judgment, "You gentlemen of the Social Revolutionaries are representatives of the petty bourgeoisie, and nothing more." Plekhanov had hailed the first book of Lenin as the epiphany of a new force in world-Socialism. That force he now found was rapidly disrupting his party.

During 1902 Lenin and his wife were in London living in poor lodgings in Whitechapel. Trotsky tells how he found them there one autumn day that year after his escape from

[1] Quoted Miliukov, "Bolshevism: an International Danger," pp. 64-5. (Italics mine.)

Siberia. He was so excited at the prospect of exchanging views with Lenin that though he arrived in London at an unearthly hour in the morning he hurried off at once to Whitechapel. He had been told on his way across Germany how many knocks he must give before that door would open. Mme. Lenin let him in and made him tea : " In her room was almost always the smell of burnt paper, and she often complained with her gentle emphasis that people wrote little, or mixed up the ciphers, or wrote in chemical inks in such a way that one line crawled over another, and so on." Later that day Lenin took Trotsky to see the sights of London. " That is their famous Westminster," he said, indicating the Houses of Parliament. Trotsky explained that " their " did not mean " belonging to the English " but " belonging to the enemy." And so it was with Lenin to the end. Everything was either " theirs " or " ours." It is hard for us, heirs of a more tolerant tradition, to realize the terrible concentration implied by those simple words, " That is their famous Westminster." If a thing or an institution were " theirs," he could admire it, but only as a general may admire the dispositions of an able enemy.[1] But to end this digression :

Events came to a head at the Congress held at London in 1903, at the Third Congress of the party. Already at the Second Congress, Lenin began to detect a certain weakening in the revolutionary fibre of the party. Men like Martov and Plekhanov began to play with Struve's ideas. The articles and pamphlets of Lenin proclaiming the indefeasible claims of revolutionary Marxism as interpreted by himself against any hint of co-operation with bourgeois parties, " reformists," all who imagined it possible that a revolution might be avoided —the claims of this little " Iskra " group consisting of Lenin, Kamenev, Zinoviev, and Rykov, became the apple of discord at the Congress. All attempts at a compromise failed, and the party broke into two wings, the Bolsheviks (Maximalists ; from Russian word " Bolshinstvo," a majority) led by Lenin, and the Mensheviks (Minimalists ; Russian, Menshinstvo, minority) led by Martov. The party was not completely disrupted, but from now on united action by the two wings became increasingly difficult.

The split took place not only over questions of tactics but on those involving fundamental principle. On the

[1] Article by Arthur Ransome, *Manchester Guardian Weekly*, 8th August 1924, quoting Trotsky's book " Concerning Lenin."

question of principle, Bolsheviks and Mensheviks were divided by the old question of a choice between revolutionary or evolutionary Socialism. It cannot be too often repeated that the Bolshevik insistence on mass revolutionary action as the purpose of the Russian Social Democrat Labour Party (R.S.D.L.P.) arises from the conception of the State held by Lenin and his followers and derivable from the doctrines of Marx and Engels. Lenin formulated his position in the astounding formula of Engels " The State is the product and the manifestation of the irreconcilability of class-antagonism." This purely negative and apparently paradoxical definition of the State becomes clearer if we place beside it the words of Engels : " The State has tended to become the State of the most powerful and predominant class politically, thereby obtaining new means for the oppression and exploitation of the oppressed classes." Obviously, if this is true, nothing can be done until the machine of the State has been wrested from the hands of its present controllers by violent means. To believe in Socialism as capable of being realized in the State by evolutionary and constitutional means involves the belief that the State is the organ for the reconciliation of classes instead of the organ for the oppression of one class in the interests of another. The Bolsheviks, accordingly, charged the Mensheviks with " correcting " Marx in terms of their evolutionary heresy.[1]

Flowing from this fundamental doctrinal difference was a corresponding conflict over methods. The Mensheviks desired to subordinate illegal to legal opposition to the autocracy, while the Bolsheviks wished to create a far-flung network of secret societies, which would control the legal societies. The Bolsheviks wished to subordinate the whole party to the Central Committee, in order to strengthen its efficiency as a revolutionary organization, while the Mensheviks aimed at fostering local initiative along legal lines.

Plekhanov, in the interests of party unity, co-operated with the Bolsheviks for some years after the split, which, however, continued to widen with the steadily increasing ascendency of Lenin. In the summer of 1905, the Bolshevik wing held its first party congress. At this, a development in doctrine is to be observed in Lenin's speech urging the Congress to abandon all idea of allowing a bourgeois republic to be formed

[1] " Report of the Emmott Committee to collect information on Russia," (Russia No. 1) (1921) Cmd. 1240, Sec. 20.

in Russia on the outbreak of revolution. In his view, European Social Democratic parliamentarism was rotten through and through with its many compromises with capitalism. Though complete Socialism probably could not be realized at once, yet, he asserted, the Russian Revolution would stand on the borders between a bourgeois and Socialist revolution.[1]

The *Iskra* had passed after the split into the hands of the Mensheviks, those " agents of the bourgeoisie," as the Bolsheviks called their rivals, whereupon Lenin founded the *Vperiod* (Forward). From this small sheet he directed his ceaseless attacks on the Mensheviks, who were well provided both with cash and papers. In spite of these advantages, when the disasters of the Russo-Japanese war precipitated the revolutionary movements of 1905, the Mensheviks found themselves at a disadvantage.

Throughout the crisis of the autumn of 1905, Lenin, though in Petrograd, did not play any public part. He appeared only two or three times at the meetings of the famous first Soviet of Petrograd, of which Leon Trotsky was the flamboyant President. The situation was so precarious that the party would not allow Lenin to expose himself to the danger of arrest. Seated in the high audience gallery, day after day he looked down upon the first Soviet at its sessions in the " Free Economic Society." " Perhaps, in those days, he already foresaw, in a dream as it were, the time when there would be a Soviet State ; when the Soviets . . . would become the sole authority in the country." [2]

The Bolsheviks took the lead, though the Mensheviks held the majority in the Soviet. The policy of armed insurrection prevailed over the caution of the moderates, and the Revolution was crushed through the inertia of the peasants, whose intervention could alone have saved the proletariat in their struggle with the autocracy. True to their principles, the Bolsheviks boycotted the elections to the first Duma, and their abstention aided the returning reaction that again gripped Russia in its blood-stained talons.

For Lenin, the Revolution was one of those glorious failures that render ultimate victory assured—the Revolution had discovered the Soviet, it had proved that the Russian proletariat could act together and, well led, could conquer power. In spite of the reaction, which the Mensheviks asserted was

[1] Zinoviev, " Lenin : His Life and Work," p. 20.
[2] Zinoviev, *Ibid.*, p. 23.

largely due to Bolshevik intransigence, Lenin's grip on his followers was unshaken, and his propagandist activity was winning recruits steadily. He remained in Russia after the Revolution till 1907; hunted from one refuge to another, living for the most part in the little village of Kuokalla in Finland, constantly escaping arrest by a miracle but never caught; and then, when the net seemed certain to close round him, he again made his way out of Russia and passed into his second exile.

Though they could not catch him, the Tsarist secret police knew well the man they were seeking. Here is an extract from their archives giving an admirable description of Lenin at this period: "Short of stature, thick-set with short neck and round red face; his moustache and beard he has shaved; nose slightly turned up, piercing eyes, bald with high forehead, nearly always carries on his arm a waterproof cape, constantly changes his headgear from a sheepskin fur hat to a Finnish cap of English tweed, with a peak like a jockey's; walks with a firm gait." [1]

His pamphlets, books and articles flowed out in a ceaseless stream, his capacity for work was inexhaustible; yet in the early years of his second exile were times of real privation. During his stay in Paris, he was ill and always living below subsistence limit, yet the clear flame of his spirit never wavered. The present Bolshevik Commissary for Education, Lunacharsky, relates that he met Lenin for the first time at the International Socialist Congress at Stuttgart in 1907. They discussed the prospects of the Socialist revolution in Europe, and Lunacharsky took a pessimistic view of the near future, saying, that, at the best, they would probably all be very old before the revolution came: "When I elaborated my views I noticed real grief on Lenin's strong and clever face, and I understood how passionately this man desired in his own lifetime not only to see a Revolution but to take a prominent part in it." [2] There was nothing vulgar or self-seeking in that passionate desire for power. Lenin was compelled by his inmost nature to seek to translate his ideas into action, and with this spirit that fearlessly asks for power and accepts its responsibilities with joy, he has imbued the Bolshevik party, which alone among the Russian enemies of the autocracy was

[1] Quoted, R. H. Bruce Lockhart, "Lenin: the Man and his Achievement," *Edinburgh Review*, April 1924, p. 299.

[2] Farbman, "Bolshevism in Retreat," p. 51.

not afraid, when the time came, to accept, nay to desire, sole responsibility.

The emphasis that the Bolsheviks, convinced by 1905 that the proletariat was the only force vital and courageous enough to attack the autocracy, laid on conspiracy and armed revolt led inevitably to fierce efforts against them by the secret police. The constant surveillance and pursuit, the knowledge that numbers of secret police had penetrated into their organization, developed a tense atmosphere of secrecy and suspicion in the party. Very few members knew the real names of more than one or two of their fellow-workers. The discipline and centralized control of the party helped to obviate the grave psychological disadvantages under which the Bolsheviks worked. An elaborate organization existed for smuggling members across the frontier and for importing literature for distribution, for the most part among the industrial workers of the cities. One of the centres of this activity was a lonely country house situated amid the vast forests and marshes round Suwalki. There members and party-workers assembled to receive their false passports and await a moment for slipping across the frontier. In this way Lenin himself paid several flying visits to Russia after 1907. In Berlin was another house for the reception of members travelling across Germany. To divert the suspicions of the German police it was actually maintained as a brothel and in this way those arriving or leaving at unusual hours escaped attention.[1]

In the year following Lenin's return to Western Europe, (1907-8) practically the whole of the secret Bolshevik organization was destroyed or dislocated by a series of wholesale arrests. So serious was the disaster that for the time even Lenin abandoned the idea of restoring the shattered organizations and advocated a policy of concentration on equipping future agitators by an intensive training at various centres. Maxim Gorky directed a propagandist school on the island of Capri; there was another at Bologna and one near Paris. Mensheviks, as well as Bolsheviks, were concerned in these schools, but the direction was for the most part in the hands of the extreme left wing of the R.S.D.L.P. —the Bolsheviks of the Left or the "Vperedovtsy," "Forwards," who frequently charged the strict Leninite section of

[1] "Report of the Emmott Committee to collect information on Russia," Russia, No. 1 (1921) Cmd. 1240, Sec. 24.

the party with making too many concessions to the Mensheviks and abandoning Bolshevik doctrine in the interests of party unity. This sufficiently rebuts the oft-repeated assertion that Lenin was a wholly disruptive force, and that nothing but complete subordination to his will and acceptance of his Marxian inspiration could satisfy him. The points that divided him from Martov and the Mensheviks have been indicated. They represent profound differences in philosophy and method, yet, though Lenin made his position uncompromisingly clear, he continued to co-operate with the Mensheviks and so to keep the R.S.D.L.P. in being right on to his *coup d'état* of 1911, to which we must return later.

During the darkest hours of the reaction, even the stoutest revolutionary wavered. The Mensheviks worked furiously for the " liquidation " of revolutionary enterprises in Russia and the substitution of wholly legal methods. They jeered bitterly at the Bolsheviks as a collection of cranks, and a special comic paper was published by them in Paris to ridicule the followers of Lenin. One of its jokes was to the effect that " a reward would be offered of half a kingdom to the person who could name a fourth Bolshevik in addition to Lenin, Zinoviev, and Kamenev." [1]

Amid all this depression and bitterness, Lenin with enormous difficulty managed to found yet two more Bolshevik papers, *The Proletariat* and *The Social Democrat*, published at Geneva, and later in Paris. He then buried himself in the National Library in Paris and devoted two years of unflagging research to a book directed against the various " semi-Marxians who endeavoured to traverse the philosophical foundations of Marxism and present it in one or other " reformist " disguise. Above all, he fought for " the living soul of Marxism, its revolutionary character," [2] and produced a vigorous defence of the materialist conception of history. Even those most inclined to sneer at his philosophical excursus were astounded at the vast mass of books Lenin managed to digest into one of his usual lucid and trenchant expositions in the course of two years' reading.

From 1909 onwards, signs were not wanting that the reaction was slackening its grip. The Bolsheviks were allowed to establish two " legal " papers in Russia, the *Zvezda* (Star) at Petrograd and a monthly periodical *Mysl* (Thought) at

[1] Zinoviev, " Lenin: His Life and Work," p. 27.
[2] N. Lenin, " The Collapse of the Second International," p. 25.

Moscow. The moving spirit and devoted contributor was, of course, Lenin, who with his little group of followers had moved from Paris to Galicia as soon as the party was allowed a legal press again in Russia, in order to be as near Russian events as possible. For two years after 1909, and the General Conference of the R.S.D.L.P. held in London that year, Lenin and his Bolsheviks were more or less reconciled to the Mensheviks on the basis of the carefully elaborated party platform there constructed.

The programme bears signs of being a compromise, for while it asserts that the " indispensable condition " of the social revolution is the dictatorship of the proletariat, it goes on to state that the " most immediate " aim of the R.S.D.L.P. is " the overthrow of the Tsarist autocracy and its replacement by a *democratic republic* " which would proceed to realize a long list of constructive reforms—" the centralization of supreme power in the hands of a legislative assembly," national free and obligatory education, the eight hours' day, national insurance, employers' liability, etc.

The years 1909-11 were a time of truce between Bolsheviks and Mensheviks. A small labour group directly inspired by Lenin secured seats in the Duma. Under his inspiration, they took up an attitude of irreconcilable hostility to the Government and virtually to the Duma itself, using it merely as a platform from which to address the wide world of Russia on the horrors of the capitalist system. When the Bolshevik deputies came to see him to consult him as to what attitude they should take to this or that measure, the budget or the policy of this or that party, Lenin would laugh heartily and then explain to his rather startled hearers: " . . . What do you want a budget, an amendment, a bill for? You are workmen and the Duma exists for the ruling classes. You simply step forward and tell all Russia in simple language about the life and toil of the working class . . . and fling into the face of this reactionary Duma that its members are scoundrels and exploiters!" [1]

By 1911, Lenin was convinced that continued co-operation with the moderate wing of the R.S.D.L.P. was progressively paralysing revolutionary activity in Russia. The " liquidator legalists " of the party, as he termed the Mensheviks and their allies, were still hard at work closing down the illegal organizations with a view to confining their activities in the future

[1] Zinoviev, " Lenin: His Life and Work," p. 30.

solely to constitutional opposition. Lenin, as has been shown, did not refuse to hold relations with "legal" organizations, rather he encouraged them, but what he held with reason to be the deepest treason to the revolutionary cause was the abandonment in principle of "illegal" work. You cannot be a revolutionary and refrain from the revolutionary deed. To drop illegal propaganda must involve ultimate absorption in the liberal bourgeois political bloc. At the same time, he fully recognized that the illegal societies in Russia were, owing to the successive blows of the secret police and the disintegrating activities of the "liquidators," in a state of complete confusion. He desired the party to close down organizations that were no longer effective, and concentrate its energies on the formation of a special professional unit of propagandists who would broadcast legal and illegal literature among the masses and so prepare the ground for the ultimate reconstitution of the secret societies and the launching of the revolution. For all these ends he began to agitate in the spring of 1911 to bring about a meeting of the Central Committee of R.S.D.L.P. through the agency of the Foreign Bureau. These organs need further description. The Central Committee of the R.S.D.L.P. was permanently split into two sections. The Foreign Bureau resided in Western Europe and endeavoured to keep in touch with the Russian section and in conjunction with it to organize and control to a greater or less degree the work of the party in Russia. Obviously, this system made it extremely difficult to assemble a full meeting of the Central Committee without an enormous expenditure of time and money in getting the members of the Russian section safely across the frontier. In addition, his opponents secured the rejection of the proposal in the Foreign Bureau.

Lenin then summoned Alexander Rykov (later his successor as President of the Council of People's Commissaries), who had just fled from exile in Russia, to confer with him in Paris. Rykov was a member of the Russian section of the Central Committee, and his support was of the greatest value to Lenin in the development of his plans. They organized a private conference of Bolsheviks at which Lenin emphasized the prevailing inefficiency of the Foreign Bureau, its refusal to summon a meeting of the Central Committee, and the disruptive activities of the liquidators. He therefore proposed to the Conference that the Bolshevik representative and those who co-operated with him on the Foreign Bureau should withdraw, and that Rykov, as the only member of the Russian section at liberty, should summon a full meeting of the Central Committee. The Conference agreed to these suggestions and Semashko, the Bolshevik representative, accordingly left the Foreign Bureau of which he was Secretary and Treasurer, apparently carrying the funds with him. Rykov's invitation to those members of the Central Committee available met with but a poor response—only eight persons attended the meeting and only five of them appeared without reservations at the Conference—viz., Lenin, Zinoviev, Kamenev, Rykov, and Tishko who remained a member of the Foreign Bureau in order to report the moves of the opposition. Since four Mensheviks who were invited did not answer, and three members of the Conference came merely as observers and would take part only with a consultative voice, it was impossible to regard the meeting as a plenary conference of the Central Committee. Lenin was thus thrust back on the expedient he had strongly desired to avoid—a representative conference of the party itself.

His object was now to secure a Bolshevik majority at all costs, and the "Organizing Commission" to engineer the secret elections in Russia was constituted accordingly. If at the forthcoming conference the Bolsheviks obtained a clear majority, the R.S.D.L.P. could be finally identified with its extreme wing controlled by himself, and the "liquidators" and other sections would be driven into the wilderness. His instructions to the Organizing Commission were definite. "If in any organization there are a hundred Mensheviks or a hundred followers of Trotsky, and only five Bolsheviks, then the representatives to the conference must be sent from these five and not from the remaining hundred."

The Commission met with the greatest difficulties in Russia—the all-important Rykov was arrested in Moscow; it was found impossible to get into touch with some of the disorganized secret groups; the machinations of the Bolsheviks became generally known. By the end of 1911, the Commission had been able to send to Paris only five Bolsheviks and two Mensheviks. The credentials of the "representatives" would not in the circumstances bear too close an examination, and in any case a conference of seven persons could not possibly pose as reflecting the views of the R.S.D.L.P. throughout the Russian Empire. Meanwhile, Lenin heard that a strong movement was developing for the summoning of a conference of all sections of the R.S.D.L.P. to re-establish the party's unity. Working against time, Lenin sent out another band of his agents to Russia. They were successful and a sufficient number of representatives reached Western Europe to justify the meeting of a conference, which accordingly sat in Prague from 19th-30th January 1912, and held twenty-three sessions. Eighteen members of the R.S.D.L.P. attended, fourteen from the organizations in Russia and four from the party abroad, representing the leaders. With the exception of two Mensheviks, they were all devoted followers of Lenin.

The Conference began its proceedings by unanimously voting itself a general party Conference of the R.S.D.L.P. and the supreme authority of the party. Lenin then proposed (as a convenient test of the revolutionary fervour of the working-class delegates present) that in view of the disorganization of the party all illegal associations should be dissolved and that the R.S.D.L.P. should concentrate wholly on legal propaganda electing a committee to supervise the work. He was delighted to find that the delegates were willing to continue their secret activities at all costs, and a resolution was passed for introducing secret associations into the existing legal workers' institutions.

As one of the motives, though not the chief, for the assembling of the schismatic Bolshevik Congress, had been the urgent necessity of deciding on what attitude to adopt towards the approaching elections for the fourth Duma, it spent some time in deciding on its policy. After the rejection of the Menshevik proposal to form an electoral bloc with the whole Liberal opposition to the autocracy, the Congress resolved that the party should maintain a strictly independent attitude to all other groups, at least during the first phase of the election.

It then elected a new Central Committee of the party of seven members including Lenin and Zinoviev, who, it was decided, should remain abroad as the Foreign Bureau of the party, as the permanent centre which could not be broken up by the activities of the secret police. The other members of the Central Committee were to work in Russia, and each was to have the right to co-opt other members who would be ready to serve in the probable event of the arrest of one or more of the original members by the secret police.

As Lenin had managed to secure the Bolshevik share of the party funds and in addition a subsidy of 40,000 francs from the trustees who sympathized with his *coup d'état* as likely to invigorate the party, the Congress was in a position to exert financial pressure on its opponents. Accordingly, it decided to withdraw the subsidy granted to the *Pravda*, a paper which showed Menshevik leanings, and to constitute the existing *Rabochaya Gazeta* as the official organ of the party, with Lenin, Zinoviev, and Kamenev on the editorial staff.

In closing the Congress, Lenin in his concluding speech as President announced his joy at having lived to see the day when " the workers, hitherto relying on the leadership of the intellectuals, now showed themselves capable of taking into their own hands the conduct of party affairs." He then returned to Paris and in an address to the newly constituted Foreign Organizing Commission defined the policy of the new R.S.D.L.P. towards the Duma elections. They must concentrate on winning seats and devote themselves, once in the Duma, to the task of making the position of the Government as difficult as possible.

In August, 1912, the indefatigable worker returned to Prague and later settled at Cracow in Galicia, to be the closer in touch with his agents in Russia. He ignored all overtures from the other sections of the former R.S.D.L.P. whom his stroke had thrown into catastrophic disorder. With great difficulty the Mensheviks succeeded in holding a Conference in Vienna in August 1912. The followers of Trotsky, who presided, were unable to come to any agreement with the Mensheviks led by Martov. Alexinsky, leader of the " Forwards " or extreme Bolsheviks, left the meeting as the result of a violent attack on him by Martov, and Trotsky actually failed to carry a resolution declaring the Conference a general meeting of the R.S.D.L.P.[1] The silence of Lenin was impregnable. Henceforth it was clear to every anxious worker in the fight against the Tsardom that he must be either for Lenin or against him. Lenin had but said " Come ye out from among them," and the secession of his followers had left the R.S.D.L.P. in ruins. He had stolen Excalibur, confident that he and he alone could wield it. His uncanny prescience, revealed in his tremendous fight for the control of the party, told him that the sands were running out. Like the Zulus, he smelt the blood of future slaughter.

On 8th October 1912, Montenegro declared war on Turkey,

[1] For the preceding paragraphs on Lenin's *coup d'état* of 1911-12, see " Report of the Committee to collect information on Russia," Cmd. 1240, Appendix VI.

and a few days later the Balkan League embarked on its great campaign against that decaying incubus, the Turkish Empire, whose recent convulsions under the régime of the Young Turks had as usual been hailed as signs of resurrection by Western pundits. To Lenin's ears the overture to the World War had begun. " You see—I was right ! " he exclaimed to Maxim Gorky, " The dissociation is beginning ! The threat of being poisoned by the pus of a dead body, should now be clear to all who look events in the face. . . . That is the beginning of the catastrophe. We will yet live to see a European war. A wild slaughter. It is unavoidable. The proletariat, I think, will not find the strength to prevent this struggle from breaking out. It will, of course, suffer more than the other classes—that is its fate. But the criminals will sink into the blood which they will shed. The enemies of the people will be exhausted. That is also unavoidable." Clenching his teeth, he looked out of the window, into the distance. " No—you only think ! What makes the satiated send the hungry to a mutual slaughter ? Can one reconcile onself with this ? Can you point out to me a less excusable, a sillier crime ? The workers will have to pay terribly for this, but finally it is they who will win. Such is the will of history."[1]

From Cracow Lenin for two more years directed the movements of proletarian Petrograd, years of vigorous propaganda and hard but pertinacious spade-work. The tremendous days of August, 1914, found him living in a " God-forsaken little mountain village in Galicia."[2] Zinoviev relates how he had a bet with Lenin that the German Social Democrats would not dare to vote against the war-credits in the Reichstag but would salve their consciences by abstaining. Lenin was convinced that, though they would not resist war, at least they would not betray their own oft-proclaimed principles of abstention, but would register an academic protest in voting against the credits. Both parties to this bet were wrong. The German Social Democrats rushed to the support of the Imperial Government. " When the first number of the *Vorwärts*, the organ of the German Social Democrats, arrived with the news that they had voted the war-credits, Lenin at first refused to believe. " It cannot be," he said, " it must be a forged number. Those scoundrels, the German bourgeois have specially published such a number of the *Vorwärts* in order also to compel us to

[1] Maxim Gorky, " Nicolai Lenin—the Man," p. 6.
[2] Zinoviev, " N. Lenin : His Life and Work," p. 32.

go against the International." Alas, it was not so. It turned out that the Social Patriots really had voted the war-credits. When Lenin saw it, his first word was: "The Second International is dead." [1]

The outbreak of the war threw the Socialist parties into the greatest moral confusion. The Second International, founded in 1889, and representative of all the Socialist organizations of the world, had again and again discussed the probability of a general war precipitated by autocratic governments or Jingo militarist parties, and the questions how to prevent the outbreak and how to smother it if kindled. At its Conferences at Paris, 1900, Stuttgart, 1907, Copenhagen, 1910, and Basle, 1912, it had passed resolutions against war providing for international strikes. Yet all these pacificist programmes remained so much ink and paper when the Socialists found themselves in a position to decide whether or not they should be translated into action. Alexinsky, a member of the "Forwards" group of the R.S.D.L.P., as has been mentioned above, and Plekhanov, the founder of Russian Social Democracy, both supported the war. In all countries, by far the most impotent of the paralysed Socialists were the pacificists who refused to support the war actively but had to bow to events and for the time lost all influence over the masses.

Alone in the earthquake Lenin stood firm. He refused to deviate by one hair's breadth from the principles he—and the rest—had so often and so vehemently proclaimed. In the autumn of 1914, he published his "Theses on the War." It was a characteristic title; at all the great turning-points of his adventurous career, Lenin was in the habit of analysing the situation in a series of theses which he would publish just as an academic publicist would issue a monograph. In his thesis of 1914, Lenin nailed the red flag to the mast. He asserted uncompromisingly that the war of 1914 was a bourgeois Imperialist scramble for world-markets; he denounced the Socialist leaders who had rallied to their governments and thereby proved the bankruptcy of the Second International—a bankruptcy he ascribed to the influence of petty bourgeois opportunism. The Third International, which he already foreshadowed, must work for the final emancipation of Socialism from the corroding influence of the bourgeoisie. What, then, was the present task of the Social

[1] Zinoviev, "N. Lenin: His Life and Work," p. 33.

Democracy, especially of the R.S.D.L.P.? He thus defines his programme: the transformation of the European war into the civil war of the exploited and murdered workers against the reactionary governments and parties of all countries. There must be intensive propaganda among the troops with a view to impressing upon them that their duty was to direct their weapons, not against their brothers, "the hired slaves of other countries," but against the bourgeoisie that battened in their blood; finally, there must be a strong republican propaganda throughout Europe. He proclaimed that the military defeat of Russia was the essential preliminary to the downfall of the Tsardom and the ousting of the Russian bourgeoisie by the dictatorship of the proletariat. Even Trotsky shrank from such a conclusion to the great argument. Would not Germany, if victorious over Russia, extinguish the very revolution for which Lenin was prepared to pay so high a price? But Lenin was willing to take the risk—since he was convinced that the social revolution once begun would become a world-wide avalanche. He firmly refused to compare the war of 1914 with the earlier wars of the nineteenth century. Those former wars were a "continuation of the policy of long national movements of the 'bourgeoisie,' movements against a foreign yoke and against absolutism. . . . There was no other question at that time save whether you preferred the success of one bourgeoisie or the other. One cannot be a Marxist without admiring the great bourgeois revolutionaries who had a historic right to speak in the name of their bourgeois 'fatherlands,' which were raising new nations . . . to a civilized life and sending them to battle against feudalism. At the same time, one cannot be a Marxist without despising those Socialists who speak in the defence of their countries in connection with the stifling of Belgium by German Imperialists and the plundering of Austria and Turkey by the Imperialists of England, France, Russia, and Italy."[1]

In the pamphlet from which this extract is taken, published in 1915, Lenin confronts the renegade Socialists with the various manifestos which they and he had from time to time signed; he analyses the various arguments of Karl Kautsky and Plekhanov in relation to their own principles in a particularly venomous style. Towards the end of this grim exposition the tone rises, and Lenin proclaims the necessity

[1] N. Lenin, "The Collapse of the Second International."

of civil war: "If to-day you are handed a voting paper, take it and organize so that you may beat your enemy, but do not use it for the purpose of sending men to parliament for the sake of soft jobs, at which they clutch, for fear they may be sent to prison. If on the morrow they take away your voting paper and hand you a rifle, a magnificent quick-firing gun, built in accordance with the latest requirements of machine technique—take these instruments of death and destruction, don't listen to sentimental whimperers who fear war. In this world there still remain many things which must be destroyed by fire and iron before the working class may be free. And if exasperation and despair are on the increase amongst the masses; if there exists a revolutionary situation, be ready to create fresh organizations and *to employ the useful instruments of death and destruction against your own government and bourgeoisie.*" [1]

The harsh originality of Lenin's position; his fearlessness in maintaining it against any Socialist who differed from him in the interpretation of the 1912 Basle Manifesto of the Second International; the note of utter conviction that runs through the passionate but closely knit arguments of his pamphlets rallied his followers to him in ever more convinced devotion. His position had the strength of one who is not afraid at any time to break the closest ties of friendship and stand alone on a question of principle. Paradoxical as it may sound, his vehement assertion that the world war must be converted into civil war in all countries was not only deducible from the terms of the Basle Manifesto, but flowed naturally from the principles he had maintained during his whole career as a revolutionary. The war did not drive Lenin further to the Left, but it compelled him to define his position in more uncompromising terms.

A few extracts will suffice to give the salient ideas running through the Basle Manifesto of the Second International: "Should . . . war break out, it is the duty of Socialists to intervene with the object of putting a speedy end to it; *it is their duty to make use of the economic and political crisis in their fullest possible measure to rouse the common people and thus accelerate the downfall of the domination of Capital.* . . . Let the governments remember that the Franco-German war was followed by the Commune. . . . The governments must be

[1] N. Lenin, "The Collapse of the Second International," pp. 58-9, in translation of A. Sirnis for Socialist Labour Press.

totally blind or mad, if they have not yet grasped that the mere suggestion of a monstrous world-war must call forth the indignation and revolt of the working class. The proletarians regard as a crime shooting at one another for the sake of increasing the profits of the capitalists, satisfying the ambitions of dynasties, or for the glory of the secret treaties of diplomacy."[1]

One wonders whether the moderate Socialists who signed this Manifesto, and some of whom at this day occupy exalted positions in the governments of Western Europe, could have imagined it possible " to make use of the economic and political crisis " precipitated by a great war " to rouse the common people and *thus* accelerate the downfall of the domination of Capital "—to do all this without a revolution, at the very crisis of national existence to rouse the people against a government armed to the teeth and fighting for its life—without a revolution ! What, again, is the significance of the reference to the Paris Commune ?

That Lenin, one of the few men whose mind was sufficiently clear to accept the consequences of his own principles, should from now on devote himself, among all his other fighting activities, to the disruption of the Second and the foundation of the Third International is not surprising. As early as March 1915, at a conference of the foreign sections of the new R.S.D.L.P. held at Berne, Lenin declared the necessity for the establishment of the Third International.

Between 5th and 8th September 1915, there assembled at the little Swiss village of Zimmerwald, near Berne, an International Congress of Socialists opposed to the war. Since the French, Belgian, and German majority Socialists, in view of the support they were affording to their governments, were not even invited, and the delegates of the British Independent Labour Party and Socialist Party were prevented by the government from attending, the Conference was dominated by the East European elements, and Lenin, Rakovsky, and Radek were the moving spirits behind the resolutions passed. Here was elaborated the famous formula " peace without annexations or indemnities on the basis of the self-determination of peoples," and though the censorship prevented more than the merest fragments of news about the Conference to leak out, it was at Zimmerwald that the Third International was born.

[1] Italics mine.

The Conference formulated the following position, embodied in the Zimmerwald Manifesto: (1) Responsibility for the war rests upon "the ruling forces of the capitalist society in whose hands the destinies of peoples have rested—monarchical as well as republican governments, secret diplomacy, powerful combines of employers, bourgeois parties, capitalist press, Churches—all these agents bear the full burden of responsibility for this war, which has originated in the social order preserved by them and nourishing them, and which is being now carried on in their interests. (2) War aims are consolidated in the formula "the struggle for 'Socialism,'" for peace without annexations and contributions, which is possible only on the repudiation of all desire for violating the rights and liberties of peoples. (3) The aim of the Zimmerwald Conference is not only peace but "we who have put ourselves not on the ground of national solidarity with the class of employers, but on the ground of the international solidarity of the proletariat and of class war, met in order to re-establish international bonds torn asunder and to call the working class to recollect their duties towards themselves. . . . Proletarians! at the beginning of the war we gave our working power, our courage, our endurance to the service of the ruling classes. Now, we must begin a struggle for our own cause, for the sacred aim of Socialism, for the liberation of oppressed peoples and enslaved classes by means of an uncompromising proletariat class war." [1]

At the moment, the definitive formation of the Third International was postponed, but the Zimmerwald Conference, before separating, set up the Internationalist Socialist Commission (I.C.S.) at Berne, which organized a second International Conference at Kienthal, another Swiss village, a Conference which met 27th to 30th April 1916. Lenin and Radek attended this Conference also, and, supported by Rosa Luxemburg, carried a resolution declaring that "all demands of the 'bourgeois or Socialist pacifism,' such as limitation of armaments, obligatory arbitration, and even the building up of 'small nations' into states, are nothing but 'new illusions,' and that 'durable' peace can be attained only by the Socialist upheaval." [2]

The intransigence of Lenin, though strongly reflected in

[1] Quoted Miliukov, "Bolshevism: an International Danger," pp. 55-6.
[2] *Ibid.*, p. 57.

the Zimmerwald and Kienthal programmes, was not unopposed, and his explosive formulæ were considerably reduced before being issued. The French Socialist, Ledebour, at Zimmerwald, voiced the real reasons for Socialist hesitancy when he exclaimed to Lenin, " It is all right for you here living abroad to issue appeals for a civil war, I should have liked to see how you would have done it if you had lived in Russia." The reply was swift, " When Marx was drawing up his Communist Manifesto he also was living abroad, and only narrow-minded Philistines could reproach him for that. I now live abroad because I was sent here by the Russian workers, but when the time arrives we shall know how to stand at our posts." [1]

Those were days of long silences, when no news came through save the endless and soul-numbing war communiqués. But ceaselessly from his refuge, first at Berne, then at Zurich, Lenin sent out the inexhaustible stream of his letters, his leaflets, papers, pamphlets. Trusty agents smuggled them into Germany and the Russian lines, and there can be little doubt that Lenin and the party, either inside or outside Russia, did much propagandist work in the trenches and among the workmen of the great industrial cities. The five Bolshevik members of the Duma were exiled to Siberia for receiving and disseminating communications from Lenin. But even with their leaders in exile or abroad, the Bolsheviks were able to make their influence felt. In the autumn of 1915, the government, compelled to attempt to broaden its basis owing to the shocking munition scandal, set up the " War Industrial Commissions " to reorganize and speed up the output of munitions. At first the Bolsheviks, by vigorous opposition, were able to prevent the election of any labour representatives to the Commissions, thus demonstrating their hold on the workers. Only after numerous arrests and government purging did the Labour Congress decide to send delegates. Needless to say, these delegates were Mensheviks.[2] But " the Russian Revolution as a whole had nothing to do with any kind of international propaganda." [3]

During the years when, like Cavor in Wells's " First Men in the Moon," he was pouring out an endless stream of messages of which he could not be sure that any were taking effect, with that almost universal characteristic of great political

[1] Zinoviev, " Lenin : His Life and Work," p. 36.
[2] See " New Europe," vol. vi., No. 77, p. 365.
[3] Miliukov, " Bolshevism : an International Danger," p. 69.

genius of never neglecting any opportunity however slight, Lenin had flung himself vigorously into personal work among the Swiss proletariat. His wretched garret in the home of a shoemaker in the poorest quarter of Zurich became the H.Q. of a tiny group of some twenty or so Swiss workers whom he had won over from the official " Social patriots." He found time to write innumerable letters to fellow-exiles of the R.S.D.L.P. in other parts of Switzerland, urging them not to think so much of Russia as to forget the Swiss. In one of his letters to Zinoviev, he rejoiced like a child because " he had succeeded in getting into the organization of Left Social Democrats seven youthful proletarians, and might, perhaps, succeed in getting an eighth."[1] His courage was not flamboyant, it was the quiet heroism of a soul driven on unrestingly by that iron will that never for an instant flagged or faltered but pressed ever up the Everest slopes of its ideal. How easy to tabulate and define his beliefs, as he so often does when engaged, as one of his friends once put it, in " boring you into conviction "—how easy yet how inadequate! In the heart of Nikolai Lenin burned some self-renewing flame of devotion, at the back of that hard ruthless intellect lurked the most potent of all forces that can possess the human soul—a dream. . . . As the war dragged on, laying ever heavier burdens on his spirit, it became obvious that he had altered. " The war and the collapse of the Second International had deeply affected him. . . . He never was very tender towards the bourgeoisie, but since the war his hatred of the bourgeoisie became concentrated and sharp like a dagger. He seemed even to have changed in his face."[2]

On the morning of Monday, 13th March 1917, four Guards' Regiments revolted in Petrograd, disarmed their officers and killed or imprisoned them. The Russian Revolution had begun. It spread with lightning rapidity. A mass movment unparalleled in modern history swept like a prolonged shudder over Russia. Within three days the Tsar, unmanned and undone, had abdicated for himself and his son; his ministers were the prisoners of the people, and the only constituted authority left in Russia, the Provisional Committee of the Duma, was vainly trying to control the national convulsion that had taken it utterly by surprise. On 15th March the Provisional Government was constructed, under the auspices of the Committee of the Duma, from the official parties.

[1] Zinoviev, " Lenin: His Life and Work," p. 37. [2] *Ibid.*, p. 38.

Twenty-four hours previously the Soviet of Workers', Soldiers', and Peasants' deputies, formed spontaneously on the model of the Petrograd Soviet of 1905, had begun its sessions in the Tavrichesky Palace where the Duma used to meet, and where at the moment the Provisional Committee was busy Cabinet building. Two authorities had come into being at the same time, the one representative of the Liberal and reformist elements of the old régime, the other the unique embodiment of the revolutionary masses.

The Russian army was the centre from which the initial revolutionary impetus proceeded. In other words, not the town proletariat but the peasant masses, who formed the vast bulk of the military forces, had taken the initiative against the incubus that was slowly smothering Russia. In any specification, however rough, of the causes of the Russian Revolution, the disintegration of the army, the progressive decay of which dated from the Polish campaign of 1915, if not earlier, must be placed first. On 29th December 1916 General Verkhovsky, later the last war minister under Kerensky, wrote in his diary: "It is hard to believe, but nevertheless it is a fact, that we mobilized 15,000,000 men and yet have only 2,000,000 combatants. The deserters number 2,000,000, while another 2,000,000 are in German prisons." The total forces in line up to the beginning of the Revolution have been estimated by a competent Russian authority to have been replaced three times along the whole battle front of 700 miles during the period August 1914 to January 1917.[1] Adequate comment on these statistics of human misery is impossible.

The preposterous legend of the Russian "steam-roller" dies so hard that the disorganization of the army is still attributed mainly to the machinations of the Bolsheviks, but the plain fact that emerges from all the vituperative legends of its enemies is that "the Revolution was not the cause but the result of the disintegration of the Russian army."[2] The objects of the war made no appeal whatever to the locally minded peasant. The curious absence of civic or national spirit in pre-revolutionary Russia is well illustrated by the story quoted by General Denikin of a group of peasant soldiers who were being harangued on the German menace. Their

[1] Report of Emmott "Committee to collect information on Russia," Cmd. 1240 (Russia, No. 1, 1921), Sec. 40.

[2] Farbman, "Bolshevism in Retreat," p. 27.

comment was illuminating, "We are from Tambov, the German will never advance as far as us." [1]

In addition, the War Office and the general administration of the autocracy were incompetent as well as corrupt. The scandals of the Court alienated the nation from the Imperial House. Finally, during the winter of 1916-17 the prevailing inefficiency culminated in a breakdown of the transport system, a breakdown hastened by blizzards, and the failure of the bread supply in the capital followed.

The rumours of pro-German influence and treachery in high places in Russia that had disturbed the Allied Governments and peoples towards the end of 1916, caused an upheaval due, primarily, to the passionate yearning of the Russian masses for peace, to be interpreted as a demonstration against inefficiency in the conduct of the war. The Russian intellectuals and bourgeoisie, constituting seven per cent. of the population, proved their own divorce from the masses they were leading by ratifying the prodigious miscalculation of the Allies that the Revolution would be followed by a new crusade of the Russians against German militarism. Revolutionary fervour for war was at first entirely absent—instead, for some weeks Russia gave herself up to charming idyllic dreams of universal brotherhood and general reconciliation. As Lenin was the first to see, a revolutionary war required a new revolutionary army, but when Trotsky, the Carnot of the Russian Revolution, created the Red Army of 1918-19, it was not for the purpose of subserving the interests of the Allies.

The key to the understanding of the period between the two revolutions of March and November 1917 has already been indicated as the co-existence throughout the length and breadth of Russia of two centres of authority—the Provisional Government and its agents on the one hand, and on the other the locally elected Soviets or Councils of workmen and peasants that sprang up all over Russia in imitation of the example of Petrograd. The famous Army Order No. 1, of 15th March 1917, prescribing the setting up of soldiers' Soviets for all the units of the army, was issued by the Petrograd Soviet without the knowledge of the Provisional Government, which was only formed on the same day. Throughout the army, Committees were everywhere created, sometimes with officers, more often without them. Their powers were not defined, with the result

[1] Denikin, "La décomposition de l'armée et du pouvoir. Février-Septembre 1917," p. 15.

that every committee was a law unto itself, and the prevailing lack of sympathy between officers and men, the heritage of the old régime, was inevitably accentuated—the officers tending to support the Provisional Government, the men turning more and more to the Soviets—the spontaneously created organs of the revolutionary spirit.

The situation was one that in the nature of things could not last—that party would triumph which rightly interpreted the mind of the masses on the two vital and revolutionary questions, peace and the land. In other words, the duty of political realists was to give the peasant soldiers peace—even at any price—and send them home with their land hunger satisfied by the complete expropriation of the Russian landowners. The instrument by which the great audacity of a separate peace with the Central Powers and the revolutionary settlement of the agrarian problem could have been carried, was the longed-for All Russian Constituent Assembly. Had the Constituent Assembly been convoked with the least possible delay after the Revolution, it could have gathered all power into its hands amid the passionate enthusiasm of a nation that had dreamed for generations of the golden day when the Supreme Senate would meet to redress the wrongs of Russia. But the tremulous masters of dwindling power were magnificently too loyal to betray the Allies, already imperiously summoning Russia to further holocausts of her decimated youth, and the Socialists, who at first shrank from power, and then dared not stand alone without the help of the interested bourgeoisie, were subjected to many influences calculated to make them hesitate before the immediate and radical solution of the agrarian problem.

Yet the questions had been asked, and the Sphinx of an inexorable fatality would sooner or later devour all persons and parties who failed to answer rightly. Perhaps the witness of those whose blood and bones were intimately involved might be regarded as somewhat biased, then could not the distracted politicians have listened to the political testament of Count Witte, the ablest of pre-revolutionary Russian statesmen, who held long before the Revolution that only a separate peace could avert a stupendous catastrophe? The sands began running out fast from the day that Nikolai Lenin returned from exile and divined in a flash of superb intuition the significance of every eddy in the roaring revolutionary torrent.

Much has been made of the famous journey in a "sealed

coach" across Germany. The symmetry of the narrative is rather spoilt by the fact that the coach was not "sealed." In any case a journey across Germany was inevitable in view of the refusal of passports by the Allies. That Germany made a point of encouraging the return of revolutionary exiles is certain—she regarded herself as immune to the visionary peace-talk of Petrograd. In these compelling circumstances Lenin applied for passports to the German minister at Berne, and a formal agreement was drawn up by which exiles of all political opinions were to be allowed to return to Russia through Germany and Sweden, and pledged themselves in return to use their influence to secure the repatriation of a similar number of German prisoners.

Before embarking on his great journey Lenin addressed a farewell letter to his Swiss converts and fellow-workers. In the face of the great fact of Revolution triumphant in Russia he reaffirms his carefully defined attitude to the war: "In 1915 we declared that should the Russian Revolution place the power in the hands of a Republican Government, and should this Government attempt to continue the Imperialist war, a war for the conquest of Constantinople, Armenia, Galicia, etc., etc., we should vigorously fight such a Government and should be opposed to the 'defence of the Fatherland' in such a war. . . . We are not pacifists, we are opponents of Imperialistic wars waged for the purpose of securing spoils. But we have always declared it an absurdity for the revolutionary proletariat to vow never to wage revolutionary wars. Such wars may be necessary in the interests of Socialism."[1] Here we find the first hint that the Bolsheviks would be prepared to support the world revolution by armed intervention. And so, characteristically definitive and analytic, Lenin began the most marvellous adventure of our day, the triumphant struggle of one man for the control of a revolution. His journey was not without incident; an important member of Scheidemann's official German Socialist party attempted to enter the carriage and was told by Lenin that he had no desire to converse with traitors, and that if the German persisted he would secure, not an interview, but a thrashing.[2]

On 16th April, the Petrograd Soviet received a wire that a party of exiles, among whom was Lenin, would arrive that evening at the Finland Station. Working against time, the

[1] Quoted Farbman, "Bolshevism in Retreat," p. 66.
[2] Zinoviev, "N. Lenin—His Life and Work," p. 39.

Soviet decided to organize a mass reception for the great revolutionary leader, rumours of whose challenging speeches at Stockholm had reached Petrograd like the growling of distant thunder on the horizon. A radio had informed the fleet at Kronstadt, and the Bolshevik sailors replied that they were coming in their ice-breaker to welcome their chief. By seven o'clock the square in front of the Finland Station was packed with an immense crowd of excited deputations, sight-seers, massed bands, and troops. On the platform stood the moderate Socialist leaders of the Petrograd Soviet, headed by Tchehidze and a number of workers' and soldiers' delegations. At 11.10 p.m. the train at length drew in and the long-awaited leader stepped out of his carriage into the tumultuous enthusiasm of the Finland Station. There were addresses of welcome from the leaders of the Soviet—Lenin did not reply to them or even acknowledge them. Turning to the crowd of soldiers' and workers' delegations on the platform, he made this speech : " Dear comrades, soldiers, sailors, and workers, I am happy to welcome in you the conquerors of the Russian Revolution and advance-guard of the world-wide proletarian army. The rapacious Imperialist War is the beginning of the civil war all over Europe. The hour is at hand when, following the counsel of our comrade Karl Liebknecht, the peoples will turn their arms against their exploiter capitalists. The dawn of the world-wide Socialist Revolution is breaking. In Germany everything is at fever heat. If not to-day, then to-morrow, any day you may expect the crash of every European Imperialism. The Russian Revolution which you made is the beginning of it, and it is the opening of a new epoch. Long live the world-wide Socialist Revolution." [1]

This challenging speech was a declaration of war on the Socialist leaders who had come to greet Lenin, and with whom he would not even shake hands.

Carried on an armoured car slowly through the dense masses of the populace, he made many other speeches on the way to his new H.Q., the palace of the famous ballet dancer, Mme Kshessinskaia. The following is the description by an eye-witness of the scene outside the station : " The official part of the reception was over. The people who had gathered in thousands and had been waiting for hours . . . were demanding that the great leader should make his appearance in the street. . . . To the tune of the ' Marseillaise,' in the

[1] Quoted Farbman, " Bolshevism in Retreat," pp. 69-70.

flare of a searchlight, and amid a welcome shouted from thousands of throats, Lenin appeared at the door of the station, and tried to get into his motor-car. But the crowd, flaunting their red banners with gold mottoes, refused to let him go away. He was then planted on the top of an armoured car from which he made a speech : " The participation in the abject Imperialist slaughter . . . through lying deception . . . burglar capitalists," are some of the few words that reached me, squeezed among the people at the entrance to the station." [1]

This uncompromising attitude of Lenin and the éclat of his reception surprised and alarmed the " Social Democrats " and the Provisional Government. They awaited anxiously the result of his first appearance before the Soviet. On Tuesday, 17th April 1917, Kerensky, the vigorous Minister of Justice, lunched with M. Paléologue, the French Ambassador. He had to dash off immediately after coffee to attend a meeting of the Petrograd Soviet, where " the apostle of international Marxism, the famous Lenin," was going to make a speech outlining his programme that afternoon. On the morning of 18th April, Miliukov, the Foreign Minister, said to the ambassador : " Yesterday, Lenin failed completely before the Soviet. He pleaded the pacificist thesis so violently, shamelessly, and tactlessly that in the end he had to shut up and leave amid hisses. He will not rise again." " I answered," writes M. Paléologue, " in the Russian manner, ' God grant it ! ' " The wise ambassador then adds this comment to the entry in his diary : " I fear that once again Miliukov may prove to be the dupe of his own optimism. The arrival of Lenin seems to me the most dangerous test to which the Russian Revolution could be subjected." [2]

It is a fact that for some weeks after his return to Russia Lenin was completely isolated. His insistent assertion that to co-operate with the bourgeoisie in the foundation of a democratic parliamentary republic was equivalent to the betrayal of Socialism, since the machinery of a proletarian state was ready to hand in the Soviets, was hard doctrine even for the Bolsheviks. His programme was rejected by a joint meeting of the Petrograd and Central Committees of the party, which, in view of what were regarded as the " delirious "

[1] Quoted Farbman, " Bolshevism in Retreat," pp. 69-70.
[2] Paléologue, " La Russie des Tsars pendant la grande guerre," iii., p. 305.

ideas of its leader, was thrown into a state of deep discouragement. On 20th April 1917, four days after his arrival, extracts from his speeches in Petrograd were printed in the *Pravda*, with the following editorial by the editor, Kamenev: "As far as the general scheme of Lenin is concerned it seems to us unacceptable. Lenin takes it for granted that the bourgeois democratic Revolution is at an end, and believes that an immediate transformation of our Revolution into the Socialist one is possible; we profoundly disagree with him." [1]

Lenin did not waver, and his articles in the *Pravda* (then the central organ of the Bolshevik party) continued to appear on his own responsibility. At the end of April 1917, he published a pamphlet entitled, "The Tasks of the Proletariat in our Revolution." To return to Parliamentary government after the creation of the Soviets would be a slip backward: "The most perfect type of a bourgeois State is a parliamentary democratic republic, but revolutionary epochs, beginning from the end of the eighteenth century, have brought to light the highest type of a democratic State. The Paris Commune is the type of this State, which substitutes for an army and police apart from the people the direct arming of the whole people. From a parliamentary bourgeois republic it is easy to return to a monarchy, as history has shown, for the whole machine of oppression remains untouched, viz., the army, police, and bureaucracy. The Commune and Soviets break up and remove this machine." [2]

But the masses, who could not follow his economic theories, knew that, beyond any question, Lenin stood for peace, and peace without any delay. The opportunity for which he waited with absorbed attention came on 1st May 1917, with the publication of Miliukov's note to the Allies on war aims. In it he declared that revolutionary Russia intended to conduct the fight against German militarism to a victorious conclusion, and reaffirmed the vital interests of Russia in Constantinople and the Straits already promised to the Tsarist Government by the Allies. The note created a ferment amongst the masses. The peace they desired above everything was to be postponed in order to achieve the "Imperialistic" programme constructed by the Tsardom and taken over by the bourgeois Liberal Miliukov. Wild demonstrations against the Provisional Government took place in the streets of Petrograd.

[1] Quoted Farbman, "Bolshevism in Retreat," p. 71.
[2] Quoted, "New Europe," vol. vi., No. 77, p. 365.

Lenin was probably surprised at the strength of popular feeling, but, in any case, he lost no time in reiterating his original marvellously accurate diagnosis of the situation and crystallizing his position in a slogan. On 3rd May, while the movement against Miliukov and the Provisional Government was growing, he published an article in the *Pravda* which winds up with the words: " Workers, soldiers, say it now, so that every one may hear: we demand that we alone, the Soviets of workers' and soldiers' deputies, should hold the power. The Provisional Government, the Government of a little crowd of capitalists, must make way for the Soviets." [1] The great formula, " All power to the Soviets," had been launched—an immediate landslide to the Bolsheviks followed, and, within three weeks of his arrival in Petrograd, Lenin was once again autocrat of the party. He demanded, in effect, that the actual centre of sovereignty in Russia should also be the legal centre, and from this moment began the deadlock between the Soviets and the Provisional Government.

The astounding mistakes of his opponents, as much as his own gigantic personality, account for the increasing ascendency of Lenin and the party under his control. The Miliukov note to the Allies had alienated the masses from the Provisional Government, the continued delay in summoning a Constituent Assembly, the failure to deal with the agrarian problem, and, above all, the singular inability of the Liberal-Socialist Coalition Ministry that was constructed after the fall of Miliukov to come to any clear agreement with the Allies on the subject of peace and the objects of the war, still further weakened the Government and brought added popularity to the Bolsheviks.

In the meantime, the Russian army was simply melting away. The peasant soldiers wanted peace, above everything. Peace and the Land—nothing else mattered. The stagnation on the front aided the loosening of military cohesion brought about by the Soldiers' Soviets, by the propaganda of the extremists, who remembered that the army had crushed the revolution of 1905, and by the sham fraternization of the Germans. The Provisional Government became more and more convinced that only an offensive could save it in face of the ever-increasing popularity of the Bolsheviks. If the offensive were successful they counted on Germany being forced to conclude peace on the basis of " no annexations and

[1] Quoted Farbman, " Bolshevism in Retreat," p. 74.

no indemnities " through the pressure of the German Socialists; the Allies were clamouring for an offensive; the Russian officers, desperate at the position of deepening humiliation in which they found themselves, urged it, in the belief that anything was better than the existing situation, and that " only a revival of the war spirit could restore to them something of their old prestige." [1]

And yet there was not a single military reason for believing that the offensive could possibly succeed. In the words of Shklovsky, who gave evidence before the Court of Enquiry held after the disaster, describing measures taken in General Kornilov's army to restore discipline: " We struggled against the dissolution of the army. We succeeded in single regiments; but we could not stop the process as a whole. . . . Our work was hopeless. The front had become a mucilage." Kerensky's method of working up the requisite fighting spirit was to tour the trenches and pour out his oratorical soul in a series of passionate orations couched in misty hyperbolic phrases that won the applause of the moment and acted like cheap alcohol for a few hours on the exhausted spirits of the men.

On 1st July 1917, the offensive started on the S.W. Front—for a few days all went well. On 18th July the Germans counter-attacked, and immediately not only were the Russian armies defeated but in a few days Russia had ceased to be a great Power. On 21st July, the Commissars at the front telegraphed to the Provisional Government: " The enemy onslaught has developed into an immeasurable calamity, . . . authority and obedience are things of the past. Entreaty and persuasion have lost all force; they are answered by threats, often even by the rifle. . . . For a distance of hundreds of versts to the rear there can be seen long files of deserters with rifles or without them, strong, vigorous men who are absolutely sure of impunity. Sometimes complete detachments desert." The heroic expedient of sending the " Women's Battalion of Death "—founded in May 1917 by Maria Botchkareva—into battle was tried in the desperate hope that the men would follow. The women attacked magnificently, fought for hours unrelieved, lost two-thirds of their numbers, and when the blood-stained, exhausted survivors fought their way back to their trenches, they found the men debating whether in the circumstances, they should advance to the

[1] Farbman, " Bolshevism in Retreat," p. 36.

assistance of the " Battalion of Death." Shortly afterwards the women had to be sent with all speed to the interior to save them from being lynched by the troops.[1] On 15th July, 1917, to the general crisis caused by what seemed the imminent break-up of the State was added an additional confusion in the resignation of the Cadet ministers. Ostensibly the bourgeois element was protesting against the excessive autonomy granted by Kerensky to the Ukraine, in reality the Cabinet was divided by profound differences over the agrarian problem. The disasters on the front and the obvious impotence of the Provisional Government was followed by the news that all over the country the peasants, weary of waiting for the Government or the endlessly delayed Constituent Assembly to deal with their special grievances, were seizing estates with violence—country houses were being gutted, and in some cases their owners murdered.

The Socialist ministers left in control of the government thought of nothing except the possibilities of another coalition with the bourgeoisie—a coalition which would save them, they hoped, from a menace which might at any moment materialize in the form of a *coup d'état*. Kornilov's measures against disintegration at the front—measures taking the congenial form of decimations and mass executions, had made him the hope of all the reactionary and conservative forces in Russia. Kerensky ratified these last efforts to reduce to order those he now termed " revolted slaves," but whom a week or two before he had hailed as the " heroes " of the Revolution. This attempt to win over the bourgeoisie by trailing at the heels of the strong-minded, honest, but limited Commander-in-Chief, was not likely to succeed. Though the bourgeois parties agreed graciously to concede another Coalition on 6th August, with Kerensky still holding office as Prime Minister, inevitably they tended to count on Kornilov who was after all certain to give them the real thing. Kerensky himself, after the failure of the July offensive, lost heart completely. He had by now hopelessly alienated the masses, and he had failed to gain the confidence of the bourgeoisie.

On 16th July, 1917, an opportunity had presented itself to the Bolsheviks of making a real bid for power. An irresponsible mass demonstration against Kerensky was joined by troops from the Petrograd garrison afraid that they were

[1] Ross, " The Russian Bolshevik Revolution," pp. 158-9.

about to be despatched to the front—more and more the Bolsheviks came to the fore, organizing and directing the mob. But Lenin did not do more than play with the idea of exploiting the disturbances in the city. For some hours it looked as though the Provisional Government would become the prisoners of the mob. Lenin met Trotsky and Zinoviev in the refreshment room of the Taurida Palace: "Shall we not attempt now?" he asked; "No, it would not do to assume power now, as nothing will come of it, the soldiers at the front, being largely on the other side, would come and massacre the Petrograd workers."[1] With his keen sense of realities he saw that the major factors were against the Bolsheviks—above all, they were in a minority on the Petrograd Soviet, which was still controlled by the Mensheviks.

With the aid of Cossacks hurriedly summoned from the front, the Provisional Government restored order in the capital, and at last nerved itself to take action against the Bolsheviks, who were held mainly responsible for the rising. Many arrests followed. Lenin at first resolved to risk arrest, but seeing the party was in danger of being broken up by the imprisonment of all its leaders, he went into hiding, first in the workmen's quarters of Petrograd, then in a frontier village of Finland.

In view of the fact that the majority of the Petrograd Soviet supported the Provisional Government during the July disturbances, Lenin now changed his tactics. Up to then he had demanded that power should be taken from "the trembling hands of the bourgeois counter-revolutionists and transferred to the capable and vigorous hands of the Soviets." In season and out of season he had proclaimed the formula "All power to the Soviets." Now he reverted to the idea of a "dictatorship of the proletariat," directed by revolutionary means, as much against the Soviets packed with "bourgeois hangers-on" as against the Provisional Government.

The Government, feeling the need of some national authority yet still unwilling to face a Constituent Assembly, convened a gathering of "representative persons" at Moscow to discuss the situation. "The State Assembly" met, 25th to 28th August, and marks the culminating point of bourgeois influence—the isolation of Kerensky between Kornilov and the Soviets became clear to all. The Commander-in-Chief appeared in person, exposed the catastrophic position at the front, and

[1] Zinoviev, "N. Lenin: His Life and Work," p. 40.

took up a dictatorial attitude to the Government. He had already demanded the extension of martial law over the railroads and factories working for the army. Acting under reactionary influence, though from the most patriotic motives, he had been meditating since the end of July a military stroke which, by displacing the vacillating Government by a military dictatorship, would check the decay of authority throughout Russia, break up the Soviets, and enable the country to continue the war.

It is difficult to imagine how Kornilov, with all the evidence in his possession, could have thought that a direct attack on the Revolution, which would inevitably throw Kerensky and the moderate Socialists into the arms of the Bolsheviks, held any elements of possible success. The breach with the Prime Minister took place on 9th September, and Kornilov began the advance on Petrograd with 70,000 men. Kerensky issued in reply a supreme appeal to those who valued the Revolution to stand by it. The Bolshevik leaders in prison rallied to the Provisional Government—Bolshevik workers mounted guard over the offices of Kerensky himself. The workmen of Petrograd swarmed out of the city and dug trenches. The redoubtable Kronstadt sailors came to lend a hand. Bolshevik agents distributed leaflets in thousands among Kornilov's troops with the result that having set out with 70,000 he reached Pskov with less than 40,000, and on the day that he had fixed for the advance from Pskov to Petrograd it was discovered that a further 20,000 men refused to move.[1] The whole adventure was liquidated in a few days and Kornilov, realizing at last that his position was hopeless, surrendered. At the height of the crisis the Cadet ministers again saw fit, on 10th September, to leave the Government in a body, thereby fatally identifying themselves with the "Korniloviad."

At this moment Lenin from his hiding-place in Finland announced another change of policy. On 16th September, just after the liquidation of the adventure, in an article called "The Compromise," he proposed his final terms. "The compromise on our side is our return to the pre-July demand of 'All power to the Soviets'—a government of Mensheviks and Social Revolutionists responsible only to the Soviets . . . now and only now . . . could such a government be organized and established quite peaceably. . . . Only for the sake of this peaceful development of the Revolution—a chance extremely

[1] Ross, "The Russian Bolshevik Revolution," p. 240.

rare in history and extremely valuable, a chance uniquely rare—only for the sake of this can the Bolsheviks, who are believers in the World Revolution and in Revolutionary methods, accept such a compromise, and, in my opinion, they should accept it. The compromise will consist in the fact that the Bolsheviks, claiming no part in the government (which as Internationalists they could assume only if the Dictatorship of the Proletariat and of the poorest peasants were established) would drop their demand for an immediate assumption of power by these two classes and for the Revolutionary methods of gaining it." [1] The one essential was that the moderate Socialists under the leadership of Kerensky would have to break definitely with the bourgeois parties, the " Kornilovists " as they were now called, who were obviously becoming more and more counter-revolutionary in their tendencies.

But it was already too late. Kerensky was hard at work again coming to yet another agreement with the bourgeois parties. He assembled another substitute Parliament, the Democratic Conference, which sat between 27th September-5th October, at first voted strongly against coalition with the Cadets, and then, shaken by Kerensky's insistence on coalition, approved of a suggested Preliminary Parliament, to which the Provisional Government should be responsible pending the meeting of the Constituent Assembly, and separated. It had contributed more heat than light to the situation. In the meantime the position was changing rapidly in favour of the Bolsheviks. A drift to their side became obvious from the middle of September and the days of the Kornilov coup. Its centre was the only body that counted, the Petrograd Soviet. On 13th September the first Bolshevik resolutions were carried, demanding the exclusion of the propertied elements from the Government; land to the peasants; workers' control of factories, and immediate peace. On 8th October Trotsky, who had been released by the Government, was elected President of the Petrograd Soviet.

Lenin, closely watching events from his hiding-place in Finland, by the end of September had reached the conclusion that the time was ripe for a successful bid for power. The Kornilov episode had converted the masses to the Bolsheviks, who had always maintained that the bourgeois parties would sooner or later attempt to assassinate the Revolution. Kerensky was playing right and left into the hands of his

[1] Quoted Farbman, " Bolshevism in Retreat," pp. 91-2.

enemies by his continuance of the policy of coalition, a policy which culminated early in October in the complete surrender of the Socialist Prime Minister to the demand of his Cadet allies that the much heralded Preliminary Parliament should have, not a controlling, but a merely consultative voice; at any moment the Germans, who had taken Riga, might occupy Petrograd and the fall of Petrograd might well mean the fall of the Revolution. Yet nobody believed in those days of trembling confusion that the Bolsheviks, the arch-critics of Kerensky, would dare to assume power alone. Every party shrank from the awful responsibility—coalition was the order of the day though coalition had again and again spelt divided counsels and political confusion. During his weeks of hiding, Lenin had occupied himself in composing two works: a short book on the teaching of Marx on "The State and Revolution," and a pamphlet entitled "Will the Bolsheviks maintain power?" The latter was Lenin's reply to those who asserted that the Bolsheviks would never dare to accept the consequences of their own attitude and assume the Government of Russia. It is one of the best, because the most buoyant, of his writings. He literally revels in the prospect of power. He asserts that, far from shrinking from power, the Bolsheviks desire it above everything, and he sketches his programme. He indicts the Government for its purely negative attitude on the questions of peace and agrarian reform. He laughs at the sentimental liberalism of his opponents: "We know that the Cadets (Liberals) are also agreeable to the teaching of democracy to the people. Cadet ladies are willing to give lectures to servants on women's rights, in accordance with the best French and English authorities. Also, at the very next concert-meeting, before an audience of thousands of people, there will be arranged on the platform a general kissing. A Cadet lady lecturer will kiss Breshkovskaia. The latter will kiss the former minister Tseretelli. And a grateful people will thus learn the meaning of republican equality, liberty, and fraternity. Yes, we quite agree that Breshkovskaia and Tseretelli are in their own way devoted to democracy and propagate it amongst the people; *but what is to be done if we have a somewhat different idea of democracy from theirs?*"[1] The pamphlet is full of a strong,

[1] Italics mine. N. Lenin, "Will the Bolsheviks Maintain Power?" p. 67. (Ed. Labour Publishing Co.) Mr H. A. L. Fisher in *The Cornhill Magazine*, March 1924, by detaching from its context Lenin's reference to the kissing on the platform (a ceremony arranged by the Cadets and announced in the papers on the day Lenin wrote these lines), endeavours

clear-cut self-confidence. It had come to this, that in all Russia, of the men who counted in politics, only one knew what he wanted and how he proposed to reach his goal.

By the end of September, Lenin was bombarding his followers with letters urging them to organize a rising without delay. On 3rd October he had expounded his views of the feasibility of a rebellion to a conference of members of the Central Committee of the party, military organizations, and representatives of the districts.[1] Though the meeting was favourable, there was much hesitation to be overcome in the party before Lenin could push it into rebellion. Zinoviev was sceptical and remarked to a friend who reported the meeting to him: "I will be with you for an armed rebellion if you can prove to me that we could hold authority for at least two weeks." [2]

The pamphlet "Will the Bolsheviks Maintain Power?" which Lenin published on 13th October, was intended not only to reply to critics but also to rally those of his followers who wanted to put off action till they had a majority on the Constituent Assembly due to meet in December, or at least till the meeting of the Second All-Russian Congress of Soviets that was to begin its sessions at the Smolny Institute on 7th November. "Do you think the starving will agree to wait two months . . . or will the German offensive, in the absence of serious steps towards peace . . . on our side, agree to 'wait' until the meeting of the Soviet Congress and the Constituent Assembly? Or have you facts that allow you to conclude that the history of the Russian Revolution, which has been proceeding so extraordinarily stormily and with such rapid *tempo* from February 28th to September 30th, will assume, between October 1st and November 29th,[3] an episcopally solemn, quiet, peaceful, legally balanced pace, excluding all explosions, leaps, defeats in the war, or economic crises? Or will the army . . . begin again to starve and freeze quietly until the date 'fixed'? Do not laugh at the 'confusion in the Smolny Institute,'[4] gentlemen! Your

to show that such childish episodes formed part of Lenin's own programme and indicate his spiteful desire to arrange public humiliations for his enemies! Rarely has an ironical passage given rise to such a misinterpretation.

[1] Podvoisky's narrative quoted Ross, "The Russian Bolshevik Revolution," p. 266.

[2] Antonov's testimony quoted Ross, "The Russian Bolshevik Revolution," p. 272.

[3] Dates are O.S. Russian calendar.

[4] Bolshevik H.Q.

own confusion is no less. You reply to the stern question of civil war by means of confused phrases and pitiful constitutional illusions. This is why I say that if the Bolsheviks were to submit to such a frame of mind they would ruin both their party and their revolution." [1]

On 20th October the new Preliminary Parliament approved by the "Democratic Conference" assembled. Kerensky, the Social Revolutionaries, and the Cadets from now on begin to founder in the maelstrom of debate which continues till the day on which the Red Guards marched in and turned the Parliament, still in a spate of talk, out of doors.

On 22nd October, Trotsky formally accused Kerensky in the Preliminary Parliament of wishing to deceive the people, after which he withdrew with all his followers from an assembly little better than a debating society. His move was generally recognized as the signal of a Bolshevik rising, but Kerensky could think of nothing better to do than to continue the endless discussions of a paralysed will. Lenin, who had failed to persuade the Bolsheviks to strike during the meeting of the Democratic Conference, 27th September to 5th October, when he had urged the Central Committee to surround the Alexandra Theatre with Bolshevik forces and disperse the Conference,[2] suddenly left his Finnish village, returned permanently to Petrograd and embarked on his great struggle with the reluctant party about the middle of October. In interview after interview he sought to convert the leaders; he preached an immediate rising, in articles and leaflets; his letters of exhortation and reproof poured from his hiding-place in a continuous stream. Hunted by the agents of the Government, he was compelled to go about disguised in a wig and false beard. Thus arrayed, he is said to have been present at the opening of the Preliminary Parliament. His victory may be said to have become assured with the forcing through the Petrograd Soviet of a resolution for the setting up of a Military Revolutionary Committee that proceeded to arrogate to itself the control of all troop-movements in Petrograd. The nominal justification for this move was the suspicion with which the masses viewed the idea of the withdrawal of two-thirds of the garrison by the Government with a view to sending more troops to the front. This proposition of G.H.Q. was looked upon as an attempt to denude the capital

[1] N. Lenin, "Will the Bolsheviks Maintain Power?" pp. 120-2.
[2] Zinoviev, "N. Lenin: His Life and Work," p. 41.

of its defenders and so to prepare the way for a German occupation. Nothing could better illustrate the mutual suspicion with which by now the Provisional Government and the Soviets regarded each other.

The Revolutionary Committee proceeded to organize rebellion under the very nose of the Government, which persisted in ignoring the fearful menace that hung over it like the sword of Damocles. Most of the Allied Representatives continued contemptuous of Russians in general and of Lenin in particular. On Friday, 2nd November 1917, Colonel Robins, Chief of the American Red Cross, met General Knox, the British military attaché: "What's wanted," said the General, "is a military dictatorship. What's wanted is Cossacks. These people need a whip. A dictatorship's the thing." When Colonel Robins suggested that perhaps there would be a dictatorship in Russia very soon, but not of the brand that General Knox seemed to desire: "What?" said the General, "You mean Lenin and Trotsky? Bolsheviks? That soap-box talk? Colonel Robins, you are not a military man. I'll tell you what we do with such people. We shoot them." "You do," said Robins, "if you catch them. But you will have to do some catching. You will have to catch several million." [1]

On Monday, 5th November 1917, the Bolsheviks seized the Fortress of St Peter and St Paul, and the Arsenal. On Tuesday, 6th November, all the Telegraph and Telephone Exchanges passed into the hands of the Military Revolutionary Committee. Early in the morning of 7th November, Kerensky, having discovered that he could not rely on any of the regiments in garrison, fled from Petrograd, hoping to return at the head of troops from the front. The Provisional Government now in continuous session retired to the Winter Palace, where the remnants of the Women's "Battalion of Death" mounted guard with a few detachments of soldiers faithful to Kerensky. All through that afternoon the forces of the Soviet crept nearer and nearer in a narrowing circle round the fateful Palace.

Meanwhile, the scene at Smolny baffled description. By the morning of 7th November, 600 delegates to the Second All-Russian Congress of Soviets had arrived. They found themselves in the midst of an armed rising. They spent their time hurrying in little agitated groups along the corridors,

[1] Hard, "Raymond Robins' Own Story," p. 52.

hustled by the stream of couriers pushing their way to and from the rooms from which the Military Revolutionary Committee was directing operations, and that other little room where Lenin awaited the long-expected distant roar that would tell him that the guns of the great fortress had opened fire on the Winter Palace. He had returned to Smolny that morning for the first time since the July days. As the evening wore on and no news came that the Winter Palace had been taken, the Congress could not be delayed any longer and assembled at 10.45 p.m. in a mood of acute anxiety. The debates began to the rattle of distant musketry. "Vladimir Ilyitch," writes Podvoisky, one of the commanders, "waiting from minute to minute for news of the surrender of the Palace, did not go to the opening of the Congress. He could not keep quiet and was pacing his little room in the Smolny Institute like a caged lion. He must at any cost have the Winter Palace: the Winter Palace remained the last obstacle in the way of the toilers. Vladimir Ilyitch swore . . . shouted . . . was ready to shoot us."[1]

At about 11 p.m. the cruiser "Aurora" and the fortress opened fire on the Palace; a few shells exploded in the corridors. The attackers surged towards the barricades and beat down the defenders. The Winter Palace had fallen. In a distant room the Provisional Government sat silent, listening to the triumphing songs of a vast multitude drawing ever nearer. So Antonov came upon them sitting at a table, and when he first saw them they seemed to him altogether "like a pale grey shivering spot."[2]

At midnight, Lenin appeared before the Congress and announced that the Provisional Government was the prisoner of the Revolution. This was his first public appearance since July, and the delegates greeted him with rapturous enthusiasm. A mighty exultation seized the Assembly as from the platform he read out decrees, which were passed almost without discussion, giving the land to the peasants, and proclaiming the control of the workers over production. "Before all things," he said, "the meaning of this revolution is, that we shall have a government of Soviets, our own organ of power, without any share in it whatsoever for the bourgeoisie. From now onwards begins a new period in the history of Russia, and this Third Revolution must finally result in the triumph

[1] Quoted Farbman, "Bolshevism in Retreat," pp. 110-11.
[2] Quoted Ross, "Russian Bolshevik Revolution," p. 279.

of Socialism." Peace would be at once offered to all the belligerents: "A just and immediate peace proposed by us to international democracy will everywhere find an ardent response in the international masses of the proletariat."[1] Lenin had triumphed. Supreme power was his, and nothing could now stay the flight of his imperious spirit. By chance a young man for whom destiny had reserved a sombre fate was present that night in the hall of Smolny. He had no sympathy for the Bolsheviks and listened idly and coldly while the revolutionary chiefs pronounced flaming speeches in celebration of their triumph. The tidal wave had landed him in Smolny, he might as well listen. Suddenly Lenin appeared and received a marvellous ovation, and then he spoke: "It was not a political speech," said the young man afterwards, "it was a cry from the soul of a man who had waited thirty years for that one moment. I thought that I was listening to the voice of Girolamo Savonarola." The listener was Leonid Kanneguisser, the brilliant son of a distinguished family. In August 1918 he assassinated Uritzky, the tyrant of Petrograd. Dark rumours spread through the city of the vengeance of the Bolsheviks on the noble-minded assassin.[2]

The course of events between the March and November revolutions of 1917 reveal how closely Lenin had adhered to the advice of his master. In his address to the League of Communists in 1850 Marx said: " . . . The workers must, during the conflict [with the autocrats] and immediately afterwards, as much as ever possible, oppose the compromises of the middle class, and compel the democrats to execute their present terrorist threats. They must aim at preventing the subsiding of the revolutionary excitement immediately after the victory. On the contrary, they must endeavour to maintain it as long as possible. . . . Against the new official government, they must set up a revolutionary workers' government, either in the form of local committees, communal councils, or workers' clubs, or workers' committees, so that the democratic middle class government not only immediately loses its support amongst the working classes, but from the commencement finds itself supervised and threatened by a jurisdiction behind which stands the entire mass of the working class. In a word: from the first moment of victory,

[1] Quoted B. Myakotin in article, "Lenin," *Slavonic Review*, March 1924.
[2] Landau-Aldanov, "Lénine," pp. 69-70.

the workers must no longer level their distrust against the defeated reactionary party, but direct it against their former allies, who would seek to exploit the common victory for their own ends. . . . Naturally, in the beginning of the movement the workers cannot propose actual Communist measures, but . . . when the Democrats propose measures which are not revolutionary, but merely reformist, the workers must press them to the point of turning such measures into direct attacks on private property; thus, for example, if the small middle class propose to purchase the railways and factories the workers must demand that such railways and factories, being the property of the reactionaries, shall be simply confiscated by the State, without compensation . . . if the Democrats demand the regulation of the State debt, the workers must demand State bankruptcy. Thus the demands of the workers must everywhere be directed against the concessions and measures of the Democrats." [1]

To attempt to follow Lenin's activity in detail for the four years of his effective dictatorship would involve undertaking the task of reconstructing the history of the Second Russian Revolution—a task outside the scope of a biographical essay. All that can be done is to select a few salient situations and crises, and indicate Lenin's attitude in dealing with the problems presented, and, as far as possible, his influence upon the course of events.[2] Those situations and crises round which the development of Bolshevik Russia revolves are: The peace of Brest-Litovsk; the attempt to realize integral Communism; the idea of world-revolution and the inauguration of the Third International; and the new Economic Policy.

The first and most pressing problem for Lenin and the Bolshevik party was to fulfil their reiterated pledge that they would secure an immediate and a democratic peace. The conference at Brest-Litovsk between the Bolsheviks and the Germans, that sat with intervals from December 1917 to March 1918, was not long in reaching the bed-rock of German imperialism. It became evident that Germany intended to

[1] Quoted Beer, "The Life and Teaching of Karl Marx," pp. 87-90.

[2] The following admirable books on the history of Bolshevist Russia are easily available:—

Farbman, "Bolshevism in Retreat" (1923). (Collins.)
Ross, "The Russian Soviet Republic" (1923). (George Allen & Unwin.)
Wiedenfeld, "The Remaking of Russia." (Labour Publishing Co., 1924.)

secure the control of all the Baltic provinces of Russia right up to the Gulf of Finland. Lithuania and Courland with the cities of Riga and Vilna were to be abandoned to Germany outright. The Central Powers would determine the fate of the great territories involved. Further, Germany was to occupy Livonia and Esthonia beyond the line defined, with a police force " until security is insured by proper national institutions, and until public order is established." [1] From a territorial point of view the terms were catastrophic. Of her Baltic coastline Russia would retain only the base of the Gulf of Finland with her European eye Petrograd, and that practically on the frontier of a hostile and independent Finland. Trotsky, the head of the Russian peace delegation, at first refused to agree to the treaty, and announced that Russia, having failed to secure a general peace in which her former allies participated, would not accept the terms proposed by the Germans, but would nevertheless discontinue the war. He fell back upon the now famous formula " No peace, no war." The reply of Germany was a general advance which demonstrated at once that the Russian army was incapable of resistance (being then engaged in demobilizing itself at the rate of hundreds of thousands of men a day) and that Petrograd could be had for the marching.

A strong party among the Bolsheviks was for resistance to the iniquitous imperialism of Germany—resistance to the death. Let the republic go down fighting to the death against the " vultures." This mood was strongly held by the Petrograd workmen. They regarded the Revolution as their work—they had saved it from Kornilov, they had won the battle against the Provisional Government. If the peasants were thinking only of peace and the land, the workers were ready to die for the Revolution. Such was their mood. The question of peace or war was debated in the Soviet at the Smolny Institute. The discussion took place amid a furious pandemonium of indignation against the Germans. In the opinion of Mr Bruce Lockhart had a vote been taken at Smolny before the arrival of Lenin, it would have been decisive for the resumption of war against the Germans.[2] The intervention of Lenin was decisive. Magnificently ironical, he asked them what particular good they would be doing by

[1] Treaty of Brest-Litovsk, art. vi.
[2] R. H. Bruce Lockhart, " Lenin: The Man and his Achievement," *Edinburgh Review*, March 1924.

throwing themselves under the German Juggernaut. Were Petrograd to fall, the Revolution would probably be extinguished. After all, the peace was but a "breathing space," at all costs the Revolution must be kept alive. What possibility of resistance was there, since, in spite of the eloquent speeches at Smolny, the Russian army would not fight. "The Russian army will never fight again until it is reorganized into a new revolutionary army." The doctrine of the "breathing space" but half-convinced the Assembly. But already Karl Radek had hit upon the same idea when he shouted at General Hoffman: "The Allies will give you a Brest-Litovsk!" The decision to sign the treaty was taken, but the ratification was left to the decision of an all-Russian Congress of Soviets. Lenin insisted on Moscow as the place of meeting. He had begun to win, but he had to work slowly. For the debate at Smolny he had characteristically prepared twenty-one theses in favour of the view that Russia would have to sign the peace. But he did not use his final arguments against Trotsky, who was convinced that the Berlin proletariat would rise against its taskmasters. For Trotsky he reserved the barbed remark, "We must not be intoxicated with the revolutionary phrase," but otherwise let him have his own way so far as talking went. "I am willing to let Trotsky see if he can put off the peace," he observed to Colonel Robins; "I am willing to let him see if he can save us from it. I would rejoice if he could. But I wanted the comrades to know what I am thinking. I wanted them to know it, so that they can remember it a few days from now."[1] It was evident Russia could not resist, but for all that Lenin's unpopularity deepened. But he pushed on. At a Soviet meeting Karl Radek rose in his place, stared at Lenin and said: "If there were five hundred courageous men in Petrograd we would put you in prison!" Lenin replied gently, "Some people, indeed, may go to prison; but if you will calculate the probabilities you will see that it is much more likely that I will send you than you me."[2]

But the workers remained. Their fury at the decision to sign the treaty culminated in an immense mass demonstration against the Smolny Institute. So dangerous did the situation become that the commandant hurried to Lenin who was working in his little room, apparently oblivious of everything

[1] Hard, "Raymond Robins' Own Story," p. 94. [2] *Ibid.*

except his papers, and demanded an order to fire on the mob. "Shoot them ?" cried Lenin, "we will talk to them. Tell their leaders to come in." They arrived grimly carrying their bayonetted rifles. Rumours had stirred among them that Lenin had fled that day to Finland. He walked towards them, "Comrades," he said, "you see I have not run away. Comrades, I was fighting for the Revolution before some of you were born, I shall be fighting for the Revolution when some of you are dead. I stand always in danger. You stand in more danger. Let us talk frankly.

"Comrades, I do not blame you for not always trusting your leaders. There are so many voices in Russia to-day ! I wonder that you have trusted us as much as you have. Among honest revolutionaries there are two voices. One of them is right. One is wrong.

"Many comrades say: 'You must go to the front and fight the Germans and die fighting. You must die fighting for the Revolution.' They do not pretend, these comrades, that you are willing to fight for anything except the Revolution. But they say, and they say truly, that the Germans are against the Revolution, and so they say : 'Go and fight the Germans.' I do not say so. I say : 'You are the new army. You are the only army of the Revolution. You are the beginning of it. What will happen if you fight the Germans ? The old army is not fighting. It cannot fight. It is exhausted. Only you, with the Revolution in you, want to fight. You know what will happen. You will fight. You will die. And the soldiers of the Revolution will be dead, and the Czar will come back. Would that be dying for the Revolution ? Comrades, when we die, let us die really for the Revolution. Let us die when, by dying, we can win victory for the Revolution. Comrades, my voice is right. They tell you I will make a shameful peace. They tell you I will surrender Petrograd the Imperial City. Yes, I will surrender Petrograd the Imperial City. They tell you I will surrender Moscow the Holy City. I will. I will go back to the Volga, and I will go back behind the Volga to Ekaterinburg ; but I will save the soldiers of the Revolution, and I will save the Revolution.

"Comrades what is your will—?

"I will give you now a special train to the front. I will not stop you. You may go. But you will take my resignation with you. I have led the Revolution. I will not share in the murder of my own child.

" Comrades what is your will—? "

" Lenin ! Lenin ! Lenin ! " The room held no other sound. It was a judgment delivered. Having heard it, the judges picked up their rifles and marched out of the room and down the corridor still delivering their judgment. " Comrade Lenin." Such was Lenin face to face with his followers. Such was Lenin the personal leader.[1] The picture is an unforgettable one.

As a supreme concession to Trotsky and the war party, Lenin approached the representatives of the Allies through Colonel Robins, and asked them to submit certain questions to their governments. He embodied his questions in a formal document. Colonel Robins asked him whether, if the document were answered affirmatively by the government of U.S.A. he would oppose the ratification of the Peace of Brest-Litovsk at the All-Russian Congress of Soviets that was to meet at Moscow on 12th March. Lenin gave him a formal undertaking to do so. The following are some extracts from this vital document: " In case the Russian Congress of Soviets will refuse to ratify the peace treaty with Germany . . . it is very important for the military and political plans of the Soviet Power for replies to be given to the following questions :—

" (1) Can the Soviet Government rely on the support of the United States of North America, Great Britain, and France in its struggle against Germany ?

" (2) What kind of support could be furnished in the nearest future and on what conditions—military equipment, transportation, supplies, living necessities ?

" (3) What kind of support would be furnished particularly and specially by the United States ? Should Japan . . . attempt to seize Vladivostok and the Eastern Siberian Railway which . . . would greatly impede the concentration of Soviet troops towards the East about the Urals—in such case what steps would be taken by the other Allies, particularly and especially by the United States, to prevent a Japanese landing on our Far East, and to insure uninterrupted communications with Russia through the Siberian route ? . . .

" All these questions are conditioned with the self-understood assumption that the internal and foreign policies of the Soviet Government will continue to be directed in accord with the principles of international Socialism and that the Soviet

[1] Hard, " Raymond Robins' Own Story," pp. 167-170.

Government retains its complete independence of all non-Socialist governments." [1]

Robins took this statement to the Special Commissioner in Russia for the British Prime Minister, Mr Bruce Lockhart, who at once sent off a long cable on the subject to the Foreign Office, urgently suggesting that the opportunity of an agreement with the Bolsheviks should be seized at once. In the course of the report he wrote: "If H.M.G. does not wish to see Germany paramount in Russia, then I would most earnestly implore you not to neglect this last opportunity. . . . If we accept it, we stand to gain considerably, and in any case we can lose nothing more than we have lost already." [2]

Neither Colonel Robins nor Mr Bruce Lockhart ever received an answer to their cables on this subject to their governments. Meanwhile Lenin, that there might be no doubt, had put off the meeting of the Moscow Congress from 12th March to the 14th. The debate on the Peace began in the Hall of Nobles at the Kremlin on 15th and continued till the evening of 16th March. Most of the delegates were against the Peace. At 11.30 p.m. Lenin waved to Robins to come to speak to him. Robins came. "What have you heard from your Government?" Robins replied "Nothing. . . . What has Lockhart heard from London?" "Nothing," said Lenin. "I shall now speak for the Peace. It will be ratified." [3] He spoke for an hour and twenty minutes. The speech has all that hard insistence, all that revelling in the mere grimness of fact so typical of one who never shrank from reality. "We were compelled to sign a Tilsit peace. We must not deceive ourselves. We must have courage to face the unadorned, bitter truth. We must measure in full, to the very bottom, the abyss of defeat, partition, enslavement, humiliation, into which we have been thrown. The clearer we understand this, the firmer, the more hardened and inflexible will become our will for liberation, our desire to arise anew from enslavement to independence, our firm determination to see at all costs that Russia shall cease to be poor and weak, that she may become truly powerful and prosperous. . . . It is unworthy of a true Socialist, if badly defeated, either to deny the fact or to become despondent. It is not true that we have no way out, that we can only choose between a "disgraceful" death—from the

[1] Hard, "Raymond Robins' Own Story," pp. 138-9.
[2] Ross, "The Russian Soviet Republic," p. 41.
[3] Hard, "Raymond Robins' Own Story," pp. 151-2.

point of view of a feudal knight—which an oppressive peace is, and a 'glorious' death in a hopeless battle. . . . A commander who leads into the interior the remnants of an army which is defeated or disorganized by disorderly flight, and who, if necessary, protects this retreat by a most humiliating and oppressive peace, is not betraying those parts of the army which he cannot help and which are cut off by the enemy. Such a commander is only doing his duty. He is choosing the only way to save what can still be saved. He is scorning adventures, telling the people the bitter truth, 'yielding territory in order to win time,' utilizing any, even the shortest, respite in order to gather again his forces and to give the army which is affected by disintegration and demoralization a chance to rest and recover."[1] When he had finished speaking the vote was taken :—

For ratification	724
Against	276

Lenin, without soliciting cap-in-hand either the approval or the help of the Allies, had offered simply a way of co-operation. Had it been accepted the war might have been shortened. As it was, Russia made a separate peace, and the misunderstanding and bitterness which that act of self-preservation provoked, was later to be exploited by war-mongers, not yet sufficiently glutted with blood and bones, until it materialized in "intervention"—an intervention in Russia on behalf of a cause unworthy of the life of a single soldier. The inspiration of that attack was fear and greed, and it achieved not even the success of creating a desert and calling it peace. It stimulated to an ever fiercer fanaticism the forces whose possible aggression afforded the excuse for the interested and the dispossessed to mobilize an ignorance as invincible as their own hatreds. It failed because it deserved to fail, because, in a word, the nations of the West are not yet altruistic enough to constitute themselves their brothers' keepers. To protect a friend from external aggression is one thing, to attempt to control his thoughts and life is another. The armed propaganda of Communism and World-Revolution was defeated at the gates of Warsaw, just as the hypocritical assumption that righteousness and Western Capitalism have kissed each other was driven in bloody ignominy from the soil of a nation determined to work out its own salvation in its own way. Not

[1] Ross, "The Russian Soviet Republic," pp. 44-5.

without reason did the Russian nation rally to the Government that was defending itself and them as against a " restoration " as infamous as that imposed by M. Thiers in the name of Republican virtue on the Communards of 1871.

One of the great problems that still confronts the historian of the Russian Revolution, and that, after all suggested explanations, still, Mr Farbman observes, remains an enigma, is that involved in the question : " Why did the Bolsheviks, on attaining supreme power, proceed to embark on the task of establishing integral Communism ? " Why did they attempt to build up in a State which, in the words of Lenin, was suffering not from Capitalism so much as from insufficiently developed Capitalism, a system which required as a *sine qua non* fully organized Capitalism on a nation-wide scale ? " Look at the map of the Soviet Republic," writes Lenin. " To the north of Vologda, to the south-west of Rostov on the Don and of Saratov, the south of Ourembourg and of Omsk, and to the north of Tomsk, there are immense territories, room for dozens of big civilized States. And in all these lands there prevails the patriarchal system, the semi-wild and the really wild. And what about the remote countryside even in the heart of Russia ? What about villages lying miles away, or even a few miles away, from railways, *i.e.*, away from material connection with civilization, capitalism, industries, and towns ? Does not the same patriarchal system, and the same semi-wild state prevail everywhere ? " [1] If Russia, as was self-evident, was in Lenin's words, " in the most primitive stage of mediæval economics," [2] how could the Bolsheviks hope to realize in such a country a system that could only come into being when the forces generated by a fully developed capitalist system " burst the integument " that could no longer contain them—— ? There is " a crack in the rattle " somewhere.

In November 1917, the Bolsheviks, apparently masters of the situation, were in reality far more constrained by circumstances than they would probably have cared to admit. In season and out of season they had preached to the slogan of " Rob the robbers ! " The expropriation of the Capitalists was to be followed by a new and better State. Accordingly

[1] Quoted Farbman, " Bolshevism in Retreat," p. 119.

[2] This of course does not contradict what was said earlier on the rapid development of Russian industry since 1880. In spite of the enormous rate of expansion *relative* to that of already industrialized countries, Russia by 1917 had only advanced a fraction of the full journey towards complete industrialization. But the point does not need labouring.

the masses themselves undertook the congenial task of closing down banks and taking over factories. This naïve interpretation of their doctrines involved, as Lenin clearly saw from the beginning, a destruction which, if not checked, must spell the economic disintegration of the Russian State. But he was the prisoner of his promises.

On the other hand, the revelation of the extraordinary weakness of the Capitalist class and the bourgeoisie may well have encouraged him to make the great experiment. The moment real pressure from the working classes was felt the Capitalists simply fled the country. There was no resistance. The Russian bourgeoisie was too little self-confident and class-conscious to offer any formidable obstacles. It was for the most part neutral in the civil war which broke out in the summer of 1918—a civil war engineered by the great landed proprietors for their own purposes, and supported by the officer class and the intelligentsia from motives of patriotism. The war, and the necessity for controlling the resources of the State, pressed the Bolsheviks farther and farther along the path of nationalization. Every failure was attributed to sabotage by the counter-revolutionaries, and was followed by redoubled efforts in the same direction. A sweeping land law in 1918 decreed that the surplus food-stuffs over and above the needs of the peasants must be surrendered to the State. The monetary economy was abolished. All public services were free. Manufactured articles—boots, clothing, agricultural implements, etc., were to be supplied by the towns to the peasants in exchange for their food. Russian industry and civic life became steadily more and more entangled by ropes of red-tape and smothered under official forms, "thick as the leaves that strew the woods of Vallombrosa." Captain McCullogh discovered that in order to secure a trouser button he was required to visit four departments placed in widely separated quarters of Ekaterinburg. Even Lenin complained that everything was being "swallowed up by formalities."[1] Yet the moral energy behind this extraordinary attempt is undeniable. A sincere effort, extending over three years, was made to apply the supreme Communist principle: "From each according to his capacity: to each according to his need." Partial nationalization begat wholesale nationalization; terrorism more rigorous terrorism. The suppression of the Capitalist press involved the ultimate

[1] Gorki, "Lenin," p. 10.

strangulation, in the interests of an official reptile press, of all forms of free criticism, whether Capitalist, Socialist, or neutral. Only in 1920 was Lenin able to arrest the final deduction of an infernal logic when he defeated Trotsky's proposal for the wholesale militarization of Labour. The debate in Communist circles became so intense that the question was submitted to the individual Soviets. Zinoviev's memorandum against the proposal was signed by Lenin, and carried the day. "They voted," exclaimed Trotsky ruefully, "not for Zinoviev's memorandum but for Lenin's signature."

Not the least of the forces urging the Bolsheviks and their leader along the path of an inflexible Communism was the conviction that the Russian Revolution was the prelude to the World-Revolution. For a long time they were convinced that only a World-Revolution could save them from ultimate destruction at the hands of the White armies. In these circumstances, every department of State became the organ of an intensive propaganda. Every decree promulgated was weighed according to its propaganda value. Russia must be sacrificed for the present to the liberation of the world from the Capitalist incubus. She was the *corpus vile* of the Communist experiment. Once Europe was free, the killing pace could be slackened. "After the proletarian revolution in at least one of the advanced countries, things will in all probability take a sharp turn; Russia will cease to be the model, and will become again the backward (in the 'Soviet' and 'Socialist' sense) country." [1]

The foundation of a new International to take the place of the organization that had collapsed so miserably on the outbreak of the world war had been Lenin's cherished ambition since 1915. In March 1919 a Congress assembled in Moscow. It was but poorly attended by Communists from Western Europe, and might be regarded as a meeting of the Russian Communist party. But the organization was in being, and the attacks of Lenin on the Second International led several Socialist parties in Western Europe to withdraw from it without, however, applying for membership in the new foundation. A manifesto signed by Rakovsky, Lenin, Zinoviev, Trotsky, and Platten was issued, addressed to the proletariat of the whole world. It would be safe to say that, as a document, it compares very unfavourably for intellectual power, construction, and relevance with the great

[1] Lenin, "Left-Wing Communism," p. 1.

manifesto of Marx and Engels published seventy-two years previously.

It begins with an excursus on the origin of the war which apparently broke out "through direct and conscious provocation of Great Britain." It then proceeds to assert that the war has accentuated "the contradictions of the Capitalist order" to the point at which they become unbearable. "The State control of social life, against which Capitalist Liberalism so strives, is become a reality. There is no turning back, either to free competition or to the domination of trusts, syndicates, and other kinds of social anomalies. The question consists solely in this: Who shall control State production in the future—the Imperialist State or the State of the victorious proletariat? In other words: Is the whole of labouring humanity to become the bondslaves of the victorious bourgeoisie, who, in the name of the League of Nations, and with the aid of an 'international' army, and an 'international' fleet, here plunders and strangles, there throws some crumbs, but everywhere holds the proletariat in chains with the sole object of preserving its dominance; or shall the working class take in hand the disordered and ruined society, in order to ensure its reconstruction on Socialist lines?" The fear expressed that the League of Nations could control an "international" army and an "international" fleet has proved somewhat premature.

The Manifesto vigorously defends the Red Terror that began in Russia during the early summer of 1918: "The wail of the bourgeois world against the civil war and the Red Terror is the most monstrous hypocrisy which the history of political struggles has hitherto revealed. There would have been no civil war if the exploiters who have brought mankind to the brink of destruction had not opposed every step forward of the labouring masses, if they had not plotted conspiracies and murders, and summoned armed assistance from without, in order to maintain or re-establish their predatory privileges."

There is every reason to believe that the worst excesses of the Red Terror were due to fear. Quite evidently the Communists from 1918-20 were fighting for their lives. That, as has been said, is one reason for their passionate concentration on the World-Revolution. The true nature of Admiral Koltchak's White government was revealed in the *coup d'état* by which he overthrew the remnants of the dispersed Constituent Assembly sitting at Omsk and constituted himself dictator. The Admiral was the prisoner of Tsarists, more anxious to avenge themselves on the Bolsheviks than to rebuild Russia as a Liberal State. The great landowners of the Ukraine during 1918 called in the Germans, recovered their estates, and proceeded, with the aid of foreign troops, to reduce their peasants again to servitude. With the armistice of 11th November 1918, the Germans withdrew, and the landlords for the most part fled with them. If on the return of the Red Army, those who had "learnt nothing and forgotten nothing" suffered terribly, it is not difficult to suggest reasons. During the same period General Mannerheim expelled the Reds from Finland after one of the most atrocious civil wars in modern history. He is said to have executed in all about 17,000 Communists in the course of a summer campaign. He and the Bolsheviks embarked on a competition in horrors. This is the background against which one must place the execution of the Tsar and the entire Imperial family in the course of July 1918. The Bolshevik chiefs, doubting ultimate success, endeavoured to bang the door on a restoration.[1]

The Bolshevik faith in the World-Revolution which was to deliver them from all their troubles culminated in the summer of 1920 during the second meeting of the Third International. The Polish war, due to the policy of adventure and land-grabbing adopted by Marshal Pilsudski, who suddenly occupied Kiev, culminated in the victorious counter-offensive of the Red Army, and the Polish forces were driven back to the boundaries of ethnographic Poland, while the Congress was in session.

The Congress had been a great success. Many parties, doubtful the previous year, had applied for admission, including the Italian Socialists. Everything seemed to hint at the approach of the World-Revolution. In these circumstances, Lenin and his colleagues had to make up their minds whether to grant Poland a just peace or to press on in the hope that the capture of Warsaw would precipitate a proletarian revolution which might spread to Germany and throughout Central Europe. Lenin showed himself indifferent to the ultimatums of Lloyd George, who shortly found himself confronted by the "Council of Action" set up by the British Labour Party with the express object of preventing inter-

[1] M. Sokolov's chain of evidence on the execution of the Imperial family goes back as far as Sverdlov, Secretary of the Central Executive Committee. Lenin's part in the tragedy remains a mystery.

vention on behalf of Poland. On the other hand, the Polish Communists warned him that the Polish workers and peasants would never allow themselves to be " delivered " by Russians. But for once the great politician allowed himself to be "intoxicated with the revolutionary phrase," and he decided in his own words " to break the crust with Russian bayonets." [1] A crusading fervour, heightened by the national hatred of the Poles, fell upon the Red Army. Some units marched twenty miles a day for twelve days—ragged, often barefoot, badly fed, shouting to the flying Poles, " You *shall* give us Warsaw ! " [2] The extraordinary atmosphere of unreality generated by the Congress and the war was suddenly dissipated by the artillery of General Weygand at the very gates of Warsaw. Under French inspiration the Poles rallied, and the counter-offensive revealed the disastrous blunder the Russian commanders had committed in allowing the army to strain its line of communications so desperately. Within a few days the Russians lost 100,000 men. The bubble had burst.

The Peace Conference assembled at Riga, and now Lenin concentrated on liquidating his adventure. He instructed the Russian negotiators to offer the Poles more territory than the Western Allies had endeavoured to secure her. Poland, swollen with lands that most patriotic Russians regard as stolen goods, was thus brilliantly neutralized as a base of operations against the Soviet Republic, since the Russian enemies of the Bolsheviks would most certainly concentrate on wrenching away from Poland territory to which she has not the slightest ethnographic claim.

Mr Farbman well compares Lenin's advance into Poland in 1920 with Kerensky's offensive in July 1917. " The Kerensky advance wrecked the March Revolution. Lenin's Polish adventure shattered his own position and made an end of the Bolshevik attempts to use the Russian Revolution as the instrument of a world-revolutionary propaganda." [3]

The failure of their hopes of a World-Revolution forced upon the Bolsheviks the obvious fact that Russia was their theatre of operations, and that in Russia, not on the great stage of the world, would they succeed or fail. And in Russia, by the close of 1920, the situation was wellnigh desperate. Reckless and inefficient nationalization had paralysed Russian

[1] Quoted Ross, " The Russian Soviet Republic," p. 310.
[2] Farbman, " Bolshevism in Retreat," p. 141. [3] *Ibid.*, p. 139.

industry in the dead hand of the State. The civil war and the blockade had cut it off from raw materials—lack of fuel was steadily killing it. The vicious circle was completed by the food problem. The peasants had replied to ruthless requisitioning by the deliberate reduction of the area of cultivated land. Determined to defeat a policy which carried off all their surplus food-stuffs, and, owing to the disorder in Russian industry, gave them nothing in return, they resolved, by a subconscious conspiracy, to grow only enough food for themselves and their families. The food returns showed a steady and continuous decline. The industrial population, in spite of unheard-of efforts by the Government, was menaced with starvation. The peasants would not grow corn because they were offered nothing in exchange by the industrial workers; the industrial workers grew more and more inefficient because they were slowly dying of inanition due to insufficient food. The hard-shelled Communists advocated the militarization of the peasants and compulsory work; the peasant delegates to the All Russian Congress of Soviets openly threatened rebellion. The attempt to carry the class-war into the villages by using the poorest peasants as the foundation of a Communist experiment was productive only of confusion. "Committees of Poverty," consisting of the poorest peasants, were set up to supervise the working out of the Decree of the All Russian Central Executive Committee of 13th May 1918, which decreed that all grain held by the peasants over the amounts needed for their own consumption and for food was to be delivered to the Government food agencies, to be paid for there at "fixed" prices which bore no relation to the cost of living. The only result of this measure was the coalition of the "middle" or independent peasants with the "Kulaks" or wealthy peasants who employed labour, against their inveterate enemies, the lazy and shiftless. The activities of the "village poverty" led to widespread disorder and local risings.[1]

The "middle peasants," the great bulk of the Russian peasantry, presented the insoluble problem. At the Eighth Congress of the Russian Communist party in April 1919, Lenin thus analysed the situation: "The proletariat, taken in its mass, is for Socialism, the bourgeoisie, also taken as a mass, is against Socialism. The relations between these two classes are easy enough to define. But when we deal with a group

[1] Pasvolsky, "The Economics of Communism," pp. 252-8.

like the middle peasantry, we find ourselves face to face with a class which has not decided views. A middle peasant is a property owner as well as a toiler on the land. He does not exploit other workmen. For decades he has borne the oppressive exploitation of the landowners. But at the same time he is a property owner." The village communes organized by the Bolsheviks were met by co-operation on the part of the middle peasants. The co-operators were independent, and individually owned the articles they lent to their societies. In the end efficiency, hard work, and passive resistance triumphed, and N. Ossinsky was bewailing in the fall of 1920 that the villages had become "the kingdom of the middle peasantry," imbued with a purely bourgeois mentality.[1] Even at the height of the class-war in the villages eighty-six per cent. of the land in Russia remained in individual holdings.[2]

In his pamphlet, "Will the Bolsheviks maintain Power?" Lenin had bitterly reproached the Kerensky Government for the peasant revolts that began in the late summer of 1917. Peasant revolts in a peasant State he had declared to be a scandalous paradox. Now he was himself faced with a series of very formidable peasant revolts, especially in the province of Tambov. Lenin, who had as early as 1918 questioned the wisdom of the policy of wholesale nationalization, now saw that the elemental force of doctrinaire Communism had spent itself. In any case, the very foundations of the State were shifting, and some way out of the impasse must be found at once.

The sense of responsibility, which Kurt Wiedenfeld regards as one of the main ingredients of Lenin's complex character,[3] drove him to appear before the Tenth Congress of the Russian Communist party in March 1921, and demand from the astonished assembly the abandonment of the compulsory food levy and the re-establishment of the free market. The peasants, after paying a fixed tax in kind, must be permitted to trade with their surplus foodstuffs as they pleased. Only so could the progressive decline of Russian agriculture and the resulting starvation of the towns be arrested, and an increased output of food stuffs be assured, carrying with it the revival of Russian industry. Had the followers of the Prophet been called upon to hear from the lips of Mahomet himself the suggestion that

[1] Quoted Pasvolsky, p. 275. [2] *Ibid.*, p. 83.
[3] K. Wiedenfeld, "The Remaking of Russia," p. 87.

Allah was after all only a convenient hypothesis, the sensation could not have been greater. "The liberty to trade with one's own produce in the open market," he said, "inevitably brings with it a division into capitalists and workers. How, then, is this measure reconcilable with Communism, and how is it possible that the Communist party can tolerate freedom of trade?" He did not reconcile the two propositions, he merely declared the proposals must be accepted. "Don't let us make any mistake: the peasants are dissatisfied with their present relationship with the State, and so it cannot continue. That is certain. The mind of the peasants is now made up. It is the mind of the overwhelming number of the toiling masses. We have to take notice of this, and we are sufficiently realists to say straight out, 'Let us revise our policy towards the peasants.' . . . Why do we propose to abolish requisitioning? Because we must give back to the small holder a stimulus, an incentive, and a push. . . . We have only to face the basic fact, and we must be in a position this very evening to send all over the world a wireless message announcing that the Congress of the governing party in Russia has decided to abolish requisitioning and to substitute for it a tax in kind, in order to give the small agriculturist a stimulus to extend his holding and to increase his sowing." [1]

He had staked the whole of his reputation and his authority on his ability to convert the party. His logic and personality beat down resistance, and he triumphed. The New Economic Policy was accepted, and all through 1921 he presided over the methodical undoing of the tangled web he had himself woven. But he took no risks. A dangerous opposition of Communist "die-hards" manifested itself—an opposition by those who alone in Russia could express themselves freely. Lenin discovered, what was a fact, that a great number of profiteers, libertines, and shady characters had crept into the Communist party, and he ordered a "cleansing." About 181,000 members were expelled—the Communist opposition was driven out with the riff-raff.

In December 1921 Lenin again defended the New Economic Policy, which had been steadily developing throughout the year, before the Party Congress. By the autumn the process of denationalizing industry had begun. "The New Economic Policy," he said, "has become necessary because the political and military alliance between the workers and the peasants

[1] Quoted Farbman, "Bolshevism in Retreat," pp. 279-80.

has not yet been followed by an economic alliance. . . . In the absence of a flourishing great industry, competent to organize itself in such a way as to supply the requirements of the peasants with all necessary speed, the gradual development of a mighty alliance between the workers and the peasants can only be ensured by a monetary system, and by the progressive advance of agriculture and manufacturing industry under the leadership and management of the workers' and peasants' State. . . . In existing circumstances, trade is the only possible link between the peasants and the workers, that is to say between agriculture and manufacturing industry. . . . For us Communists, this is an extremely disagreeable discovery. . . . The core of the whole matter is that we must replace the compulsory levy by a tax upon agricultural produce. This must be the central feature of our economic policy." [1] Already the New Economic Policy had demonstrably begun the economic regeneration of Russia. The foundations of the State had again stabilized, and the Bolsheviks were still masters of Russia, but were they still Bolsheviks? Behind the far-reaching utterances of Lenin and the radical change of policy by which, with all the intuition of a great statesman, he had again saved his party from destruction and the State from catastrophe, shone an invincible determination to retain power and so continue the great task of the remaking of Russia. It had been a prodigious effort.

But already the shadows were beginning to close on that strong spirit. All through 1921 his iron will had been lashing a tired brain and body to ever more tremendous efforts. In the midst of all that crushing labour that now no longer filled him with the enthusiasm of a schoolboy, he found time to write anxiously to his friend Gorki: "I have sent your letter on to Kamenev. I am so tired myself that I can't do a stroke of work. And you have hæmorrhage and don't go abroad? That is unheard-of, shameful, unreasonable. In a good sanatorium in Europe you will get cured, and will be able to do so much more. My word, you will, while here neither can you get a cure nor do any work—just a bustle it all is, nothing but a useless bustle! Go away, and get better. Don't be stubborn, I beg of you!—Your Lenin." [2]

At the end of 1921 he fell suddenly ill and was removed

[1] Quoted Wiedenfeld, "The Remaking of Russia," p. 90.
[2] Gorki, "Lenin—the Man," p. 11.

to Gorki, a large country house with a park, some twenty miles from Moscow. In the autumn of 1922 he recovered sufficiently to return to work and make public speeches. But this was the supreme effort. In December he was prostrated by a paralytic stroke, which for some time deprived him of speech and of the use of his right arm. He was taken back to Gorki, and there he lingered all through 1923, attended by the greatest specialists of Russia and Germany. At the end of 1923 he recovered sufficiently to walk a little, and, characteristically, he began to practise writing with his left hand, as his attendants discovered from the innumerable sheets of paper he covered with exercises. Optimistic reports were spread of his progress, and when the end came it was unexpected. On 21st January 1924, he had a sudden relapse, and died an hour later at seven in the evening. His most faithful followers were with him at the end.

For four tremendous years he had wrought mightily at the very heart of a human tempest. For yet two more his shadow had ruled Russia, and when he died even many of his enemies had mourned the passing of one of the greatest Russians of history. Great moulder of men and events that he was, he never feared to learn the lessons life had to teach him. In his speeches he loved to emphasize and dilate on the value of experience. Just because of this infinite variety and adaptability, the political edifice of his building stands unshaken. More and more it seems certain that the Russia of the future must accept the legacy of Lenin. The red star of the Soviet Republic burns in an unobscured ascendancy, and within a week of his death the British Government accorded to the new State a formal recognition.

A transformation is taking place within the Communist party. The dyer's hand is becoming subdued to his colours. And that metamorphosis, imposed by life itself and the chief sign of life, was begun by the "dreamer," who, by taking thought, had become the ruler of Russia.

"Is there not a danger of the party degenerating, of being transformed?" Radek was asked at a meeting. "Certainly," he answered, "we are being transformed daily. In Switzerland, as revolutionary exiles, we never paid any attention to rainfall, being preoccupied by Marxian discussions. And now we are more concerned with rainfall and drought than with the philosophy of Mach or of Avenarius. Ossinsky, the present Commissary for Agriculture, was then translating Verlaine, and was totally indifferent to ploughing and sowing. Now he is completely obsessed by agriculture, and fights only with locusts and other pests. Kissilov used to be absorbed in plans for annoying the bourgeoisie; now all his thoughts are given to the proper organization of the Moscow tramways. Tchicherin, then a Menshevik, was only occupied in diplomatic wars with us; now his transformation has gone so far that he busies himself exclusively with making diplomatic peace with European Governments. In former days we thought the bourgeois only worth wiping out; now we wonder if he will make a good factory director. The party of agitators has been transformed into the government of the biggest State in Europe. We are steadily, daily changing, and yet we remain the same. A party which failed to transform itself could not live two days."[1]

It is just this will to power that distinguishes the Communist party in Russia, and justifies its claim to be the only vital force as yet capable of guiding the nation. Vast and incalculable powers are at work, and not the least is the moral fervour of the Communist party. Convinced of its historical mission, it works on amid rapidly changing circumstances—adjusting itself continuously to meet the impact of new facts. In the face of all disappointments it preserves its faith that the rebuilding of Russia will vindicate its possession of power and the work of its founder. Whether that Russia will be a strong Socialist State or not cannot be yet guessed at; all that those of all classes who have joined that work know is that somehow devotion, work, patience "will make it better to-morrow."

What, then, are we to think of Nikolai Lenin? There can be no forestalling of the verdict of history, whatever that may be. And yet has history ever yet pronounced a final verdict on any of the great *personalities* that stand out in the long panorama of human life? Strafford, Richelieu, Peter the Great, Cromwell, Cavour—we know that these were men who left an indelible impress on life and events, but the exact appraisement for ever eludes our fumbling search. And so it must be with Lenin. Certain grand features of his life and character are already discernible through the mists of hatred and misrepresentation that hang thickly over his name. Was he cruel? Was he commonplace and unimaginative? Was his work a mere destruction, a hellish

[1] Quoted Farbman, "Bolshevism in Retreat," p. 303.

uproar of no more positive significance than the unearthly howlings of a demoniac in the desert? All these charges and more have been hurled at one who never feared antagonism, and who, at the darkest moments of his fortune, would repeat the words of the Russian poet, "We hear sounds of approval not in the sweet murmur of praise but in the wild shouts of rage."

Was he cruel? That he was relentless in sweeping from his path all who opposed the realization of his ideas admits of no question. But his actions were never inspired by motives of personal revenge or spite—he cared nothing for the paying back of old scores, and welcomed all who chose to help his work, protected all who acquiesced, no matter how often they had once opposed him. It did not take long for those who suffered most in the Revolution to discover that the master of the Kremlin stood between them and those of his followers (often in high places) who found an evil satisfaction in the glutting of unholy malignities. The Red Terror rises like a miasma between us, watching from safe places, and the Russia of 1918-20. Yet for every mention of the Extraordinary Commission, how often does one hear that it began its terrible work only with the outbreak of civil war and the converging advance of the White armies backed by the Great Powers of the world? For seven months after his accession to supreme power Lenin held his hand, and, when he struck, he struck with the intention of not having to strike again. "In what measure do you consider the blows dealt in a fight necessary—or superfluous?" he asked a reluctant friend.[1] The Extraordinary Commission, like the Committee of Public Safety, bound the collapsing fabric of the State together with hoops of steel. It saved Russia from anarchy on the one hand, and on the other, from the last ignominy of foreign conquest.

Was he a "commonplace little man," great by the accident of great events, absorbed in a narrow circle of ideas, imprisoned by a logic impervious to the facts of life? Were he so simple he would present no problems to the inquirer. A fanatic who never confounded the world as it is with the world reshaped "nearer to the heart's desire," a man who lived ever in the light of a great idea, and had all the instincts of a successful statesman—such was Lenin. Such must be every man who is not the prisoner of circumstance. He

[1] Gorki, "Nicolai Lenin—the Man," p. 9.

dreamed that his system could set men free from all that crushes in the mere material struggle for bread, free for the higher things of the spirit, and, because of that, his enemies accused him of thinking that men could live by bread alone. The lover of Tolstoy who rejoiced like a child to find that he knew more about Albert Dürer than the Germans with whom he was conversing, who found pleasure in poring over books on mediæval costumes, and feared that his love of great music might blunt his sense that the world of beauty was growing like a lovely isolated flower amid wastes of ugliness and misery [1]—such a man, it is safe to say, was neither commonplace nor a mean and narrow-minded economist who thought of his own abstractions as the sole reality. "I know nothing that could equal the 'Appassionata,'" he said once after hearing Beethoven's mighty music. "I could hear it played every day. Marvellous, supernatural music. When I hear it I always think, maybe with naïve, childish pride: what wonders human beings are capable of accomplishing!" He added merrily: "But I can't listen to music too often; it get on my nerves, rouses the desire to say charming nonsense, and stroke the heads of the people who, in spite of living in a dirty hell, are able to create such beauty. And to-day one can't allow oneself the luxury of stroking people on the head; they would bite your hand off, one must hit them on the heads, hit mercilessly, although, in ideal, we are against all violence to men. Hm . . . hm . . . the job is not an easy one." [2]

His friend Gorki is convinced that the Red Terror was an almost intolerable torment to Lenin, whom he could not picture "without the beautiful dream of the future happiness of all mankind, the dream of a bright and joyful life. . . ." "In this blunt politician there sometimes shines the light of an almost womanly tenderness for his fellows." [3] In his love of children he was a true Russian, Russian also in his swift transitions from patriarchal benevolence to a cold relentless fury against the "counter-revolutionaries." He never doubted the wisdom or the righteousness of the means by which for thirty years he fought the battle of the "Revolution" or maintained it, when, by a miracle of patience

[1] He told Mrs Sheridan that he objected to "bourgeois" art because it "beautified" and disguised reality. Sheridan, "Russian Portraits."

[2] Gorki, "Lenin—the Man" p. 3.

[3] Wiedenfeld, "The Remaking of Russia," p. 21.

and audacity, he had laid hold on supreme power. Half his power lay in the conviction he inspired of ascetic devotion to his idea. Not even his enemies ever doubted his motives, as they have so often doubted those of Trotsky, Zinoviev, and the rest ; and, as a former ambassador to Soviet Russia has wisely observed : " None but an ascetic can wield such immense and far-reaching powers without succumbing to the temptations of personal ambitions, or to the yet meaner allurement of personal gain." [1]

As a revolutionary leader he was unique. He was never tired of quoting Danton's great summons to France " Audacity ! Audacity ! and again Audacity ! " His estimate of the chances of success in every given situation was unerring, and his moral strength never flagged. In the dark days of 1918, when, compassed about with advancing armies, and threatened by conspiracies without and within, the Republic of Soviets seemed about to vanish in the horrors of a great revenge, it is said that some of his chief lieutenants gathered in his little room in the Kremlin in a mood of horror-stricken despair : " We cannot succeed," cried one, " We cannot fail ! " replied Lenin, and the words seemed to infuse their wavering spirits with a new and crusading ardour. His wisdom held back those who urged the Republic to go down fighting to the last against the Germans in 1918 ; his vast, almost prophetic authority, imposed the New Economic Policy in 1921.

We shall understand him best if we compare him with another great revolutionary figure—Oliver Cromwell. Captain McCullogh has noted the almost religious fervour of the Communists in those early days of fiery trial. Seeking a word to describe the force at work, he found himself saying, " Puritanism." Like Cromwell, Lenin felt himself the instrument of a " world-historic process " ; failure could never touch his spirit, for he fought on the side of irresistible forces. The impact of his personality and the ardour of his disciples worked like a ferment in the torpid mass of Russian life. Without the impetus of a great idea no party could have roused to conscious life the vast forces that had driven the peasants blindly into revolution. The stirrings of slumber passed into waking life. It matters not that Lenin's attempts to build a Communist State went down before a catastrophic economic disaster. " With one tremendous surgical operation he cut away the

[1] K. Wiedenfeld, " The Remaking of Russia," p. 23.

dead flesh of centuries." [1] The nation awoke from its mediæval dream into modern life, and, before he died, that new Russia had imposed her will even on her iron master. The duel between the old and the new begun by Peter the Great was completed by Lenin. Sooner or later Russia will take her place among the nations of the world as a modern state. One day in Gorki village, gently caressing some children, he observed: "Those youngsters will have a better time than we can; they will not have to go through the things which fell to our lot. For them life will not be so cruel. All the same I don't envy them. Our generation has succeeded in accomplishing a task marvellous in its historical importance. The compulsory cruelty of our lives will be understood and justified one day. Everything shall be made clear, everything!" [2] The great revolutionist was right—a new nation has been born into the world. It is doubtful whether he ever realized that the great dream of his life, the apocalyptic vision of a revolution heralding a new, a better world, of which Russia was the forerunner, had spent itself in building a new State. Certain it is that he felt his work to have the same eternal validity as his conviction of a mission, a conviction that gave his strange personality an overpowering ascendancy. Before he died he had already become a legendary figure—to the peasants he was Ilyitch or "Slant-eye" or "The Bald." They felt for him the mixture of love and fear in which the Paraguayans of a century ago held the tremendous shadow of Dr Francia, and at his funeral vast crowds wept in the streets of Moscow.

Talking one day to his friend Gorki, Lenin exclaimed with great enthusiasm: "It is a foolish phantasy to imagine that there are people independent of history. Even if one were to admit that there were such people in the past, they don't exist any more. Everybody is involved in the whirl of reality, entangled as never before." We miss the trumpet tones of the Great Protector, but the spirit is the same: "We care not what men will make of these actings. They, will they, nill they, shall fulfil the good pleasure of God and we shall serve our generations. Our rest we expect elsewhere—that will be durable."

[1] R. H. Bruce Lockhart, article, "Lenin: the Man and his Achievement," *Edinburgh Review*, April 1924.
[2] Gorki, "Nicolai Lenin—the Man," p. 2.

A LIST OF AUTHORITIES

BEER. " The Life and Teaching of Karl Marx." (Leonard Parsons, 1924.)

BOURDEAU. " Tolstoï, Lénine, et la Révolution russe." (Paris, 1921.)

DENIKIN. " La décomposition de l'armée et du pouvoir, Février-Septembre 1917." (Paris, 1922.)

FARBMAN. " Bolshevism in Retreat." (Collins, 1923.)

GORKI. " Ecrits de la Revolution." (Paris, 1922.)

—— " Nicolai Lenin—the Man." (*Daily Herald* pamphlet, 1924.)

HARD. " Raymond Robins' own story." (New York: Harper & Bros., 1920.)

ISWOLSKY. " Memoirs of Alexander Iswolsky." (Hutchinson, 1920.)

KERENSKY. "The Prelude to Bolshevism: the Kornilov Rebellion." (T. Fisher Unwin, 1919.)

KUNTZ. " L'offensive militaire de l'Etoile rouge contre la Pologne " (Paris, 1922.)

LANDAU-ALDANOV. " Lénine." (Paris, 1919.)

LASKI. " Karl Marx: an Essay." (Fabian Society, and Allen & Unwin, N.D.)

LENIN. " The Collapse of the Second International." (Pamphlet, The Socialist Labour Press, N.D.)

—— " Will the Bolsheviks Maintain Power?" (Labour Publishing Co., 1922.)

—— " The State and Revolution." (Contemporary Publishing Association, New York, 1921.)

—— " Thesis on Bourgeois Democracy and Proletarian Dictatorship." (1920.)

—— The Great Initiative, including the Story of Communist Saturdays." (1920.)

—— " 'Left Wing' Communism, an Infantile Disorder." (The Communist Party of Great Britain, London.)

—— " The Land Revolution in Russia—being a speech on the land question by Lenin in December 1918, together with the two fundamental land decrees." (Pamphlet, Independent Labour Party, 1919.)

LOUKOMSKY. " Memoirs of the Russian Revolution." (T. Fisher Unwin, 1922.)

MASARYK. " Sur le Bolchévisme." (Geneva, 1921.)

—— " The Spirit of Russia—studies in History, Literature and Philosophy." 2 vols. (Allen & Unwin, 1919.)

MILIUKOV. " Bolshevism: an International Danger." (Allen & Unwin, 1920.)

NAUDEAU. " Les dessous du chaos Russe." (Paris: Hachette, 1920.)

PALÉOLOGUE. " La Russie des Tsars pendant la grande guerre." 3 vols. (Paris, 1921-2.)

PASVOLSKY. " The Economics of Communism." (New York: The Macmillan Co., 1921.)

PRICE. " Reminiscences of the Russian Revolution." (Allen & Unwin, 1921.)

ROSS. "The Russian Bolshevik Revolution." (New York: The Century Co., 1921.)
—— "The Russian Soviet Republic." (Allen & Unwin, 1923.)
TROTSKY. "The History of the Russian Revolution to Brest-Litovsk." (Allen & Unwin, 1919.)
WIEDENFELD. "The Remaking of Russia." (Labour Publishing Co., 1924.)
WITTE. "The Memoirs of Count Witte." (Heinemann, 1921.)
ZINOVIEV. "N. Lenin: his Life and Work." (Pamphlet, pubd. Communist Party, N.D.)

"Report (political and economic) of the Committee to Collect Information on Russia." (Parliamentary Paper, Russia No. 1 (1921), Cmd. 1240.) [Also quoted "Emmott Committee."]
"The Manifesto of the Moscow International." (The National Labour Press, Ltd., N.D.)
Pamphlets of reprinted Russian documents published by the American Association for International Conciliation, Nos. 147-9, 159.
Soviet Russia—a description of the various political units existing on Russian territory, to which is appended the constitution of the Union of Socialist Soviet Republics of 6th July 1923. (F.O., 1924. H.M. Stationery Office.)

BENITO MUSSOLINI

" Italia fara da se."

CHARLES ALBERT, 1848.

" Ever so much lightning does not make daylight."

LESSING.

BENITO MUSSOLINI.

BENITO MUSSOLINI

Two great anti-Liberal movements have arrested the attention of Europe since the armistice of November 1918—Bolshevism and Fascism. Both these great political and social forces are anti-Liberal in that both alike deny the postulates of the idea of democracy enunciated by Abraham Lincoln in the tremendous phrase: "Government of the people, by the people, for the people." Both Fascism and Bolshevism involve the dictatorship of a class-party, and in either case only an advanced and dominant section of the class from which the ruling party is drawn is also enrolled in the party. Perhaps the word party is misleading in describing Bolshevism and Fascism, since each alike claims by its exclusive dictatorship to eliminate the whole idea of party, in the Liberal-constitutional sense of one of several organized groups who take it in turn to direct the State, according to the shifting favour of the electorate, or in other words, the people.

Such a claim by any organized body in a nation to exclusive dictatorship can only be vindicated by force, and both Fascism and Bolshevism repose upon an armed and disciplined force (in a sense the party in arms)—in the one case, upon the Fascist militia; in the other, upon the Red Army.

The parallels between the two movements are interesting and instructive, but so are the differences. In both cases general public opinion has rightly identified the two movements with two outstanding personalities—Nikolai Lenin and Benito Mussolini. But whereas the party of which Lenin was the founder and dictator, possesses a long and conscious tradition of revolutionary activity and a profoundly meditated and articulated body of doctrine, Fascism was in origin the half-conscious product of post-war reaction and discontent, and to this day has not succeeded in discovering what exactly it wishes to achieve. Therefore to a far greater extent than was the case with the Bolshevik dictatorship, Fascismo was and is dependent almost uniquely upon the life and varied fortunes of one man—Benito Mussolini. And yet just because of the singular opportunism of Mussolini's character, the study of Fascism is by no means the story of his life, but that of a veritable complex of events, influences, parties, forming and directing the blind impulse we know as Fascism which raised Mussolini to power but of which he has never yet been the undisputed master. This sounds like a contradiction in terms, but is justified by the fact that for two years after its foundation in 1919 Fascism was so confused that observers had to confess that it defied exact description or analysis, and that since 1921 Mussolini has become to an increasing extent the rallying-point of the whole movement.[1]

The exponent of a revolutionary Conservatism was a little over thirty-nine years old when he constituted himself dictator of Italy in October 1922. He was, as dictators and premiers go, remarkably young for his office. But young as he was he had packed into his eighteen years of mature life a considerable experience of politics, chiefly as a revolutionary Marxian Socialist.

Benito Mussolini was born at the little village of Predappio, near Forli, in the Romagna, in April 1883. It is not without significance that the Romagna has been throughout her modern history the storm centre of continental Italy. The elder Mussolini, a convinced Socialist, living in the region Italian Socialism regards as its stronghold, brought up Benito (" our Benit," as the villagers still call him [2]) a Socialist of the Italian semi-revolutionary type of the 'seventies and 'eighties. It is amusing to find English Conservative admirers of Mussolini rather naïvely explaining that, though a Socialist, his father was after all quite a respectable person.[3] The latter assertion is probably correct, since the elder Mussolini was the village blacksmith of Predappio.

For some time the young Benito worked with his father at his forge; he then became a village schoolmaster. This advance in status could not long satisfy his eager and restless spirit, and it was not long before he embarked on a political career by standing for a local office against a wealthy magnate. Mussolini becoming convinced of unfairness in the conduct of the election, without hesitation and with characteristic impetuosity arrested the even tenour of his rival's triumph by smashing the ballot-box.[4] The arch smasher of ballot boxes of our day had embarked upon a career that was to lead him to the high places of power.

To avoid the consequences of this first essay in iconoclasm the young Mussolini (barely twenty at the time) fled to Switzerland, and in his absence a local court found him guilty and sentenced him to a term of imprisonment. His first days in

[1] Beal's " Rome or Death," p. 243.
[2] San Severino, " Mussolini as revealed in his Political Speeches " Introduction, p. xvi.
[3] Phillips, " The Red Dragon and the Black Shirts," p. 22.
[4] Beal's " Rome or Death," p. 248.

Switzerland in 1905 were passed in a bitter struggle against poverty. He became a day labourer, at one time working as a bricklayer,[1] but throughout this time of trial he was losing no opportunity of increasing his knowledge, and his first achievement was to become proficient in French. His horizon began to clear when he met Giacomo Meneotto Serrati, still the leader of left-wing Italian Socialism, though not a revolutionary, and, as a man and a leader, notable for judgment and discretion.[2] The two co-operated in developing Marxian propaganda in Switzerland so effectively that the Swiss Government served him with an expulsion order as an "anarchist" and an "undesirable guest." It is worth noting that this order was rescinded by the Swiss Government only on Mussolini's rise to power in 1922.

A year or two of wandering in France and elsewhere followed, until he settled in the Trentino, where he edited the Socialist paper *Avanti*. A little later he co-operated with the famous irredentist Cesare Battisti on the paper *Popolo*. This association is significant. Even as a Socialist Mussolini, as we shall see, has never made the mistake of underrating national feeling as a factor in the problems that Socialism sets out to solve. The complete rejection by Italian Socialism of what he recognized passionately as a permanent element in his own nature was the primary cause of his "conversion" in 1914.

In 1910 he was amnestied by the Italian Government, and at once returned to his native province, Emilia, to edit yet another Socialist paper,[3] significantly named *The Class War*. His first notable success came to him at the Socialist Congress at Ancona in 1912. There he engaged in a vigorous controversy with Leonida Bissolati over the question of the Socialist party's attitude to freemasonry. In Bissolati he met a noble opponent, not only over a passing question of party tactics but, later, in a wider dispute for the soul of a nation.

Leonida Bissolati, not unmindful of Mazzini and of the principles invoked by Italian patriots when they set their hands to the building of Italy, never wavered in his belief that it was possible to reconcile the fullest realization of legitimate Italian nationalist claims formulated by the irredentists in Austria and Italy, with the liveliest sympathy for similar claims

[1] Beal's "Rome or Death," p. 248.
[2] Herron, "The Revival of Italy," pp. 82-3.
[3] Phillips, "The Red Dragon and the Black Shirts," p. 23.

by other nations rightly struggling into freedom or working for the completion of a process of national reunion already begun. So he proclaimed, with all the energy of a profoundly idealistic and generous nature, that Italians should rejoice at the liberation of Czechs and Poles, and equally at the successful realization by Serbia of the idea of Southern Slav unity, and by Greece of the "great idea" of an Hellenic Aegean state, embracing all the Greek communities that could be united under a national sovereignty. Bissolati was the apostle of an enlightened nationalism that believed in meting to others measures it had itself won. His gospel was destined to be eclipsed by the shoddy imperialism of d'Annunzio, proclaiming almost in the very words of his hero, Stelio d'Effrena, that he recognized "a barbarian in every man not of Latin blood." The man who was to exploit and canalize the intoxicating doctrines of the poet Commandante of Fiume met the protagonist of an older and more heroic Italy in Bissolati at the Ancona Congress, and, for that reason, the incident acquires a certain tragic significance in the history of contemporary Italy.

Mussolini's activity at the Ancona Congress won for him the position of editor of the *Avanti*, the famous organ of the Italian Socialists, which he held till the outbreak of the war brought Italy to a great dividing of the ways. In his writings and his speeches he continued to show that passion for direct decisive action which has always marked him out. "He is of the type that believes in cutting Gordian knots at one blow," and years later he was to describe his famous *coup d'état* of October 1922, as the "cutting of many Gordian knots." [1] He remains as he has lived, a revolutionary.

Among those with whom he came in contact in these days were some who divined the tendencies latent in the fiery soul of the man whose very face had something of the antique Roman in it, and yet more of the Italian despots of the Renaissance. In an oft-quoted remark, Georges Sorel, the founder of Syndicalism and the exponent of the "doctrine of violence," ventured on a prophecy marvellous in its penetration: "Our Mussolini is not an ordinary Socialist. Believe me, you will see him some day, perhaps, at the head of a sacred battalion, saluting with the sword the Italian flag. He is an Italian of the fifteenth century, a condottiero." [2]

[1] Beal's "Rome or Death," p. 250.
[2] According to the *Giornale di Roma*, quoted Beals, p. 253.

It has been suggested that the alienation of Mussolini from Socialism began with the abortive revolutionary movement that broke out in the Romagna in June 1914, and for some weeks paralysed the country, only to collapse at last in sound and fury and senseless destruction and pillage.[1] This is to suggest that the arch-apostle of direct action has an innate objection to revolution as such; that the Socialist of the extreme left was a believer (or has even since become one) in the tranquillity of a bourgeois order. Probable enough it is that he hated the Romagna movement for its ill-organized individualist confusion, for already the great problem of a truly national revolution was constantly before his mind. It was the war that pointed out the way clear before him, not *from* Socialism, but towards the Revolution of his dreams.

The decision of the Salandra Cabinet, of which the Marquis di san Giuliano was the Foreign Minister, was literally imposed upon the Government by the confused condition of the public opinion that counted in Italian politics. There was hesitancy, but both from a national and a political point of view, it soon became clear that Italy would not intervene on the side of her Allies. Italian public opinion, in view of the steady improvement in relations with France, Great Britain, and Russia—an improvement definitely embodied in a series of agreements [2] which, while within the scope of the text of the Triple Alliance, inevitably weakened even the purely political bonds that allied Italy to Austria and Germany—and for sentimental reasons, steadily imposed a period of neutrality. Germany had expected this attitude on the part of her ally, and at once devoted herself to the task of keeping Italy neutral, through a bargain with Austria-Hungary —a bargain that would have secured Italy the Italian regions of the Austrian Tyrol.

The policy of neutrality and a bargain with Austria-Hungary—a bargain strictly justified by Article VII. of the Triple Alliance, by which Austria is pledged to compensate Italy for any independent action on her part in the Balkans—was that advocated by the famous Italian politician Giolitti,

[1] As a sign that the Socialist millennium had dawned, chickens were sold at half-penny each to the peasants in the market-place of Molinella (Phillips, p. 22).

[2] Franco-Italian agreement of 1902 that if either party were attacked by one or more Powers the other would observe neutrality. Italy had always made it clear to her Allies that, in view of her geographical position, she would in no circumstances take part in a war against Great Britain.

"the dictator" of Italian politics and parties for the decade before the outbreak of war. Giolitti doubted Italian strength for the prolonged war which he anticipated, with all the lonely prescience of Lord Kitchener. Neutrality also seemed to him the inevitable consequence of the curious position in which Italy found herself in 1914, "the friend of the Entente, and the formal ally of the Central Powers, the potential enemy of Austria and France, and the lasting friend of two irreconcilable rivals, Germany and Britain." [1]

The Baron Sonnino, later the architect of the Treaty of London and Italian intervention, and, once committed, an impeccably loyal friend of the Allies, held in August 1914, from the point of view of immediate Italian interests, that Italy should intervene on the side of the Central Powers. He anticipated, along with many other Italians, the immediate victory of Germany and Austria. Timely help would reap a rich reward in Corsica and perhaps French Tunis. Many nationalists, "who later were the most fervent partisans of war against the Central Powers, and accused of treason any who differed from them, at the same time affirmed and maintained that we should take sides with our Allies in the conflict, and blamed the Government for its decision to remain neutral." [2] The abiding passion of the Nationalists was to cut a great figure in the world regardless of ends or means. In view of the immense influence the Nationalist movement was later to exercise over Fascism, it will not be out of place to discuss the origins and the philosophy of this highly organized party, that from its foundation about 1903 has played so vital a part in the development of modern Italy.

Nationalism was a protest against the corrupt government that had chequered the history of United Italy with disappointments. The colonial adventure under Crispi had ended in disaster at Adowa when the Emperor Menelek signally vindicated the independence of Ethiopia. The adventure had been inaugurated to make clear Italy's claim to be a great power; official incompetence and cowardice bade fair to make her negligible. Pareto and Mosca were the thinkers of the new doctrine. Enrico Corradini remains its most ardent exponent. Italy they thought needed regeneration by blood and fire. The nation was not spiritually

[1] A. E. F. Pribram and A. F. Braumuller, "Die Politischen Geheimvertrage Oesterreich-Ungarns," quoted Mowrer, "Immortal Italy," p. 170.
[2] Giolitti, "Memoirs," p. 384 (Eng. translation).

united yet—only war which was and remains the biological remedy of racial decadence, could cure the malady of smug and unambitious materialism rapidly becoming an acknowledged principle of government under the Liberal " dictator " Giolitti. A bold colonial policy was advocated, not in terms of " the white man's burden " or of wealth, but for the stimulating effect of death and war on the national character. Democracy, aristocracy, autocracy are all appearances under cover of which at all times strong and able men have " managed " the people or the monarch. Away with pretences then. " Government will be no more one-sided and far more efficient nationally if exercised by an aristocratic self-constituted governing class composed of those most likely to have the requisite qualities—the old nobility, that is, rejuvenated by admixture with the rich and powerful among the middle class and the exceptionally gifted from the common people." [1]

This panacea the Nationalists commended in a cloud of impassioned verbiage to the youth of the nation, and one outcome of their activities was the war in Tripoli, 1911-1912. Giolitti has explained his motives for the adventure in his Memoirs; they are political and good as far as they go. France had absorbed Algeria and Tunis, Great Britain, Egypt. They recognized Italy's prior claim on the reversion of Tripoli and successive Italian premiers had encouraged Italian economic activity in Tripolitana. The advent of the Young Turks to power at Constantinople was followed by the growth of anti-Italian feeling in Turkey, manifested in a hostile diplomatic attitude. Italy felt that her Allies, in view of their considered Turcophil policy, were not backing her sufficiently and that she must act for herself and so both clear up her relations with Turkey, and improve her position in the Triple Alliance. The moment seemed favourable. France, Great Britain, and Germany were deeply entangled in the Moroccan web, and far too occupied to be able to spare time to thwart Italy's expansion. Such a favourable conjuncture was not likely to recur—the Young Turk provocation and the pre-occupation of the Powers. Though France had recognized Italy's claims, her occupation of Tunis had filled Italian public opinion with an incurable fear that the French Colonial Expansionists would somehow and sometime force the hands of their Government and round off the French North African Empire with Tripoli. " . . . The moment had to come, and from

[1] Mowrer, " Immortal Italy," pp. 157-8

my point of view had come, when we would find ourselves faced by this alternative: either to assert our rights or to renounce them."[1]

Giolitti does not tell us that the country, or rather the young and ardent elements in it, were growing tired of his benevolent and corrupt dictatorship, and that he was always ready to throw sops to Cerberus when he could afford them. The State finances under the Italian Walpole were in admirable condition, the Nationalists clamoured that the national prosperity should be manifested in great deeds, and that Italy should vindicate with high gestures the grandeur of her "Roman past."

The national weakness of the Italians is to become intoxicated with alarming ease on mere words. "We Italians," observed Signor Nitti to a group of American correspondents, "do not make revolutions, we make speeches."[2] "For all his shrewdness, the average Italian is completely taken in by praise and hyperbole. Tell him he is a good fellow and you like him; he remains cold. But call him a noble Roman, the legitimate child of Latin virtue and civilization, the younger brother of Dante—announce that his country, his army, his customs, his women, his intelligence, his nobility of soul outshine those of other countries as the sun the moon—and he's yours."[3]

The people that counted wanted war, but the masses were pacific and indifferent, as they usually are. So the self-appointed task of the Nationalists was to conjure up a mirage of more than Babylonian glory and wealth. "Libya, a miserable country, became, in their words, a land of riches, running with mythological springs amid garden scenery. It could, they said, be made the second home of Southern Italians, the real answer to the problem how the surplus population could continue to emigrate and not be lost. Naturally, Southern Italians were enthusiastic."[4] And the end of it all was that much rich Italian blood was poured out on the sand of an African desert.

Only the Socialists remained aloof and scornful of an adventure that brought Italy some prestige but more disappointments. Equally they stood out against the rising tempest of nationalism in 1914–15.

[1] Giolitti, "Memoirs," p. 254, also see generally cap. xi.
[2] Quoted Mowrer, "Immortal Italy," p. 40.
[3] Mowrer, "Immortal Italy," p. 39.
[4] Mowrer, p. 160.

Before the war the Italian Socialist party had been one of the most consistently radical in Europe. Since its official organization in 1892 however, when the anarchists were expelled, it has like other Socialist parties contained two sections, a radical group, later syndicalist in tendency, standing for a root and branch destruction of the existing social order, and a body of evolutionary Marxians ("Reformists," as Lenin contemptuously called them), who took an active part in national life and, under the influence of Giolitti, seemed likely to be converted to a monarchical Socialism resembling that of the followers of Scheidemann in Germany. The expedition to Tripoli did much to injure the Reformists, and as a result the Party Congress in 1912 declared that "on account of its revolutionary essence, the Socialist party can be only a party of agitation and education, not a governing party." [1]

The Radical tendencies of the Italian official Socialist party were clearly revealed on the outbreak of the war. Alone of the powerful European Socialist parties it endeavoured to act in the spirit of the many resolutions of the Second International as to the attitude of Socialists to international war. On Italian intervention it announced its official formula to be "neither to help nor to hinder the war." The significance of this cannot be exaggerated. From the '90's onwards Italian Socialism had been steadily gathering strength. It had successfully exerted an increasing pressure on the Liberal state, especially in the more vigorous North. True to its general attitude of "agitation and education" it had, as we have seen, successfully eluded Giolitti's effort to dilute his Cabinets with Socialism, with the result that the Italian premier, in order to retain power, was forced to make more and more concessions to the masses organized by the Socialists. For instance, he evaded popular indignation at the results of the Libyan war by the timely concession of universal suffrage in 1912. More and more it came to be an accepted axiom that the only alternative to the graft and corruption of the "dictator" was Socialism. More and more Socialism was accepted as sooner or later inevitable.

Since the day when at the Ancona Congress in 1912, Mussolini had made a great fighting speech against the placid semi-bourgeois mentality of the "reformists," he had acquired a more and more commanding position in Italian

[1] Quoted Mowrer, "Immortal Italy," p. 308

Socialism as the marvellously energetiç editor of *Avanti*, the most influential organ of the party. It was a great achievement for a young journalist of twenty-nine and by the summer of 1914 he was looked on as the strong man of Italian Socialism. Then came the war and with it the spiritual crisis Sorel had foreseen. Mussolini was not long in convincing himself that with the defeat or victory of the Central Powers was bound up the rise or fall of European Socialism and with it the cause of integral revolution. In the struggle against German militarist aggression he felt the Italian proletariat would at once help in freeing the West from a menace stultifying alike to Liberalism and Socialism, and, disciplined in the fiery ordeal, would be thus equipped for the task of revolution—a revolution that should be a transformation and renaissance of Italy at last made one in blood and fire. Thus did he reconcile his Socialism still revolutionary, with the intense consciousness of Italy a nation. He had taken over the doctrine of war from the Nationalists because, like them, he felt that the unity of Italy was as yet political only, the legacy and life work of Cavour must be made one in spirit as in body.

He did not hesitate to promulgate the necessity of Italian intervention on the side of the Allies and to co-operate with all who followed this great idea, but he did not leave the Socialist party until he was first deprived of the editorship of the *Avanti*, and finally, on 25th November 1914, expelled from the party. At the meeting at Milan, before the Socialist section which decreed his expulsion, he re-affirmed his Socialism in memorable terms: "You think to sign my death warrant, but you are mistaken. . . . You have not seen the last of me! Twelve years of my party life are, or ought to be, a sufficient guarantee of my faith in Socialism. Socialism is something which takes root in the heart. What divides me from you now is not a small dispute, but a great question over which the whole of Socialism is divided. Amilcare Cipriani can no longer be your candidate because he declared, both by word of mouth and in writing, that if his seventy-five years allowed him, he would be in the trenches fighting the European military reaction which was stifling revolution.

"Time will prove who is right and who is wrong in the formidable question which now confronts Socialism, and which it has never had to face before in the history of humanity, since never before has there been such a conflagration as exists to-day, in which millions of the proletariat are pitted one against the other. . . . You must not think that the middle classes are enthusiastic about our intervention. They snarl . . . and fear that the proletariat, once armed with bayonets, will use them for their own ends.

"Do not think that in taking away my membership-card you will be taking away my faith in the cause, or that you will prevent my still working for Socialism and Revolution." [1]

Already, on 15th November 1914, he had launched another paper, the *Popolo d'Italia,* and became its editor, to preach with all his unwearying pertinacity the necessity of Italian intervention. He stumped the country on speaking tours, inveighing trucelessly against the "flabby and frightened" foreign policy of the Salandra Government. "We should not explain," he said at Parma on 13th December 1914, "the universal phenomenon of war by attributing it to the caprices of monarchs, race-hatred, or economic rivalry; we must take into account other feelings which each of us carries in his heart, and which made Proudhon exclaim, with that perennial truth which hides beneath the mask of paradox, that war was of 'divine origin.' . . ." After examining the various lines of pacificist argument developed before the war, he turns to the programme of the Second International. "The Germans, who ought to have set the example, flocked as a man to the Kaiser's banner. The treachery of the Germans forced the Socialists of the other countries to fall back upon the basis of nationality and the necessity of national defence. The German unity automatically determined the unity of the other countries. It is said, and justly, that international relations are like love: it takes two to carry them on. . . ." He reminds his hearers yet again that the bourgeoisie is neutral in spirit. "As a conclusive proof, compare the tone of the middle-class papers to-day with that shown at the time of the Libyan campaign, and note the difference. The trumpet-call which then sounded for war is muffled now. . . . The secret is out, and ought to make the Socialists, who are not stupid, stop and think. On the one side are all the conservative and stagnant elements, and on the other the revolutionary and living forces of the country. It is necessary to choose." Almost in the very words of Machiavelli's "Prince" he produces his last argument: "It is necessary to act, to move, to fight, and, if necessary, to die. Neutrals have never dominated events.

[1] San Severino, "Mussolini as revealed in his Political Speeches, Nov. 1914—August 1923," pp. 5-6.

They have always gone under. It is blood which moves the wheels of history!"[1]

The campaign for intervention continued to gather momentum. "Fasci di azione rivoluzionaria"—groups to agitate for intervention sprang up all over northern Italy, with Milan as their centre. In these "Fasci for Revolutionary Action" we see the origin of post-war Fascism. Its very name makes clear the revolutionary outlook of these early interventionists. Most of them, like Mussolini, were members of the Socialist party. Some, like Mussolini, had been uncompromising advocates of revolutionary as against reformist methods; others, like Alcesti de Ambris, were leaders of the revolutionary tendencies in the Trades Union movement. They were supported by such Syndicalist theorists and writers as Panunzio and Mantica. They believed in intervention because the war in their opinion was generating a world-revolutionary situation; they were assisting at the awe-inspiring overture to the universal triumph of Socialism.[2]

To these early "Fasci" rallied the Republicans, followers of Mazzini, and the Nationalists, both alike worshippers of the idea of national unity, to be realized by a crusade against Austria, whose crime in Mazzini's words was "not that she defends herself, but that she exists."

Socialists are often accused of being indifferent to problems of nationality and territorial sovereignty. There is a certain justification for the charge, but the truth is, that Socialists have held that territorial problems, whose moral significance they do not deny, can be peacefully solved once the social question has been settled. The universal triumph of Socialism will bring the automatic settlement of all territorial and racial questions. The patent fact, however, that it is the national, not the social problem that comes perpetually to the front in times of international crisis, led the Italian Socialist Interventionists to elaborate theories to meet the reality. In this way they reached the conclusion that problems of territory and independence perpetually stultify and push into the background efforts for far-reaching social change. "Hence arose the idea that it was only after the achievement of national unity that the forces of social revolution could be brought into play."[3]

Mussolini's attitude at this time is clearly indicated in his

[1] San Severino, "Speeches," pp. 10, 11, 13, 17.
[2] Odon Por, "Fascism," pp. 26-7.
[3] *Ibid.*, p. 28.

speech at Milan, 25th January 1915: " . . . the *Fasci* of action have this object, to create that state of mind which will impose war upon the country. To-morrow, if Italy does not make war, a revolutionary position will be inevitably decided, and discontent will spring up everywhere. . . . Then we shall say to the dominant classes: 'You have not proved yourselves capable of fulfilling your task; you have deceived us and destroyed our aspirations. Your first care should have been the completion of the unity of the country, and you have ignored it. . . .' This will be a case which will surely end in condemnation, in condemnation which cannot be other than capital. . . . The old forces of the political and social life of Italy will fall into fragments."[1]

The romanticism and the political irresponsibility of such views need no comment. But fulminated in clouds of burning rhetoric by a d'Annunzio, apocalyptic nationalism made headway. The masses of the country were ignorant and inert. On the whole they inclined to neutrality and Giolitti. There was a strong anti-war movement in Piedmont.[2] But in the classic land of political violence the interventionist jingoes and romantic revolutionaries were not at a loss for means of persuasion. A campaign of incredible abuse and slander was organized against Giolitti. At a meeting held at the Costarzi Theatre, close to his house in Rome, d'Annunzio openly incited the crowd to kill one of the few men in Italy who dared to count the cost in terms of reality.[3] He was accused of having taken twenty million lire from Austria and Germany. Crowds of excited youths, spoiling for a fight, followed him about the streets, shouting, "Abbasso!" On one such occasion when he had been escorted by his friends through such a demonstration, the old man turned at the door of his house and said to the crowd: "Just for once shout, 'Viva l'Italia!'"[4] It will not be difficult for English readers to recall to mind the similar, if less virulent, persecution of an eminent politician by interested parties in this country at the outbreak of war.

The campaign of d'Annunzio, Mussolini, and the interventionist groups was of the utmost parliamentary value to the government, once the Baron Sidney Sonnino had convinced himself and his colleagues that the negotiations with Austria, begun by him in December 1914, for territorial com-

[1] San Severino, "Speeches," pp. 23-4.
[2] Giolitti, "Memoirs," p. 393. [3] *Ibid.*, p. 400. [4] *Ibid.*, p. 397.

pensation for Italy as the price of her neutrality, were likely to break down. The government and the parliamentary interventionists calculated on a short war, and believed that Italian intervention would be decisive in turning the tide in favour of the Allies, who, against all expectation, had succeeded in holding the German assault. Three or four months, they reckoned, would decide the struggle.[1] In the Secret Treaty of London, of 24th April 1915, whereby Italy pledged herself, in return for the acceptance by them of her territorial programme, to enter the war on the side of the Allies within one month, it was arranged that Great Britain should give Italy facilities for a loan of £50,000,000, "a sum less than what every month of the war cost us, nor was any provision made for freightage or supplies of coal, iron, corn, and other things which we lacked, and which were indispensable for a war of any duration." [2]

A final indication of the anxiety of Italy to enter the war before it ended is to be found in the otherwise meaningless inclusion in the Italian Green Book of telegrams, during March and April 1915, from the Italian ambassadors in Petrograd and Berlin, and from the Italian minister at Nisch, reporting the possibility of a separate peace between Russia on the one hand and the Central Powers on the other.[3] As a result Sonnino concluded an advantageous agreement with the Allies, which, by allotting a considerable section of Slav Dalmatia to Italy, violated one of their most emphatic principles—the liberation of oppressed nationalities. The treaty was a model of the old secret diplomacy, and fortunately for the ultimate peace of Europe, it contained within itself the seeds of its own destruction, for its fundamental presupposition was that Austria-Hungary would survive the war, merely trimmed of some of her outlying provinces. Mussolini and not Sonnino was right in regarding the war as essentially revolutionary, for the world in which the Baron lived and moved and had his austere being went up in clouds of smoke at the Armistice. The credit or discredit of this evil treaty rests on the Baron Sonnino, not on the Allies fighting with their backs to the wall for very existence, to whom a bill was presented that they could not refuse to foot.

During May 1915, largely owing to a furious campaign of intimidation by the interventionists, the Government was able

[1] Giolitti, " Memoirs," p. 385. [2] *Ibid.*, pp. 385-6.
[3] The Italian Green Book, Nos. 57, 61, 66.

to beat down parliamentary opposition, and Italy entered the war a divided nation. Mussolini, rejected at first as a volunteer for the front, eventually joined the 11th Regiment of Bersaglieri as a private, and with them he served during the next two and a half years. He had put his faith to the supreme touch, and he never wavered. As a corporal he seems to have started and edited a trench newspaper. Military duties absorbed him, until, in 1917, he was desperately wounded by the bursting of a trench mortar. He hovered for some time between life and death, and on recovery had to be invalided out of the army. It is worth recording that King Victor Emmanuel, in the course of a visit to the hospital where he lay, spent some time in conversation with his future prime minister, and is said to have remarked to his "aide" that he thought Corporal Mussolini would go far. By the time that Mussolini resumed his seat in the editorial chair of the *Polopo d'Italia* there was much work to be done. It was the eve of Caporetto.

The Italian soldier, peasant or worker, had gone to the front without much enthusiasm. He had fought well through pride, or force of example, or national pugnacity, as most men do, but the moral stimulants demanded by the Western democracies were not served out to him, because the Italian governing class did not believe in democracy, or the rights of oppressed nationalities, or a new international order, even sufficiently to treat those ideas as valuable propaganda. It believed in the balance of power, in the Italian hegemony of the Adriatic, in "sacred egoism." [1] The army was controlled by a cold, strong-willed, but rather incompetent autocrat, General Cadorna, who believed above all things in a repressive discipline, decimations, censorship. The Italian is always restive under discipline, and even when ignorant, he is rightly sceptical of the truth and honesty of "principalities and powers." The sense of nationality in, say, a southern Italian peasant, is weak. Often the privates did not know the names of any of their immediate officers, but that did not hinder their scepticism finding an outlet in mordant and untranslatable squibs. But they fought well and bore hardships unbelievable even on the Western Front, until the stupidity of things dawned on them, and they became very weary. An incomprehensible mythology, invented by people who do not speak the same language or think the same

[1] The famous phrase of the premier, Signor Salandra, on the motives of Italy in entering the war.

thoughts as yourself, is, after all, not a very effective specific against moral exhaustion.

The news of the Russian Revolution, even when interpreted by General Cadorna as a passionate eagerness on the part of Russian peasants to go on fighting, had told the Italian soldier that one nation at least had broken the vicious circle, and actually seemed to be engaged in kicking out its rulers from the seats of the mighty. There was a certain amount of direct revolutionary propaganda among the troops—propaganda eagerly seized upon by Conservatives as the sole explanation of what followed. Far more important as factors were the bitter letters from home from those who knew from the soldiers on leave, that most of Cadorna's bulletins were deliberate lies. "Let all letters from home be destroyed," suggested Cadorna. Incompetence in the high command, starvation rations, lack of sympathy between officers and men, wasteful and brutal frontal attacks—these elements, in the psychological complex, were infinitely more significant than Socialist propaganda.

At 2 a.m., on 24th October 1917, the Austro-German offensive began. In five days it had broken completely through, and the Italian armies were in headlong retreat. A mob of 1,000,000 soldiers and civilian refugees fled under a grey October rain—it was the "greatest migration" that the world records accomplished in so short a time.[1] When the army at last rallied on the Piave, leaving Venetia in the hands of the enemy, out of 1,000,000 men in line at the beginning of the offensive, 700,000 had vanished. Out of 2,062,000 in the fighting ranks, 800,000 were lost in a few days. In November 1917 the Italians on the Piave faced 400,000 Austro-Germans with 280,000 men. All of the immense army stores, valued at 6000 million lire, machinery, rolling-stock, food, winter clothing, fell into the hands of the enemy.

The demoralization seemed complete; bodies of men surrendered singing to the enemy, doubtless believing that such conduct, if universal, would end the war. The blow was staggering, not only to Italy but to the Allies. For a moment it seemed that the cause would be lost before the weight of American intervention could turn the scale.

And then out of the very depths of the catastrophe the Italian people, made one at last by a marvellous moral recovery, wrested victory out of the jaws of defeat. If the Austro-

[1] Mowrer, "Immortal Italy," p. 228.

Germans could not by their hammer-strokes drive Italy out of the war, they and not the Italians had been defeated. Even before the arrival of Allied help, the tide had been turned on the Piave. The enemy was held.

The full revelation of the deficiency, the intolerable aspect of defeat, the invasion of the Fatherland, transformed the nation. All classes co-operated in national work, bitterness was replaced by enthusiasm. A crusading ardour filled the hearts of all ranks; the repentant army, officers and men, worked together with sympathy and self-sacrifice.

It was this great moral effort that carried Italy through 1918: the revived tenacity and patriotism, ably directed by the new commander-in-chief, General Diaz, carried the re-organized army to victory at Vittorio Veneto—a victory as spectacular as the defeat of Caporetto, and the immediate precursor of the catastrophic collapse and disappearance of the Dual Monarchy. New nations sprang into being on the advance of victorious Italy, and the dark shadow of the House of Habsburg passed from the Danubian lands.

That the reorganization of the Italian forces was splendidly seconded by the Allies, Great Britain and France, whose armies played no insignificant part in the final triumph of Italian arms, is an undeniable fact that finds scant recognition in Fascist Italy. A few days before the *coup d'état* that carried him to power, Mussolini, in his speech at Naples, sneered at the welcome assistance of British troops at Vittorio Veneto as being "absolutely derisory."[1] We shall see that this attitude is part of the studied policy of the new and anti-Mazzinian Italian nationalism.

In the dark hours of defeat and danger and with the revival of hope in the future, the Italian Government had been lavish in promises of a reconstructed and a better Italy. One man at least took the promise of a regenerated nation seriously, for he had dedicated himself to the task when, in 1914, he had fired the "Fasci of revolutionary action" with his own deep passion. All through 1918 Mussolini, in speeches and writings, bent his whole energies to the task of steeling Italy to hold on to the end. In the speech delivered at the Teatro Communale, Bologna, on 24th May 1918, he envisages the future: "The returning battalions will move with the slow and measured tread of those who have lived and suffered much and who

[1] Dr William Miller in *Contemporary Review*, Aug. 1923, art., "Nine Months of Fascismo."

have seen innumerable others suffer and die. They will say, we shall say: 'Here upon the track which leads back to the harvest-field, here in the factory which now forges the instruments of peace, here in the tumultuous city and the silent country, now that the duty has been done and the goal reached, let us set up the symbol of our new right.' Away with shadows! We, the survivors—we, the returned, vindicate our right to govern Italy, not to her destruction and decay, but in order to lead her ever higher, ever on, to make her—in thought and deed—worthy to take her place among the great nations which will build up the civilization of the world to-morrow." [1]

Profound disillusionment was the lot of Italy after the Armistice. The official view of Vittorio Veneto, that it was the decisive action of the war, contrasted dramatically with the facts of the international situation. Very shortly the bourgeois parties, who had promised the masses a new heaven and a new earth when the tide of war ebbed and flowed doubtfully round the banks of the Piave, began to explain their own inability to meet a single post-war problem by the reiterated assertion that the Allies, and, above all, President Wilson, had robbed Italy of the fruits of victory.

The bankruptcy of the existing régime was revealed in the reverberating diplomatic defeats sustained by the Baron Sonnino at Paris. Awaking too late to the grave defects of his cherished creation, the Treaty of London, which had formally allotted the Italian town of Fiume to a future Croatian State, he endeavoured to placate national feeling by insisting on the cession of this vigorous and self-conscious community that had long enjoyed a privileged position under the Hungarian Crown, to Italy, according to the clearly applicable principle of nationality. At the same time he demanded the pound of flesh he had won under the treaty—an important section of the Dalmatian coast-line and islands, containing a mixed population of which the Italian element represented some three per cent. It is really inaccurate to call the population mixed, since the Italians, when they were present, were usually congregated in little communities. The plain fact was that the treaty was constructed with a view to making the Adriatic an Italian lake. The arguments by which this unquestioned Imperialism was justified in public were, as was inevitable, a curious mixture of sentimentalism and ancient history.

[1] San Severino, "Speeches," p. 48.

President Wilson, outraged by what he regarded as the clear attempt of Italy to effect the economic and political strangulation of the newly-born Jugoslav State, resolutely refused to countenance the Italian occupation of the Dalmatian coast—an occupation that had been skilfully effected by Sonnino under the terms of the armistice with Austria. At the same time he gravely weakened the moral consistency of his contentions by permitting the cession to Italy of the wholly German districts of South Tyrol up to the Brenner Pass, while resisting the justifiable Italian claim for Fiume on the ground that the city was necessary to the economic life of Croatia. The latter view finds formal expression in the secret Treaty of London itself, but the President failed to realize that Fiume was a vital question of sentiment. A diplomatic tangle was created that not only endangered the peace by desperately embittering the relations of Italy and Jugoslavia, but a deep conviction of injustice and disappointment developed in Italy—a conviction that was to poison the vital springs of national life.

On 10th June 1919, the *Corriere della Sera*, greatest of Italian newspapers and a firm friend of the Allies, wrote as follows: "Nearly every one has been able to come to an agreement with Wilson by endorsing the famous Fourteen points: Poles, Jugoslavs, Czechs, and English have secured from him plenary indulgences; Clemenceau and Japan have secured extensive limited indulgences. It is, unhappily, for Italy, Wilson's lightning conductor, that have been reserved all the blasts of his obstinacy. Others have been allowed to pass freely. Only Italy is in quarantine. To Italy is denied every square inch of territory that lies outside her linguistic frontiers. But Jugoslavia is pardoned the continued occupation, seven months after the Armistice, of the German town of Klagenfurt. The one is treated like an enemy, a kind of "Aunt Sally"; the other like a schoolboy for whom the master reserves all the privileges. How can this inequality of treatment fail to offend and wound us?"[1] In an organ, *La Vraie Italie*, published in French and devoted to the cause of intellectual co-operation with other countries, under the editorship of Giovanni Papini, Ardengo Soffici could write of France as Italy's "cold and spiteful rival, more pertinaciously bitter than any other in thwarting her claims, prepared for any intrigue and treason, and solely bent on establishing in her

[1] Quoted Alazard, "Communisme et 'Fascio' en Italie," pp. 18-19.

own favour that hegemony that we thought to have shattered for ever in beating down our enemies." [1]

Little as the masses and most of the ex-soldiers cared for Adriatic hegemony and the balance of power, they knew that prices were soaring, and that the Government made no attempt to redeem its promises. Steadily the conviction grew throughout the country that the whole war had been a futile and inexcusable waste of blood and treasure, a monstrous mistake. The happiness of millions had been staked on a barren adventure.

The Socialists were not slow to see their advantage. They alone had refused to have part or lot in the war. Disdainfully they had stood aside, and though again and again they had shown in quiet and unobtrusive work for the nation during the war, that no party or class has a monopoly of patriotism—least of all those who proclaim it from the housetops—the temporary restoration of solidarity and good feeling was soon dissipated in the disappointments, ill-luck, and recriminations of the period after the Armistice.[2]

All the disillusioned, discontented, hungry, turned to Socialism—the one party uncompromised in the war that every one wanted to forget and live down—and recruits flowed in from all quarters. In 1914 the official Socialist party contained some 42,000 adherents ; in 1919 its active members rose to 100,000. The General Confederation of Labour—closely allied to the Socialist party—embodied some 300,000 members before the war; in 1919 the numbers went up to more than 1,200,000.[3]

Not unmindful of the insults to which they had been subjected, the Socialists took the offensive with wholesale denunciation of the war and its defenders. On 15th April 1919, the Socialist leader Treves, in a speech before a large crowd, invited it "to sweep the streets of Milan of interventionist filth." [4] Deserters were hailed as national heroes; the premier, Nitti, hastened to give them an immediate amnesty; and one, Misiano, was later elected to Parliament—Naples and Turin disputing as to which should have the honour of returning him. "Italy after the Armistice presented the unusual spectacle of a victorious country trying by all means to obliterate its victory and abase the authors thereof." [5]

[1] Quoted Alazard, p. 20.
[2] Odon Por, "Fascism," p. 32.
[3] Alazard, "Communisme et 'Fascio' en Italie," p. 34.
[4] Quoted Mowrer, "Immortal Italy," p. 318.
[5] *Ibid.*, p. 318.

Quite apart from this characteristically vehement manifestation of the after-war malaise another force was at work in Italian life—that of the example and doctrines of the Russian Bolshevik Revolution. Russian influence had begun in Italy with the Zimmerwald and Kienthal Conferences, 1915-16, where a " defeatist " programme had been sketched by Lenin, and the scaffolding of what was to become the Third International run up by the great revolutionary and the representatives of European Socialist parties opposed to the war. As usual the Russians generalized from Russian experience. Great concessions had been wrung from Tsardom only by military defeat—after the Crimean and Russo-Japanese Wars. " Defeatism," therefore, had a *raison d'être* in the case of Russia, though Trotsky doubted the wisdom and usefulness in allowing the militarist reaction in Germany and Austria-Hungary to win the war, and thereby run the risk, as Mussolini had asserted in 1914, of seeing them stamp out the revolutionary movement on the Continent.

Lenin had apparently been vindicated by events. He was the ruler of a mighty nation, and was generally believed to be engaged on the architectural plans for the New Jerusalem he proposed to build in Russia. In March 1919 came the foundation of the Third or Communist International, and the news literally stampeded the Italian Socialist party towards revolution. A powerful group of Social Communists sprang up in the body of the inflated Socialist party, and it was this group which set about preparations for engineering an exact copy of the Second Russian Revolution in Italy. The programme was quite clearly formulated: a proletarian revolution and the expropriation of the bourgeoisie was the goal; there must be no co-operation with the existing State; whatever the Government proposed or did the Socialists must obstruct. So doctrinaire were the extremists that since the Russian Revolution had followed military defeat, and unfortunately Italy had not undergone that necessary preliminary to regeneration, they decided that the required " defeatist " atmosphere must be created by the systematic vilification of the war, the bourgeoisie, officers, soldiers, and police.

For the time being the Russian mirage completely blinded the Socialists to realities and to the foundations of their own power. Before the war they had made great progress and won notable concessions by a tacit co-operation with the State.

Progress was only possible with its approval. To come out openly for revolution was to compel the State in desperation to look elsewhere for support.

State constructive work was absolutely vital if Italy was to solve her two great internal problems—Agrarian and Labour. The agrarian disorders, acute both in North and South Italy, differed considerably in the two regions. The South is the region that still awaits its '89. It is a country of large estates, successors of the ancient latifundia. Once it was the garden of the Mediterranean, now, with poverty as a motive, a reckless deforestation has ruined the fertility of the land. The woods and forests formerly caught the rain, bound the thin soil together, and fertilized it with leaf moulds. Now the peasant has to scrape the surface of a sun-baked, inhospitable, all but waterless waste. The picturesque villages that crown the sugar-loaf hills are centres of an unutterable though teeming squalor. Water has to be brought too far, and is much too precious to justify its waste on the human body. Even wealthy landowners may sometimes find themselves compelled to use wine instead of water for washing purposes.[1] Millions must be spent on the South before it can recover, as some day it may, its old natural fertility. To add to the troubles of the peasant of South Italy and Sicily, he was cursed with a decayed feudal system. A pre-war inquiry revealed that 787 persons owned one-third of Sicily. Most of these great landowners lived in Rome or abroad, leaving their estates to be managed by "gabellotos," who rented them at a fixed rate. The gabelloto was "the type of all implacable usurers." Frequently he sub-let to exploited sub-gabellotos, who in turn sub let plots to the more than exploited peasant at exorbitant rents. The pre-war Southern peasant was ignorant, superstitious, and inert. The soldier back from the trenches, who had learnt many things and had consolidated his pre-war Socialism, found a quick way out of an iniquitous position. Scarcely had the demobilization been completed when the governing classes were startled by the spontaneous and widespread seizure of lands by peasants, led by the ex-soldiers, and the general expulsion of gabellotos all over Sicily and the South.

Signor Nitti, who fully realized that the agriculture of South Italy belonged to the eighteenth century, and that he must accept the new movement or run the risk of a

[1] Mowrer, "Immortal Italy," p. 135.

Jacquerie, acquiesced, with the result that on 2nd September 1919, the famous Visocchi Decree gave the peasants "the right to take possession of all land insufficiently cultivated." Many years before, Giolitti had publicly proclaimed that the development of a strong class of peasant landed proprietors was the only effective method for stemming the tide of Socialism in Italy, and the Visocchi Decree, vague as it was, led the way in the direction indicated by the "dictator."

By the end of 1920 a system had been elaborated whereby a regional commission composed of proprietors, peasants, experts, and representatives of the Government, authorized the occupation of uncultivated ground. A *modus vivendi* between the peasants and the landowners was not impossible once the curse of the gabelloto had been removed.[1]

In the North, where Socialism and the organization of labour had made much further progress than in the South, the problem was different. There the movement, inaugurated by the Catholic Popular party and some of the ex-soldiers, in favour of the development of a small landed proprietary met with vigorous resistance on the part of the existing Labour Land Leagues, dominated by the Socialists. The elections of 1919 gave the Socialists 3 out of the 4 deputies for the region of Ferrara and the Lower Po; in the municipal elections of 1920 they captured every one of the 21 communes and secured a majority on the provincial council. With the aid of this administrative machinery thus completely in their hands, the 200 Red Leagues of the province secured an absolute monopoly of labour. The proprietors had to employ the number of labourers allotted to them by the local League or do without labour altogether.

When the proprietors, worn out with ceaseless restrictions and vexations, tried to escape their troubles by selling out to their own labourers—the Leagues checked the possible rise of peasant proprietors by a ruthless use of the boycott. Such conditions were general in North Italy after the war. The peasant Leagues were in many cases a thirty years' growth, and represented the inevitable tendency of labour to constitute itself in self-protection a monopoly. "The free market in labour" is the inevitable prelude of "wage-slavery" and economic depression. The after-war problem hinged on the transformed spirit of these Leagues which, under the guidance of the extremist Socialists, and hypnotized by

[1] Alazard, "Communisme et 'Fascio' en Italie," p. 59.

the message from Moscow, began to regard themselves as the advanced guard of Revolution. The strength of the Leagues was shown by the devastation wrought by the succession of agricultural strikes, such as that of February 1920, when 60,000 labourers of the province of Ferrara came out, followed immediately in March by the 200,000 of Lombardy.[1] In both cases, the animals were abandoned. Their weakness lay in their subordination to the idea of a Revolution which never materialized, but was to justify the dictatorship of the League Executives—a dictatorship that inevitably bred much secret discontent that only lacked opportunity to break into open revolt against the Communist bosses.

In Italian industry after the Armistice two forces began swiftly to show themselves. In the first place, a highly interesting and significant agitation in favour of "workers' control," originating in the increasing self-consciousness and improved status of the workers, and only later passing over into the revolutionary movement of 1920; and in the second place, the political effervescence due to the example of the Russian Revolution, and manifesting itself in a long series of disastrous strikes.

Since they were purely political the least thing was sufficient to start a strike. In January and February 1920, two general strikes on the railways paralysed the country twice in a few weeks. Engine-drivers would keep expresses waiting long hours in stations until an officer or soldier in uniform who happened to be in the train was by this means frozen out. Strikers paraded the streets of Milan insulting men in uniform. One officer was stripped in order that his persecutors might beat him with greater effect and ignominy.[2] It became dangerous to appear well dressed in public. Posts and telegraphs were constantly dislocated by strikes. The garbage men of Rome struck twice in hot weather, and for days the streets of the city were polluted with accumulated refuse that might quite easily have caused an epidemic.[3] Slight quarrels regularly ended in murder. The strike atmosphere seemed to have entered the Parliament itself, and riots in the chamber were of regular occurrence. On one occasion Signor di Rodino, rushing to the rescue of Signor Maury, whom he saw fainting and covered with blood, amid the crowd of

[1] Alazard, "Communisme et 'Fascio' en Italie," p. 59.
[2] *Ibid.*, p. 47.
[3] Mowrer, "Immortal Italy," p. 320.

his assailants, was himself bitten severely in the arm by an enraged Socialist deputy![1] "Life became a sinister carnival."[2]

Turati had the moral courage to protest against "this long chain of strikes, let loose under every pretext—the only consequence of which was the aggravation of a situation already difficult enough." He was powerless to control the elemental forces at work in the country—forces far more the consequence of the post-war disillusionment working on the volatile spirits of the nation than the product of a deeply laid or well-co-ordinated plot woven by the Red Wizard of the Kremlin. The Socialist party itself, apparently moving with irresistible will to the clearly conceived goal of revolution, was in reality paralysed behind the scenes by the desperate faction fights between the moderates and the adherents of Lenin.

All through 1920 the struggle continued evenly balanced. In the spring the Italian Socialist party decided to send delegates to the famous Second Congress of the Third International that met in the exalted atmosphere produced by the first victories of the Red Army over the Poles, and the headlong advance on Warsaw. The Supreme Pontiff of the new faith now decided that "all the postulates for world-revolution exist." All Communist parties were required to accept the famous twenty-one points drafted by Zinoviev, with all their disastrous disruptive consequences for the Labour and Socialist cause in Western Europe.[3]

These points were in substance that every Communist party must accept its name, organization, programme, and even tactics, from the Executive Committee of the Third International sitting in Moscow; it must call itself a Communist, not a Socialist party, and must rigidly exclude from its membership all "social patriots," "social pacifists," and "reformists." In short the Italian Socialists were required to work for world-revolution and Soviet Russia under martial law administered from Moscow. Serrati, extremist as he was, did not feel inclined to accept such terms for less than the Millennium in full working order. His researches in Russia left him still more unconvinced, and the man who had set out on his pilgrimage to the Kremlin favourable to the idea of joining the new International, returned to report to his party that he had found

[1] Alazard, "Communisme et 'Fascio' en Italie," p. 55.
[2] Mowrer, "Immortal Italy," p. 320.
[3] See Farbman, "Bolshevism in Retreat."

Russia the land of "hunger, pestilence, and the gallows,[1] . . . there is nothing left but a brute mass, incapable of organic conception, hating work, resigned to misery, to obedience, and to death . . . there is no liberty of the Press or personal liberty, but terrorism holds subject more than a hundred million people. . . . The ignorant masses are grouped in peasant labour armies, which do little work and do that little badly." [2]

During the critical year when the revolutionary and counter revolutionary storm was brewing, the State had been administered under the guidance of Signor Nitti. He succeeded Orlando, discredited by his inability to make headway against the Allies at Paris, and represented the return of the Liberal Giolittian neutralists of 1914—the aged dictator himself still kept in the background. Since no interventionist would co-operate with him, he was compelled to surround himself with the neutralists of former days. But in the circumstances of Italy at the time, as has been mentioned above, this was no particular drawback to him. Great hopes were entertained of his premiership. For an Italian premier he was still young, he was unquestionably clever, and held broad and far-sighted views on foreign policy, regarding Italian troubles as a detail in the general European confusion. He aimed at liquidating the Adriatic question by the abandonment of the preposterous claim on Dalmatia on the lines of the settlement concluded by his successor. He seemed at last to have paved the way for an entente with Greece by the Tittoni-Venizelos agreement over the Dodecanese, whereby eleven of the twelve Greek islands, occupied by Italy during the Italo-Turkish War, 1911-12, were to be ceded to Greece on the conclusion of the general peace with Turkey, while Rhodes was eventually to pass to Greece after a plebiscite, provided Great Britain held a similar plebiscite in Cyprus.

But his efforts to secure an Adriatic settlement were hopelessly jeopardized by d'Annunzio's adventure, and the record of his internal administration is the story of a drift towards the abyss. He adopted a policy of "Olympian calm" before the disorder in the country, or in other words an attitude of complete inertia towards the revolutionary menace. As a result the extremists multiplied instead of diminishing their efforts to precipitate a convulsion. He believed that the only quality required in a statesman was a certain nimbleness and

[1] Mowrer, "Immortal Italy," p. 337.
[2] Quoted Herron, "The Revival of Italy," p. 83

parliamentary dexterity—accordingly he gave way to the opposition in parliament or country on every possible occasion, and when he left office in June 1920, Italy was on the verge of social revolution.

In the hope of clearing up the situation Nitti secured the passing of a law for proportional representation, under which the elections of 16th November 1919 were held. The nation had been dowered by Giolitti with universal suffrage in 1912 as a sop to the masses after their Tripoli disappointment. The elections of 1919 ought, under proportional representation and universal suffrage, to have been clearly representative of the nation. In effect they added to the existing confusion. The bourgeoisie, disgusted with the divisions and general ineffectiveness of the constitutional parties generally abstained in a fatalistic mood of acceptance of the inevitable revolution, which every one took for granted.

The election held one great surprise, the rise of the new Catholic Popular Party, under the leadership of the Sicilian priest, Don Sturzo. Up to 1904 the Vatican had imposed abstention from elections as the rule of all strict Catholics. This attitude of hostility to the Italian State originated in the occupation of Rome by the forces of United Italy in 1870, and the consequent extinction of Papal territorial sovereignty. By 1909 the ineffectiveness of this protest was fully realized, and electoral campaigning was permitted, with the result that fifteen Catholic deputies entered the Chamber. In general the Catholic vote was given to the Liberals, who had accepted the most important points of their programme, with the result that in 1913 the *Osservatore Romano*, the official organ of the Vatican, was able to assert that 228 deputies owed their seats to the Catholic vote.[1]

On 18th January 1919 the deputy Bertini and Don Sturzo drew up an appeal for the formation of a new Catholic "Popular Party," independent of the Liberals, and with a clear platform of its own. They launched a large programme of economic and social reform on strictly constitutional but radical lines. Representation of economic interests and social classes in parliament, and the creation of technical councils where intellectual and manual labour would be represented ; thorough organization of the industrial capacity of the nation, attention to agriculture and irrigation ; the development of a strong class of peasant proprietors ; proportional representation and

[1] Alazard, "Communisme et 'Fascio' en Italie," p. 29.

women's suffrage; the reform of the Senate along electoral lines (instead of the existing system of nomination by the King on the recommendation of the Prime Minister) and the representation in it of various organized groups, educational, political, and economic; the conclusion of international agreements guaranteeing the rights of labour and conditions of work; the acceptance of the Fourteen Points of President Wilson as the basis of Italian foreign policy—these are some of the items of the programme of the new party.[1]

This Catholic radicalism of Don Sturzo has its roots in the famous Encyclical "Rerum Novarum" of Leo XIII., in which the great Pope boldly adopted the watchword "Social Justice," and promulgated an idea that Christians might be expected to accept, but which in fact opened a Pandora's box of controversy: "Wages should not be less than are necessary to maintain a frugal and sober worker." The new party gave a great impetus to the Catholic Labour groups. In 1914 these counted 103,326 members; in 1922 their numbers were 1,180,000, of whom 935,000 were agricultural labourers.[2] The Popular party went into the election expecting, with the aid of proportional representation, to win 70 or 80 seats, it actually returned with 100. The Socialists calculated on winning at the outside 100 seats, they actually won 156. Populars and Socialists together controlled the majority in the chamber, but were incapable of co-operating for longer than was necessary to defeat the Government. The Liberals and Conservatives formed a confused mass of changing opinion, on which the Government could not rely, since Nationalists and Moderates were as much divided against each other as the Popolari and the Socialists. Violent anti-monarchical demonstrations by the Socialists marked the State opening of the Chamber on 1st December 1919. A short time afterwards Modigliani, an influential Socialist leader, ended a speech on foreign policy with a peroration in favour of a Republic, and for ten minutes the Assembly foundered amid the uproar of 300 deputies shouting "Long live the King!" and 180 replying, "Long live Lenin!" Nitti, whose ministry was in a precarious position at the moment, with great dexterity seized the opportunity, and exclaimed, "I desire the maintenance of the monarchy," thus giving the Moderates of all parties clearly to understand that his fall might spell the fall of the dynasty. In this way the ministry

[1] Beals, "Rome or Death," pp. 117-18, and Alazard, p. 30.
[2] Beals, "Rome or Death," p. 119.

"existed" until the middle of 1920. Nitti simultaneously clung to office with the tenacity of a limpet, and continued his policy of concessions and acquiescence. The Social Communists continued to flout nationalist sentiment, apparently with the sole object of enraging all those who were proud of the part Italy had played in the war. Even this pettiness Nitti was prepared to condone, and on his instructions the first anniversary of the Italian Armistice of 4th November 1918 passed unobserved.

After various highly discreditable manœuvres on the part of all concerned,[1] the Popolari, who had declared war on the Nitti government at their congress at Naples, 8th April 1920, eventually overthrew it on 9th June, and the King, as a last resource, turned to Signor Giolitti, who came back to power after a silence that had lasted practically unbroken since May 1915.

The great deputy for Dronero found the State almost on the verge of dissolution, yet in spite of this, under his wise guidance, Constitutionalism made its final effort — an effort far more successful than is usually imagined. Two great problems confronted him after his accession to office—d'Annunzio and the liquidation of the Fiume movement, and the culmination of the revolutionary unrest in Italy in the famous occupation of the factories by the workers during August and September. The difference between inertia and political flexibility was never more clearly demonstrated than in his masterly handling of an all but desperate situation.

On the night of 11th to 12th September 1919, Gabriele d'Annunzio transformed the interminable Fiume debate by occupying the city at the head of a chosen band of nationalist enthusiasts. He was assisted by volunteers of the regular army and he had behind him the passionate sympathy of all Italians not absorbed in the difficult task of persuading their fellow-countrymen to believe that in Russia alone was Orthodoxy to be found. Since it was generally agreed that the constitutional leaders of Italy had made a desperate mess of the peace, two lines of thought or rather passion developed from this realization. On the one hand, as we have seen, the war was regarded as a monstrous villany perpetrated by the bourgeoisie for their own nefarious ends, a view developed in the Social Communism that looked towards Moscow as the new Mecca; on the other hand, patriotism became a mono-

[1] See Alazard, "Communisme et 'Fascio' en Italie," p. 67.

mania and d'Annunzio the frenzied hierophant of a new mysticism. In either case the Liberal state became the rapidly disintegrating target of the missiles hurled simultaneously from Right and Left.

The Fiume raid was organized in the city itself by a group of seven junior Italian officers who, convinced through a misunderstanding that the Allies were contemplating, with the connivance of Nitti, the surrender of Fiume to the Jugoslavs, took the vow " to save the city or die in the attempt." They offered the command to d'Annunzio, the prophet of ultra-nationalism, who welcomed as a magnificent adventure what was a question almost of life and death to the young military enthusiasts who had dared to take on their own shoulders the responsibility of defying military discipline. But " the expedition had found a leader whose fame could shield his followers." [1]

To his followers d'Annunzio was the prophet of Italy, in his own words, " a column of never-consumed fire," a definition which would tend to confirm the average Englishman in the view that this great Italian figure is at best a vapouring litterateur and at worst a dangerous lunatic. " We think of an aged and somewhat decayed voluptuary, the hero of a thousand beds, and instead we find him at fifty-six directing a complicated undertaking in its least details, manifesting an unrivalled physical and intellectual energy. This is but the latest of his surprises; his has been a life of continual renewals. From the sensual, talented boy, eager for the obvious prizes of life, he passed to the disdainful superman, the philosopher meditating on his own death, the emotional voluptuary toying with ideas of suicide. The fleeing debtor became the intellectual lion of Paris. Then, at the age of 52, 'the dandy put on uniform, the poseur showed a contempt for death, and the voluble boaster a capacity for firm instant action.' " [2]

Egoism and devotion to everything Italian are the two threads that can be traced through the whole variegated web of a life spent as he would have it " among women, sculptors, musicians, poets, princes, as in a Decameron." " I would rather die," he told the French actor Le Bargy, " than lead a mediocre life."

It is possible that his intervention prevented a weak and pusillanimous government from handing over Fiume to the Jugoslavs, but even this is highly improbable. But once

[1] Mowrer, "Immortal Italy," p. 280.
[2] Mowrer, " Immortal Italy," p. 282.

that unlikely disaster had been averted, he rapidly became an intolerable nuisance, if not an actual menace, to the Government of Italy and the peace of Europe. Most of the original expedition who had been inspired by the sole desire to save Fiume for Italy soon wearied of him and his heroics, but he did not lack recruits attracted by his offer of a " joyous life." Existence at Fiume passed in an endless round of carnivals, gorgeous processions and superb speeches from the poet-dictator. His followers, maintained by the subscriptions of admiring though distant multitudes, passed their time in a vast many-coloured orgy. In the words of the inspired Commandante, " the name of all the women of Fiume is Ardour." As for the worst of the legionaries, their conduct ranged " from murder to robbery, from cocaine to pederasty." [1]

D'Annunzio drifted steadily into more and more irresponsible courses. He adopted an openly provocative attitude towards Jugoslavia; he endeavoured to undermine by propaganda the loyalty of the Italian regular army; he defined Italy's new malady, Fiumanism, as " a great and universal spiritual ideal of liberty and justice that interests all peoples and spreads out marvellously beyond the narrow circle of a territorial question." Accordingly he tried to get into touch with every subversive movement in Europe, offering money to the " Irish Republic," and writing to Tchitcherin to request material and moral aid from Bolshevik Russia to a " fellow-revolutionary." He ended by openly making preparations for a march on Rome, to be followed by the deposition of the King, and a d'Annunzian dictatorship. It became increasingly evident to Giolitti that the dangerous deadlock over Fiume must be ended without delay.

The situation was favourable to a compromise. The responsible parties immediately concerned were anxious for a settlement; Jugoslavia realized that with the elimination of President Wilson as an effective force in Europe, she could not hope to win Fiume, and she was anxious to secure Italian support against a possible Hapsburg restoration in Hungary, threatened by the attempt of the Emperor Karl; Great Britain and France were willing to support any agreed settlement. In these circumstances the intermittent negotiations were renewed and culminated in the treaty of Rapallo, 12th November 1920, a treaty marking an important, though not final, stage in the liquidation of the Adriatic question.

[1] Mowrer, " Immortal Italy," p. 295, quoting.

Italy acquired the whole of Istria, the best possible strategic frontier in Venetia Julia, the Italian town of Zara in Dalmatia, and a few islands; in return she relinquished the zone of occupation in Dalmatia and agreed that Fiume should assume the status of an independent city within defined boundaries.

The Commandante had now to be dealt with and he spurned the treaty with furious vituperation as the betrayal of the city he had won for Italy. All attempts at a compromise whereby his "constitution of the Regency of the Carnaro"—an interesting and ingenious attempt to embody the ideal of the Guild Socialists in the formal machinery of a state [1]—should be confirmed as the fundamental law of the free city set up by the treaty, were repulsed by the poet-dictator who, by now, had lost all sense of reality through living so long in his "gorgeous mediæval dream." The threat of force he welcomed as an opportunity for further heroics: "The crime is about to be consummated, fraternal blood about to be shed . . . those about to die salute you. . . . This was written and this was marvellous." Not for a moment did he believe that Giolitti, "that heap of poor filth," would dare to vindicate the pledged word of Italy.

The Prime Minister ordered General Caviglia to attack Fiume on 24th December 1920. The time was well-chosen, as on Christmas day no papers appeared. When the astonished public realized on the morning of 26th December, that the long-feared "fratricidal struggle" had broken out, the final bombardment had begun.

D'Annunzio confidently awaited a revolution in Italy or a mutiny in the navy, in which he counted many supporters. He loudly announced that in any event he would leave his "bloody body" between Fiume, his Fiume, and her assassins. On the afternoon of 26th December, the battleship "Andria Doria" steamed close into shore and fired three well-directed six-inch shells into the palace of the Commandante, who was stunned and slightly wounded. Obviously Giolitti meant business. Placing his resignation in the hands of the National Council of the city the Dictator announced that the Italians were "a people of cowards for whom it is not worth while to die." The National Council hastened to surrender the city to General Caviglia—the "gorgeous mediæval dream" had ended after a short nightmare. Signor Giolitti had success-

[1] For text, see Appendix I. Odon Por, "Fascism."

fully carried out the " simple police measure " necessary to vindicate constituted authority.

This was the second great triumph of the aged statesman. The first problem in order of time with which he had to cope after his return to office was that created by the dramatic seizure of factories by the workers at the end of August 1920. As it leads on directly to the intervention of Fascism in Italian politics as a powerful force that had grown from small beginnings, it will be as well to consider this famous crisis here though out of its chronological order

The Italian Federation of metal workers (F.I.O.M.) and the Owners' Association (A.M.M.A.) had co-operated before the war in the development of the Metallurgical Industry through institutions known as the Internal Committees of Workers, which played a definite but vigorously defined part in the economy of every factory. The compromise worked well until the post-war period of grave social and political unrest. Constant friction in the industry arose from the demand of the Internal Committees for larger powers of control. The owners, exasperated by what they considered the increasing ill-will of the men, seized the opportunity afforded by a wage dispute to order a "lock-out." The men immediately countered by seizing the factories and organizing their famous " lock-in." It was a full-blooded attempt to apply integral Syndicalism. The movement rapidly spread from Milan all over Northern Italy and even reached Sicily. Soon no less than 500,000 men were involved, in occupation of more than 600 workshops and factories.[1] It was a magnificent and audacious movement, but from the first it lacked strong and effective direction

The great industrial magnates who had allied themselves with the Nationalist admirers of d'Annunzio against Giolitti, because he had threatened them and all other war profiteers with crushing taxation,[2] now expected him to rush to their assistance. It is said that some of the industrialists had not scrupled to finance Bolshevist attempts at revolution in the hope of discrediting a Premier who had dared to attack their interests. To their consternation he announced with an indifferent air that he intended to remain neutral. Then the magnates realized for the first time that the man they had been plotting to overthrow, held them in the hollow of his hand. At the height of the crisis the country was amazed to hear that the

[1] Odon Por, " Fascism," p. 66. [2] Alazard, p. 71.

Premier had left for a short holiday. Faced with the fact that the 500,000 men involved, though they maintained strict order, were in no yielding mood, the Premier refused to precipitate what would have amounted to a civil war for the barren satisfaction of expelling workers from factories that would infallibly have vanished in smoke at the first attempt to "vindicate the law." "What do you wish me to do?" he is said to have asked an infuriated owner. "If necessary you should not hesitate to bombard the factories," was the answer. "Very well," said Giolitti, "I will begin with yours."

Very soon the enormous intrinsic difficulties of the position became obvious to the "locked-in" workers. The slow failure of their credit, even though bolstered by heavy subventions from the Trade Unions, drew their attention to the seriousness of the situation. On 10th September 1920 the representatives of the great Trade Unions, the Directorate of the Socialist party, the Socialist deputies and the Labour leaders of Italy, met to decide on the line of policy to adopt in face of the factory seizures. For the first time the question of revolution—obviously the consequence of the factory seizures if they were maintained—was openly debated. At the end of thirty-six hours continuous session a motion for peace and for an agreement with the owners was carried in a block vote by 592,245 to 409,569. Revolutionary Bolshevism had been decisively defeated by moderate Socialism. How had classical evolutionary Socialism managed to triumph at a moment when industrialists and bourgeoisie alike expected an immediate attempt to seize control of the State by revolutionary action?

The revolutionary impulse was checked not by fear of what Giolitti could do, but by the realization of the terrible complexity of the problem. The Russian experiment and its disastrous consequences were by now sufficiently understood; Italy was in the very trough of industrial depression—so bad was the position that some owners were anxious to sell their concerns to their workers. "The Trade Unions did not see how they could possibly carry on the factories and give employment to all the workers, satisfying all the demands which would infallibly be made on a Labour State."[1] The Conference also faced the prospect of an immediate blockade by the Western Powers in the event of a proletarian revolution.

[1] Odon Por, "Fascism," p. 68.

"It was impossible for the social revolution to take place as a result of the occupation of the factories—or of any purely industrial cause—in a country that was predominantly agricultural. . . . What seemed impossible to a minority, viz., the industrial workers, was believed to be impossible for the whole country. . . . It never entered the head of any of the leaders of the Socialist movement that the industrial difficulty was, to a great extent, artificial. . . . It never occurred to them for a moment that the right thing to do was to put an end to the industries or to reduce them at once to the minimum required for the supply of the country itself, and transform them into industries dependent on home agriculture instead of on the supply of raw materials from abroad. To set about at once intensifying agriculture, to shift great masses of workers from industries where they had not long been employed into rural districts, to create organic relations between agriculture and industry—such measures would have afforded the only possible solution, because it corresponded with the actual economic conditions in the country." [1] A sense of responsibility to the nation had caused the Socialists to turn back from what looked like almost certain victory. The decision showed that all along, influential though the revolutionary section of the party had been, it had never been sufficiently strong to carry Socialism on to a definite revolutionary course under the central direction of a G.H.Q., subordinating everything to the attainment of power. Without such organization success was impossible.

Giolitti was not slow to drive a wedge into the rift his prescience had led him to calculate on the occupation of the factories producing in the ranks of Socialism, between the classical evolutionary and the Social Communist groups. He compelled the now thoroughly cowed industrial magnates to agree to the introduction of Trade Union control of industry, under the supervision of the State, by means of workers' committees in each factory. The new strength his wisdom had won for the Liberal State was demonstrated when the neutralist of 1914 issued stringent instructions to all local authorities for the celebration throughout the country of the second anniversary of the Armistice with all possible brilliance. The decisive stroke against d'Annunzio and the extreme Nationalists followed, as we have seen, in December

[1] Odon Por, "Fascism," pp. 68-9.

1920, with its clear hint to the Communist revolutionaries that they would meet with the same short shrift if they appealed to arms and organized rebellion.

In February the great Liberal statesman reviewed the situation of which he seemed to be master in a speech to the Chamber: "The present events," he said, "are only the consequence of the profound social transformation which began in Italy thirty years ago. One saw the first manifestation of this drift in Sicily in 1892, when 'Fasci' sprang into existence. It was wrong to adopt a policy of violent repression then, as in 1898—repression in no way checked the movement of events: the social logic was not to be resisted. From 1904 to 1908, as Minister of the Interior in the Zanardelli Cabinet, I secured absolute respect for the liberty to strike. In a word, I thought then as I think now, that the workman's labour is his inviolable possession. . . . From 1904 to 1914 took place a continuous upward movement of the proletariat. The war accelerated this movement. The causes are easy to diagnose: exaggerated promises made during the war, propaganda in the trenches, the scandalous spectacle of the immense riches accumulated by the profiteers. All these influences have begotten this spirit of violence whose consequences ought not to surprise us. The culminating moment of the crisis was the occupation of the factories. It was impossible to hinder this occupation. For where would we have found the agents to re-establish order in the streets if one had employed them to guard the factories? To undertake a pitiless repression would have been to inaugurate a period of bloody struggles over a question of economics. In any case the occupation of the factories has demonstrated to the working class that in present conditions it cannot direct a factory. *And so the proletariat has lost its illusions.*" [1]

Throughout the winter of 1920-21 the Premier drove home his advantage against the Communists. For the local administrative elections a constitutional "Party of Order," formed under his direction, took the field. With all his old tactical genius he arranged that the elections should be held in "safe" areas first, as an example and encouragement to the doubtful. In this way Naples, Rome, Florence, and Turin were won back from the Communists.[2]

It is at this moment that the new Fascist organization came

[1] Quoted Alazard, "Communisme et 'Fascio' en Italie," p. 74. (Italics mine.)
[2] *Ibid.*, p. 75.

prominently to the fore in the horrible riots at Bologna on 21st November 1920. Giolitti had watched its activity not without hope that he could use it in his struggle to extricate the State from the menace of Communism on the one hand and maniacal Nationalism on the other. At this point we must go back again to the beginning of 1919, after this long but necessary digression, and resume the task of following, through all his transformations, the subject of this essay.

It cannot be too often repeated, in view of the later apotheosis of Mussolini, that he left the fighting line, resumed the editorship of *Popolo d'Italia*, and embarked on the politics of the stormy period after the Armistice, not only as an intense Nationalist, sharing the ideals of Enrico Corradini and of his party, but in vehement contradistinction to the reaction for which the Nationalists stood, he still retained his faith in revolutionary Syndicalism. He had entered the war because he believed that the Italian proletariat, disciplined and made one in the fiery struggle against the European militarist reaction, would emerge strong enough to undertake the revolution against the Liberal State and the bourgeoisie. In 1919 he was unchanged except for a deepening of his Nationalism.

In those first days of Fascism there was no thought of a political reaction. The sole quarrel (though an important one) between Mussolini and the Socialists was over the persistent refusal of the latter to see any good in the national idea or the war. It was an extraordinary error in judgment—an error that reveals their fundamentally doctrinaire tendencies—on the part of the Socialist extremists to attack and vilify the men whose belief in radical revolution was as strong as their own, but who persisted in affirming that through the ordeal of war Italy had won something that must never be surrendered—the sense of the nation as above every class or party, as an organic unity capable of regenerating itself. It is almost impossible to formulate the ideas of the early Fascisti without becoming as vague and pseudo-mystical as their own theorists. We can at least say they were Nationalists out and out, upholding every Italian claim, whether for Fiume, for Dalmatia, or for the opportunity of colonial expansion. They had discovered the nation—an idea of wonderful, nay, primitive clarity—which was to carry them to power, and to renew them in every transformation, like the lifegiving flames that consumed the Phœnix. The Fascisti were ex-soldiers, proud of the war record of the Italian army, outraged and made self-conscious by the insults of the Socialists and the spectacle of the brood of vampire profiteers literally gorged on the blood of their comrades. Their unexpressed aspiration was contained in the question: " Why should the splendid unity of the last year of war be shattered by the scandalous bickerings of party politicians and the struggle of selfish interests? The idea of the nation united us then, it must be made to unite us now. Away with parties which confuse and embitter the issues, let us return to the days of dicipline, work, and self-sacrifice in the service of Italy."

This is a mythology of immense power, almost as impervious to criticism as that of the "world-revolution," conceived in the powerful intellect of Lenin as the goal of the present historical epoch. To the question, Where will the moral idea be found capable of recapturing that sense of unity realized by the nation in the face of a great external challenge to its independence? —a challenge embodied in the grim, tangible reality of the Austro-German armies pouring through Venetia—the answer is, Unity will be realized through *disciplined* devotion to the idea of the nation. And in the end this means that the idea of national unity is vindicated by the discipline of sticks, revolver shots, castor-oil, and a Terrorist organization. The moral dream is transformed into a physical nightmare. But we are anticipating.

After the war the former interventionist groups, the "Fasci di azione rivoluzionaria," revived under the name of "Fasci di Combattimento," spontaneous associations of ex-soldiers for the most part in North Italy. These groups held their first meeting on 23rd March 1919, under the inevitable presidency of one of the most famous of the interventionists of 1914—Benito Mussolini—like most of the members of the new groups, a Socialist who had broken with Socialism on the great question of peace or war, nationalism or exclusive internationalism. The programme, in view of the later evolution of the movement, deserves attention. It was ambitious, and may well be described as revolutionary. Its authors demanded a Constituent Assembly to sit for three years, and as its first work undertake the revision of the Constitution; the formation of occupational national councils on guild Socialist lines, elected by members of trades and professions, with legislative rights and the power to designate as Cabinet ministers (one for each council) the commissary-generals elected by the national councils; proportional representation, and women's suffrage ; the lowering of the age limit for electors and deputies, and the abolition of the Senate ; the passing of a law to confirm the eight-hour day, and the granting of a minimum wage for all industrial and agricultural workers ; the inauguration of a system of workers' control in factories, and where possible the carrying on of industry and public services by Labour organizations ; the institution of a national militia for home defence ; " a heavy special tax on capital of a progressive nature, which would take the form of a true, though partial, expropriation of wealth ; the sequestration of the possessions of religious bodies, and the abolition of episcopal revenues ; . . . the revision of war contracts and the sequestration of 85 per cent. of war profits." [1] The Nationalist side of early Fascism finds expression in the demand for a strong national foreign Policy worthy of a great Power after a victorious war.

Perhaps the most startling features of this remarkable programme—an admirable reflection of Mussolini the revolutionary Socialist tempered by Mussolini the Nationalist—are the open attacks on the two future pillars of Fascism, the Senate and the Church. Finally, a further point requires emphasis. Fascism was, to begin with, strongly Republican in tendency, and retained this feature, as we shall see, until a much later period in its eventful history.

During the greater part of 1919 the movement remained weak, but the Nationalist element in it strengthened steadily. Its activities were for the most part devoted to the systematic persecution of the German and Slav inhabitants of the territories annexed to Italy at the peace. The first demonstration of importance by a Fascist unit seems to have been the burning of the Nardoni Dom, the headquarters of the Slav Nationalist organization in Trieste, 13th July 1920, but for a whole year previously the beating and baiting of foreigners had been endemic in the occupied regions.[2] The admirable efforts of the Government to conciliate its new subjects were thwarted by this self-constituted movement for " Italianizing the barbarians."

The first attempt of the new party to enter domestic politics at the elections of November 1919 met with little success, Mussolini receiving only a small percentage of votes for his

[1] For this passage and preceding paragraph, see Odon Por, " Fascism," pp. 102-3.

[2] Beals, " Rome or Death," p. 43.

candidature at Milan. He polled 5000, while his opponent, Turati, was returned with 100,000 votes in his favour. His Socialist opponents accordingly treated Mussolini and his party as negligible. As for his general political attitude at the time of the formal inauguration of the Fascist groups of ex-soldiers, it is sufficiently indicated by his speech to the workmen of Dalmine (Bergamo), on the occasion of the first movement of factory occupation in March 1919, the prelude to the far more important wave of Syndicalism that swept over Italy during the summer of 1920. "I have often asked myself," he said on 20th March 1919, "if, after the four years of terrible though victorious war, in which our bodies and minds have been engaged, the masses of the people would return to move in the same old tracks as before, or whether they would have the courage to change their direction. Dalmine has answered. The order of the day [for the occupation of the factories] voted by you on Monday is a document of enormous historical importance, which will and must give a general direction to the line taken by all Italian labour; . . . you are the producers, and it is in this capacity that you vindicate your right to treat the industrial owners as equals, . . . and I tell you that you are on the right road, because you are freed from your protectors, and have chosen from among yourselves the men who are to direct you and represent you, and to them only have you entrusted the guardianship of your rights. . . . Upon the flagstaff of your building you have run up your flag, which is the tricolour, and around it you have fought your battle. You have done well. The national flag is not merely a rag, even if it has been dragged in the mud by the bourgeoisie; . . . it still remains the symbol of the sacrifice of thousands and thousands of men. . . . I say that I shall not cease fighting against the party [the Socialists] which during the war was the instrument of the Kaiser. They wish, at your expense, to try their monkey-like experiments, which are only an imitation of Russia. But you will succeed, sooner or later, in exercising essential functions in modern society, though the political dabblers of the bourgeoisie and semi-bourgeoisie must not make stepping-stones of your aspirations so as to arrive at winning their little games."[1]

The speech reveals the singular originality of Mussolini's attitude. The Syndicalist of 1912 and 1914 is still the convinced Syndicalist of 1919, openly approving of that anathema

[1] San Severino, "Speeches," pp. 63-6.

of the bourgeoisie and their supporters in Italy or elsewhere, the occupation of the factories, and the expropriation of the magnates. Though the individual occupation may end in compromise, the workers of Dalmine have given " the general direction " to the Labour movement. The old revolutionary enemy of the bourgeoisie hates them as cordially as ever. But the note of an intense nationalism thrills through the rejoicing periods of this fighting speech. A year later and his attitude had not changed. During the great " factory seizures " of 1920 Mussolini announced his neutrality in no uncertain terms. These are facts that need emphasizing if what may be called the Mussolini " legend," assiduously put about by interested parties since his accession to power, is ever to be dissipated.

It was the Fiume adventure that first brought the Fascisti notably to the foreground. Mussolini became the right-hand man of the Poet-Dictator in organizing the flood of irresponsible propaganda with which he deluged Italy throughout 1920. Fascism grew with the intensity of the hatred it roused. Finding that it could not compete by its radical programme of 1919 against the Socialists for the leadership of the masses, it naturally tended to fall back more and more upon the nationalist aspect of its mission. Powerfully reinforced by the existing Nationalist party with its strong anti-Socialist and anti-Labour bias, all through 1920 Fascism tended to draw to itself an increasing body of intellectuals, professionals, students, and ex-officers, attracted by its exploits among the Germans and Slavs, and at Fiume, and stimulated by the mystical and idealist apotheosis of patriotism, which is its most notable characteristic. Inevitably, with the influx of young and idealist elements, it absorbed a far larger " crowd who joined Fascism or backed it from sheer personal or class interest," and as a result it " was diluted and contaminated, just as Classical Socialism was, by inflation." [1]

In the course of the summer of 1920, on his famous visit of reconnaissance to Moscow mentioned above, Serrati told Lenin that far from " all the postulates of revolution " being present in Italy, signs were not wanting of the imminence of a great bourgeois reaction. Then came the final Socialist revolutionary wave, marked by the factory seizures, and followed by the defeat of Bolshevism through the moderate evolutionary Socialists and the tactical genius of Giolitti. It was at the very moment when the Socialist bark was tacking into the

[1] Odon Por, " Fascism," pp. 105-6.

teeth of the failing revolutionary gale that the side squall of reaction struck and capsized it.

In the course of the administrative elections of December 1920, so carefully and successfully organized by the Premier in circumstances already discussed, it became obvious that the Red Leagues of Ferrara and the Lower Po had secured what amounted to a territorial sovereignty. The towns had long been completely at their mercy. The discovery by Fascism of all the possibilities of its favourite weapon, violence, dates from the bloody affray between the Fascists and the Communists on 21st November 1920, at the official opening of the new Municipal Council of Bologna, on which the Social Communists had just secured a majority. In the course of the desperate riot that began outside the municipal palace a young lawyer ex-officer, Giordano, widely known and esteemed for his gallantry and patriotism, and a member of the Liberal minority on the Syndic, was murdered by a panic-stricken Communist in the Council-chamber itself.

The disastrous events at Bologna helped the Fascists by creating a wave of indignation throughout the country. They seized the opportunity to organize the famous expeditions against the Red Leagues in the country districts round Bologna. Agrarian Fascism began to assert itself, operating from the towns in the form of " a sortie by a besieged garrison." " It became from this moment the pitiless counter-revolution to a revolution *manquée*." [1] The Fascio of Bologna literally rose in rebellion; aided by volunteers from the army they forced the Council to resign, and the disorders in the famous revolutionary city culminated, on 24th January 1921, in the burning of the local Chamber of Labour. " That night," wrote Enrico Corradini, " I saw the fortress of the enemy, the Chamber of Labour, disappear in flames. Cheering citizens assisted at the spectacle, while policemen, carbineers, guards, and soldiers watched the flames devour the building, with their arms at rest." [2]

Raids were organized into the country, strongly supported by officers of the regular army burning to requite the insults of which they had been the targets. Skilfully planned, the raids were amazingly successful. Villages were sacked, labour leaders tortured and murdered; in South Italy the landowners connived at the assassination by Fascists of leading peasants

[1] Odon Por, " Fascism," p. 106.
[2] Quoted Mowrer, " Immortal Italy," p. 355.

concerned in the land seizures of 1919. Almost immediately the peasants counter-attacked and mercilessly exterminated any Fascist they could lay hands on. Not for another year did Fascism make its appearance again in the South, and then in a very different guise. The success of Fascism in North Italy and its failure in the South are instructive. In the North bourgeois elements organized in groups, often under the skilful direction of professional soldiers, struck at a mass of labourers tyrannously organized by the Red Leagues at the head of which stood the Communist bosses. Once the organization was dislocated by the destruction of the Labour headquarters and the murder or flight of the directors, all the elements among the agricultural workers who had only submitted perforce to the Red tyranny, joined the Fascists, attracted by their programme of land to the individual workers and the building up of a class of small-holders ; in the South, on the other hand, where Fascism assumed a purely reactionary complexion, it foundered on the strength of the peasants defending their newly-won position.

Delighted by the revelation of the essential weakness of the Red strongholds in North Italy the bourgeoisie hastened to join Fascism in crowds. In defence of their economic interests landowners and bourgeois heavily subscribed to the coffers of the new party. They were anxious to break the labour-monopoly of the Leagues, and re-establish the " liberty of Labour," or in other words, the liberty of wealth to exploit a disorganized mass of workers. The fall of Fiume and the expulsion of d'Annunzio's fire-eaters, brought a number of invaluable recruits to the Fascist organization—capable of any crime or any heroism, they were utterly careless of their own lives or the lives of others.

Mussolini and his co-workers, seeing from what source their recruits were coming in, definitely ran with the crowd and infused the fluid programme of earlier Fascism with the doctrines of the bourgeois reaction. The new striking force, brilliantly directed by a secret headquarters, made rapid progress by means of the edifying measures so enthusiastically described by Sir Percival Phillips. Yet Fascism as a capitalist reaction failed, " simply because it was directed against a revolutionary plan that had been abandoned by all but the most visionary of its adherents." [1] During the first half of 1921 the movement against Bolshevism rapidly degenerated into a wholesale

[1] Mowrer, " Immortal Italy," pp. 344-5.

assault on every type of Socialism and upon any institution that could remotely be connected with Socialist activity. Systematic violence broke down any attempt at resistance.

It is often asserted that Fascism was the spontaneous reaction of a society in deadly peril acting for itself in the face of a state too distracted to fulfill the elementary duty of protecting life and property. The fact that often receives no attention from the exponents of Fascism outside Italy, is the extent to which Signor Giolitti, anxious to avoid the odium of more repressive measures than were absolutely imperative, encouraged the earlier Fascist offensive. The regular army and the police were in open collaboration with lawbreakers whom they should have been hunting or shooting down. The Fascisti were allowed to turn national barracks into private arsenals, the police made a point of arriving late on the scene of every armed Fascist outrage against unarmed Socialists for the purpose of terrorizing a legally elected mayor or town council into resignation. "That is the way the wind is blowing," remarked the prefect of Emilia, when he was asked why he did not attempt to repress the Fascist orgies.[1] Giolitti's encouragement was probably based upon the calculation that the activities of the Fascisti would enable him so to reduce the Socialist representation in parliament at the elections he was planning, that a stable Liberal and democratic bourgeois bloc could be formed capable of giving his government assured support. But, great tactician that he was, he could not foresee that the success of the Fascist offensive to which he had lent the support of the State, could not stop with the discovery by the bourgeoisie that they had been terrorized by a hollow turnip, but would become a veritable landslide just as threatening to the Liberal state as the Communist menace of 1919-20.

A few statistics will illuminate the nature of Fascist activities between January and June 1921. The figures refer to the institutions and buildings destroyed by the Fascisti operating along military lines often with the co-operation of regular officers.

12 Newspaper offices.
26 Clubs.
60 Labour Union H.Q.'s.
86 Co-operative Societies.

[1] Mowrer, p. 361.

43 H.Q.'s of peasant Leagues.
34 Socialist H.Q.'s.
17 Schools, libraries and cultural societies.
36 Workers educational circles.

During the same period the casualties were :—

202 Killed by Fascisti.
44 Killed by the police or army.
1144 Wounded by the Fascisti.
4258 Wounded by the police or army.

5648 Casualties.[1]

The numbers of those of the contending forces (if a persecution can be called a contention), arrested by the police are significant of the tacit pact between the police and the Fascisti :—

2240 Workers, Socialists, and Communists.
102 Fascisti.[2]

That arising out of the destruction, usually by arson, of 314 buildings, 2240 of the frequenters of those buildings should be arrested and only 102 of those responsible for the destruction, argues, to say the least, an unusual outlook on the part of the guardians and administrators of the law.

The successful liquidation of the Adriatic question which gave Italy her natural frontiers and re-established friendly relations with Jugoslavia, relations that promised to develop into an alliance ; the obvious defeat of Bolshevism ; and, in spite of the Fascist disorders which at first did not alarm the Government, the steadily improving financial situation of the country whose national deficit, thanks to the abolition of fixed prices for bread, Giolitti's savage taxation of war-profits, and the operation of the super-tax, had been reduced from fourteen thousand million lire in 1919 to slightly more than four thousand million lire at the beginning of 1921 [3]—all these factors inclined the Premier to dissolve the Chamber and hold a general election for all Italy within her new frontiers, in the hope that the constitutional as opposed to the subversive elements in the Chamber might be strengthened.

[1] Beals, " Rome or Death," pp. 58-9, from calculations based on a comparison of the files of the *Corriere della Sera* " (Liberal), and *Avanti* (Socialist).
[2] Mowrer, p. 364, based on files of the *Avanti*.
[3] Giolitti, " Memoirs," p. 443

The administrative elections of the previous winter had revealed to the Fascist directory the extraordinary hold that Socialism still retained on the masses—accordingly they multiplied their blows and a "month of violence preceded a day of terror" when the elections were held, 15th May 1921. According to the *Osservatore Romano*, the official organ of the Vatican, on election day 40 people were killed and 70 wounded throughout Italy. In many districts of the Romagna, Emilia, Tuscany, and Umbria, bodies of Fascisti and State Carbineers lay in wait at the polling-booths and drove off the Socialist voters in some cases with rifle fire.[1] In spite of these unheard-of efforts, under the system of Proportional Representation, proof against any abuse except the Hungarian method of State prevention of voting, the unconstitutional opposition of Socialists, Communists, and Republicans was reduced by only 30. They retained 122 seats. The Facists returned a small group some 30 strong and the Popolari maintained their strangely amorphous party in being, as strong in numbers as before, only the Liberal constitutional groups failed to improve their position and remained distracted and without a programme. Yet though the relative position of parties in the Chamber remained more or less unchanged, the Prime Minister could rightly congratulate himself that out of an electorate of eight millions, half a million more votes had been cast for the constitutional parties than in 1919.[2]

By 1921 the phrase "anti-constitutional" must be used of the Socialist party with caution. The events following the factory seizures had convinced Lenin that it was better to have one really devoted soldier for the proletarian revolution than a hundred sympathizers. Accordingly, he ordered his followers to secede from the Socialist party and constitute themselves an independent Communist body definitely working for revolution under the orders of Moscow. At the Seventeenth National Congress of the Italian Socialist party at Leghorn in January 1921, the Moderates under the disillusioned Serrati, triumphed over the Leninites who, accordingly seceded, carrying with them only one-quarter of the party members. The Bulgar Kabakcheff read Lenin's sentence of "excommunication," which was greeted with derisive shouts of "Habemus pontificem"—the words with

[1] Mowrer, "Immortal Italy," p. 368.
[2] Giolitti, "Memoirs," p. 444.

which the election of a new pope is announced to the Roman people.[1]

But even after the secession of the Communists, the Socialists, though presenting a united front in the Chamber, were still paralysed with dissensions behind the scenes. By the municipal elections of October 1920 the Socialists had gained a splendid victory. With 2500 of the 8000 Communes in their hands, with 25 provincial administrations and 156 parliamentary representatives (reduced to 122 in May 1921), they should have been able to develop a strong positive programme and make up their minds either to secure seats in the Cabinet or support Socialist measures vigorously when introduced by the Government. The Reformists led by Turati favoured collaboration with the Government in the carrying of the Socialist programme. He rightly argued that voting in elections and sitting in parliament were forms of collaboration with the bourgeois state, and that if the Socialist party was not a revolutionary secret society, it must be prepared to take the consequences of such a moral collaboration by accepting power in the constitutional course of events.

The extremists who remained after the secession of the Communists, and still hankered after the flesh pots of Bolshevism, even though they were not prepared to take their orders from Moscow, insisted that the party was still in spirit with the Third International. The deputies in parliament should be strictly subordinated to the Central Executive Committee of the party and instructed " to exert pressure from the outside upon the bourgeoisie, using all the weight of their numbers and moral strength to limit the power of the executive, to safeguard all the public power already captured by us, and, on the other hand, to impose upon the bourgeoisie . . . the proposals that the group might formulate." [2] The doctrinaire extremists received a clear majority at the Convention held in the Lyric Theatre at Milan in November 1921, controlling two-thirds of the voting strength. The Moderates acquiesced though announcing their intention of ultimately converting the party. Not only then did Socialism weaken under the wind of reaction all through 1921 and 1922, but the party was simultaneously breaking up owing to the explosive struggles going on within it.[3]

Let us return to the campaign of violence against Socialists

[1] Mowrer, p. 342.
[2] Beals, " Rome or Death," pp. 181-2.
[3] *Ibid.*, p. 182.

waged without cessation by the Fascisti during the first half of 1921. At the conclusion of the May elections, commenting on the shocking outrages that marred them, Guglielmo Ferrero, the eminent historian, wrote wisely that "the burning of the chambers of Labour, the Co-operatives and the Labour Headquarters," had "balanced in the public mind all the errors and foolishness committed by the Socialists after the elections of 1919."[1] Not until July did Mussolini detect one of those changes in public opinion to which he always responds. Shortly before he had announced, at the conclusion of the May elections, that the Fascisti deputies "being essentially republican in tendency" would not be present at the State opening of parliament, thereby deliberately offending his Nationalist and Conservative supporters, but confident that the Fascisti successes enabled the party to dispense with allies. Perhaps his declaration is his own deduction from an assertion of his made about the same time, that events pointed to the speedy accession of d'Annunzio to power. Certainly the poet had been formerly heard to remark that his sleep beside the waters of Lake Garda would not be long. But by the summer of 1921 signs of yet another reaction began to manifest themselves. Policemen and Fascisti in large numbers were stabbed by night on lonely roads. Catholic groups of anti-Fascists, known as "God's arditi," and a body founded by Argo Secondari, the "Arditi of the People," caused terror to many Fascist raiding parties by the ferocity of their revenges. The middle classes and the landed proprietors, fearing the possibility of a Jacquerie, began to protest against the tale of senseless burnings and beatings and murders organized by the Fascisti. A wave of indignation swept over Italy at the news of the Fascist outrage at Treviso on 12th July 1921. The local clericals and republicans had dared to protect some labourers of the neighbouring village of Ca' Tron from exploitation by two grasping landowners, who were subscribers to the secret reactionary organization which was not long in answering their appeals. Fifteen hundred men, swiftly and secretly mobilized from districts as far apart as Istria and Tuscany, arrived in the dead of night in 100 armoured camions armed with rifles and hand grenades and wearing steel helmets—their equipment having been issued to them out of stores of the regular army. They proceeded to sack the offices of the local clerical paper *Il Piave,* then those of the Republican

[1] Mowrer, "Immortal Italy," p. 366.

organ *Riscossa,* the latter building after a seige of several hours. Where then was the new Terrorism going to draw the line? After the Socialists, the Clericals and Republicans, perhaps, in a moment of inexplicable aberration, even the Conservatives.

Mussolini quickly grasped the fact that Fascism was in danger, through its excesses, of alienating the country and raising up against itself a resistance fatal to its prestige based on its successes over the Socialists. He announced accordingly in parliament in July 1921, that the time had come for Fascism to sheath its sword. Bolshevism in Italy had been crushed, and the Fascists who had now entered parliament should take their place in the national life as a party that had still to realize its programme of reform and reconstruction. Fascism should make no more dangerous martyrs, "Violence is often an injection of oxygen that rouses a dying evil to life again."[1] On 3rd August 1921, Socialists, Fascists, and representatives of Trade Unions, brought together by the Speaker of the Chamber of Deputies, signed a pact to put an end to acts of violence. But this attempt of Mussolini to put a brake on what had become an avalanche was too late. Many Fascist local organizations openly refused to respect the pact; outrages multiplied. Still hoping to regain control, Mussolini resigned from the Fascist Central Council and commenced a vigorous campaign in the columns of the *Popolo d'Italia* against those he termed the "false Fascists," who constituted apparently the bulk of the party: "Fascism," he wrote on 7th August 1921, "is no longer liberation, but tyranny; no longer the safeguard of the nation, but the upholding of private interests and of the most grovelling and unenlightened classes existing in Italy."[2] "How is peace to come about?" he asked in the *Popolo d'Italia* of 18th August 1921. "Perhaps you think you can get it by wiping out the two millions of citizens who voted for the Socialist party? But are you not running the risk of perpetuating civil war? Or of finding yourselves in rebellion against the whole spirit of the nation? Or of being obliged to submit to a Socialist peace to-morrow, owing to some other quite probable turn of the tables? Do you not see signs of this? Will not the single anti-Fascist front, destroyed by the agreement, form up again to-morrow almost automatically?"[3]

[1] Odon Por, "Fascism," p. 113.
[2] Quoted Odon Por, "Fascism," pp. 115-16.
[3] Odon Por, "Fascism," pp. 117-18.

Cesare Rossi, later the hero of the famous storming of Ancona by thirty-two Fascisti, in July 1922, an intimate friend and the right-hand man of Signor Mussolini, until, in the June of 1924, he was thrown into prison by order of his chief for being concerned in the murder of Signor Matiotti, wrote about the same time in the same paper: " Fascism has become, in truth, an entirely conservative and reactionary movement. . . . It reacts with foolish and purposeless cruelty against everything that tells of progress and achievement in the life of to-day, against all that has been gained, all that makes for peace. . . . That very character, in fact, of petty overbearing tyranny, of which we used to accuse the Socialist party in the days, bright or dark, of their supremacy, has now been transferred to the very heart of the Fascist movement." [1]

Fascism had indeed reached the parting of the ways and so had the Liberal state. The new Chamber, elected in May and opened by the King on 11th June, consisted of 535 members (27 additional seats having been assigned to the liberated provinces), of whom 275 were organized in the various discordant Liberal and Democratic groups (as against 239 in the previous Chamber); the Popolari had increased their numbers from 101 to 107 and the Socialists had fallen from 156 to 122. There were 16 Communists, 7 Republicans (as against 13 in the previous Chamber), 4 Germans from the Alto Adige, and 5 Slavs from Venezia Giulia.[2] The Fascists entered parliament 35 strong and the Nationalists 10. This distribution of forces gives the following general results: Constitutional Liberals—uncertain supporters of the Government, one or other of whose groups might at any moment go into opposition—275. Constitutional and anti-Constitutional opposition on some elements of which the Government might generally rely, 306. Obviously this was a position of extremely unstable equilibrium. Strong attacks were launched on the Government's foreign policy, too conciliatory for the Nationalist groups. Giolitti had announced that he intended to eliminate the already reduced national deficit by the thorough overhauling of the monstrously inflated, and at the same time badly paid, bureaucracy. The wholesale dismissals and concentration of offices he contemplated would inevitably rouse up against him, a powerful opposition based on injured private interests. In these circumstances the fact that, on 26th June 1921, the Government on a vote of con-

[1] Odon Por, " Fascism," p. 118.
[2] Villari, " The Awakening of Italy," p. 128.

fidence only secured a majority of 34, and that many of these 34 votes were cast with reservations, convinced the Premier that his position must in the near future become untenable.[1] Accordingly he insisted on resigning with his whole Cabinet, and left office on 1st July 1921.

Other reasons that persuaded Signor Giolitti to resign before he had been actually defeated in the Chamber were probably his realization that he was rapidly losing control of the Fascisti, whose activities were, as we have seen, causing a reaction in the country, and his disappointment at the failure of his efforts to win over the Socialists to the support of the Government.

In the previous winter the Government, true to its promises, made the moment the Factory seizure movement had been liquidated, brought forward three Bills of the utmost importance. A scheme for workers' control in factories, for the setting up of a Labour Parliament for the purpose of legislating on economic questions and for transforming, in favourable circumstances, private industrial and agricultural enterprises and even public services into Co-operative Societies. " This last act," said the Minister Labriola in introducing the Bill in the Chamber of Deputies, 22nd November 1920, " will be the crowning touch to the work of reforming the State in social matters. We desire, by its means, to secure the right of the workers in any business undertaking to form themselves into a Co-operative Society for the purpose of purchasing or renting the business, which would then no longer be conducted on a wage basis. Such management should be absolutely free. A body of workmen engaged in the business, who considered that they were capable of carrying it on, and had not the means to do so, would be enabled to gain possession of it, or to lease it, on payment by instalment to the proprietor; provision being made to prevent such co-operators from transforming themselves into proprietors of a private business. In every way, the principle of the economic sovereignty of the State would be upheld, and its right to participate in the profits of Co-operative enterprises as established under this regime." [2]

But the predominant anti-constitutional section of the Socialist party, with their doctrinaire refusal to collaborate in any form with the " bourgeois " State, took up the grotesque

[1] Giolitti, " Memoirs," p. 445.
[2] Quoted Odon Por, " Fascism," p. 95.

position of voting against their own programme, introduced by a Government prepared to assign hundreds of millions of lire to finance their schemes. Such a position could not last. Reactionary elements, encouraged by the absurdly impracticable attitude of the Socialists, began to regain courage and to embark on a policy of obstructing the application of Workers' control, which in a moment of panic they had themselves accepted.[1] " All along the line, in every field of action, was shown the incapacity of the Social Communists to give expression to any definitely thought out policy." [2] As for the Liberal State, after the resignation of Giolitti it drifted like a rudderless hulk helpless on the rising flood of Fascist reaction, as it had been helpless, for the most part, in the earlier tempest of revolutionary disorder. Giolitti had, by his decisive energy and his wise inaction, proved that in capable hands the State could have weathered the storm. He had saved Italy from civil war and enabled the moderate Socialists to save her from Bolshevism; he had dramatically pricked the d'Annunzian bubble and delivered a resounding blow to romanticist nationalism. His skilful hand had steered the State unerringly between the Scylla of revolution and the Carybdis of reaction. The moment his hand was withdrawn the State rapidly became the inert toy of every wind and wave. At the end of 1921 the Baron Sidney Sonnino, watching from the tranquil retirement of his magnificent library, observed that " if Italy was to be saved from disintegration some form of *coup d'état* was necessary." [3]

Fascism passed through the crisis that overtook it, during the summer of 1921, to emerge an organized party in November. Realizing the strength of Fascist intransigence Mussolini was not long in withdrawing his resignation and again taking a share in the control of the movement. He understood clearly that if Fascist energy was not to dissipate itself in aimless violence it must be co-ordinated and disciplined not only by a more centralized control, but by the formulation of a programme which by its attractiveness would win the bourgeoisie to a tolerance of Fascist methods. The truce with Socialism had broken down because the initial impetus to violence in the Fascist groups could not be controlled so long as they were confronted all over the country by the strongholds and organizations of the very enemy against whom they were the armed

[1] Odon Por, p. 96. [2] *Ibid.*, p. 101.
[3] Villari, " The Awakening of Italy," p. 148.

protest. Besides, no man can serve two masters, and in many districts pacts existed between the local Fascists and the land-owners and industrialists, the more anxious, with their increasing success, to press to the end their armed advantage over the disordered Socialist ranks.[1] If, then, bourgeois public opinion could be conciliated by the programme, it would cease to react against Fascist violence, especially if the violence were systematic and of obvious value to the middle classes, as in the case of strike-breaking.

A way was opened for the attainment of supreme power to be wrested from a vacillating Government and a discredited Parliament, and concentrated in the hands of one who had known, uniquely, how to win the passionate devotion of masses of the young men, their hearts aflame with the idea of an Italy made great by the love and self-sacrifice of her sons. The secret of Mussolini is that he has known how to call fellow-workers, in terms of discipline and sacrifice, to the realization of his vision of a regenerated people. Every great idea that can stir that "desire of the moth for the star" in the heart of youth, and summon it to battle in terms of self-devotion—whether it be expressed in the frigid dogmas and academic formulæ of Lenin, or the gorgeous rhetoric of d'Annunzio, has in its service the moral energy that defended the dictator of the Kremlin from the vengeance converging from every quarter of the compass, and carried the armies of the Red Republic to victory over those who fought for the dead past and the interests of the dead past—the moral energy that swept the squadrons of the Fascisti to the conquest of the Eternal City.

On 4th November 1921, the body of the Italian Unknown Soldier, after its journey from the Cathedral of Aquileia to Rome past many tiny towns, where great crowds had wept and prayed at its solemn passing, and some had called the names that lay nearest to their hearts, was laid to rest in the "Altare della Patria," in the presence of the King and a great gathering. On the tomb were inscribed the words, "Ignoto Militi."[2] With the genius of great leadership, Mussolini summoned the Fascista Congress that was to formulate the programme of the new party to meet in Rome on 6th November 1921.

The work of the Congress was promulgated in December as "the programme of the National Fascist Party." The

[1] Odon Por, "Fascism," p. 118.
[2] Villari, "The Awakening of Italy," p. 183.

preamble states that " Fascism has constituted itself a political party in order to stiffen its discipline and define its creed. The nation is not merely the sum of the inhabitants of the country, nor is it merely an instrument of the parties within it, for carrying out their purposes, but an organism embracing an indefinite series of generations in which each individual is but a transient element ; and the supreme synthesis of all the possessions of the race, material and immaterial." The programme then defines the attitude of the Fascist Party to the State : " *The State is to be reduced to those functions which are essential, the political and judicial.* The State should confer powers and responsibilities on certain associations." National Technical Associations, representative of trade and industry, should control the economic activities of society.

With regard to the great problem that fascinated Dr Neville Figgis, the programme continues : " Fascism cannot fail to recognize as an historical fact, the development of corporations : its desire is to co-ordinate that development to national ends." It declares itself in favour of a legal eight-hour day, provision for the accidents, sickness, and old age of workers ; the representation of workers of every industry in the management *in so far as it is concerned with the employees* ; and the diffusion of small holdings in districts where agricultural conditions render them likely to be productive.

In home politics the Fascist party aims at re-establishing the ideal of the administration of " public affairs not in the interest of cliques or parties, but in the supreme interest of the nation."

In foreign affairs Fascism affirms Italy's " right to complete unity, historical and geographic, *even in cases where that right has not yet been attained. . . .*[1] Fascism does not believe in the vitality and in the principles that inspire the so-called League of Nations, inasmuch as not all the nations are represented in it, and those that are represented do not find themselves on a footing of equality." In the sections devoted to financial and economic reconstruction, the chief points affirm the need of drastic economy and reduction of the bureaucracy, with a view to balancing the budget ; a settled scheme of public works, with a view to development of the railways and their electrification, improvement of roads, and extended use of water-power, the equipment of a few carefully selected ports

[1] Presumably an oblique reference to French Corsica, British Malta, and the Swiss canton Ticino.

with the most up-to-date facilities. Finally, to restore "to private enterprise those industrial undertakings which have proved unsuitable for State management; especially telephones and railways." This policy to be eventually completed by the surrender of the State monopoly of posts and telegraphs to private enterprise.

The section devoted to social policy begins: "The State recognizes the social function of private property, which is at the same time a right and a duty. It is the form of administration which has been assigned throughout historical times to the individual by Society for the increment of the wealth of the community." The Fascist Party goes on to assert that the interests of the State require that the quarrels between classes and categories should be brought under control, and therefore decrees: "Legal recognition of labour and employers' organizations and of their consequent responsibility." Strikes in the public services are to be prevented by the institution of arbitration tribunals composed of representatives of the Government, of the workers, of employers, and "of the public that has to pay."

The interesting and ambitious section devoted to educational policy begins: "The aim of the school should be to train persons capable of ensuring the economic and political progress of the nation, of raising the moral and intellectual level of the workers and of providing for the constant renewal of the governing class by developing the best elements in all classes." The first point in the educational programme is the declaration of war on illiteracy. Elementary schools should be reorganized for the "introduction of national sentiment . . . so as to make them suitable for the moral and physical training of Italian soldiers." The section on justice advocates the extension of therapeutic and preventive methods of dealing with crime, and that on national defence declares that "the army, in conjunction with schools and with clubs organized for sport, ought to train our citizens for combat and for patriotism."[1]

In January 1922 the various Fascist Trade Unions were formed into the Confederation of the Fascist Corporations. The basic idea underlying the Fascist Trade Unions is thus defined: "The nation—considered as the synthesis of all the material and spiritual values of the race—shall be above individuals,

[1] See text of the Programme (Dec. 1921) of the National Fascist Party. Odon Por, "Fascism," Appendix II. (Italics mine.)

categories and classes. Individuals, categories and classes are instruments made use of by the nation for gaining a great position. Individuals, categories, and classes hold all rights and privileges on condition that these are consistent with the higher national interest." Among the aims of the Confederation, which consists of seven Corporations representing agriculture, industry, commerce, transport and communication, public and private employees, liberal professions, and art, the chief is "to assist workers to outgrow gradually their position as apprentices and wage-earners, . . . so as to enable them to attain a state of independence and well-being as holders of property"; to ensure a decent existence for workers by the periodical fixing of a minimum wage, and the encouragement of co-operative societies and "undertakings on an industrial or agricultural share-basis. The Confederation and the Corporations were strongly centralized and subject to a rigid discipline and not the least of their activities was "to combat all tendencies and political measures of an anti-national nature."[1]

A comparison of the programme of December 1921 with that of March 1919 will reveal how far Fascism had travelled in two and a half years. Nationalism remains, and in 1921 has been deepened by the impressive formulation of the idea of a nation-state as an organic and harmonious unity. In both programmes there is a clear recognition of the importance of economic corporations, but the earlier Syndicalism has disappeared. The appeal of 1921 is directed primarily to the bourgeoisie and to all who desire to join the ranks of the bourgeoisie: "The Confederation declares that the increase of production and means of production implies, not only the increase of the productive types, but at the same time the increase of the middle classes and an ever-growing diffusion of wealth and property; which also means that it will afford to the proletarian élites the possibility of acquiring and directly managing the instruments and materials of production and of rendering themselves indispensable both socially and technically."

The language of most Fascist programmes and pronouncements tends to be cloudy and diffuse. Frequently all meaning founders in a cloud of abstractions, but in the case of the 1921 programme there is much to attract, from the vision of a

[1] See extract from the Statutes of the Confederation of Corporations. Odon Por, "Fascism," Appendix III.

nation, " where none are for the party and all are for the State," to the all but apocalyptic opening of the cornucopias of a middle-class prosperity. Presumably the rigid Trades Unions of the Fascists will gradually " wither away " as each assisted worker joins the middle class, becomes independent, and renders himself " socially indispensable." The programme is tinged with the neo-romanticism which lies at the heart of the Fascist movement and finds expression in constant allusions to the Roman past of the Italian people, and their duty to work for Latin civilization in the Mediterranean—a duty interpreted in such phrases as " the restoration of the Empire." The nation is to be disciplined and unified in order that it may undertake a dimly adumbrated programme of imperialism.

The root fallacy of this vague but attractive formulation of post-war discontent interpreted in terms of an exclusive nationalism, is the idea that one party can acquire a monopoly of patriotism and because of that monopoly, claim a perpetual control of the State. The State is thus conceived of as above party, whereas what is envisaged is the capture of the State by a party claiming to be the embodiment of the national idea. That the normal life of the State should be above party it must be above the control of organized public opinion—in a word, it must be an autocracy or dictatorship of some kind, self-renewing, absolute, amenable only to the ultimate control of popular insurrection. Those who denounce party politics for corruption and inefficiency dream of a united public opinion electing and obeying its executive,—the nation becomes the party. This is pure romanticism. To escape parties the reformers must escape division of opinion—this they will never do so long as the major issues of life remain complex and the answers to its questions far from self-evident. Those critics of representative government who have probed deeper have not shrunk from the idea of a dictatorship or a strong monarchy,[1] conceived of as representing the ultimate interests of the nation, subject to some slight control by a senate of " best men," an " aristocracy of talent," in a word, an oligarchy of " superior persons," who will see further and act more wisely than the deputy elected by the votes and reflective of the mentality of those who do know on which side their bread is buttered. Since government is regarded as an art as delicate as painting on vellum or carving ivory balls in the Chinese manner, the conception of self-government as a duty

[1] *E.g.* Mr Hilaire Belloc.

as plain as, say, washing one's ears, and as essential as air and exercise to a healthy life, becomes a crazy paradox. The basis of the reaction, by no means confined to Italy, is discontent with the weaknesses of human nature revealed in election manœuvres and the manipulation of parliamentary groups—it will have succeeded if it renovates the parliamentary machine in the direction of making it more rather than less representative of the national life. If that life is stagnant the parliament from which emanates the government will probably be stagnant. It will live the life of the nation from whom it springs, if great issues are raised before a people made responsible by self-government, the parliament of that people reflects the answer given by the majority of the citizens. But the minority will also be present in the national assembly to contribute to the national education by full discussion of measures projected by the predominant party or group of parties. The cause of group intrigues and weak government is the bankruptcy of national life in clear political thought. Greek parliamentary institutions appeared to be bankrupt in 1909, until a great leader rallied the nation to a great programme of national reconstruction, submitted to their free discussion. Leadership is required, but leadership is not, as some imagine, incompatible with truly representative government. The leader to be efficient should not be elevated so far above criticism that he hears it merely as "the winding of a shell on the far-off seashore." Rather his place is in the thick of the wordy battle from which emerge measures of national policy tested by criticism.

The creation of a national party unified by a profoundly anti-Socialistic programme calculated to rally all who had been terrified by the Red menace, and to make a special appeal to national sentiment stimulated by the memory of a victorious war and the senseless campaign of national self-depreciation that followed it; the creation of a new Trade Union movement penetrated by the nationalist ideals of the new party, completed the structure rendered necessary by the frank acceptance of violence as a political weapon. Fascismo had become a centralized military force by the organization of the Fascist Militia in January 1921. A conference of leaders had organized the Fascist groups according to the plans of General Gandolfo, Italo Balbo, and the Marchese Perroni. Italy was divided into twelve zones, and in each zone the Fascist volunteers were organized along the lines of the ancient Roman military system. The fighting force, the "Principi," and the reserve, the "Triarii" had, as the primary unit, the "squadra," of fifteen to twenty men, under the command of a "capo squadra."

3 Squadre form a Manipolo, under a Decurion.
3 Manipoli form a Centuria, under a Centurion.
3 Centurie form a Cohort, under a Seniore.
3 to 6 Cohorts form a Legion, under a Consul.
3 to 6 Legions form a Group of Legions, under a Group Commander.

There were also organized "cohorts" of cyclists, and "manipoli" of motor-cyclists. The unit of discipline and control was the legion. The value of small units was, however, repeatedly emphasized in the secret orders of the G.H.Q. Constant practice at rapid mobilizations of small units under the general direction of mobilization officers, trained them in rapid concentration at given points in a district, and equally rapid dispersal. The force, which at the end of 1922 numbered some 300,000 men, was subject to a rigid discipline, both in military matters as in those of personal conduct. These are extracts from some of the secret orders: "The Fascisti party is always a militia. The Fascisti militia is at the service of God and of our Italian country. Every soldier must serve Italy with purity, pervaded by a profound mysticism, sustained by an unshakable faith, dominated by an inflexible will, as disdainful of opportunism and prudence as he is of cowardice, convinced of his holy call to save his great common mother, Italy, and to give her strength and purity. The Fascisti soldier knows only duty. He has no rights, save that of being allowed to perform his duty, and duty is his only joy. He has a moral code of his own. The usual moral code, which is prismatic, with many facets, with many meshes, is of no use to him. Honour is for him what it was for the ancient knights, a law which strives for though it never reaches the apex of perfection. It must be outside, as it is always above, the written or formal code."[1] The romanticism of the movement, an aspect of Fascism not usually emphasized sufficiently, lends whatever significance there may be to this curious passage, so illustrative of the national weakness for "insignificant speech." It is not difficult to see wherein lies the appeal of a society offering a Black Shirt, discipline, adventure, and much romantic, patriotic sentiment, to a youth of

[1] Quoted Phillips, "The 'Red' Dragon and the Black Shirts," p. 44.

the middle classes, too young in many cases to have experienced the blood-stained reality of the trenches, his eyes full of star-dust, and led on by adored leaders, for the most part men with splendid military records. But just because Fascism is a youth-movement the future for Italy is full of hope.

By the beginning of 1922, then, Fascism was at once a political party, a Trade Union movement, and an armed and disciplined militia. The supine acquiescence of the Liberal State had allowed the development of what was indeed "a State within a State."

The reorganization of the party during the winter of 1921-22 had placed in the hands of Mussolini a magnificent weapon. It must be used if it was not to rust, and used for the supreme purpose of conquering political power. The truce with the Socialists had broken down and the consequences must be accepted. The Socialist strongholds were the communes. They must be conquered. Once local government was in the hands of the Fascists, Rome would be theirs for the taking. "The Social Communists from the first made Rome their objective, aiming at the conquest of the central power, and afterwards, through it, of the country; the Fascisti, on the other hand, conquered the country first, and Rome fell into their hands afterwards like a ripe fruit."[1] Throughout 1922 the assault on the Socialist communes and Trade Unions continued trucelessly. The attack on the Socialist communes took the character of a national conquest, for the Socialists to the end flew the red flag from all the municipal buildings in their hands—the hauling down of that hated emblem and the hoisting of the national Tricolour became a symbolic assertion of the central dogma of Fascism, the supremacy of the nation-State, and the denial of all Internationals, whether Red or Black or Green.[2] "The National Fascist Party affirms that during the present historical period the prevailing form of social organization in the world is national Society, and that the essential law of world-life is not the unification of various societies into a single immense Society 'Humanity,' according to the Internationalist creed, but the fruitful and, we may hope, peaceful co-operation between nations."[3]

[1] Odon Por, "Fascism," p. 111.
[2] Bolshevik (Communist), Clerical, Peasant.
[3] Programme of National Fascist Party (Dec. 1921); Odon Por, "Fascism," Appendix ii.

The methods were the usual variations on the theme of violence, but more and more systematic. Socialist mayors and councils were threatened and beaten into resignation. To many, large doses of castor-oil were administered. Labour centres were ruthlessly attacked, and, short of immediate submission to Fascist orders, burnt. Then began a strange stampede: union after union seceded from the General Confederation of Labour, and went over to the Fascists. As many as seventeen agricultural Red Leagues joined in a single day in Ferrara.[1] By absorbing the seceding Labour organization into their newly constructed Trade Unions the Fascist Directory was able to eject the former Socialist leaders and break the back of Socialist organizations.[2] To save the Co-operative Societies, which represented enormous sums of money and decades of splendid and patient labour—to save these societies from ruthless destruction, the Socialist workers went over in masses to the Fascists.[3] Once the labour monopoly in a given district had been won for the Fascisti, the ruthless application of the boycott soon secured the surrender of the few dissidents.

Yet another transformation insensibly worked a "sea-change" in Fascism. By the wholesale absorption of masses of men who up to the last moment had been Socialists, the movement began to lose its exclusively bourgeois character. By the middle of 1922 the agrarian Fascisti had definitely escaped from the control of the landowners, who had previously financed them for their own purposes. Owners of idle or ill-cultivated lands were coerced into putting their estates in order. In other cases, the estates were seized in the interests of the labourers. Proprietors were compelled to contribute to the maintenance of the Fascist agrarian squads. By December 1922 the organ of the proprietors, *The Bulletin of the Agrarian Association*, was complaining that the Fascists had forcibly prevented the Association from holding a meeting. The paper had discovered that "not even the Bolshevik aberration resorted to such measures."[4] In the presence of this remarkable evolution—in itself a sign of the vitality of the Fascist movement—Claudio Treves, a leader of the Reformist Socialists, was able to say in Parliament, on 9th August 1922: "In future, Fascism, too, has its responsibilities before it.

[1] Beals, p. 142.
[2] Odon Por, "Fascism," p. 111.
[3] *Ibid.*, p. 127.
[4] Quoted Beals, "Rome or Death," p. 143.

The iron rod will have its *raison d'être*. If this is to be Trade Unionism we do not fear it. We already see it resorting to the monopoly of labour, refusing the right of working to all who do not carry its badge—the very gravest accusation that it brought against our Trade Unions. The truth is that all the working classes, in whatever manner they are organized, tend to form for themselves a monopoly of labour."[1] The attempt of the reactionaries to secure what is euphemously called "the freedom of Labour" had been decisively defeated by forces within the Fascist body. Mussolini did not hesitate to say that as far as he could see Fascism was leading towards a Trade Union State.

The final demonstration of Fascist strength came with the last effort of the Socialists—the general strike of 31st July 1922. It was officially announced as a "legalitarian strike," a protest against the continued inertia of the Facta Government in face of Fascist outrages. All sections of the Socialist party co-operated in ordering this attempt to rouse the Liberal State from its coma. Turati, the reformist, who all through the summer had been feverishly working to secure Socialist collaboration in the formation of a Government capable of stemming the tide of reaction, hoped by means of the general strike to presuade the Popolari to co-operate with the Socialists in the formation of a Government which would supplant the Facta ministry. Signor Facta, an honest politician and a devoted follower of Signor Giolitti, had presided with dignity at the ill-fated Genoa Conference, but, in spite of his promising programme (of which Senator Scialoja remarked that it had been signed Facta in error for Verba[2]) had otherwise merely contemplated with tranquillity the rising tide of Fascism.

Mussolini and the Fascisti Directory took the general strike to be a challenge, which they at once accepted. They ordered a Fascist mobilization, and launched the following ultimatum at the Government: "We give the State forty hours in which to give some proof of its authority to all who depend upon it and to those who are making attempts upon the very life of the nation. When this time has elapsed, Fascism will take upon itself full liberty of action, and will take the place of the State that will have once more shown its impotence."[3]

[1] Quoted Odon Por, "Fascism," p. 129.
[2] Villari, "The Awakening of Italy," p. 142.
[3] Quoted Odon Por, "Fascism," p. 125.

It was a clear declaration of independence, the frank recognition that in Italy there were two centres of political authority.

The Fascisti proceeded to replace the railway staff, and organize the tramways and essential public services. Masses of the workers refused to obey the order for the most useless of all the innumerable strikes which had paralysed Italy since the war. By the time Signor Facta had instructed the prefects to hand over their powers to the military, the strike had been called off. But the Fascist offensive continued. On 3rd August the Black Shirts occupied the municipality of Milan—the commune most notorious for the maniacal financial recklessness of the Red administrators. Between 1918 and 1922 the deficit had steadily increased from 16,000,000 to 375,000,000 lire. As a result of the Fascist action the syndic was dissolved and taken over by the Government. The new inspector, Dr Ricci, succeeded in a year by the ruthless cutting down of expenses in converting a deficit of 375,000,000 lire into a surplus of 17,000,000.[1]

It is administration such as that of the Social Communists in Milan and elsewhere which lends colour to the accusation that their object is to demonstrate the failure of the "Capitalist system" by deliberately ruining every concern they control. An orgy of reckless extravagance (such as the Esperanto courses at Milan, the innumerable municipal bands, the free summer holidays at the seaside or the mountains for favoured employees, etc.[2]) followed by incontinent bankruptcy, will, it is hoped, produce the requisite revolutionary unrest. If after large expenditure on such purposes as those which occupied the municipality of Milan to the neglect of the city's drainage system, the budget is found to balance, men of good will (after suggesting perhaps that the sanitary arrangements would be improved by a little extra expenditure) should be the first to applaud. Continuous and deliberate over-expenditure, and the accumulation of a dead weight of debt dragging the concern to bankruptcy, is the sort of offence against society against which Fascism reacted at Milan. As we have seen, it followed this up by the forcible dissolution of innumerable other Socialist syndics legally elected and in many cases efficient. But reaction does not pick and choose. At the end of September the squadrons of the new State invaded the German districts of the Alto Adige (the district

[1] Villari, "The Awakening of Italy," p. 160. [2] *Ibid.*, p. 157.

of the South Tyrol annexed to Italy by the Treaty of St Germain) and compelled the resignation of Dr Perathoner, the German Mayor of Bolzano, and the dissolution of the German police force. Dr Perathoner's offence was the refusal to permit Italian schools, his notoriously anti-Italian attitude, and his neglect to obey an order by the Governor of the province ordering that official notices and the names of streets should be in Italian as well as in German.[1]

The spectacle of a Government too weak to enforce its own orders, even in the annexed territories, and of an extra-legal organization superseding at all points the legal authorities, produced an intolerable sense of strain. The feeling grew that a solution must be found either by the absorption of Fascism by the State or the absorption of the State by Fascism. Mussolini, with his unfailing perception of the underlying psychology and motives of every shifting manifestation of public opinion, saw that the irritant of Fascism had by now goaded the nation into the conviction that anything, even the armed overthrow of the Liberal State and the substitution of a Fascist dictatorship, would be preferable to the existing chaos. At any moment the strain might produce a revulsion and show itself in a wild outburst of hatred against Fascism. There were at work also other powerful motives for immediate action. The development of Fascist Trade Unionism and the actions of the agrarian Fascisti had so alarmed the great industrialists and landowners that they had begun to withdraw their subscriptions, without which the complicated and expensive organization could not be kept in being.[2] The great adventurer knew that an increasing pressure was being brought to bear on Signor Facta to induce him to undertake a supreme effort with all the forces of the State against Fascism, an effort that would, it was believed, raise the Liberal State once more triumphant over a ruined Socialism and a suppressed Fascismo. He has never been one to shrink from heroic measures or to hesitate at the parting of the ways, and in these compelling circumstances Mussolini decided to play for high stakes.

Between 1st and 3rd October there sat in Rome a Congress of the Socialist party. At a moment when it was menaced as never before in its history, the mephitic forces within the party finally rent it to pieces. The party now comprised only

[1] Villari, " The Awakening of Italy," p. 166.
[2] Odon Por, " Fascism," p. 144.

61,225 registered members, as compared with 100,000 eighteen months previously. The great issue before the congress was the question of collaboration with the Liberal State. The votes of the members were cast by their representatives as follows :—

For Collaboration : 29,119.
Against Collaboration : 32,106.

The anti-collaborationists did not consider the question one that could be decided by a majority. It was a question of expelling from the party those "social patriots" and "reformists" who were compassing the betrayal of the proletariat. By a majority of 2987 votes Turati and his followers were expelled and immediately formed themselves into the "Unitarian Socialist Party." The triumphant extremists who remained took the name of "Maximalists," and then broke into two groups over the question of allegiance to the Third (Communist) International.[1] At the moment when Moscow, alarmed at the menace of Fascism, was urgently advising "purification by unification" (in 1921 it had as emphatically enjoined "purification by schism"), the Italian Socialist party blew up after spontaneous combustion. As Claudio Treves put it, the party "had been Balkanized." Only the Parliament stood between Mussolini and supreme power.

Yet as the days passed in ever deepening anxiety, the Parliament through which the great Cavour had worked in building up the fortunes of little Piedmont before he had launched her on her superb adventure, the making of Italy, and summoned all Italians to fight not only for a united but a Liberal nation, became more and more a whirligig of distracted phantoms. At the centre of impotent activity, half seen, as through a gaseous Fata Morgana of party intrigue, might be discerned the wavering form of Don Sturzo—the Punchinello of Italian politics.

Towards the end of September 1922, the Fascista Directory met at Rome, and after discussion conferred full powers on Mussolini to take at his discretion any action, political or military, to carry Fascismo to power.

Like Louis Napoleon preparing for the formal restoration of the Empire, Mussolini now went on a political pilgrimage.

[1] Villari, "The Awakening of Italy," p. 167.

The speeches he delivered were in effect the proclamation to all the Fascisti of " the state of danger of war." Into the confused babel of Italian life his words rang out clear, insistent challenges to the existing order and its supporters. With the skill of a great artist and a great politician he gradually quickened the pulse of the speeches—the call to revolution becomes more definite. Not only was he preparing the Fascisti for their adventure, he was watching the effect of the ever plainer hints he dropped for the benefit of public opinion. He saw incredulity, hesitation, a certain hope, but no signs of reaction, no rallying in the defence of the discredited Government.

At Udine, on 20th September 1922, the anniversary of the capture of Rome by the Italians in 1870, Mussolini began that " second march on Rome " that was to lead him to the high places of power. He asked his hearers to think of Rome as the symbol of Italian unity. " We want to make Rome the city of our ideals, a city cleaned and purified of all those elements which corrupt and defile her ; we wish to make Rome the throbbing heart, the living spirit of the Italy of which we dream." To be worthy of this task, " we must first firmly discipline ourselves, otherwise we shall not have the right to discipline the nation. And it is only by the discipline of the nation that Italy can make herself heard in the councils of other countries. Discipline must be accepted. If it is not it must be imposed. We put aside the democratic dogma that one must for ever proceed by sermonizing and lecturing in a more or less liberal manner. At a given moment discipline must show itself under the form of a command or of an act of force." He justifies Fascist violence as necessary, but it must not become a habit, it must have a moral end, and it " must be proportionate to the necessities of the moment." He discusses Fascist Syndicalism, into which he claims Fascism has infused a new doctrine, that of " the State above all classes," " the task of Fascismo is to make the people organically one with the nation, so that they may be ready to-morrow, when the nation has need of them, as the artist takes his raw material in order to create his masterpiece." Fascismo does not " adore the masses, even if they have got work-worn hands and brains," it knows that " history proves that it has always been the minorities, a handful from the first, that have produced profound changes in human society " ; but the fact remains that " only with the masses forming an intimate part of the life and history of the nation can we have a foreign policy." In foreign policy Fascismo stands for the firm assertion of her rights and the end of the policy of renunciation. National unity itself is not yet complete, "because perfect unity cannot be spoken of until Fiume and Dalmatia and the other territories have come back to us, thus fulfilling the proud dream which we carry in our hearts." Fascism is challenged to produce a programme: "Our programme is simple: we wish to govern Italy." As to the charge of republicanism, "I think that the regime can be largely modified without interfering with the monarchy. . . . To-day there are many indifferent to the monarchy who to-morrow would be its supporters, and who would find highly respectable and sentimental reasons for attacking Fascismo, if it had dared to aim at this target. I do not think that the monarchy has really any object in opposing what must now be called the Fascista Revolution. It is not in its interests, because by doing so it would immediately make itself an object of attack, in which case we could not spare it. . . . " Fascism proposes to renovate the State first by shearing it of all unnecessary functions. "We have had enough of the State railwayman, the State postman, and the State insurance official. We have had enough of the State administration at the expense of the Italian tax-payers, which has done nothing but aggravate the exhausted financial condition of the country." "*We must have a State which will simply say: 'The State does not represent a party, it represents the nation as a whole, it includes all, is over all, protects all, and fights any attempt made against her inviolable sovereignty.'*"[1]

The speech is remarkable for its calm assertion of the Fascist will to power, though the possibility of a revolution is not stressed, and for the clear definition of the Fascist attitude to the monarchy. The monarchy will be preserved if it is not hostile to Fascismo. Doubt as to its attitude towards the monarchy had alone restrained large numbers, especially of the officer class, from joining the movement. Now, on the eve of great events, when everything might depend on the action of the army, the question of the regime had to be settled.

Five days later at Cremona, 25th September 1922, the note of the short speech is pitched in a higher key: "What is that feeling which stirs you when you hear the song of the Piave? It is that the Piave does not mark an end, it marks a beginning. It is from the Piave, it is from Vittorio Veneto, it is from our

[1] San Severino, "Speeches," pp. 143-57.

victory—even if it was mutilated by a mistaken diplomacy—that our standards move on! It was on the banks of the Piave that the march was begun that cannot stop until Rome is reached." [1]

On 6th October, in a speech at Milan, he again outlines his programme. This time he proclaims the necessity for ending the unreality in Italy by revolution. The speech opens with the celebration of the glories of Fascista violence, "the great, wonderful, relentless violence of the decisive hour; . . . we cannot accept the humanitarian, Tolstoyan moral standard, the moral standard of slavery." There are two States in Italy, the Liberal legal State and the Fascista State—one State too many. Fascismo, he asserts, by its daily acts, its independent organization, has proved itself the actual though not yet the legal State. There is still a way out, "if the whole of Rome were not suffering from softening of the brain"—let the Government pass an Electoral Reform Bill (to end the regime of P. R.) and then appeal to the country. A crisis in Parliament is no good: "thirty crises in the Italian Parliament as it is to-day would mean thirty reincarnations of Signor Facta." "The Liberal State is a mask behind which there is no face, it is a scaffolding behind which there is no building." Fascismo means new life-blood to the State, that is new men—the Italy which has come from the trenches is strong and full of life. "That is why Fascismo thinks more of men than measures." "Fascismo represents a reaction against the Democrats, who would have made everything mediocre and uniform, and tried every way to conceal and to render transitory the authority of the State, from the supreme head to the last usher in the Law Courts. . . . Democracy has taken 'elegance' from the lives of the people, but Fascismo brings it back; that is to say, it brings back colour, force, picturesqueness, the unexpected, mysticism, and in fact all that counts in the souls of the multitude. We play upon every chord of the lyre, from violence to religion, from art to politics. We are politicians and we are warriors. We are syndicalists and we also fight battles in the streets and the squares." A mighty task lies before Fascismo when it has undertaken, as it surely will, the government of Italy. But in the days to come Fascists will be able to say "to the children who are growing up, and who represent the eternal spring of life, . . . 'Great was the effort and hard the sacrifice, and pure was the blood that was shed;

[1] San Severino, "Speeches," p. 160.

and it was not shed to safeguard the interests of individuals, class, or caste; it was not shed in the name of materialism; it was shed in the name of an ideal, of all that was most noble, beautiful, and generous in the human soul.' " With such spirit-stirring words did the great leader prepare for the General Congress of the Fascist Party, to meet at Naples on 26th October 1922.[1]

Naples was occupied by an army of 50,000 Fascisti, who, amid scenes of delirious enthusiasm, marched past their chief. The speech he delivered, punctuated by the insistent voice of the mighty gathering, crying, "To Rome! To Rome!" revealed that he recognized that the unique moment for action had at last arrived. He told his audience that the Fascist Directory had demanded of the Government electoral reform, the immediate dissolution of Parliament and new elections, and the handing over to Fascist ministers of the portfolios of the Ministries of Foreign Affairs, War Office, Admiralty, Labour, and Public Works, in fact the government of the nation. Mussolini declared he did not desire to enter the ministry, preferring to reserve to himself his polemical freedom. Fascism wanted power, he declared, and would attain it, if not by legal then by illegal means. He reiterated the acceptance of the monarchy: "There is no doubt that the unity of Italy is soundly based upon the House of Savoy." As for Parliament, Fascismo did not want to do away with "the people's toy Parliament," but it did not believe in democracy: "If democracy had its uses and served the nation in the nineteenth century, it may be that some other political form would be best for the welfare of the nation in the twentieth." The situation, in a word, was such that in the fine metaphor of the chief: "The moment has arrived when the arrow must leave the bow, or the cord, too far stretched, will break." [2] The Government of Signor Facta made no satisfactory reply, and the same evening the Fascist Quadrumvirate was constituted to direct the approaching *coup d'état,* consisting of Michele Bianchi, Dr Italo Balbo, Signor De Vecchi, and General De Bono. The Naples Congress broke up, and Mussolini returned to Milan.

On 26th October 1922 the messengers of the Quadrumvirate got into touch with the Government and the King through the Liberal ex-Premiers Orlando and Salandra. As a result of

[1] San Severino, "Speeches," pp. 161-70.
[2] *Ibid.*, p. 172.

their pressing representations, Signor Facta decided to resign, but continued to hold office until a new Government could be constituted. In the meantime De Vecchi and the Fascist staff established themselves at Perugia, and ordered a general Fascist mobilization. Within a few hours the brilliantly co-ordinated forces of the Fascists were converging in an ever-narrowing circle on the Eternal City. On the 28th the Government, at last awake to the gravity of the position, issued an order declaring martial law throughout the country. The military authorities at Rome took steps for the defence of the city, and Italy seemed on the eve of civil war. The regular army was the one force dreaded by the Fascist chiefs. They had taken an immense risk in deciding to cut their way to power, sword in hand, but they had gambled on the cowardice of the Government and the success of their own propaganda in undermining the loyalty of the officers. They were not, however, so sure of the extent of their moral ascendancy as to be other than gravely perturbed by the eleventh-hour stroke of Signor Facta.

The same morning the Premier had sought an interview with the King to obtain his signature to the decree already published. Victor Emmanuel was confronted with a momentous decision, and he did not hesitate. He resolved at all costs to spare the nation a civil war, and he not only refused to sign the decree, but hotly ordered the Prime Minister to revoke at once an order that should never have been issued without the previous consent of the monarch.

But the King, true to the intensely constitutional attitude he has always adopted, at once sent for Signor Salandra, as the Parliamentarian most likely to be able to construct a Cabinet. Salandra accepted the mandate, and offered portfolios to De Vecchi, Grandi, and Ciano. Before accepting they wired to Mussolini at Milan for permission to take office, and on 29th October received his decisive refusal: "I refuse, because I do not wish the Fascista victory to be mutilated."[1] Signor Salandra then informed the King that he could not form a Cabinet, and advised him to send for Mussolini. As a hundred thousand Fascisti were converging on Rome from all quarters of Italy, and a conflict with the regular army might break out at any moment, the King summoned Mussolini from Milan by telegram the same day. On the morning of 30th October he arrived in Rome just as the first Fascist columns

[1] Villari, "The Awakening of Italy," p. 179.

entered the city. The occupation was entirely peaceful, save for the usual murmur of a few Communists.

The man whose hands were now at last closing on the reins of supreme power proceeded at once to the Quirinal, and, still wearing his black shirt, presented himself before the King: "I beg your Majesty's forgiveness for appearing in my black shirt, but I have only just returned from the battle, fortunately a bloodless one, which we have had to wage. I bring to your Majesty the Italy of Vittorio Veneto, reconsecrated by the new victory, and declare myself the devoted servant of your Majesty." The black shirt of Mussolini and the occupation of Rome by the Fascist forces were both finely deliberated gestures. Something was required to show that there had been a revolution. Who had won, Victor Emmanuel, who, with a masterly preservation of all the constitutional forms, had opened the door and invited in one who was about to breach the wall with dynamite, or the Premier, who accepted office wearing the insignia of revolution? That silent duel has not yet been decided. The same day the new Cabinet was announced. Mussolini had prepared his list at Milan. It included members of all the Constitutional parties, and the King, on perusing it, remarked: "The excellent and well-balanced composition of the list could not have been happier." [1] The anti-democratic revolution had begun.

No final verdict on Mussolini's work can yet be passed, chiefly because it has not yet been completed. Only a brief review can be attempted in an essay of this length.

After securing a vote of plenary confidence from the Chambers, which it was impossible for the House of Representatives to refuse, confronted, as it was, with the *force majeure* of organized Fascism, the Government secured full powers for one year to take any measures necessary for bureaucratic and financial reform by a majority of 275 to 90, on 25th November 1922. Mussolini's intention was to keep the existing chamber in being as long as possible in order to be able to carry through it a measure of electoral reform, and then at the end of his period of plenary power to dissolve and go to the country. There were many good reasons, for avoiding a general election. Fascism, though it had captured the central machine, had not yet fully occupied the State. By the early months of 1923 all functionaries of any importance throughout the kingdom whose whole-hearted acceptance of

[1] Villari, p. 182.

the new regime was in any way doubtful had been removed, and the grip of the party on the heartstrings of the nation consolidated. A stringent press law was promulgated, but not for the time enforced. It was a weapon for future use.

"Order and Economy" were the immediate watchwords of the Dictator. The first was his objective in creating, in January 1923, the "Volunteer Militia for National Safety." The existing Fascista squadre were disbanded, and picked elements were reabsorbed into the new militia. It was placed upon a territorial basis, and its duty was to assist the army and the police "in maintaining internal public order, and to prepare the citizens for the defence of Italian interests in the world." It was dependent on the orders of the Prime Minister alone, took no oath of allegiance to the King, and was recruited solely from among the Fascisti. In a word it was a party organized as an army, and its regional heads exercised more power and influence than the prefects of the provinces. The organization of the militia strengthened the grasp of the party on the national life, and, at the same time, completed the extraordinary duplication of the legal and the revolutionary State: Parliament and Fascist Grand Council; army and Fascist militia; prefects and Fascist regional heads of militia.[1]

The problem of economy was faced heroically. Previous Governments had indeed begun the necessary task of balancing the budget and reducing the deficit. But they tended to rely on heavy taxation, which beyond a certain point complicates problems by strangling national assets. Mussolini realized that Italy was suffering, in common with most Southern countries, from a plethora of officials and State employees. He began by amalgamating overlapping ministries and suppressing superfluous offices. A ruthless cutting of staffs in the various ministries was inaugurated, designed to discover the exact point at which the services could be maintained in a state of efficiency. In the six months ending 30th April 1923, 17,232 men were dismissed from the railways, which since the war had become under State management hopelessly over-staffed and inevitably insolvent.[2] Notice was given that by the end of 1923 the staff must be reduced by another 300,000. The stupendous disorder of the State railways can be gauged by the fact that after these amputations[3] they

[1] Ferrero, "Four Years of Fascism," p. 91.

[2] Villari, p. 217.

[3] These necessary reductions were made the excuse for partisan dismissals of Socialist railwaymen—however good their records.

increased in efficiency. It is confidently expected that the railway deficit will be extinguished by 1926, when, in pursuance of a general policy of ridding the State of its economic commitments, Mussolini hopes to hand over a working system to private companies. So far does he carry this denationalization policy that eventually he proposes to surrender even the Government monopolies of posts and telegraphs.

Another reform in the direction of economy was the drastic suppression of the host of mushroom law courts United Italy had inherited from the former separate Italian States. In March 1923, on the proposal of the Minister of Justice, over 600 courts, varying in importance from four courts of appeal to 550 magistrates' courts, were abolished.[1] At the end of a year the Fascist Government could point to increased economy and efficiency of the public services, and to a budget wherein national expenditure had ceased to rise, and real reductions, not a mere piling on of taxation, had been effected.

To impress upon his colleagues and the nation the immense importance he attaches to economy and strict finance, the Prime Minister made the occasion of his handing over to the Finance Minister, De Stefani, of his budgets for Home and Foreign Affairs for revision at the Treasury, a formal state ceremony: "We must consider," he said, "that the money of the Treasury is sacred above everything else. It does not rain down from heaven, nor can it even be made with a turn of the printing-press, which, if I could, I would like to smash to pieces. It is made out of the sweat, it might be said of the blood, of the Italian people, who work to-day, but who will work more to-morrow. Every *lira*, every *soldo*, every *centesimo* of this money must be considered sacred, and should not be spent unless reasons of strict and proved necessity demand it. The history of peoples tells us that strict finance has brought nations to security. I feel that each one of you believes in this truth, which is fully proved by history."[2]

It was not long before it became obvious that though the Prime Minister was ready to accept the co-operation of all who were equally prepared to accept the dictatorship of Fascismo, he regarded the slightest manifestation of political independence as the declaration of a truceless war. This attitude sprang from the profound conviction which animates the Fascist party that it has a divine right to the government of Italy. In April 1923, after the Turin Congress of the

[1] Villari, p. 224.
[2] San Severino, p. 273.

Popular party, where it had, under the leadership of Don Sturzo, reaffirmed its faith in parliamentary government and proportional representation, and its defence of the Catholic religion, while disclaiming opposition to the Government, Mussolini expelled the "Popular" ministers in his Coalition, thus forcing the party into opposition.

This high-handed act naturally led the Fascist party to face the prospect of an election, with the powerful Popular party in opposition. Though justly proud of their reforming achievements, the Fascist leaders were perfectly aware of the intense hatred with which they were regarded by the victims of their ruthless economies and reorganizations. Yet they could have afforded to laugh at such opposition so long as they had the support of all the constitutional parties. Once their inevitable assumption of infallibility had begun to alienate the constitutional parties, they were forced to consider ways and means for assuring the political supremacy of Fascism. The result of these considerations was the famous Electoral Reform Bill introduced in the summer of 1923.

Proportional representation, hastily introduced, had evidently proved a failure in Italy. It is devised admirably to test the real strength of parties, provided they are content to appear honestly before the people, stand on their own legs, and submit their programme. Issues are hopelessly confused, if, as in Italy after its introduction, parties make previous arrangements with each other. The obvious alternative to any form of proportionalism was the British system of representation. Fascisti who have considered the question of electoral reform solely as a problem in political science, have urged such a measure on Mussolini. But this group, headed by Signor Farinacci, have not been concerned primarily with the problem of securing a majority at all costs.

The Government determined to force through Parliament an extraordinary scheme, originally proposed by Michele Bianchi, and considerably modified by Signor Acerbo, the Secretary for the Cabinet. The country is divided into fifteen constituencies, for which each party is to present lists, thus preserving some element of territorial connection between the deputies and the constituents. But the result of a general election is not determined in the constituencies. For this purpose the whole of Italy is regarded as one constituency. The party which secures relatively the largest number of votes in the whole country is at once entitled to two-thirds of the seats in the future Chamber.[1] The remaining third is distributed on the basis of proportional representation among the other parties in the field. The two-thirds majority is then a prize awarded to the party that secures a bare majority over any other party. The suggestion of the Opposition, that unless the winning party secured 40 per cent. of the total votes cast it would not receive its prize of seats, was rejected. The Fascist leaders were not prepared to gamble on winning 40 per cent. of the votes.

It appeared inevitable that the Government's Bill would be rejected by the "Popular" vote in Parliament, in which case Mussolini would have been confronted with the choice of assuming an open dictatorship or dissolving with a real chance of defeat. His superb parliamentary performance of 16th July 1923, and the sudden intervention of the Vatican, saved him. The Pope was by now convinced that the Fascist Government was stable; Mussolini had hastened to concede the demands of the Church with regard to religious education in schools. Pius XI liked the political radicalism of the Catholic Populars no better than had Benedict XV, and he was convinced that the rejection of the Government's proposals might mean civil war and would certainly precipitate the outbreak of violent Fascist anti-clerical demonstrations that had already begun. He hastened to indicate that the Popular party did not represent the views of the Vatican by intimating to Don Sturzo that he had better resign. As a priest he could not refuse, and at a stroke the Popular opposition was dislocated.

The speech of the Premier in defence of the Bill was a marvellous oratorical achievement. He did not go into details, but he reviewed the situation that in his opinion made the Fascist Revolution necessary. He did not threaten, but there was no escaping the significance of his words: "We have left many dead on the road to Rome, and naturally anybody who deludes himself is a fool. We have the power, and we shall hold it. We shall defend it against anybody! The Revolution lies in this firm determination to hold power. . . . I have also the duty of telling you—and I tell you from a debt of loyalty—that on your vote depends in a certain sense your fate! . . . Do not let the country have once again the impression that Parliament is far from the soul of the nation, and that this Parliament, after having manœuvred for an entire week in a campaign of opposition, has achieved

[1] Villari, p. 247.

sterile results at the end. Because this is the moment in which Parliament and country can be reconciled. But if this chance is lost, to-morrow will be too late, and you feel it in the air, you feel it in yourselves. And then, Gentlemen, do not hang on political labels, do not stiffen yourselves in the formal coherence of the parties, do not clutch at bits of straw, as do the shipwrecked in the ocean, hoping vainly to save themselves. But listen to the secret and solemn working of your conscience; listen also to the incoercible voice of the nation!"[1] A vote of confidence in the Government was carried by 303 to 140. On 14th November 1923, the Electoral Bill was voted by the Senate by 165 to 41.[2]

On 25th January 1924, the dissolution of the Chamber was decreed after the Premier had surrendered the extraordinary powers he had secured a year before. At the same time the ministerial minute to the King, submitting the decree and reviewing the reforming efforts of the Ministry, was published. The task that remained even after the prodigious efforts of a year was formidable: "For carrying this out, the new Assembly, if your Majesty is pleased to accept the proposed decree, will have to give its assistance by means of a conscious, assiduous collaboration with the Government, which recognizes the true virtue of an elected representation, constituting it, if no longer the fulcrum around which all public life gravitated in the years of political decadence, one of the fundamental elements which, in harmony with others, contribute to the regulation of the life of the State." There could be no better formulation of the Bismarckian conception of the State. In future, deriving from the King, the Executive would presumably submit new laws to the elected representatives of the people, but administration, with all that the word spells of power and the conduct of the external affairs of the nation, would be outside their control, if not outside their criticism. The Premier, though he naturally desired a majority, would not feel obliged, any more than did the maker of modern Germany, to resign if he lost it. This conception of the working of the State—a conception formulated by Strafford and King Charles I before and during the English civil wars—recurs again and again in the speeches of Mussolini.

He conceives himself as the representative of the Italian people, or rather of all that merits the name of Italian in loyalty, patriotism, discipline, work. Italians who do not

[1] San Severino, pp. 347-62. [2] Villari, p. 248.

conform to his interpretations of these virtues and qualities are not part of the nation, they are pariahs and must be subject to strict discipline.

The fundamental problem of government, the relations of the leader and the led, a problem that the Liberal tradition has solved by representative government, or in other words, by "power with responsibility," is ignored and left unanswered. Sooner or later "co-ordinate powers" will give rise to the old debate as to where the real sovereignty lies. The same mystical sense of mission inspired Lenin, who, in spite of all his scientific thought, was content to the end to regard himself as "the infallible prophet of an infallible mass." [1] He preferred to leave undefined the relations of the prophet to the mass. But in politics mysticism, whether Bolshevik or Fascist, is not enough.

The elections for the new Chamber took place on 6th April 1924. On 23rd March, the Premier made his only election speech. Fascism, he declared, unlike most revolutions, had refrained from punishing its opponents: "But I am convinced, and we must shout it aloud so that all may hear, that if it were necessary, in order to defend our revolution, to do to-morrow what we did not do before, we should not hesitate to do it." As for the political pressure exercised on the nation by the Fascist party and its army of 500,000 men, "if it is desired that Fascismo—the Government and the party—should reduce that pressure, our adversaries must accept the accomplished fact. . . . We must go forward. We must make Italy great. That is the infallible aim of Fascismo." [2]

In order to win votes in the predominantly anti-Fascist South, various Liberal politicians were included on the Government list of candidates, among them the ex-Premiers Salandra and Orlando. The election passed off comparatively quietly, and of the 7,628,859 electors who voted that day by the curiously crude method of striking a line through the emblem of their party inscribed on the ballot-papers,—the bundle of rods and the axe, the *fasces* of Fascismo; the cross on a shield of the Popolari, etc.,—it was found that 4,693,690 had voted for the Government; nigh on 3,000,000 electors had, however, declined to vote for the Government; 1,039,762 votes had been cast for the two Socialist bodies and the Communists. The Popolari came next with 619,738 votes; the Constitutional Liberal opposition, that refused to accept

[1] Masaryk, "Sur le Bolchévisme."

[2] Villari, pp. 280-1.

places on the Government's list, fared badly with under 96,000 votes.

The composition of the new Chamber was as follows: 374 members pledged to the Government—260 Fascisti, 114 Liberals, and 31 Constitutionalists, representing various other groups. Of the Opposition there are 64 deputies representing the Socialists and Communists, 40 Popolari, 14 of the Constitutional Opposition, 7 Republicans, and 4 deputies from the German and Slav annexed territories. In a House of 535 members, 405 support the Government. Even if the extremely diverse Opposition united it cannot muster more than 129. If the Opposition in the Chamber was negligible, it was evident that there was a numerous if divided body of opinion that refused to accept the ideal of a "national Government" under the guidance of Mussolini. But with such a Chamber Fascismo might hope to embark seriously on the task of constitutional reform. When the new Chamber assembled the situation appeared secure.

If we turn for a moment to Mussolini's foreign policy it can in general be described as at once firm and dignified. His expressed intention on assuming office was to secure for Italy her due share of influence in the counsels of the Allies as a Great Power. He made quite clear that he would continue the Entente on no other terms. Too long had Italy been treated as a politically negligible factor by France and Great Britain. The extremely anti-British tone of his speeches, as late as the early days of October 1922, seemed to hint at the possibility of a diplomatic revolution, in view of the fact that Poincaré was on the eve of the occupation of the Ruhr, an occupation that was to strain the Anglo-French Entente to the breaking-point. After some obscure diplomatic manœuvres, apparently looking towards a continental combination directed against Great Britain, the new ruler of Italy came down on the side of caution.

He at once announced his readiness to ratify and put into action that Fascist bugbear, the Treaty of Rapallo with Jugo-Slavia, settling the status of the Free City of Fiume. "The fundamental principle upon which our foreign policy is based," he declared in a speech to the Chamber on 16th November 1922, "is that treaties of peace, once signed and ratified, must be carried out, no matter whether they are good or bad. A self-respecting nation cannot follow another course. Treaties are not eternal or irreparable; they are chapters and not epilogues in history; to put them into practice means to try them. If in the course of execution they are proved to be absurd, that in itself constitutes the possibility of a further examination of the respective positions."[1]

The Free State of Fiume was not long in proving an absurdity. Negotiations with Jugo-Slavia were resumed, and after a long and tortuous course, concluded with the settlement of January 1924, whereby Italy secured the faithful city, and Jugo-Slavia obtained the neighbouring harbour, Porto Barros, and a small strip of what was the rural district of the defunct Free State. It was the deserved triumph of a patient and able displomacy, and has paved the way to the conclusion of an agreement, almost amounting to an alliance, between the two Adriatic Powers. In his election speech the Premier was able to exclaim with telling irony: "It is true that the Tricolour is to-day on the Monte Nevoso. But if we had followed the suggestions of the Liberalism of Dronero the Tricolour might at most be waving over the station of Cervignano, and perhaps we should never have reached Salorno. Monte Nevoso we might have seen, if you will allow me to use a trench-warfare expression, through a binocular. Symbolically, we might have placed Giolitti's *palamidone*[2] on its summit, whereas the glorious Tricolour is now waving up there."[3]

In the Ruhr controversy, Italy's influence has usually been thrown on to the side of a settlement by agreement with Germany. Only in the Corfu crisis was a glimpse afforded of the nationalistic licence of which Fascism is the embodiment.

The Corfu crisis requires a domestic background. Throughout the early summer of 1923 the Dictator was having considerable difficulty with the dissentient Fascists, who resented the various measures of the Government designed to transform the revolutionary squadre into a civil though partisan militia. The Electoral Reform Bill, as we have seen, gave rise to much discussion, and was not safely through till November. In spite of the profound secrecy in which they were conducted, it was known that the "conversations" with Jugo-Slavia had become highly strained, and seemed likely to fade into silence.

This was the situation when, on 27th August 1923, General

[1] San Severino, p. 210.

[2] Long overcoat of which Giolitti wears a peculiar cut (Villari, p. 280, note).

[3] Quoted Villari, p. 280.

Tellini, two officers, an interpreter, and a chauffeur—part of the Italian delegation on the Commission dispatched by the Ambassadors' Conference to delimit the Greco-Albanian frontier, were murdered on Greek territory in an ambush, not far from Janina. The relations of Italy and Greece had recently been more than usually strained, owing to a violent campaign in the Greek press accusing General Tellini of deliberately favouring Albanian as against Greek claims. In view of this fact, and not without an eye to the acrimonious discussions going on in Italy, Mussolini decided on violent action. A brief note was dispatched to Greece, on 29th August, in the form of an ultimatum, demanding not only ample apologies, but an indemnity of £500,000, to be paid within five days of the receipt of the Italian note. The complicity of the Greek Government in the murder was assumed from the first. From that day to this, in point of mere fact, no evidence of such has ever been forthcoming, nor is it known whether the murderers were Greeks or Albanians. Greece replied by accepting some of the demands and rejecting others, including the demand for £500,000; but just reparation to the families of the victims was promised. At the same time the Greek Government had requested the Council of Ambassadors to appoint a commission of inquiry, whose findings she would accept.

The Greek reply was considered unsatisfactory by Mussolini, who ordered in consequence the immediate occupation of Corfu "as a pledge." The occupation took place on 31st August. Five minutes after the Admiral of the raiding squadron had received a note from the Greek commandant to the effect that the Citadel—which was dismantled—was packed with Greek and Armenian refugees, the Italian warships opened fire, killing sixteen children and four adults among the refugees from Turkish barbarism. There were in all 100 casualties. Italian landing parties followed up the bombardment, and, wearing gas-masks, they proceeded to "storm" the undefended and ungarrisoned Citadel in a series of short rushes. Doubtless they discovered the bodies of the child garrison.

A wave of indignation passed over Europe. Greece appealed to the League, and Lord Robert Cecil asserted the competence of that body to intervene against the threats of Signor Salandra, the Italian representative, that Italy would withdraw from the League sooner than allow a matter affecting her honour to be discussed. M. Poincaré for a moment supported the British stand, but hastened to join Mussolini when the latter gave him to understand that it would be the turn of France next to be put into the dock by the British Government, which had but recently asserted the illegality of the Ruhr occupation. Italy agreed to allow the Ambassadors' Conference to decide the issue that affected its own Commission, and Great Britain, aware of Poincaré's defection, accepted the transference of the question from the League. As a compromise, it was able to insist on the Ambassadors using the Greek reply rather than the Italian ultimatum as the basis of the demands they now formulated. Apologies were to be presented to the representatives of Great Britain, France, and Italy, not Italy alone; honours were to be rendered to the warships of the three Allied Powers, which were to return the Greek salute shot for shot. The Italian ultimatum had demanded that the Greek fleet should render honours to the Italian flag in the presence of the Italian squadron—the Greek fleet flying the Italian flag. A Commission of Inquiry, composed of delegates of Great Britain, France, Italy, and Japan, was to inquire into the outrage. Finally the Greek Government was to deposit £500,000, "to be given in whole or in part to the Italian Government on the decision of the Permanent Court of International Justice at the Hague." Greece accepted this note of 7th September. On the 14th the Ambassadors' Conference had with extreme difficulty persuaded the Italian Government to evacuate Corfu by 27th September "in any circumstances," the Conference reserving to itself the right to decide, on the basis of the report of their Commission of Inquiry, what reparation, if any, Greece owed to Italy. This penalty "may consist, for example, of the payment to Italy of the 50,000,000 lira (£500,000)."

The Commission of Inquiry, given only five days in which to inquire, reported on 22nd September. The British, French, and Japanese had satisfied themselves that the Greek Government had done all in its power to facilitate the search for the murderers. Certain Greek authorities had been negligent, "but the observations made up to this date are not complete or decisive enough to allow the Commissioners to judge whether the Greek Govermennt ought to be held responsible for the cases of negligency revealed, or whether these negligencies are the result of the defective organization of a police administration which disposes of imperfect means of criminal investigation. For the moment the Italian Commissioner, for reasons more particularly of a moral order, inclines rather to the first hypothesis, while the other three Commissioners incline to the second."

The Ambassadors met on 25th September to consider the report. On 26th September the Conference announced that several cases of negligence had been reported, and that in consequence, by way of penalty, it decided that Greece should pay the £500,000 deposited with the Swiss National Bank as security. What had happened? Briefly, Mussolini had instructed the Italian Ambassador to carry off the £500,000, failing which Italy would remain in Corfu. Lord Crewe, the British Ambassador, refused to sign such a document without instructions, which he duly received. In this way Italy was compensated for an act of pure piracy by a fine levied—in the teeth of the evidence—on a poverty-stricken country grappling with the greatest refugee problem in the world.[1] That Italy did evacuate Corfu on 27th September 1923 is perhaps a matter of congratulation in any case, since Mussolini had been observing irrelevantly that Corfu had once belonged to the Venetian Republic.[2]

Unquestionably this terrible display of violence had focused an indignant world public opinion on the Dictator, who obviously realized that he was in a false position, but from a domestic point of view the coup had been a great success, and the nation had supported the Premier.

When the new Chamber assembled Fascismo, with its enormous majority, appeared unassailable. The revision of the Constitution, in the Bismarckian sense already discussed, was anticipated. The Opposition appeared to accept the situation in so far as giving up all thought of other than parliamentary opposition can be called accepting the situation. Most people were content to judge by results, and the results had not been bad.

In a somewhat tense atmosphere the Matteotti murder of 6th June 1924 exploded like a bomb. This able and moderate Socialist leader had not spared the Fascist administration; he was believed to be in possession of damaging information. He was kidnapped in broad daylight outside his home and borne away in a motor. Many weeks later his body was found trampled naked into muddy ground with a file through the heart. Within a few days it became certain that men of the

[1] See Glasgow, "The Janina Murders and the Occupation of Corfu," *Contemporary Review*, Oct. 1923, and Anglo-Hellenic League Publication, No. 53.

[2] Matteotti, "The Fascisti Exposed," p. 54.

highest influence in the Fascist party were implicated, and a wave of horror and indignation swept over Italy. The Premier did not shrink from action. Caesare Rossi, one of the heroes of Fascism, and Aldo Finzi, Under-Secretary to the Ministry of the Interior, were arrested and a searching enquiry instituted. The future trial hangs like a great cloud on the horizon.

Yet, within a short time, it became obvious that the Premier was not prepared to break completely with the extremists. To do so would have spelt an abandonment of the "Revolution." The long-suspended Press decree was issued and put into force. It is widely regarded as a flat violation of the constitution which guarantees liberty of the Press. Though it has been used against violent Fascist organs with a low circulation, it has proved an invaluable weapon against great Liberal papers like the *Stampa*, which in Milan has a daily circulation of 80,000 as against the 4000 odd of Mussolini's personal organ edited by his brother, the *Popolo d'Italia*."

The Premier had so often promised "normalization" that the Opposition began to demand some signs of it. What was the status of the Fascist militia ? How long would it continue to be a party army. In the end the Opposition withdrew in a body from Parliament, refusing any longer to co-operate in the piecemeal destruction of the constitution. The position is now as uncertain as it ever was, and with the passing of time the Premier seems to be drifting more and more into a position of complete dependence on the party he is unable to control. The violence of the language with which he alternately offers the olive branch, brandished as a club, to the Opposition "on the Aventine," or threatens, as in a recent speech at Badia San Salvatore, to make "litter for the barracks of the Fascist militia with the corpses of the chiefs of the Opposition," is not reassuring.[1] When the *Stampa* ventured to comment on these words to the effect that they made co-operation with Fascismo impossible, since they showed "that the leader of Fascism has no conception of the possibility of any other means of government than those created by violence and kept up by violence," it was confiscated.

A candid observer is driven to the conclusion that dark clouds overhang the future of Italy because her fortunes are in the hands of a man who has the temperament of a revolutionary. Mussolini is not driven into revolution by facts,

[1] Quoted, *Manchester Guardian Weekly*, 26th September 1924.

revolution constitutes his sole method of action. "It still lies with him whether the medicine of Fascismo is to be a bone-building tonic or merely a useful dose of castor oil." [1]

"He is not profound," said the Minister Drouyn de Lhuys, of Napoleon III., "he is merely a surface that changes rapidly." In view of the extraordinary procession of phases we have observed in the career of Benito Mussolini, the judgment might well have been applied to him. Like Louis Napoleon he is a believer in nationality—his own—but, unlike the Emperor, he does not believe in the *principle* of nationality. For principles he has substituted a belief in force, the heritage of his Socialist revolutionary period, and in the counsels of Machiavelli. He admits that both consent and force are necessary for the maintenance of the State, but in opposition to the Liberalism he so profoundly distrusts, the emphasis he loves to lay, both in speech and action, is upon force.

Commenting on chapter iii. of Machiavelli's Discorsi in an article in the Fascist magazine, *Gerarchia*,[2] he wrote that he endorsed the famous judgment on humanity which can also be found up and down the great Florentine's work: "Of men it may generally be affirmed that they are thankless, fickle, false, studious to avoid danger, greedy of gain, devoted to you while you confer benefits upon them, and ready, as I said before, while the need is remote, to shed their blood, and sacrifice their property, their lives, and their children for you; but when it comes near they turn against you." [3] "If I were asked," wrote Mussolini, "for my judgment on my fellows, I could not in any way soften down the judgment of Machiavelli, I should probably have to make it more severe."

There is a profound political immorality in his attitude to the means required for the supreme end which was also Machiavelli's—the building of a strong nation state. Well might he say at Naples, on the eve of the *coup d'état*, "We play upon every chord of the lyre, from violence to religion, from art to politics." He has disarmed the clerical radicalism of Don Sturzo and the Popolari by taking over that part of their programme acceptable to the Vatican, religious instruction in State schools and the freedom of religious processions Something may be done to increase the stipends of the clergy. The

[1] Coote, "The Fascist Victory and after," art. *The Nineteenth Century*, Oct. 1923.
[2] 24th April, 1924.
[3] Machiavelli, "The Prince," cap. xvii.

man who in 1919 advocated the sequestration of the possessions of religious bodies and the abolition of episcopal revenues, in 1921 discovered that the Vatican was an asset to Italian nationalism: "I maintain that the Imperial and Latin tradition of Rome is represented to-day by Catholicism. If, as Mommsen said thirty years ago, one could not stay in Rome without being impressed by the idea of universality, I both think and maintain that the only universal idea at Rome to-day is that which radiates from the Vatican. I am very disturbed when I see national churches being formed, because I think of the millions and millions of men who will no longer look towards Italy and Rome. For this reason I advance this hypothesis, that if the Vatican should definitely renounce its temporal ambitions—and I think it is already on that road—Italy ought to furnish it with the necessary material help for the schools, churches, hospitals, etc., that a temporal power has at its disposal. Because the increase of Catholicism in the world, the addition of four hundred millions of men who, from all quarters of the globe, look towards Rome, is a source of pride and of special interest to us Italians." [1]

It would be difficult for cynicism to go further.

When, in the summer of 1923, he had surmounted the first crisis in the Fascist party after its attainment of power, he seized the opportunity presented by the assassination of General Tellini and his staff in Greek territory to rally the lately divided Fascists by the occupation of Corfu, and the employment of overwhelming force at a moment's notice against a State whose responsibility, even contingent, is becoming more and more improbable. Greece was unpopular in Italy, an attack on her under any colourable pretext, would enable the nation to experience that unity of national sentiment, which he has set himself to stereotype; it might also and incidentally disarm the critics who were troubling him in the bosom of Fascism itself.

So little does Mussolini believe in the constitution which is the legacy of the heroic and tragic days of 1848, that though he has asserted again and again that the nation is behind him, he declined to consult it until by means of a fantastic electoral law he had rendered the representative system a poor farce. The Opposition, enraged by the Matteotti crime, has now withdrawn from the Chamber, thus rendering all pretence of constitutional government impossible. They will not return,

[1] Speech in Chamber, 21st June 1921; San Severino, pp. 202-3.

they say, until Fascism has ceased to dominate the country through the instrumentality of an enormous party militia, and has made up its mind to restore the Liberal constitution.

Is it possible for one who loves to cut Gordian knots by some dramatic stroke, dictated to him by his impatience and his inexhaustible energy, to cultivate the laborious art of untangling political webs in a parliament of which he will be a leader only so long as a normal election gives him a majority? Probably he desires to return to some form of legality—though certainly and naturally not to the legality of Giolittian Liberalism—but his problem is the same as Cromwell's that he derives all his authority from an extra-legal force. The constitutional idea embodied in the Parliament and the revolution personified in the Fascist militia, cannot continue indefinitely side by side. Yet Fascism is the militia and the militia is Fascism in action. To an increasing extent the nation has set its heart upon the attainment of a normal constitutional existence. The forces against Fascism are still powerful and none more so than the Liberal idea embodied in the constitution and made a sword in the hand of that "son of liberty"—Cavour.

The founder of modern Italy defined the malady that has since his day afflicted her, "Free states cannot endure unless the principle of responsibility be largely diffused through all classes of citizens." A dictatorship such as Mussolini's need not necessarily be incompatible with a firm intention of renovating a system of government that has broken down through just that lack of the sense of responsibility diffused through all classes of the citizens. Dictatorship with him, however, appears an end rather than a means—the pursuit of the impossible task of setting up a state that shall be above class and party; a state, in a word, which shall itself be a party perpetually installed and above all others because able to suppress them.

Yet it would be idle to deny the positive benefits Mussolini has conferred upon Italy. He has given her a greater measure of peace than she has had since the war wrecked the Liberal régime debilitated by Giolitti's "system." He has by a firm and successful foreign policy, following closely on the lines laid down by Giolitti, Nitti, and Sforza (save for the disastrous exception of the Corfu episode), considerably raised Italian prestige throughout Europe. He has solved the interminable Fiume question in favour of Italy and with the consent of Jugoslavia; he has settled in a statesmanlike and skilful way the Jubaland dispute with Great Britain and thus won a valuable extension of Italian Somaliland. He realizes more vividly and in a more practical way than his predecessors the vital need of financial stability and he seems well on the way to achieve it.

He has embarked, with much that is young and vital in Italian life, upon a prodigious adventure in nation-building, involving a new constitution and new organs of public life. He dreams of a Trade Union State where the "corporations" infused with the national idea will co-operate in a harmony of work, discipline, and sacrifice. Though Mussolini seems to have turned his back on the very idea of representative and responsible government, nobly vindicated by Cavour when he proudly wrote: "Thirteen years' experience has convinced me that an honest and energetic minister, who has nothing to fear from revelations of the tribune, and who is not in a humour to allow himself to be intimidated by the violence of extreme parties, can only gain by parliamentary struggles. I never felt so weak as when the Chambers were closed," [1] there is room for hope that his marvellous energy and vivid personality will be converted, by facts that he always respects, to the realization that a dictatorship without national consent is nullified and that such a consent cannot long be wrung from any people with so great a tradition of liberty as the Italian. Let him build new and lasting institutions in which the discontent that produced Fascism can find a satisfaction more abiding than that afforded by the cheap alcohol of a nationalism liable at any moment to lead the nation into some fatal aberration. By such institutions Fascism will be judged; only by such institutions can she teach anything to the world worth learning.

Of the singular man who holds the fortunes of Italy in his hands to-day, it may be said that even if he affects to be actuated by a profound pessimism, the creative activities of his life belie him. Under his touch situations are transformed —he is the apostle of the creative deed. He brings to the service of Italy a love as deep as Garibaldi's, of whom it has been said that "he believed in Italy as the saints believe in God." Stronger than his belief in the precepts of "The Prince" is his vision of a new Italy worthy of her ancient greatness. He will not cease from fighting till life fail him

[1] Cavour to Mme de Circourt, 1860.

or triumph crown his efforts, for of him might have been written the burning words :—

> " Sir, in my heart there was a kind of fighting
> That would not let me sleep : methought I lay
> Worse than the mutines on the bilboes. Rashly ?
> Then praised be rashness for it. Let us know
> Our indiscretion sometimes serves us well
> When our deep plots do pall."

A LIST OF AUTHORITIES

ALAZARD. "Communisme et ' Fascio ' en Italie." (Paris, 1922.)
ASSAN. " La question du contrôle ouvrier en Italie." (Paris, 1922.)
BARNES. " The Basis of Fascism." (Article in *The Edinburgh Review*, July 1924.)
BEALS. " Rome or Death : the Story of Fascism." (John Long, 1923.)
FERRERO. "Four Years of Fascism." (P. S. King & Son, 1924.)
GIOLITTI. " Memoirs of My Life." (Chapman & Dodd, 1923.)
GORGOLINI. " The Fascist Movement in Italian Life." (T. Fisher Unwin, 1923.)
HERRON. " The Revival of Italy." (Allen & Unwin, 1922.)
LÉMONON. " L'Italie d'après guerre, 1914-21." (Paris, 1922.)
MATTEOTTI. " The Fascisti Exposed—A Year of Fascist Domination." (Independent Labour Party Publication Department, 1924.)
MIRTIL. " Et l'Italie." (Paris, 1921.)
MOWRER. "Immortal Italy." (Appleton & Co., 1922.)
PHILLIPS. " The ' Red ' Dragon and Black Shirts." (*Daily Mail*, 1923.)
POR. " Fascism." (The Labour Publishing Company, 1924.)
VILLARI. " The Awakening of Italy." (Methuen & Co., 1924.)

ELEUTHERIOS VENIZELOS

"If the fact be so, why should we sport with it?"

OLIVER CROMWELL.

"Faith, like a jackal, feeds among the tombs, and even from these dead doubts she gathers her most vital hope."

HERMAN MELVILLE.

ELEUTHERIOS VENIZELOS.

ELEUTHERIOS VENIZELOS

ONE afternoon in the autumn of 1899, M. Clemenceau called on the Comtesse de Noailles in Paris. He had just returned from Athens, and from a holiday in the Levant. "Ah, and what are your impressions of Greece?" "Well, Madame, I am not going to talk of the grandeur of the Acropolis, nor do I intend to torment you with a lecture on archæology. I have been to see strange and picturesque lands, among them Crete. You will never guess, though, my most interesting discovery in the island, one more interesting by far than the splendours of the excavations. I will tell you. A young advocate, a M. Venezuelos—Venizelos?—Frankly, I cannot quite recall his name, but the whole of Europe will be speaking of him in a few years."[1] The story is one more proof of M. Clemenceau's penetration, for twelve years were to pass before the life of Venizelos was to become the history of Greece.

The European public has observed Venizelos since 1910—yet the average newspaper reader's impressions are kaleidoscopic and melodramatic rather than coherent; the great Greek has appeared at irregular intervals on the crest of some dramatic event: rescuing the Greek monarchy, and inaugurating a national risorgimento; launching the Balkan League on its brief but meteoric course; appearing and disappearing in his historic struggle with King Constantine; conducting a revolution at Salonika; building up by imperceptible degrees the startling fabric of a new Mediterranean State; swept from power at the most astounding general election of modern times; and emerging in these last days from the retirement of an exile to guide again the destinies of his country at one of the decisive and most tragic moments of her history; and by the sole exercise of his gigantic moral authority against a victorious revolutionary faction, insisting on the surrender of East Thrace, and so making possible the armistice of Mudania and the Lausanne Conference, as the preliminary of an attempt to rebuild the fallen fortunes of the Greeks.

The justification or the condemnation of a statesman must lie in the total tenour of his political life, rather than in the varying aspects in which it may be regarded. To secure this general view we must begin far behind 1910 or even 1898—we must go back to the days of a boyhood and a youth spent in the shadow of Turkish tyranny.

[1] Quoted, S. B. Chester, "Life of Venizelos," p. 5.

Eleutherios Kyriakos Venizelos was born at Mourniés, a village not far from Canea, in Crete, on 23rd August 1864. He was the fourth son of his parents, and as his three brothers had died in infancy, great anxiety was felt for the safety of Eleutherios. For this reason two Mahomedan "hodjas" and two Greek priests prayed ceaselessly for two days before his birth.[1] This anxiety probably prompted the choice of his romantic name, as it certainly did the curious ceremony that was peformed soon after his birth.

The boy was placed on a heap of sawdust by the side of the road, and not far from his home. Some friends of the family, who were in the secret, were concealed a short distance away. After a pause, they proceeded down the road, and expressed due astonishment at discovering the child by the way-side. Picking little Eleutherios up, the friends hurried to his parents, and solemnly explained to them that they had come upon him abandoned on the road. They added that as they knew that M. and Mme Venizelos were childless, they had brought him to them in the hope that perhaps they might choose to adopt the boy. This generous act the father and mother of Eleutherios expressed their intention of doing, and as the child lived and thrived, the neighbours said that unquestionably the device, a local custom to meet these very circumstances, had succeeded, and M. and Mme Venizelos had in this way successfully deflected their evil fortune.[2]

The elder Venizelos, a small merchant member of a family that had emigrated from the Morea after the rebellion of 1770, intended his son to succeed him in his business. For some years, up to the age of eighteen, Eleutherios worked in his father's office, until his remarkable ability attracted the attention of a family friend, M. George Zigomalas, the Greek Consul-General at Canea, who urged the elder Venizelos to send the youth to the University of Athens.[3]

The merchant yielded to the advice of his friend and the enthusiasm and importunity of his son. At Athens, Venizelos, who became an LL.D. in 1887, at the age of twenty-three, and was shortly after called to the Bar, laid the foundations of that profound knowledge of the history and geography of the Near East by the studies he has prosecuted throughout his

[1] Kerofilas, " Eleftherios Venizelos," p. 1.
[2] Chester, " Life of Venizelos," p. 1.
[3] Kerofilas, " Eleftherios Venizelos," p. 5.

later life, a knowledge that was to constitute him the formidable foe of hostile experts at Paris in 1919 and 1920.

The political aspiration for liberation from the Turkish yoke and union with Greece was traditional in his family. The elder Venizelos took part in the great rebellion of 1866, and had been compelled to fly with his family to the Greek islands, where he spent some years (until he was amnestied in 1872), during which he acquired Greek nationality, a circumstance that his son was in after years to find valuable.

At Athens, Venizelos consolidated his boyish faith by his studies, and formed those wide views of the destiny of Greece to which he has dedicated his life. The idea of Hellenism, the ultimate liberation of all the Greek communities of Turkey that could be united in a single Ægean State, has been his inspiration from the beginning, and where he differs from his political opponents of later years is that the aspiration of every generous-hearted Greek youth has been the life-long vision of this man of genius, who has worked always in terms of the larger world of unredeemed Hellenism, rather than for the "quiet time" that seems the *summum bonum* of most old politicians.

Venizelos returned in 1887, and for two years practised as a barrister in Canea, where he attracted great attention by the logical brilliance of his cases. At the same time he began to take part in local politics, and was elected a deputy to the Cretan Assembly in 1889, in time to take part in an insurrection, during which he had to fly to Athens.

During the nineteenth century Crete was the Turkish Ireland that eventually became an international question. Since 1821, when the Cretans took part in the Greek War of Independence, there had been constant risings, until, under European pressure, the Porte modified a previous semi-liberal experiment by the Pact of Halepa in 1878.

One great cause of trouble had been that the Cretan Moslems were of the same race as the Cretan Christians, and. like all such minorities, were intensely self-conscious. The Pact of Halepa gave the Christians a slight advantage. There was to be an annual assembly consisting of 49 Christians and 31 Moslems, freedom of the Press was conceded, and Greek was to be the official language of the law courts and the legislature. The provision that half the surplus revenue was to be spent on the roads and harbours of Crete promised a remedy to the complete neglect of the centuries of Turkish rule.

In 1889, after the rising to which I have alluded, a firman was issued repealing the Pact of Halepa and reducing the numbers of the Assembly and the proportion between Christian and Moslem. After the usual union with Greece had been proclaimed by the insurgents, a pacification was arranged by the Powers, and the Sultan appointed a Christian governor as an experiment. The discontent, however, continued, as the Christians sighed for the Pact of Halepa, and the Moslems resented the Christian governor.[1]

From 1889 to 1896 Venizelos was active in political life, endeavouring to construct a truly national Opposition to Turkish power. He had become leader of the Liberal party soon after 1889, when his maiden speech had been a protest against the accepted habit of forcibly ejecting the Opposition from the Assembly after a successful election! " A party," he said, " should not be founded solely on numerical strength, but it also needs moral principles, without which it cannot do useful work or inspire confidence." [2] Such doctrines were startlingly paradoxical in the Cretan Assembly of those days.

In 1896, the stringent repressive measures of the Turkish Government against a further outbreak, in which Venizelos took an active part, caused such an exodus of Cretans to Greece, where national feeling rose to a sympathetic fever heat, that the British Government intervened and brought pressure to bear at Constantinople for a restoration of the Pact of Halepa. But the Christians were no longer satisfied with the privileges of 1878; they clamoured for union with Greece, which the Powers were determined to prevent at all costs.

It is at this point that we first catch a glimpse of M. Venizelos, not as a successful barrister nor as a straight shot among the Cretan hills, but as an imaginative statesman seeing an opportunity for a positive half-step forward. M. Caclamanos, then editor of the *Asty*, now Greek minister in London, tells the story :—

" I was young, very young for the editor of a newspaper. The Cretan question had entered a new and acute phase. The concert of Powers suggested a hybrid solution, viz., a return to the famous Pact of Halepa. Greek hopes and aspirations were once more frustrated. We carried on a most violent campaign, without respite or indulgence, against the Government. We demanded union with the mother country.

[1] Miller, " A History of the Greek People," pp. 103-4.
[2] Kerofilas, " Eleftherios Venizelos," p. 7.

The Greek Government was annoyed. . . . Ministers . . . had vainly interceded with me. The King himself had delegated one of his aides-de-camp to expostulate, but my staff and I remained immovable.

"On a certain evening, one of the active leaders of the Cretan revolution was announced. It was M. Venizelos. . . . At the moment I was writing an article. The Cretan leader was a man I admired both for his indomitable courage and gallantry, but I did not accept him as a source of inspiration for my article, which I continued to write. M. Venizelos, with eyes glittering behind his professorial spectacles, seated himself before me. He had a small, dark beard; he was wearing a soft collar, a black suit, and Cretan boots coming to his knees. His physiognomy, the expression of his remarkable eyes, and especially his smile—that mysterious smile which Greek journalists have humorously compared to the smile of Leonardo's Gioconda—had surprised me. But he had begun to speak. I put down my pen. A vague uneasiness had changed swiftly into a vivid interest. I listened to this Cretan chief, this 'highlander,' as I had thought him to be, only to learn new lessons in history, politics, and diplomacy. During half an hour he held my closest attention by his wonderful eloquence. Without coming into collision with my opinions, he asserted that although the solution involved by the revival of the Pact of Halepa was less than complete, it was in the interest of small nations not to oppose the policy prescribed by the Powers. In other words, that the little States must adapt themselves to circumstances, and endeavour to realize their national aspirations by degrees. He alluded to Cavour and Italy. He prophesied an epoch when the world, uplifted by a sense of the iniquity of despotism, would rise for the realization of a democratic ideal, the accomplishment of the wish of the people. He made some pleasant remarks about my paper, discreetly adding that its energies might be utilized to greater advantage in the future.

"I confess that M. Venizelos charmed and subjugated me. Profound and instinctive admiration rose within me. It seemed that a new star was about to show itself and shed a brilliant light on the Hellenes. I felt somewhat in the same frame of mind as an astronomer who detects a new and luminous body in the heavens.

"Before M. Venizelos left me, I explained some of my sensations to him. 'Monsieur,' I said, 'there is only one man with the power to make me alter my opinion. You are that man.'

"On the following day, an article which was considered very clever appeared in my journal. This article was nothing in reality but a summary of M. Venizelos's speech to me in my office. It put an end to the campaign of the *Asty*.

"My sudden conversion was attributed to various influences. No one, however, knew anything of my interview of the previous day, nor did anyone guess the real cause of my changed policy." [1]

But the affairs of Crete remained in a confused condition; feeling between Christian and Moslem mounted higher every day. On 4th February 1897 Venizelos, returning from an electoral campaign in the country, arrived on the heights overlooking the city. In his own words: "I saw Canea in flames; it had been set on fire by the Mussulmans, who had thus started the great revolt." [2] The Cretan insurrection of 1896 at once revived in strength. Venizelos assumed the leadership of a Cretan Christian Defence Force, and established himself on the Akrotiri, or "Peninsula," that separates Canea from the famous Suda Bay.

The allied Admirals of the European fleet that now arrived in Suda Bay had been sent with the usual instructions; the *status quo*, in other words, Turkish sovereignty, was to be maintained pending the further decisions of the Powers. As a first step, an ultimatum was served on Venizelos, demanding the hauling down of the Greek flag on Akrotiri. He refused firmly, and on 21st February 1897 the allied fleet began the bombardment that continued till the Greek flag had been carried away by a shell. It is both amusing and significant that the future Premier decided that, as he was quite likely to interview the English Admiral shortly, the situation demanded that he should devote his spare time to the study of English. Accordingly, while the English and allied warships were taking leisurely aim at the Greek flag and watering his camp with occasional shells, Venizelos began his first English exercises.

From the first he took up an attitude of intransigence on the question of union with Greece. Yet his was not the obstinacy of a fanatic leader, even in those early days, when he was passing through the apprenticeship of a statesman. His interview with a British naval officer sent by the Admirals

[1] Quoted Chester, "Life of Venizelos," pp. 27-9.
[2] *Ibid.*, p. 35.

to persuade him to surrender illuminates with a flash of light both the motives of the great insurgent, and, as in a parable, the secret of the Eastern Question since then. The officer found Venizelos, a quiet, reasonable young man, ready to see the difficulties of the Powers in dealing with Turkey, but equally emphatic that he would not sacrifice Crete on the altar of their convenience. "Your Foreign Office," he said, "is in a tight place, and you can go as slow as you like with the Sublime Porte. Make a feint of coercing us if you feel you have to. I shall restrain my men. But it must be only a feint. If your soldiers and mariners, for whatever reason, go beyond a certain line I shall indicate to you, we shall open fire. Then you will be up against a guerilla war that will not pay, and that will not help you a bit with your diplomatic game at Constantinople." "Why do you not put yourselves in our hands?" asked the officer; "you know we have already freed Crete, all except in name, and if you work with the Powers, your day will come more quickly than by forcing our hand and compelling us to oppose you." The reply of Venizelos showed that he had grasped the only way of escape from the Turkish curse, the lesson taught to the oppressed nationalities by a century of European diplomatic impotence: "European policy is invariably the maintenance of the *status quo*, and you will do nothing for the subject races unless we, by taking the initiative, make you realize that helping us against the Turks is the lesser of two evils." The comment of the envoy is characteristic and unanswerable: "Damn it all, the beggar is right!" he wrote, "and I hope we shan't have to shoot him." [1]

As a reply to the open Greek co-operation with the Cretan insurgents, Turkey took the bull by the horns by declaring war on Greece on 17th April 1897—the allied fleet having already proclaimed the blockade of Crete until the insurgents should express their willingness to accept "autonomy" under Turkish suzerainty. The crushing defeat of the Greeks under the Crown Prince Constantine in May, and the occupation of Thessaly, compelled Greece to sue for peace, and at the same time divided the Cretans into two parties, the Autonomists, who wanted to accept the allied terms, and the "Unionists," under Venizelos, who still held out on Akrotiri. In August he was elected president of the insurgent committee against the Autonomists, but resigned in October, when the Cretan Assembly

[1] Quoted H. A. Gibbons, "Venizelos," pp. 26-7.

decided for the Admirals' programme. But he would not yield his position on the Akrotiri. To accept autonomy, he had declared in the Assembly, was to betray both Crete and Greece: "I shall never let history," he cried, "accuse me of being a traitor. For what other name can be given to a man who would accept autonomy? Have you forgotten that it is on your account that the mother country is involved in an unfortunate war? Have you forgotten the heavy sacrifices that she has made in order to come to your help? Now that she is suffering in the hour of trial, shall we be so base as to betray her, forget her, and abandon her? Neither I nor the volunteers at Akrotiri wish to become traitors." [1] At these stinging words the Assembly broke into wild disorder. A deputy, drawing a knife, rushed upon Venizelos as he stood by the table: his life was saved only by the intervention of a moderate member, who tripped the would-be assassin. But for some time he went in danger.[2] Before he made his way back to his camp on the Akrotiri, the house in which he was staying was set on fire by a howling mob—he escaped after a speech in which he denounced his assailants as traitors to Hellas! [3] Of these Akrotiri days he said later, "that 1897 was one of those critical moments when the voluntary compromising of a principle would have been more disastrous than failure to secure its triumph by holding out as long as was humanly possible." [4]

His attitude seems curious in view of his readiness, as has already been indicated, to accept even the Pact of Halepa in 1896; but, apart from the question of honour, the events of February 1897 had convinced him that even if Crete could not secure union, she should not give up the claim until a much more generous measure of autonomy was granted than that conceded by the Pact. First and foremost in his demands he placed the withdrawal of all Turkish troops from the island, without exception, as the preliminary of all discussion.

Facts converted the Powers to this point of view. On 3rd September 1898, a detachment of British bluejackets were massacred by the fanatical Moslems of Candia. At once the attitude of the Powers stiffened. On 4th November, they announced that they were taking over Crete. English, French, Russian, and Italian forces landed at various points, and ordered the Turks out. The last Turkish troops left on 25th

[1] Kerofilas, "Eleftherios Venizelos—His Life and Work," p. 22.
[2] H. A. Gibbons, "Venizelos," p. 31.
[3] *Ibid.*, p. 32.
[4] *Ibid.*, p. 29.

November 1898. Meanwhile the Powers had offered the High Commissionership of Crete to Prince George of Greece, the younger son of the King. The new High Commissioner landed in December. On 21st December, Turkish effective sovereignty had ended, and Venizelos and the intransigent Unionists gave in their adhesion to the new Government that the Powers had commissioned the Prince to construct.

In the events that preceded and those that followed the installation of Prince George, we must bear in mind that Venizelos throughout kept the thought of union with the kingdom constantly before him. Whenever we find him advocating autonomy, or Cretan independence, or anything else, it is always as a move towards a better position whence to effect union. He became Councillor of Justice in the new Government, and in that capacity helped to draft the Constitution. The Prince was left with considerable powers. He was to be assisted by five Councillors appointed by himself, and was entitled to nominate ten members of the elective Chamber that met annually and was renewed biennially. The naturally autocratic disposition of the Prince was given too much scope in the Constitution, and here we find the explanation of the revolution of 1905.

Prince George could not stand his masterful Minister for long, and Venizelos became increasingly estranged by the dictatorial tendencies of the Prince. In the spring of 1901 the clash of these two temperaments was precipitated by a startling speech of Venizelos, in which he advocated the erection of Crete into an independent principality. He had several motives for this sudden *volte-face*. He felt that if Crete could get her independent status recognized by the Powers, the international forces stationed in the island would have to be withdrawn. Experience had taught him that such a force was the chief obstacle to union. It had also come to his ears (and was indeed sufficiently obvious) that King George[1] and his son were working for a settlement by which Crete would be constituted a viceroyalty under one of the Greek princes. Venizelos had not fought the Turks in order to create an appanage in Crete for the Greek Royal Family, hence, if union and nothing but union was the goal, the best way to counter Prince George's plans would be the advocacy of an independent Crete. The answer of the enraged Prince was

[1] King George of Greece, father of Prince George, the High Commissioner of Crete.

the immediate dismissal of Venizelos, who from 1901-5 was leader of the Liberal opposition to the increasing autocracy of the Government.[1]

The personality of Prince George became the centre of political interest, and, realizing the precariousness of his position with Venizelos in opposition, he took to active participation in the elections, undertaking canvassing tours in the country on behalf of his candidates, on one occasion in the august company of the Archbishop. Posts in the Government service were distributed and manufactured for the benefit of the subservient. In 1903, he used his discretionary power to suspend the liberty of the Press. Criticisms, made even in private letters, of the mal-administration of Crete were punished by imprisonment. He elevated his private secretary, one Papadiamantopoulos, into chief minister. His self-confidence increased with time until one day, in March 1905, the Prince and the Powers were startled by the news that Venizelos had once more taken to the hills.

" One fine March evening . . . a tall, thin man of about forty, with a sparse brown beard, was walking towards Canea by the coast road which leads from the suburb of Halepa to the capital.

" At this time of year it is already spring in the island of Minos, and the white villas of the suburb are half-hidden in greenery. High walls surround them, but yet not so high that they prevent the passer-by from catching glimpses of gay flower-beds. . . . In this little corner of an earthly paradise, Prince George's palace, the consulates, and dwellings of the more wealthy Cretans are hidden among the winding paths. The man of whom we are speaking was just going down the steep hill at the bottom of which stands the building of the International Club, facing seawards, when a closed landau passed him going in the same direction. Thinking the carriage was empty the man hailed it, and the coachman, although he had a fare, stopped as soon as he recognized the stranger.

" The carriage door was opened, and the Prince's private secretary put his head out. He also recognized, or rather guessed, who the stranger was in the half-light and . . . he hurriedly got out in the hope of a private conversation, which, under the critical circumstances, would, he thought, be particularly desirable.

[1] Chester, " Life of Venizelos," pp. 81-3.

" But his illusion was short-lived. M. Venizelos (for it was no other than the leader of the Opposition), in a few courteous words, explained his mistake.

" The two opponents bowed coldly, and the private secretary resumed his drive towards Canea, while Venizelos, after stopping a few moments at the International Club to see his friends, entered the first vehicle he saw, and was driven into the country, to the village of Mourniès, at the entrance to the deep gorge which leads by impossible goat-paths to the impregnable position of Therisso. The revolution of 1905 had begun." [1]

At Therisso, a village a few miles from his birthplace Mourniès, a revolutionary committee proclaimed the political union of Crete and Greece.

As a political move it was a master-stroke. Had Venizelos taken to the hills in the name of Liberal reform and as an opponent of the autocratic methods of the High Commissioner, it is improbable that he would have roused the country or seriously alarmed the Powers. But by identifying the cause of Liberal reform with the most passionate aspirations of the people he converted a local parliamentary issue into a first-class European question ; he created a moral vacuum round Prince George to such an extent that the Cretans seemed actually to forget him in rallying round the old flag once more nailed to the mast by the defender of the Akrotiri. At the same time, the confidence of the Powers in the competence of Prince George was fatally shaken.

In August 1905, the Powers, whose fleets had arrived as usual in Suda Bay, proclaimed martial law and undertook a punitive expedition into the interior. At the same time, they appointed a commission to suggest internal reform.

On 15th November 1905, after lengthy negotiations, Venizelos surrendered to the forces of the Powers and a general amnesty was proclaimed. Yet, though the Powers were still resolute to prevent the union, which they feared would lead to another Greco-Turkish war, the insurgents of Therisso had convinced them that an autocracy would not work in Crete. Prince George, feeling himself more and more neglected and ignored by the Commissioners, resigned his office in May 1906.

In July, Mr Alexander Zaimis was appointed High Com-

[1] Kerofilas, " Eleftherios Venizelos," pp. 38-40, quoting Van den Brule, " L'Orient Hellénique."

missioner; a man of Liberal sentiments, who at once gave his confidence to Venizelos. The new regime began well. Prince George had been bundled out, but the European detachments remained. The insurgent and diplomat of Therisso had taken one more patient step forward. But the Greek Royal Family had been bitterly offended. Prince George devoted himself to the vilification of Venizelos (during the Therisso crisis he had actually persuaded the Cretan Bishops to excommunicate the rebel!) and to those days we may trace back the ultimate suspicion of King Constantine for the opponent of his brother;[1] the tragic "malaise" that underlay what was certainly at one time a genuine admiration for his great Prime Minister, yet ten years later was to emerge at a tragic dividing of the ways.

The next stage in the Cretan story brings us to 1908. The Cretans, after the Bosnia-Herzegovina crisis and the proclamation of Bulgarian independence of Turkish suzerainty, seized the opportunity of declaring again in favour of union. The Assembly, under the leadership of Venizelos, declared, in the absence of M. Zaimis, the office of High Commissioner abolished. A Coalition Government was set up with Venizelos as Prime Minister, which announced its intention of holding the island for the King until the moment for union should come.[2] Europe was faced with the old problem, and again the allied fleet appeared in Suda Bay.

Meanwhile, the Cretan action had precipitated a fresh crisis in Greco-Turkish relations. The Sultan demanded an immediate disavowal of the Cretans. Greece was divided between a peace and a war party. In the end, the Prime Minister Theotokis, supported by Rhallis, assured the Powers and Turkey that he had "nothing to do" with Crete. The dilemma for Theotokis was complete. The Cretans had announced that if the Greek Parliament were dissolved, the Cretan Assembly would follow suit, and the elected deputies would present themselves in Athens as members of the Greek Chamber. Turkey, on the other hand, vehemently announced she would at once declare war if the Cretan deputies were admitted.

The Powers once again cut the Gordian knot at Canea by landing detachments and hauling down the Greek flag. But, from the Cretan point of view, one more step had been taken

[1] Miller, "A History of the Greek People," p. 113.
[2] Chester, "Life of Venizelos," pp. 124-5.

towards union with the final withdrawal of the International forces on 26th July 1909.[1]

The diplomatic humiliation of Greece was too much for the long discontented army, and on 28th August took place the *coup d'état* of the Military League at Athens, and King George found himself face to face with a dictatorship. The League was not anti-monarchical, but it demanded a drastic reorganization of the army, and a thorough reform of the political system. Its members lacked experience and administrative capacity—if the revolutionary movement was not to fail the League must find some one to whom it could confidently surrender its powers. The old politicians were waiting in the background for what they felt would be the inevitable failure of the League—yet who could tell if the fall of the League would not also prove the fall of the monarchy?

In this extremity the League, itself revolutionary, turned to the great Cretan revolutionary on whom all Greek eyes were at the moment fixed.

On 10th January 1910, Venizelos arrived in Athens and gave his advice to the King. He was, at the moment, the only man capable of intervening between King George and the League. He asked the King to copy the Cretan remedy and summon a National Assembly with a mandate to revise the constitution. Both the King and Theotokis feared that a National Assembly would call the monarchy in question. The answer was unhesitating: "Sire, on the day the National Assembly meets the Military League will be dissolved." Evidently the Cretan possessed the confidence of the hated League. "I hope Venizelos will soon be hanged from the mast of a battleship," was the private comment of the King.[2]

However, the National Assembly was convoked, and after he had suggested a "carry on" ministry to restore normal conditions and prepare for the Assembly, Venizelos returned to Crete as President of the Executive Committee. His programme was clear: "I shall strive for the recognition of Greek annexation, for the preservation of order, for the protection of the Mahommedans and for the maintenance of the sympathy and goodwill of the protecting Powers, coupled with reforms in our administration." It was evident that everything pointed to Venizelos as the future Premier of Greece—he was a candidate for the Greek National Assembly; his father's naturalization

[1] "Annual Register," 1909, p. 339.
[2] Chester, "Life of Venizelos," p. 129.

as a citizen of the kingdom was of use to him. Athens was agog, but, like Napoleon, he knew the power of the enigmatic. His hands were already on the reins of power—he all but controlled the League; his election to the Assembly was a certainty and the "old parliamentary hands" faced with horror the prospect of the man from nowhere rising to power at a bound over the heads of the laborious under-Secretaries who had toiled up the painful hierarchies of bureaucracy.

In August, Venizelos left Crete for a holiday in Western Europe, where he saw many ministers and persons of interest and influence. The impression he made on them was enthusiastically favourable. He could count on the benevolent support of the Powers.

The National Assembly was opened by the King on 14th September 1910. It consisted of 358 members, of whom 190 belonged to the Coalition party formed by M. Theotokis and M. Rhallis. Ten Socialists appeared for the first time, and there was a group of 45 Thessalian deputies who formed an agrarian party, pledged to the gradual expropriation of the feudal Thessalian landowners in the interests of the cultivators. There remained a body of 80 Independent deputies who represented the national reaction against the corrupt and incompetent record of the older parties. Their chief demand was that the Chamber should constitute itself a Constituent and not a "Revisionist" Assembly. On 16th September they caused a riot in the Chamber by endeavouring to prevent the majority from taking the oath prescribed by the Constitution instead of taking it "as a constituent body deriving its mandate from the sovereign people." Order was restored only on the appearance of a body of troops with fixed bayonets. As a result of these quarrels between the Independents and the other parties, no work of any kind was done by the Assembly for several weeks.[1]

Venizelos had been elected to the National Assembly—his Greek citizenship disarmed the indignation of Turkey, determined at all costs to prevent Cretan deputies from sitting in the Greek Chamber. The movement in Greece in his favour steadily increased. Venizelos must come to Athens to be ready to take over the Premiership, which the nation clamoured should be his. A deputation of Members of Parliament and notabilities set sail from Greece to take him back to Athens. He had already placed his resignation of the Cretan

[1] "Annual Register," 1910, p. 350.

Presidency of the Council in the hands of the Assembly. The Cretans had made up their minds to lose him, though they looked forward with apprehension as well as hope to the future. The supreme ability of the man had impressed itself upon the fierce and excitable temperament of his fellow Cretans. That genial and gracious personality had wound itself into their hearts. They knew that every hour of his day was theirs, and that the indefatigable minister, the ubiquitous organizer, the generous fighter, was the friend of the humblest of them.

September 17th, 1910, was the day fixed for the departure of the Greek deputation with their guest. A huge farewell banquet was given and the citizens attended. Speeches were delivered dwelling on the past and the fine team work that had pulled that gallant island through, and then it came to Venizelos to reply. He rose to speak and had spent much thought on preparing what he intended to tell the Cretans. He was going to dwell on the future, the realization of their dearest hopes. He was going to promise that union, if it could not be realized from Crete, would be brought about from Greece, and then he intended to ask them to lift their eyes to horizons still more distant, and to remember that Crete and Greece were but parts of the great world of Hellenism, and to dedicate themselves anew to the splendid mission of liberation. As he looked round on the citizens of Canea, many of whom were weeping at the prospect of losing that strong arm and great heart in many a remembered fight, the words he had prepared failed him. He could only say, " My dear fellow citizens "—but it was enough, and so the great adventurer embarked upon his Odyssey.[1]

On 18th September 1910 a vast concourse met him at the Piræus and escorted him to his hotel. From the balcony he addressed the excited crowd. Greece needed reform throughout. There must be a national effort, a " risorgimento " against the corrupt and incompetent past. In order to preserve the continuity of the State and ensure constitutional reform, the National Assembly must be revisionist, not constituent. In other words, the fundamental institution of Greece, the monarchy, must not be discussed. At this point the crowd interrupted with repeated cries of " Constituent! Constituent! " " Revisionist," replied Venizelos. " Constituent," repeated the crowd, with rising excitement. Every

[1] Kerofilas, " Eleftherios Venizelos," pp. 60-1.

time they cried, " Constituent ! " Venizelos repeated as clearly and as firmly as before, " The Chamber must be Revisionist." At the end of perhaps ten minutes of this the crowded square was reduced to complete and wondering silence. Those who were present at this historic scene and who had come in any doubt of the real quality of the Cretan, went away satisfied that the man required by the situation had beyond question arrived.

On 18th October, King George requested him to form a Ministry ; and two days later he met the National Assembly. At once it became obvious that the party leaders—all ex-Prime Ministers—were not prepared to give this " new man " the unconditional vote of confidence he demanded. They resorted to the old Greek parliamentary trick of absenting themselves from the Parliament with their parties, and as the Greek Constitution of 1864 required the presence of half the members of the House as a quorum, this was a favourite device for hanging up business. Venizelos at once resigned. The news of his resignation caused consternation throughout Greece. An indignation meeting of 10,000 people convoked by the University and the Trade Guilds denounced the old political parties and carried a resolution urging the King to maintain Venizelos. On the following day, Venizelos, whose resignation had been refused by the King, appeared in the Chamber and demanded for the Government a vote " expressing the complete and unreserved acquiescence of the Chamber in its declarations." [1] M. Theotokis announced that he was ready " to accord tolerance to the Government." M. Mavromichalis said he would vote against the Government, and M. Rhallis that he would abstain. In the result, the Government received a vote of confidence by 208 to 31.[2]

The superb parliamentary instinct of Venizelos told him that the behaviour of the party " bosses," in withholding a vote of confidence, had finally discredited them in the eyes of the people. It was also clear to him that with such a House it would be impossible to carry any really far-reaching measures. He therefore converted the King to his views, and on 25th October launched one of the most audacious political thunderbolts of modern history in the form of a decree dissolving the National Assembly and ordering new elections.

Between the dissolution and the elections in December he conducted a Midlothian campaign throughout Greece. He

[1] " Annual Register," 1910, p. 351. [2] *Ibid.*, p. 351.

indicted the historic parties before the nation and urged it to sweep them out of existence. On the eve of the elections, fixed for 11th December 1910, he issued an address to the people. It struck a new note in Greek politics: "I do not promise that the Government now or in the future will inaugurate the Golden Age: since the illness has been grave, the cure will be long; what I do promise is that the cure shall be serious and radical. The first duty of a politician is to know how to sacrifice his personal interests and those of his party to the general interest of the Fatherland. It is equally his duty always to tell the truth to great and small alike without concerning himself about the discontent his words may cause. Leaders must set the example of absolute submission to the laws, otherwise how can they compel respect for them on the part of all citizens? . . . The statesman ought to seek power not as an end, but as the means of realizing an elevated and patriotic goal. He will not hesitate, then, to relinquish it, if his maintenance at the head of the Government has to be purchased by the abandonment of his programme." [1]

In a speech from the balcony of his hotel, he pointed out that the maladministration of the older parties had led to the existing debilitation in Greek finances. The result of their mismanagement had been the Revolution of 1909. The new Revisionist Assembly need not confine itself to those clauses in the Constitution indicated by the dissolved Chamber. The King had no objection to the extension of its reforming activities, provided the fundamental institutions were left untouched. What was wanted was the extinction of the mode of government existing before the Revolution. As for the dynasty, he declared that in all Constitutional countries the Crown played a most important part in curbing political faction. Unfortunately, in Greece, the Crown had not fulfilled its duty in this respect, though rooted in the affections of the nation. "He hoped the Crown would henceforth play a more energetic part in the Government." For himself, he had left Crete, not as the leader of a party, but as the champion of the great cause of Hellenic regeneration.[2]

There is a grim, unconscious irony in this reference to the part he hoped the Crown would in future play in Greek political life. The old King knew his Greece even better than M.

[1] "La Politique de la Grèce," preface by Joseph Reinach, pp. 7-8.
[2] "Annual Register," 1910, p. 352.

Venizelos, and on this question he was wiser than his great minister, as events, only too tragic, were to prove.

The answer of the people must have exceeded the expectations of the most enthusiastic Liberal, for in the Revisionist Assembly of January 1911, of 364 deputies, 300 were Venizelists.[1]

The year between the meeting of the Revisionist Assembly and its dissolution on 3rd January 1912 was a year of national reorganization, that may well be called regeneration. I can but briefly indicate the nature of the reforms passed by the Revisionary Assembly. The " spoils " system was abolished, and the civil service made permanent. The quorum in the Chamber was reduced from half to one-fifth. A Council of State was instituted to control the civil service. A thorough reform of the franchise and redistribution of seats took place. The agrarian problem of Thessaly was solved by the abolition of the feudal system that still obtained in that province. The national finances were overhauled by a strong commission that managed to create order out of a traditional chaos. Foreign experts were called in for finance ; a British Naval Mission, under Admiral Mark Kerr, reorganized the navy, and a French Military Mission, the army. Agriculture was placed under a ministry that devoted itself to the spread of scientific methods and knowledge through model farms under European experts. Education was made universal, free, and compulsory. Centres were established all over the country for the free distribution of quinine for a scientific war against malaria. A tremendous programme of road and railway construction was inaugurated. Under the tireless vigilance of the Government the Greek merchant marine and carrying trade began to boom in the Levant. In connection with the agricultural revival and the anti-malarial measures, a programme of marsh-draining was begun. It will be right to add here that these reforms were completed during the period between the second Balkan War and the outbreak of the Great War, 1913-14, by the passing of a series of Acts for employers' liability, sickness, and old age pensions, the prevention of cruelty to animals, and university extension.

The centre of all this tremendous activity that was rapidly bringing Greece into line with the advanced nations of the West was the Prime Minister ; his hand was everywhere, and he found time for everything. He was to be seen at every

[1] " Annual Register," 1910, p. 352.

lecture of importance, he patronized all the efforts of literary and historical societies to spread a knowledge of the Greek classics, and to infuse the new language with the ancient. He attended the Athenian Theatre regularly, and gave the revived drama every encouragement. Working for long periods of time, for eighteen hours a day, without a holiday save that afforded him by the restless and abounding interest he took in every manifestation of the national spirit, he imbued all with whom he came in contact with the splendid and commanding energy that won for this man of forty-seven the devotion and enthusiasm of all that was young and idealistic in the life of Greece. Here is an arresting description of Venizelos in the great days of the national revival.

"In the ante-chamber of Venizelos one meets the queerest visitors, from ministers and generals with whom he regulates the affairs of State, to the lowliest peasant whose crops are not promising, to the woman whose rheumatism does not let her sleep—every one demands a personal interview of Venizelos to state his grievances and his desires. Venizelos must know that Demetrios, whose goat has been stolen, is not pleased with the internal administration. After Demetrios, he must receive the old grandmother who has been waiting for two hours to explain to the Premier that the overcoat which was given to her grandson in the army is somewhat worn, and that Venizelos must write immediately to the military authorities, that they may replace it with one worthy of the physique of her strapping boy.

"Once there came a request from an unhappy husband, who begged Venizelos to lead his wife back to the right path. 'If you, Mr President,' wrote the petitioner, 'would only summon my wife and admonish her, I am sure that she would listen to you, and that she would change her conduct, and so, thanks to you, I should find my lost happiness again.' How, with all his goodwill, does Venizelos find time to occupy himself with the affairs of Greece, the goat of Demetrios, the vegetables of the peasants, the grandson's overcoat, and the unfaithful wife? For he does do so!" [1]

The width of his outlook is proved by the fact that he did not become the tool of any class. Though Venizelos was backed by manufacturers and shippers and the wealthiest Greeks, a leading Socialist, commenting on his programme, declared: "The hopes of a million struggling, despised, and

[1] H. A. Gibbons, "Venizelos," p. 163, quoting Dr Antonios P. Savvidis.

wronged working men and women are centred in the present Government."[1]

But at the very moment when his whole energy was apparently focused on internal reconstruction, Venizelos was inaugurating the negotiations which led up to the most famous and dramatic diplomatic revolution of modern times—the Balkan League.

A Balkan alliance against Turkey, with the object of compelling the Porte to recognize the rights of its Christian populations in Europe to some form of local self-government, had often been mooted before, but chronic racial antagonisms between Bulgar, Serb, and Greek had rendered all previous negotiations abortive.

The Turkey of Abdul Hamid had exploited these antagonisms and allowed the pot to boil with only an occasional stir of the bayonet, but the new Turkey of the up-to-date revolutionists of 1909 decided to inaugurate a policy of "Turkey for the Turks," in other words, a wave of artificial Turkification swept over the European provinces, and the subject Christian races were brought closer together by the common menace which threatened each one with a loss of all the privileges and exemptions Europe had from time to time been able to secure for them.

In May 1911, Venizelos sent indirectly through Mr Bourchier, the famous *Times* correspondent in Sofia, a proposal for a Græco-Bulgarian defensive alliance, having for its object the protection of the Macedonian Christian population and the maintenance of their various privileges.[2] These negotiations were conducted in profound secrecy, M. Gueshoff, the Bulgarian Premier, and Venizelos ciphering and deciphering their own dispatches. The Greek offer was well received, but no treaty was concluded until the parallel Serbo-Bulgarian negotiations, initiated by Russia, had culminated in a treaty in March 1912.

Obviously Venizelos at this time regarded the prospect of a war with Turkey—inevitable sooner or later if the intolerable condition of Macedonia remained unchanged—with equanimity, convinced as he was of the radical change for the better in the moral discipline and equipment of the Greek army effected under the guidance of the French Military Mission.

[1] Quoted Dr E. J. Dillon, *Contemporary Review*, Jan. 1911.
[2] Gueshoff, "The Balkan League," pp. 36-7.

During the lull in the negotiations with Bulgaria he seems to have contemplated seizing the opportunity afforded by the Turco-Italian war, which broke out in October 1911, and was followed by the occupation of Tripoli. He offered to join the Italians in the war against Turkey, and proposed to invade Macedonia with 150,000 men. "As it was not to our interests at the time, however," writes Giolitti, "to bring the Turkish question to a head, we not only refused the offer, but even advised Venizelos to be prudent and keep the peace."[1] The naïve assumption behind these words, that a Great Power, in pursuance of economic interests and a desire to make a splash in the Mediterranean big enough to vindicate Italian prestige against France in Morocco and Great Britain in Egypt, is at liberty to attack a State in time of profound peace and almost at a moment's notice, while, at the same time, counselling a small Power "to keep the peace" in face of the intolerable regime to which its nationals were being submitted by its ancient tyrant just beyond its border,—such an assumption is evidence of the "light heart" with which Signor Giolitti inaugurated the overture to the great war.

In October 1911, Turkey, probably influenced by panic at the Italian aggression, suddenly mobilized against Bulgaria. Venizelos seized the occasion to renew his overtures for an alliance by instructing M. Panas, the Greek minister in Sofia, to call on M. Gueshoff and announce that if Bulgaria would "intervene in the event of a Turkish aggression on Greece he was authorized by his Government to declare that Greece, in her turn, will fight should Bulgaria be attacked by Turkey."[2]

In view of the critical position in which Bulgaria found herself this assurance from Greece, coming as it did before negotiations with Serbia had been concluded by a definite alliance, and at a moment when it was far from certain that any agreement would be reached,[3] was, as M. Gueshoff saw, of capital importance. He was authorized by the King and Cabinet to reply that Bulgaria would assist Greece in a war with Turkey "on conditions which must be specified in a defensive treaty."

Not until 27th April 1912 (after the conclusion of the Serbo-Bulgarian alliance) were negotiations for an alliance between Greece and Bulgaria taken up in earnest. At once

[1] Giolitti, "Memoirs of my Life," pp. 356-7.
[2] Gueshoff, "The Balkan League," pp. 37-8.
[3] Nekludoff, "Diplomatic Reminiscences."

it became apparent that there were grave differences between the Greek and Bulgarian attitude to the future status of Macedonia. M. Gueshoff frankly stood for "autonomy" with equal rights for all nationalities. Greece regarded Macedonian "autonomy" as a stage in the process of absorption into Bulgaria, and declined to accept M. Gueshoff's formula. From the Greek point of view the only solution of the Macedonian question was partition, but, as we shall see, partition was not discussed. M. Gueshoff made it clear that Bulgaria would not sign a treaty "which did not at least recognize an obligation to fight for those rights of the Christians of Turkey which were based on treaties."[1] After a long silence Venizelos consented to the following formula which was inserted in the preamble of the treaty: "Bearing in mind that the peaceable existence of the various nationalities in Turkey, based on real and genuine political equality and on the respect of all the rights of the Christian nationalities in the Empire, whether they derive from treaties or have been conceded to them in a different way, constitutes an indispensable condition for the consolidation of peace in the East, . . . etc."[2] The remaining clauses of the treaty briefly provide for mutual help in case of war. Obviously Gueshoff still felt that a pacific solution was possible along lines of autonomy for Macedonia within the Turkish Empire. Venizelos also believed that Turkey, confronted by a Balkan League, could be compelled to put her house in order without war. Nevertheless, he must have faced the prospect of war, since he had, as we have seen, offered the Greek alliance to Italy.

He was prepared for war; and the thorough reform of the Greek army he had inaugurated, and the conviction that it was an effective fighting force, had finally convinced the Bulgarians that the Greek alliance was worth having. Since he was prepared for war, where, as his opponents in Greece afterwards asked, are the obvious provisions for an eventual division of the spoils? The Serbs and Bulgars had minutely delineated their future frontiers. Why had Greece neglected this elementary precaution and not even staked out a claim? The treaty is the measure of the diplomatic genius of Venizelos. For him the *sine qua non* of a successful war against Turkey

[1] Gueshoff, "The Balkan League," p. 39.

[2] Text of Treaty Gueshoff, Appendix vii (English); French text, "History of the Eastern Question," F. O. Handbooks, No. 15, Appendix xiii.

was the possession of Salonika and its hinterland. If war broke out, he believed the Greek army could occupy Salonika before either the Bulgars or the Serbs. The *fait accompli* would, he hoped, lead to an amicable agreement, but he knew that the most powerful political parties in Bulgaria (whatever M. Gueshoff might be ready to concede) were determined to secure Salonika, the chief port of Macedonia, for the Bulgaria that the Russians had sketched at the Treaty of San Stefano in 1877,—the "Great Bulgaria," that had been so ruthlessly truncated by the Powers at the Congress of Berlin. To mention Salonika would wreck the negotiations and hopelessly antagonize the ally without whom Greece could not hope to defeat Turkey. Greece, he realized, must win Salonika by her own exertions, and so he concluded the treaty and by his silence made possible the League that in the superb campaigns of October and November 1912 overthrew the Turkish Empire in Europe. In the words of M. Take Jonescu, the famous Roumanian Premier, "not to have discussed the partition beforehand places Venizelos on a level with Cavour and Bismarck."

The treaty was signed on 29th May 1912, and was completed by a declaration of vital importance: "The first article [providing for mutual assistance] does not apply to the case of a war breaking out between Greece and Turkey in consequence of the admission into the Greek Parliament of the Cretan deputies against the wishes of Turkey. In that event Bulgaria is only bound to observe towards Greece a benevolent neutrality. . . ." It was this declaration, rendered necessary by the ever-imminent danger of a war between Greece and Turkey over the status of Crete, that confronted Venizelos with a final test of statesmanship before he was able to launch Greece on the victorious war of liberation.

On 3rd January 1912, the Revisionary Chamber was dissolved on the conclusion of its momentous labours; the new elections took place in April, and once more the Venizelist Liberals were returned with an overwhelming majority, in spite of an intensive campaign of personal slander and abuse on the part of the old politicians, whose regime had been desperately wounded by the reforming Assembly. But a grave crisis was suddenly precipitated by the decision of the Cretans to hold simultaneous elections, and to send deputies to Athens, as they had tried to do under Venizelos himself, in 1909.

Once more a European fleet appeared in Cretan waters, but the assiduous deputies, after being turned back once, managed to evade the peaceful picket of warships and arrived in Athens. If they were allowed to take their seats, a war with Turkey was almost certain to break out immediately, yet the secret treaty Venizelos had just concluded provided that in such circumstances the Bulgarian alliance did not come into operation. The Cretan deputies must be excluded at all costs. The Chamber was opened by the King on 1st June, and all roads leading to the Parliament were strongly held by cavalry, infantry, and police, while a strong cordon of troops encircled the building.

Hardly had the sitting begun, before a Cretan deputy, who had managed to enter the House disguised, jumped to his feet and demanded that his fellow-members of Parliament should be admitted in the name of the Cretan people. At the same moment, a strong phalanx of deputies who, by sheer determination, had broken through the lines of not unsympathetic troops holding the main road, rushed vociferating upon the cordon that surrounded the Parliament. Immediately the Opposition surged on to the floor of the House, and in a few moments pandemonium reigned within and without the Parliament. A deputy was seen making his way to the door, revolver in hand, shouting that he would shoot all who opposed him.

In the company of one or two of his friends Venizelos managed to escape from the House, and with tremendous difficulty persuaded the Cretans to send a deputation to meet him in his private room. The news immediately produced a temporary lull in the uproar. There in his study, with the treaty in his pocket, the Prime Minister urged the Cretans, with the aid of every conceivable argument, except the one decisive one, to wait a little longer and so enable him to arrange matters. They were adamant. With a dramatic gesture he produced, not the treaty, but a prorogation of Parliament to 1st October. The bewildered deputies, Greek and Cretan, poured out into the sunlight. There was no longer a Parliament about which to dispute.[1]

The prolonged negotiations among the Balkan States as to the exact reforms they intended to demand were suddenly cut short by the mobilization of Turkey on 30th September 1912. All through the summer Europe had been watching

[1] Chester, "Life of Venizelos," pp. 153-4.

the Balkans—the Albanian revolt had brought the intervention of the Balkan States nearer. The agitation throughout Turkey caused by the temporary fall of the Young Turk party, due to the disaster in Tripoli, had stiffened the Porte in its determination to refuse all external intervention.

The Great Powers came forward with suggestions for administrative decentralization and were met with studied evasions. It was now the turn of the Balkan Alliance, which launched its famous ultimatum on 12th October 1912, demanding administrative autonomy of the provinces of European Turkey on an ethnic basis, Belgian and Swiss governors, elective local Assemblies, educational liberty, and local militias. No answer was returned by Turkey, and on 18th October the three Allies—Bulgaria, Greece, and Serbia, declared war. Montenegro had already done so on 8th October. At the moment when he launched the ultimatum, Venizelos proclaimed the union of Crete and Greece, and the deputies, now at last enlightened as to the profound motives that underlay their exclusion in June, took their seats.

On that same 18th of October 1912, the main squadron of the Greek fleet put to sea from the Piræus in the presence of the King and the Prime Minister. The speech of Venizelos is characteristic of the man in its hard, almost metallic, yet moving appeal. " There are moments in the lives of individuals when they regret the career they have chosen. I must own that I find myself in this predicament just now. I regret that my career has brought me to the helm of the State, instead of being one of you, no matter who, be it an officer, a petty officer, or even an able seaman.

" Yes, I assure you at this moment I envy you all, even to the common sailor, for it is to you that our country is now entrusting her fate with every hope !

" We enter the struggle full of confidence on land, for have we not our Allies ? but our confidence is no less great at sea, where our Allies have entrusted their fate to us.

" We are full of hope, for we know the stuff you are made of, and that you are well prepared, and above all we know the courage that inspires you all.

" Our country expects you not merely to die for her, for that is little indeed ; she expects you to conquer ! That is why each one of you, even in dying, should be possessed by one thought alone—how to eke out his strength until his last breath, so that the survivors may conquer.

"And you will conquer! I am more than sure of that!"[1]

Meanwhile the race for Salonika had begun. Early in November, when the Allies were marching from victory to victory, and Turkish resistance was crumbling on all sides, Venizelos heard with consternation that the Crown Prince Constantine, whom a year before he had restored to the military status of virtual Commander-in-Chief (lost as a result of the revolution of the League in 1909), was contemplating a movement towards Monastir—a movement dictated primarily by strategic considerations. In the middle of the night on which he heard of the contemplated deflection, Venizelos got into touch by telegraph with the King, whose headquarters were within easy reach of the Crown Prince. He impressed upon the King the gravity of the proposed deflection of the advance, and ended by asserting that he would hold the Crown Prince personally responsible for any movement that delayed by an hour the occupation of Salonika. "Salonika at all costs—without Salonika all other acquisitions are worthless." The King at once visited his son and persuaded him to continue the forced march on Salonika. On 9th November the city was occupied by the main Greek forces. Within twenty-four hours a flying Bulgarian column was at the gates![2]

Long before the conclusion of the definite Treaty of Peace with Turkey on 30th May 1913, by which Turkey in Europe west of the Enos-Midia line was ceded to the Allies, profound discords had begun to disturb the harmony of the Balkan League. The diplomatic breach between Serbia and Bulgaria, arising out of the Serbian demand for a revision of the treaty (a demand Austria and Italy had foreseen when they deprived Serbia of a port on the Adriatic, and bolstered up an inflated Albania destined to become the special preserve of Italy) widened steadily with the increasing ascendancy of the war-party in Bulgaria. Instead of conciliating Greece and endeavouring to detach her from Serbia, the Bulgarian war-party, forgetful that there was also a Greek war-party (headed by King Constantine, who had succeeded to the throne on the assassination of King George in March) that Venizelos was endeavouring to curb, took up an attitude of increasing hostility to the Greek claims on Salonika.

The attitude of Bulgaria had seriously alarmed Venizelos

[1] Quoted D. J. Cassavetti, "Hellas and the Balkan Wars," p. 38.
[2] Chester, "Life of Venizelos," p. 159.

during the first Conference with the Turks in London. He found that Dr Daneff, the chief Bulgarian delegate, made a point of avoiding all discussion on the question of the future Græco-Bulgarian boundary. This attempt to postpone the allocation of Salonika seemed to Venizelos the confirmation of his worst fears. After many attempts, he seized the opportunity of broaching the question to Dr Daneff, when he had for the first time called on his Greek colleague unaccompanied. He had come to discuss the question of breaking off the Conference with the Turks, who had characteristically succeeded in exhausting the patience of the Allies by endless tergiversation.

"When we had finished our discussion," Venizelos relates, "M. Daneff rose to leave. I said to him point-blank, 'As we are alone, let us talk about Salonika.' Much embarrassed and on tenterhooks, he replied: 'This is hardly the moment.'

"'Still we have a little time in which to settle the foundations of our future discussions.'

"'I have received no instructions from my Government; I know nothing about the business.'

"At this point, I could not resist saying sharply: 'Let us talk seriously, and try to arrange matters.'

"'With pleasure; but Salonika is at this moment in the hands of the armies. Politics have nothing to do with it now; we will speak of it after peace has been signed with Turkey.'

"We were both standing near the door. Summoning all my self-control, I replied, 'Salonika is not in the hands of the armies, but under the Government of the King of Greece. Salonika belongs to Greece by historical right and by the right of conquest. And I can tell you this: Greece will consent to any other sacrifice in order to maintain the Balkan Alliance—but give up Salonika—Never. Never!' . . ." Dr Daneff went out without a word.[1]

During the first week in March 1913 Venizelos visited Belgrade. After conferring with the Serbian ministers he returned home by way of Sofia to make another attempt to reach an agreement with Bulgaria. M. Nekludoff, then Russian minister at Sofia and intimately concerned in building the Serbo-Bulgarian alliance, has recorded his impressions of the Greek statesman with whom he sought an interview on the question of the future partition of Macedonia: "I have rarely seen a

[1] Kerofilas, "Eleftherios Venizelos," pp. 102-3.

man who, at the first meeting, has produced such a favourable impression on me as M. Venizelos did. An astonishing simplicity, an absolutely frank and open way of expressing his opinions and convictions—which one feels to be deep—constituted and still constitute the strength and prestige of this true statesman. I felt at once that I was in the presence, first, of a perfect gentleman, and then of a scrupulously honest politician. No phraseology, no desire to deceive his questioner were apparent in the clear, precise, and modest expression of his thoughts. The very fact that he, promptly and without any preamble, broached the principal question—that of Græco-Bulgarian demarcation—predisposed me enormously in his favour." [1]

Venizelos worked out Greek claims on a map for the benefit of the minister. Briefly, Greece must have Salonika and just enough territory in its hinterland (including the Chalcidic Peninsula) to ensure the strategic safety of the city. The line he indicated seemed to Nekludoff so reasonable that he promised to press the Bulgarian ministers to accept it. "What is bad," said Venizelos at the conclusion of the interview, "and what makes me anxious, is the fact that nothing on earth will induce the Bulgarians to enter into negotiations with us, as we have repeatedly suggested they should do. They always elude the subject, as if they were on the watch for fresh occurrences or some new situation; and yet amongst us public opinion is very much excited over the tone of the Bulgarian press, which even disputes our possession of Salonika!" Greece and Serbia were being forced into an alliance, though he had not yet concluded it.[2]

When Nekludoff impressed these views on the moderate Bulgarian Premier and urged him to resolve at least one of the many problems confronting him by concluding a definite settlement with Greece, a settlement sure to have the effect of abating Serbian demands, he found Gueshoff in perfect agreement. But his Cabinet was a Coalition, and he could not act without the fire-eating Daneff. King Ferdinand's attitude also was enigmatic. More and more, Gueshoff inclined to escape from a situation of which he had lost control, by resigning.[3]

Meanwhile, Venizelos had returned to Greece to fight his own chauvinists. Early in March 1913, a memorial was

[1] Nekludoff, "Diplomatic Reminiscences, 1911-17," p. 139.
[2] *Ibid.*, p. 140. [3] *Ibid.*, pp. 141-3.

sent to the Greek "Boulé"[1] from the Greeks of Thrace and Eastern Macedonia, including the Greek towns of Serres, Drama, and Kavalla, that Venizelos was prepared to see incorporated in Bulgaria. On 14th March the memorial was submitted to the Chamber, and on 15th two deputies challenged the Government's policy. The whole Opposition, not without the backing of a considerable body of public opinion, attacked the Premier. "Are such," cried Theotokis bitterly, "are such the declarations of the 'Liberator of Hellas?'" The reply of Venizelos was worthy of the man who believed that the Balkan League offered a way of escape from the hideous rivalries that paralysed South-Eastern Europe.

"I am aware," he said, "that there are those who are trying to stir up trouble among the Greek populations which without question will remain outside the Greater Greece. I want these populations to know from the lips of the responsible head of the Greek Government that those who urge on them such an attitude are the true enemies of their country, the true enemies of Hellenism. In other days—three years ago or more—it would have been difficult, perhaps, for a Prime Minister to dare to make such unpalatable revelations. But I, gentlemen, who have only been a few years among you, have come to the conclusion that in three years a tremendous change has come over the soul of the Greek people. Every one does not see it; but it is so great that it permits, nay, that it compels, the responsible head of the Greek Government to tell the truth to the people.

"It is natural that difficulties should have arisen as to the division of the conquered territory. One knows how strong national exclusiveness is. Each of the nations that have shared in this struggle for freedom, impelled by the national instinct, tries to obtain as large a share as possible. Each, in good faith, claims to have contributed most to the common cause. But the truth is different. All have contributed to their utmost. Each of the Allied nations has concentrated all its resources, moral and material, to win a result which never would otherwise have been won.

"I have a conviction that the partition of the conquered territory will not be made by the military authorities, who have a limited horizon and look at matters from a merely military point of view, nor by the too fervid patriots of this State or that, but by these States' responsible Governments.

[1] Parliament.

. . . I hope their patriotism will be so lofty that they will not shrink from such sacrifices as will be inevitable if the partition is to ensure the continuance of the alliance, even if they are bound to be called traitors by the fervid patriots of their own race." [1]

But Bulgarian intransigence remained unshaken; open military attacks on the Greek and Serbian forces multiplied. In these circumstances, Greece and Serbia concluded a Convention on 5th May 1913, binding themselves to conclude a formal alliance. Still hoping against hope that a compromise with Bulgaria was possible, Venizelos delayed the signature of the alliance and the parallel military convention until 1st June 1913. Later in the year, Stratos—in revenge for what he considered the high-handed action of Venizelos in ordering him to resign—taunted his former chief with having subordinated Greek to Bulgarian interests, "and with having been thrown into complete despair by the repeated aggressions of the Bulgarians during the month of May in the district of the Panghaeon." To have shrunk from war was an offence to this little-minded man, for whom fate had reserved so baleful an influence on his country's future fortunes. Replying to these attacks on 25th November 1913, Venizelos declared that the fact that the Bulgarian war had had a favourable issue did not make him regret having dreaded it. "My critics," he said, "forget the misfortunes of the State which for thirty years has held the hegemony of the Balkan Peninsula." [2] In Dr Burrows' words, "the remark shows the greatness of the man."

On the 30th June Bulgarians flung themselves on the Serbian and Greek forces in a sudden and unannounced offensive. It is now certain that King Ferdinand ordered the general attack without the knowledge of the Bulgarian Ministry. A swift and brilliant counter-offensive, and the dramatic intervention of Roumania, brought Bulgaria to her knees. By the end of July, the former Allies met at Bucharest, and on 10th August the treaty was signed that secured for Greece not only Salonika, but Serres, Drama, and Kavalla, Greek cities that Venizelos would have sacrificed then, as later, to a Balkan League as a permanent political combination, but was not prepared to relinquish once Bulgaria had definitely revealed her intention of securing the hegemony of the Balkans.

[1] Quoted Ronald M. Burrows, "The New Greece," pp. 11-12 (Anglo-Hellenic League Publications, No. 14).
[2] *Ibid.*, pp. 12-13.

At the close of the second Balkan War, Venizelos confidently looked forward to a long period of peaceful development. To quote his own words: "I was careful to insert in the first paragraph of the King's Speech that Greece considered that she had realized her national programme almost in its entirety. I put that phrase on the King's lips, although I still had the widest views for the future of Hellenism, because I was firmly of the opinion that the national interest required us to secure, as far as it lay in our power to do so, a long period of peace. I was ready to pray that the solution of our other national questions might be postponed for a whole generation. For a whole generation Greece would have to be occupied in the extensive development of her doubled dominion, and during this period of development she must either hope that the Greeks in Turkey would find a tolerable *modus vivendi* under the existing system, or else be certain that, when the time came for the break-up of the Turkish Empire, a leading place would be taken by a strong Greece, strong enough to solve by her own effort the problems which await a national solution."[1]

These are wise words, but Greece was to have but one year of uneasy peace, during which the all-powerful C.U.P.[2] developed on an increasing scale the policy of expelling the Greek populations of Asia Minor, before she found herself compelled to decide on some policy to adopt towards the world war of August 1914.

The escape to Constantinople of the *Goeben* and *Breslau* seemed to Venizelos the prelude to a Turkish attack on Greece, either as the ally of Germany or alone. The relations of Greece and Turkey were the worst possible. The Turks had refused to recognize the allocation to Greece by the Powers of the islands she had occupied lying along the coast of Asia Minor, and, as a result, the two countries were not so much in a state of peace as in one of suspended war.

Venizelos persuaded the King to agree to his making a general, but none the less formal, declaration of solidarity with the Entente Powers, in which he recognized that the place of Greece was beside the three Powers who guaranteed her.[3]

[1] "The Vindication of Greek National Policy, 1912-17. A Report of Speeches delivered in the Greek Chamber, August 24-26, 1917, by E. Venizelos and others," pp. 70-71.

[2] Turkish "Committee of Union and Progress."

[3] By Convention of 7th May 1832, and Treaty of London, 13th July 1863.

The result was immediate. The Entente, while thanking Greece for her declaration, announced that if the reinforced Turkish fleet entered the Ægean to undertake operations against Greece, the Allies would attack it. On the other hand, Sir Edward Grey felt it necessary to decline the immediate aid of Greece for fear Turkey would regard it as an aggression. The Turkish menace had been countered, yet Greece still possessed considerable liberty of action.[1] The policy of Venizelos between September 1914 and March 1915, the occasion of his first breach with the King, is marked by a steady evolution towards intervention on the side of the Entente. Practically every Greek politician agreed that if there was to be intervention at all, it must be on the side of the sea Powers—the choice was always between intervention and neutrality.

At the Cabinet Council, held in the presence of the King early in August 1914, which decided that Greece must for the moment maintain neutrality, Dr Streit, later one of the leaders of the Germanophil party, then Minister of Foreign Affairs, exclaimed gleefully: "Then we are all of one mind that we shall remain neutral." Repoulis, suspecting the motives of the remark, turned to Venizelos: "Do I understand, Mr President," he asked, "that Greece is to remain neutral to the very end, or are we to watch for an opportunity of coming in?" "Not only shall we watch for an opportunity," replied the Premier, "but Greece, like a midwife, will help circumstances to be born, so that she may join the Allies."[2] As we have seen, he was not long in taking the first step. But many considerations urged Venizelos to adopt a policy of intervention on the side of the Allies. From the most general point of view, he regarded the cause of European Liberalism as bound up with the fortunes of the Western Powers. He believed quite definitely that, with all weaknesses and shortcomings, the Allies were the guardians of European liberty. Repetition has vulgarized, if not made hypocritical, the proclamation of this truth that, in the last analysis, the cause of European civilization, interpreted as the continued growth of her political institutions towards democracy, depended on the victory of France and Great Britain. It is a view from which Venizelos has never swerved. "Even if those two

[1] "The Vindication of Greek National Policy, 1912-17." Speech of Venizelos, delivered 26th August 1917; Churchill, "The World Crisis," i., pp. 485-6.

[2] D. Vaka, "Constantine, King and Traitor," p. 66. *Θὰ ἐκμαιεύσωμεν τὰς περιστάσεις*

nations are beaten," he said, "it is better for Greece to be beaten on their side than to win on the side of Germany."[1]

The alliance with Serbia remained a lien to bind Greece to the Allies, for it pledged her to intervene on behalf of Serbia against any attempt by Bulgaria, by an attack on Serbia, to upset the balance of power in the Balkans created at the Peace of Bucharest. The mere facts that Bulgaria inclined to the Central Powers, and that Turkey, by the end of October 1914, had definitely joined them only made the issues for Greece clearer. Greece was wholly dependent on the sea, and inevitably her interests gravitated towards the sea-powers. A final consideration remained, and that the old one formulated by Machiavelli in "The Prince," but ever self-evident: if your fortunes are being decided by two powers greater than yourself, it is your elementary duty to decide which of them you desire to win, and, having made up your mind, to assist to the limit of your power the friend of your choice. Win or lose, your fate is being decided in any case, and you have not passed under the ignominy of leaving to others the sole voice in your destiny. Your contribution, for all you know, may be decisive. Be at least sure of this, that your real friend will always ask for your services, your secret enemy will press you to remain neutral. If Greece was at any time to attempt to realize the dream of a re-united Hellenism, "the great idea," that time had come, for Turkey was the prison-house of the Asiatic Greeks—a prison-house now besieged by the forces of the Entente.

In January 1915, after several vague overtures from the Entente, Sir Edward Grey appealed to Greece to intervene to save Serbia, then believed to be in danger from an Austro-German attack. He accompanied the appeal by the offer of considerable territorial concessions in Asia Minor.

In his famous memoranda to the King Venizelos advocated the acceptance of this unique recognition of the claims of Hellenism. Yet he faced the danger of a Bulgarian flank attack by suggesting, as we shall see, territorial concessions in the Kavalla region as the price of a reconstituted Balkan bloc. The sacrifice would be slight if the Hellenism of Asia Minor could be rescued from its age-long tyranny. The dominating thought, repeated in every variation, is that Greece was faced by a clear issue. Either she would expand

[1] Demetra Vaka (Mrs Kenneth Brown), "Constantine, King and Traitor," p. 204.

into Asia Minor and absorb the Greek populations in one Greek Ægean state, or Turkey by pursuing the policy inaugurated by the Young Turks in 1909, which had already led to the expulsion of 200,000 Greeks, would succeed in exterminating Hellenism in Asia Minor.

The memoranda of January 1915, were elaborate arguments designed to persuade the King to accept Sir Edward Grey's famous offer. Throughout the memoranda Venizelos lays the greatest possible emphasis on the duty of seizing the opportunity afforded by the Entente offer, of finally liberating the Ottoman Hellenes from Turkish oppression. The last words of the memorandum of 11th January are worth quoting: "Even in the event of our failure, we shall have a clear conscience, knowing that we have fought to free those of our countrymen still held in subjection by Turkey, and knowing that we had fought also for the general interests of humanity and for the independence of small nations, which a Turco-German triumph would jeopardize irreparably. And finally, we should retain the esteem and friendship of those powerful nations which created Greece and have helped and supported her so many times. While our refusal to carry out the obligations imposed by our alliance with Serbia would not only destroy our moral existence as a nation . . . but it would leave us without friends and without credit in the future. Under such conditions our national life would be endangered." [1]

Cynics are in the habit of suggesting that such arguments are used by politicians only on a public platform—Venizelos used them in an ultra-confidential memorandum to his Sovereign. He was prepared to take gigantic risks in terms of a great idea—a re-united and liberated Hellenism. He had no doubt of the goal—the infinite combinations and expediencies of practical politics were subordinated to a vision as noble as that which inspired the wisdom of Cavour and the soul of Mazzini.

When it became evident that the joint intervention of Greece and Roumania on the side of the Entente was impossible, and that Roumania was not to be drawn from her enigmatic neutrality, Venizelos boldly advocated the sacrifice of substantial territories (the Drama and Kavalla district) to

[1] Text of Memorandum, 11th January 1915. Chester, "Life of Venizelos," pp. 224-7, and "Eleutherios Venizelos and English Public Opinion" (Anglo-Hellenic League Publication, No. 19).

Bulgaria in order to win her to reconstitute the Balkan League and intervene on the side of the Entente. He pointed out that the concessions offered by the Entente in Asia Minor more than compensated for the undoubtedly heavy sacrifice of Kavalla. In a further memorandum to the King, dated 17th January 1915, he wrote : " I firmly believe that we ought to lay aside any hesitation. It is improbable that such an opportunity as that offered to Hellenism to-day will ever arise again. If we do not take part in the war, whatever the result, the Hellenism of Asia Minor will be lost to us finally. If the Powers of the Triple Entente are victorious, they will divide among themselves or with Italy [Italy had not yet intervened] both Asia Minor and the remains of Turkey. If Germany and Turkey are victorious, not only will the 200,000 Greeks, who have already been driven from Asia Minor, have to renounce all hope of returning to their homes, but the number of those who will ultimately be expelled may assume alarming proportions. In any case, the triumph of Germanism would mean the absorption of the whole of Asia Minor. . . . " In view of the magnitude of the opportunity the risks are worth running and the price worth paying : " To your Majesty, still, happily, in the prime of manhood, it may be given not only to create by your sword the Greater Greece, but to confirm your military success by a complete political organization of the new State. To you it may thus be given to transmit to your successor, when the fulness of time demands, a work of such magnitude as has been given to few monarchs to achieve." [1]

The news that Bulgaria had contracted a loan on the German market convinced Venizelos that she could not be drawn from her neutrality on to the side of the Allies, and the King was unsympathetic, backed as he was by the weight of the opinion of the Greek General Staff.[2] But Venizelos continued to work for intervention in the face of the growing hostility of the Court and army circles, who were convinced of an ultimate German victory.

The first breach with the King took place in March 1915. Telegrams from Constantinople continually reached Venizelos to the effect that the Turkish Government was meditating

[1] Memorandum of 17th January 1915. Text Chester, "Life of Venizelos," pp. 227-31, and Anglo-Hellenic League Publication, No. 19.

[2] " Vindication of Greek National Policy, 1912-17—a Report of Speeches in the Greek Chamber, August 24-26, 1917," p. 81.

flight to Konia and that Gallipoli was only weakly held. At the same time, the Allies again requested intervention. He knew Great Britain at the moment was experiencing difficulty in raising a force strong enough to attack the Gallipoli Peninsula. The situation once more seemed to Venizelos to have changed in favour of Greece. Instead of pushing forces up to the Danube to aid Serbia, who for the moment was out of danger, the far easier task was proposed of sending a small Greek expeditionary force to Gallipoli to co-operate with the British fleet. Venizelos laid these views before the King in a fourth memorandum of this period which has never been published. Constantine was frankly afraid that a war against Turkey would inevitably mean a war against Germany, and he doubted whether Greece could absorb the territories in Asia Minor the Allies were promising her. A dramatic interview with the Prime Minister ensued. The tremendous vision of a liberated Hellenism that had opened out before Venizelos; the conviction that the issues were now quite clearly set, either Greece must absorb the Greek populations and so expand into Asia Minor or the Turks would eject the minorities, lent his overwhelming personality peculiar and added ascendancy. At the end of a prolonged argument, Constantine consented. "Very well, then, in God's name!"[1]

Hardly had he left the King when he was faced by a crisis provoked by the resignation of Colonel John Metaxas, the Chief of the General Staff. Venizelos at once proposed to the King the assembling of a Crown Council to decide the issue. It was an audacious move, as most of the members of the Council were his own political opponents. In two sessions he had converted them and removed the chief objections of the General Staff as to the danger from Bulgaria, by reducing the proposed expeditionary force from one army corps to one division, calculated as sufficient to deal with the isolated Turkish garrisons. Only Theotokis was opposed to the idea of the expedition, but he hastened to make clear that the King could not rely on him as an alternative Prime Minister. "You know my opinions," he said, "but I am bound to admit not only that my opinions may be regarded as out of date, but also that they are not shared by the Greek people; consequently, your Majesty must not depend on the fact that if you

[1] "Vindication of Greek National Policy, 1912-17—a Report of Speeches in the Greek Chamber, August 24-26, 1917," p. 85.

choose to follow another policy, you might find me disposed to undertake its application.[1] Rhalles, an ex-Prime Minister, and later a Constantinian, exclaimed, "Courage, Your Majesty, courage," and to Venizelos, "Mr Prime Minister, it is your duty to go forward."

It was at the very moment when Venizelos had converted the Opposition chiefs to the feasibility of a Dardanelles expedition, that the King suddenly gave a strong personal lead in the opposite direction, and thus founded by his success a party that, in the strict sense of the word, was Constantinist. He refused to accept the recommendations of the two Crown Councils, held under his presidency, and Venizelos resigned on 6th March 1915. Not the least cause of Constantine's sudden swing round at a moment when his hesitation seemed on the point of vanishing, was the development of strong Russian opposition to the idea of a Greek expedition to the Dardanelles. At a moment when they had realized their desperate position in face of the beginning of the great advance of the Germans across Poland; at a moment when the opening up of direct communications with the Allies was a matter of life and death to Russia, the Imperial Government chose to revive their old jealousy of the Greeks. On 3rd March 1915, Sazonov, the Russian Foreign Minister, declared to the British Ambassador: "The Russian Government could not consent to Greece participating in operations in the Dardanelles, as it would be sure to lead to complications . . . the Emperor had, in an audience with him (Sazonov) yesterday, declared he could not in any circumstances consent to Greek co-operation in the Dardanelles." In Athens the Russian Minister, Prince Demidov, devoted himself to discouraging the Greeks. If they came in at all, he said, they must direct their forces against Austria and in aid of Serbia, not merely against Turkey. He impressed on Constantine that in no possible circumstances would Russia permit him or his forces to enter Constantinople.[2] Since Constantine's inclinations were all for keeping out of the war, which, he felt convinced, would end in the decisive victory of the Central Powers, though he had begun to waver about the prospects of a separate war with Turkey and an expedition to Constantinople, this insulting attitude on the part of one of his prospective Allies merely confirmed his doubts, and he shrank back into neutrality. And so the only available

[1] "Vindication of Greek National Policy," p. 85.
[2] Churchill, "The World Crisis," vol. ii., pp. 201-2.

striking force capable of attacking the fateful Peninsula and freeing the line of the Straits was thrown away. Great Britain began laboriously to build up her magnificent expedition. But the sands were running out, even before that epic assault was launched. Venizelos resigned on 6th March; the fortification of Gallipoli began the following month.

In his famous speech in the Greek Chamber on 26th August 1917, Venizelos, referring to those March days, made a great claim: "Five days after the decree of mobilization, the Army Corps which I asked for would have been mobilized, and in another nine days, with the abundance of material which we and our Allies had at our disposal, we should have found ourselves with our Army Corps, or even with our one Division, in occupation of the Peninsula, which was unguarded, ungarrisoned, and unfortified . . ." [1]

The Gounaris Government that succeeded Venizelos spent its time enraging the Allies by a series of shifty proposals for intervention, accompanied by such a rigmarole of conditions and provisions that M. Delcassé cut matters short by declaring, almost in the exact words, that Greece could come in or stay out as she chose, but that he could not waste his time haggling over what seemed insincere proposals, such as the suggestion "that the Allies should be prepared to contribute forces which, combined with the Greek, would equal the united Turkish and Bulgarian forces (in view of Bulgaria's doubtful neutrality), and that the sphere of Greek action should be limited to the *West* of the Gallipoli Peninsula; but it was agreed that if the Allies wished it, they should have the military assistance of Greece on the Gallipoli Peninsula too, *provided that they landed their own troops first.*" [2] As for Constantine, he felt he had to make some offers to the Allies, however guarded, to conciliate the people whose "sympathies," as he told Mrs Kenneth Brown, "were with the Entente . . . but every time I made an offer, I can tell you I trembled in my boots for fear they might accept it." [3]

To aid his nominee, Gounaris, in his political campaign, the King thought fit in April 1915 to give him the confidential

[1] "Vindication," p. 86.

[2] Zographos to Greek Minister, Paris, 14th April 1915; quoted Abbott, "Greece and the Allies, 1914-22," p. 36. (Italics mine.)

[3] D. Vaka (Mrs Kenneth Brown), "Constantine, King and Traitor," p. 187.

memoranda of Venizelos, not for his information but for publication. They both hoped that the suggested cession of Kavalla to Bulgaria would rouse public opinion against the Liberal leader. At the General Election in June, the Liberal Party was returned to power with a reduced, but still substantial majority; the Opposition winning 130 and the Liberals 184 seats. M. Gounaris, however, remained in power till late in August, on the pretext that the state of the King's health precluded a change of Government.

On his return to power, Venizelos defined his policy to meet the situation arising from the evident failure of the Dardanelles expedition and the policy of neutrality pursued by Gounaris. He reaffirmed his determination to defend Serbia against any attack by Bulgaria, and the policy was ratified by the King. On 22nd September Bulgaria suddenly mobilized, and on the 23rd Venizelos had the most famous of all his interviews with King Constantine. He informed the King that the Government was about to submit to him an order for the general mobilization of the Greek army as a reply to the Bulgarian menace, and to place Greece in a position to come to the aid of her ally, Serbia, if necessary. The King was quite blunt about his view. "You know I don't want to help Serbia, because Germany will win, and I don't want to be beaten." After a long argument about the military aspect of the situation, Venizelos played his last card: "Your Majesty," he said, "having failed to persuade you, I am very sorry, but it is my duty, as representing at the present moment the sovereignty of the people, to tell you that this time you have no right to differ from me. By the elections of 13th June, the people have approved my policy and given me their confidence; and the electorate knew that the foundation of my policy was that we should not allow Bulgaria to crush Serbia and expand overmuch so as to crush us to-morrow. At this point, therefore, you cannot depart from this policy: unless of course you are determined to set aside the Constitution. . . ." The King replied: "You know, I recognize that I am bound to obey the popular verdict when it is a question of the internal affairs of the country; but when it is a question of foreign affairs, great international questions, I think that so long as I believe a thing is right or not right, I must insist upon its being done, because I am responsible before God."

Venizelos has described his feelings on hearing this astounding claim: "I remember that a feeling of distress overcame me, and with clasped hands and a melancholy movement of the head, I said: 'Alas, this the theory of monarchy by the Grace of God, unhappy Greece!' And after a little, I said to the King that in the circumstances of the time I could not undertake to fight for the Constitution—'after calling Your Majesty's attention to the Constitution, I feel I must offer my resignation, which I beg you to accept.'" [1]

The King then declared that he could see no reason for resignation. After all, Bulgaria might not attack Serbia; *per impossible*, her declaration that her mobilization was defensive and for the purpose of maintaining an "armed neutrality" might be true. In which case, his disagreement with Venizelos vanished. So he persuaded Venizelos to remain in office and counter-sign the mobilization order. Before the conversation ended, a way out of the difficulty flashed on the Premier. The objections of the King, backed by the General Staff, all hinged on the fact that Serbia, because she was engaged on holding back the Austrians on the line of the Danube, could not put into the field against a possible Bulgarian attack the 150,000 men stipulated for in the Serbo-Greek Military Convention. What if the Allies would send 150,000 men to take the place of the Serbian contingent? The King agreed. Venizelos left the Palace, returned to the Ministry, and urgently summoned the Ministers of the Entente. By 8 p.m. on 23rd September 1915 the famous invitation had been despatched. At 8.15 an urgent message came from the King requiring Venizelos not to despatch the message. "Kindly inform His Majesty," replied Venizelos, "that the *démarche* has already been made." [2] The change of mind was characteristic: "Of course Venizelos will take you in," Constantine told Mrs Kenneth Brown, who was about to visit the great rebel at Salonika, after seeing the King one March day in 1917. "He has a way of his own of convincing. He would convince even me, who knew everything, and only after he had gone and I thought things over, would I see how wrong he was; but while he was talking to me I could never withstand him." [3]

Conscious as he was of the all but open hostility of the King, due to Constantine's profound conviction that Greece would be beaten if she intervened against Germany in a war

[1] "Vindication," p. 105. [2] *Ibid.*, p. 108.
[3] Demetra Vaka (Mrs Kenneth Brown), "Constantine, King and Traitor," p. 192.

he thought certain to end in the victory of the Central Powers, Venizelos determined to fight on to the end. "My relations with my King are as bad as possible, and are becoming worse, but I shall remain to keep out the Germans as long as possible," was his comment at the time.

The opposition of the General Staff, under the inspiration of the King, to any abandonment of neutrality; the brilliant German propaganda of Baron Schenck, the German minister; the failures of the Entente in the Russian Campaign and the Dardanelles Expedition, all combined to shake public confidence in the great minister. The Salonika expedition was deeply resented, and the Opposition, conscious of the secret support of the King, challenged the issue on the night of 4th October 1915. Summoned by his opponents to say what would happen if, in the course of a war against Bulgaria, Greek troops should find themselves face to face with the German army, he made his way to the tribune amid scenes of unparalleled excitement. In a long and brilliant speech he defended his policy of intervention, in the course of which, reverting to the challenge and dominating with his voice the rising tempest in the Chamber, he used the memorable words: "If, in pursuing our national policy, fulfilling the duty that our honour demands, honouring our treaty of alliance, defending the vital interests of the country, we should find in our path the great ones of the earth, I am sure that while expressing our regret, we should do our duty." [1] The issue had been stated and the challenge accepted. A vote of confidence was carried by 151 votes to 102.

Yet, the next day, the King sent for the Prime Minister and informed him that the speech had gone further than was justified. He could not agree to it. Though the Allied forces were at the moment landing at Salonika, the King refused to accept the consequences of the situation. Constantine had triumphed in his long struggle—the fight of a weak man to emancipate himself from the influence of a personality so overwhelming that he could not trust his judgment when face to face with "the Cretan." But the shadow of the great minister was always falling across his spirit. Long afterwards, when waiting to receive one or other of his many puppets, Skouloudis, or Calogeropoulos, or the learned Lambros, he would fall into a reverie and then, rousing himself and

[1] Speech, 4th October 1915. Text, "La Politique de la Grèce," p. 36.

pulling out his watch, he would say to his Secretary, "Is Venizelos there yet?"[1]

Nothing remained for Venizelos but to resign. The Bulgarian invasion of Serbia was launched at once, and the great refusal of M. Zaimis to honour the treaty obligations of Greece ensured its success. Those treaty obligations had been repeatedly recognized by Greece since the outbreak of war. Gounaris, leader of the "Constantinian" Opposition, had himself recognized the duty of Greece to defend Serbia from a Bulgarian attack.[2] The contention that the Treaty was of purely Balkan scope and did not apply to a general war is refuted by the fact that the validity of the treaty was recognized again and again during the period when Serbia was fighting Austria, and, therefore, definitely involved in the European war. Very rarely has one Government addressed to another such a tissue of contemptible sophistries as is contained in the dispatch of M. Zaimis to the Serbian Government of 11th October 1915. One quotation will illuminate its character. "The Royal Government . . . was always ready to face the Bulgarian danger even in case it should appear in the course of the European war, although Serbia was already struggling with two great Powers. For that reason, it hastened immediately to answer the Bulgarian mobilization by a general mobilization of its army. But it had always in view a Bulgarian attack undertaken *separately, even though in connection with* the other hostilities undertaken against Serbia. The hypothesis of an attack concerted with that of other Powers was and ought to be outside of its anticipations . . . etc."[3]

The year that followed was one of successive humiliations for Greece. A series of ephemeral Prime Ministers, dependent on a Chamber for which the Liberal party had refused to vote, on the advice of Venizelos, in December, administered with increasing difficulty the personal policy of the King. The reasons for this refusal to co-operate in the normal working of the Constitution were given by Venizelos in a manifesto to the electorate on 21st November 1915—a manifesto the news of which the Royalist censorship made every effort to prevent reaching the outside world. He denied the right of the

[1] G. M. Mélas (former Secretary to King Constantine), "Ex-King Constantine and the War," p. 121.
[2] Greek White Book, 1917, Nos. 28, 29, 31.
[3] *Ibid.*, Document No. 34. (Italics mine.)

King to dissolve the Chamber on an issue that had already been placed before the people a few months before. "At what moment," the manifesto continues, "and in what conditions has [the Government] proceeded to these elections? A large number of Liberal deputies are with the Colours and consequently will find it impossible to take part in the electoral campaign. All the men that can be mobilized are with the Colours. Only old men, the unfit, the shirkers, and the disabled will be called to the ballot. These are they who alone, and to the exclusion of the others, would decide by their vote the fate of the nation! Not only is the Government keeping with the Colours—as a result of the mobilization—half the electors, but it has resolved—and its friends make no mystery about it—to give its partisans leave of absence before the elections in order to enable them to vote. Those of the mobilized men who are not the friends of the Government will be retained with their regiments, under military discipline. . . . It is the duty of the Liberal party to refuse to take part in this political comedy in order to avoid giving an appearance of legality to what should be denounced . . . as the violation alike of constitutional law and of morality. . . . When the crisis abroad has ended, and if the disasters which the Government's policy is preparing for us do not assume such a magnitude as to shake our faith in the future of Hellenism, the Liberal party will be ready to undertake the struggle into which the country is being pushed for the defence of its constitutional liberties." [1]

What had the Royalists to show for "neutrality at any price"? "Where, at least," asked Venizelos in the Chamber, "are your thirty pieces of silver?" The continuous mobilization of an army that neither took the offensive nor defended its neutrality; that was ordered to evacuate Eastern Macedonia and surrender Fort Roupel without firing a shot; that was compelled to hand over Kavalla and its forts and stores to the Bulgars and to submit to the internment of a Greek army corps in Germany—as if a belligerent could under any circumstances invade a neutral's territory and intern his army! All this when the whole kingdom was under arms—then why not demobilize? The answer was simple—having once embarked on the tempestuous sea of absolutism, the King could not get back to port. The consciousness that he would lose a free general election, only possible on

[1] "La Politique de la Grèce," Appendix ii, pp. 202-4.

demobilization, dictated to him the execrable policy of keeping the army on a war footing in order to justify a wide application of martial law and censorship. Athens was oppressed by a heavy cloud of German propaganda. Ten of the fourteen newspapers were bought up outright and used as the medium of carefully distorted news. Political absolutism was openly preached in the Royalist press. It was in such circumstances as these that Venizelos resolved on resorting to the last expedient—rebellion.

On 25th September 1916, he left Athens and went to Crete, where he proclaimed the setting up of a provisional Government of national defence.[1] Most of the islands joined the new movement. A revolt had already broken out at Salonika. After rousing the islands, Venizelos and his allies joined the Salonika Committee, and began to raise troops in order to take part in the war in the Balkans. From the first, he emphasized the fact that his movement was not anti-dynastic. When the King, shaken by the news, privately sent to ask him whether, if the Government entered the war on the side of the Allies, he would demand his own return to office, the answer of the great rebel was worthy of him:[2] "If the King will abandon the neutrality that is ruining the country and pursue a policy dictated by the vital interests of Greece, neither I nor any of my friends will demand any offices in the Government entrusted with the task."[3] But Constantine was not long in finding his feet again, and, though compelled by the Allies to demobilize half his force, withdraw the other half to the Morea, expel the enemy ministers, and surrender the control of posts and telegraphs, he still clung to his personal policy, with his authority daily shrinking and his personal humiliations multiplying.

As a result of the sanguinary conflict, on 1st December 1916, between the forces of Constantine and Allied naval detachments landing to carry out a further demand for the surrender of field batteries, Royalist Greece experienced the miseries of a strict blockade. It was, however, able to gratify its feelings by a massacre of Venizelists on 2nd December 1916; the "discovery" of a long letter from "the

[1] The story of the great adventure is delightfully told in J. C. Lawson's "Tales of Ægean Intrigue."

[2] See G. M. Mélas, "Ex-King Constantine and the War," pp. 73-7.

[3] "Vindication," p. 152. See also Abbott, "Greece and the Allies," p. 132.

Cretan " to an adherent purporting, in so far as it was intelligible, to advocate the assassination of his opponents; and the ceremonial cursing of Venizelos on 26th December 1916, by the Archbishop of Athens, who stood for the occasion on " a cairn of stones in the midst of a great multitude." [1] Eight bishops, representing every district of Old Greece, participated in the scandalous ceremony reminiscent of the Dark Ages. The formula was comprehensive: " Cursed be Eleutherios Venizelos, who has imprisoned priests,[2] who has plotted against his King and his country." Each participant cried " Anathema ! " and cast a stone upon the cairn.[3] At the same moment, not far from the infatuated bigots, small groups of women were lighting votive candles before sacred images for the life and health of the great rebel, and at the dawning of the next day the cairn of cursing was found strewn with flowers.[4]

The charge that Venizelos at this time was either plotting a rising in Athens with the connivance of the Entente ministers, or advocating the assassination of his political enemies, is too serious to be ignored. This famous Korakas forgery was subjected to a critical study by the late Principal of King's College, London, Dr Ronald M. Burrows, who illustrated his remarks with photographic facsimiles.[5] By a chain of eleven distinct proofs he demonstrated that the letter is ungrammatical; that the writer mis-spells an ordinary abstract word meaning " imposition " five times in the course of the letter; that the writing is cramped and often illegible, not in the least resembling the clear bold writing of Venizelos; that, though written on large quarto sheets of paper, in a letter of 1000 words there is not a single paragraph, whereas Venizelos is in the habit of paragraphing very carefully; that " individual words and letters are, without exception, unlike the genuine examples "; that the writer ends his letter with a false concord impossible for an educated man, viz., " I greet *thee*, always *yours* "; that the style is wordy and obscure, whereas (as anyone can verify) the dispatches and speeches of Venizelos are models of lucidity. In a word, Dr Burrows proved that the letter was a clumsy forgery.

[1] Abbott, " Greece and the Allies," p. 175.
[2] And was yet to imprison more, not to speak of bishops!
[3] Paxton Hibben, " Constantine I and the Greek People," pp. 521-2.
[4] Address of Alexander N. Diomedes, formerly Greek Minister of Finance, 16th Feb. 1917 (Anglo-Hellenic League Publication, No. 31, p. 27).
[5] Vol. v. of " The New Europe," No. 57, 15th November 1917.

Mr G. F. Abbott, in a book, "Greece and the Allies," published in 1922, writes of the letter, "the publication of this document, with a photographic facsimile, had confirmed the apprehensions which had long haunted the popular mind. Nor did M. Venizelos's indignant denial of its authenticity . . . shake the conviction that the big coup was planned for first December."[1] There is no mention of the fact that the forgery had been exposed five years before.

Mr Paxton Hibben, in his book, "Constantine I and the Greek People," written in 1917, but not published till 1921, quotes the most preposterous sentence in the whole letter, "It is not my custom to calculate on the basis of dry logic and historical fact, but rather on the sudden psychological changes, together with the law of compulsion and imposition, which is stronger than all laws, whether written, unwritten, real, or hypothetical," as a characteristic specimen of the literary style of Venizelos. The most that can be said of it is that it reads like an exposition of Fascist political theory.

Once he was installed at Salonika the agonizing doubts that had distracted him in the last months before the rebellion passed from the mind of Venizelos. There had been doubts as to whether he should stake all on his ability to break away from the incubus that oppressed Greece—stake his good name on an adventure, the dangers and disappointments of which he knew by long experience; divide the country, shake the throne, endanger the fabric of the State. The other rôle of revered prophet, strictly constitutional when all his enemies were denying every clause in the fundamental statutes, pointing a moral instead of adorning a tale, talking instead of acting, in a word, doing his legal best—this course appealed to his years, but a fearless and unsparing analysis of the springs of his thought, an analysis he laid before the Greek Chamber in a fascinating passage of the most famous of all his speeches, convinced him that to be passive so long as there was the energy in him to be up and doing was at bottom fundamentally selfish and due to a mere shrinking from duty.

It is not necessary to detail the history of the Salonika movement. The new Government raised in a few months a force of 60,000 men, and there can be little doubt that, but for the veto of the Allies, the war could have been successfully carried from Salonika to Athens. The decision of the Allies to depose the King themselves in June 1917 by the exercise

[1] Abbott, "Greece and the Allies," p. 166.

of their treaty rights, is to be deplored, for it placed Venizelos in the false position of returning to Athens in their baggage train, though it probably averted a civil war. Not to have insisted on occupying Athens with his own forces is probably the greatest political mistake in his life. He saw the risk, but he could not fully foresee the remorseless use the Royalist party was to make of this psychological blunder of returning to Athens behind the Allied forces and entering a city held by Allied troops. " After all," he said to General Regnault, who had occupied Athens, " it is certain that people will always say that I returned to Athens only with the support of the Allies." [1] They would have said it, however he had returned, but he had lent the saying a deadly authenticity. When Major Mélas, on the Allied warship in which the great Cretan returned, told him of his fears as to what history would say of this foreign intervention, Venizelos replied, with tears in his eyes, that he had aimed at occupying Athens only with Greek troops, but after the events of December 1916, he had felt unable to insist further.[2]

The two Governments of Athens and Salonika were under Venizelos fused, and after the reconvening of the dissolved Chamber of June 1915, Greece entered the war. The vast energy of the Premier that had rallied the youth of Greece around him at Salonika did not fail him now. At the eleventh hour he had brought his country into the war in time to vindicate her national aspirations. The problem before him in 1918 was to place the Allies under a definite obligation to Greece. The Greek army must play a decisive part in the final offensive, it must prove itself formidable—only so could it regain its fatally injured prestige, and enable Greece to plead the cause of Hellenism before the Peace Conference.

On 26th August 1917, Venizelos, in the greatest political speech of his life, and perhaps the greatest oratorical achievement of modern times, reviewed the past and envisaged the future before the Greek Chamber. He demanded a vote of confidence, after holding the attention of the House and galleries for nearly eight hours of sustained and closely reasoned argument. To read this speech attentively is in itself a political education. The final passage, when he faces the immense problems that lay before him, deserves quotation.

[1] Regnault, " La Conquête d'Athènes, Juin-Juillet, 1917," p. 101.
[2] Mélas, " Ex-King Constantine and the War," p. 237.

"I am not blind, Gentlemen, to the picture which is presented before me. That which I feared when I left office in October 1915 has unfortunately come to pass. The Greece of 1917 does not even distantly resemble the Greece of 1915, which we then handed over to *their* keeping. The men who pursued a German policy can boast of the truly alarming success that has attended their efforts. I see our ally, Serbia, overthrown, even though her overthrow is only temporary, and will be followed, as I feel assured, by the restoration of her full national unity. I see Bulgaria overwhelmingly aggrandized, and ready to fall on us to-morrow to crush and subjugate us. I see the regime of internal corruption risen from the dead with a fresh impetus and a fresh vigour. I see the economic wreck. I see the Royal Army almost in a state of dissolution. The Greece of 1917 does not resemble the Greece of 1915 in either a territorial, a moral, a financial, a military, or a political sense. Nevertheless, with all these disadvantageous conditions, my optimism does not desert me. A nation which for no less than three thousand years has passed through such great trials without disappearing; a nation which only yesterday recorded the victories of 1912 and 1913; a nation which, although betrayed by its rulers, succeeded in finding within itself sufficient moral strength to create a new State, and raise a new army, and write, as I have often said, some of the brightest pages of our military history—I am unshakably convinced that such a nation still conceals within itself enough vitality, even at this last moment, to achieve its own salvation.

"Gentlemen, the nation is aware that I have never promised it anything that was not attainable. The nation knows that I have never fallen short of the undertakings I have given. In taking part in this world-wide war at the side of the democratic nations, which have been brought together in a common cause, in a truly holy alliance, by Germany's claims to the empire of the world, whose clients are our two hereditary enemies, we shall not only regain the national territories we have lost, we shall not only re-establish our honour as a nation, we shall not only effectively defend our national interests at the Congress of Peace and secure our national future, but we shall also be a worthy member of the family of free nations the Congress will organize, and we shall hand on to our children such a Greece as generations past have dreamed of, whom we must show ourselves not unworthy to succeed, such a Greece as we ourselves foreshadowed in our recent victories of 1912 and 1913." [1]

In the last year of the war, Greece raised 300,000 fighting men, besides great numbers of labour gangs for work behind the lines. In the final offensive, through the insistence of Venizelos, Greek divisions took part in all the major operations, and they more than justified the unquenchable optimism of a statesman whose faith was not without its influence in buoying the flagging spirits of leaders less endowed with penetrative imagination.

December 1918 found him already installed in Paris. His assets at the Peace Conference were his own immense prestige, the services of Greece in the Allied cause, the political genius that amazed that miscellaneous assembly, and the fact that the Greek army was kept fully mobilized and ready to act on the frontier of Greece at the moment when war weariness first laid its grip upon the Western nations, and left them at the Peace Conference with little stronger sanction than prestige and the similar, if more deadly, exhaustion of their enemies.

His achievement in the face of determined Italian and American opposition is the political miracle of recent years. The work was realized in stages; the occupation of Smyrna took place on 15th May 1919, and was due to the fear of France, England and the United States, that Italy, who had just created the famous crisis over Fiume, might try to occupy Smyrna, a city which she had been promised at the Conference of St Jean Maurienne in April 1917. That promise had been made dependent on the consent of Russia, but since then the Provisional Government of Kerensky had fallen, and Lenin reigned in his stead. President Wilson sympathized with the Greek claim to Smyrna, if he opposed other parts of the great Cretan's programme.[2]

Italian landing parties in April and May had been creeping up the coast from town to town, and the Allies had reason to fear a *coup de main*. Italy at Smyrna, in their then mood, was an intolerable prospect. But where to find the forces to prevent it? Venizelos was asked to lend them—his claim to Smyrna had not yet been considered by the Allies, but his were the only available forces.[3]

[1] "Vindication of Greek National Policy, 1912-17—a Report of Speeches in the Greek Chamber, August 24-26, 1917," pp. 160-1.

[2] Baker, "Woodrow Wilson and World Settlement."

[3] Toynbee, "The Western Question in Greece and Turkey," p. 77. Baker, "Woodrow Wilson and World Settlement," ii., p. 194.

The same troops that were now landed in Smyrna had early in the year formed the two divisions that Venizelos lent to the French in their ill-starred expedition to Odessa against the Bolsheviks. The expedition had been a failure from the French point of view, since it was terminated by a mutiny in the French Black Sea Fleet. It is alleged that 180 sailors were executed on a single Allied warship off Sebastopol.[1] French bondholders were vicariously wreaking a vengeance which they would otherwise have exacted from the mocking dictator of Red Russia. The expedition cost Greece 286 men in a cause not her own, but it had placed the Allies under obligation, and whereas Greek troops went to Odessa at the convenience of France and returned again, they went to Smyrna for the convenience of the Big Three—Clemenceau, Lloyd George, and Wilson—and would they return? Venizelos had learned the lesson of Cavour who began to make the kingdom of Italy out of the mud of the trenches round Sebastopol. One of the results of the expedition to Odessa was the assurance of the eventual reversion of N. Epirus.[2]

In the vilayet of Aidin, the chief city of which is Smyrna, Venizelos claimed the pre-war population as consisting of 1,188,359 Greeks and 1,042,050 Turks.[3] It is certain that these figures are unreliable, but it is equally certain that within this area are great and wealthy Greek communities—not by any means confined to the coast and especially to the capes, as the average ethnographical map would suggest. The geographical considerations that point to this area are sufficiently obvious from a glance at a physical map of Asia Minor. Venizelos proposed to detach what is a geographical subdivision of Asia Minor—a central plain extending inland some distance from the sea, protected on either flank by mountain bastions and bounded to the east at the space between the converging massifs, by the high wall of the tableland that constitutes the interior of Anatolia. The eventual line of the Sèvres treaty, embracing an area smaller than the lowland plain, certainly gave to Greece the core of the Greek communities, but in deference to Italian opposition the predominating Greek city of Aidin was excluded. The

[1] Proceedings of Greek Revolutionary Tribunal for Trial of Ministers, *Empros*, 11/24 November 1922.

[2] Testimony of George D. Rhalles before the Revolutionary Tribunal, *Empros*, 4/17 November 1922.

[3] "Greece before the Peace Congress of 1919—a Memorandum dealing with the rights of Greece, submitted by Eleutherios Venizelos," pp. 21-2.

frontier was indefensible and in practice, Turkish hostility even at its weakest, necessitated the holding of a far wider flung line.

The attitude of Venizelos to the Hellenism of Asia Minor has been sufficiently indicated. He was convinced that after 1909 the alternatives had been, either Greece would occupy these largely Greek lands or in the course of a few years their Greek character would be obliterated by wholesale expulsion. That the attempt ought to be made he was convinced. But the dangers of such expansion had been obvious to him from the first and he never disguised them. The *sine qua non* of effective occupation in the Smyrna area was European support for a number of years. The power upon whose help he chiefly relied was Great Britain. A friendly and a powerful Greece on the Ægean would be a buttress to British sea-power in the E. Levant. France was not unfriendly—only Italy, forgetful of Cavour, regarded him with undisguised malignity as the architect of a state possibly a rival sea-power in the future.

By the acquisition of E. and W. Thrace he secured, with the Smyrna coast, practically the whole Ægean sea-board. The new Greece was now based on the Ægean with wings on the Adriatic and the Black Sea. Once the Allies had detached W. Thrace from Bulgaria (Treaty of Neuilly), and then for the time refrained from allotting it to Greece in deference to American opposition ; and once they had resolved to deprive Turkey of all territory in Europe except the Constantinople area, the problem could only be solved either by an Allied occupation of the provinces and the establishment of an administration under their own control, or by ceding them to Greece. To occupy Thrace was a responsibility they did not care to undertake in the face of a suspicious public opinion and grave exhaustion.

In June 1920, the Turks started revolutionary movements near Adrianople and grave trouble threatened. All this time the Greek army had been kept by Venizelos on the Thracian frontier. Once more his patience and foresight were justified ; the Allies gave the word, and in July 1920, King Alexander entered Adrianople and order was speedily restored. In his memorandum on Greek claims presented to the Conference, Venizelos did not assert the Greeks were a majority in these two provinces, but he argued that since the Greek element constitutes a fringe round the whole coast, practically continuous to the Black Sea, and the interior is inhabited by an inextricable mixture of Greeks, Turks, Bulgars, Armenians, Jews, and others, and since the Greek element is the most important and progressive as well as only slightly less than the Turkish element in numbers (the only other numerically considerable nationality) it was reasonable to allow the Greek State to embody these geographically continuous Hellenic communities. He studiously refrained from making any claim on Constantinople; but urged that it should be internationalized under the League.

Practically, the dreams of Hellenism had been realized by this amazing man who, as Signor Nitti, his opponent, has written in a generous tribute, "always seemed to be conceding something when his claims were granted." By the time that the Treaty of Sèvres of 10th August 1920 was signed, Venizelos had not only won for Greece that foothold in Asia Minor that he dreamed of, making the city of refuge for the persecuted Anatolian Greeks, but seemed to have made good the claims of Greece on N. Epirus and the Dodecanese. Over both questions he had to make painful headway against determined Italian opposition.

N. Epirus, with its Greek towns of Argyrocastro and Korytsa, had been occupied by Greek forces during the Balkan War, but the whole of this territory had been assigned to the new Albania by the International Commission appointed to determine the frontier, in deference to Italy's expressed determination to prevent Greece extending her coast line so as to control both sides of the Corfu Channel.[1] This would apparently constitute a naval menace to Italy. The Italians feared the establishment of a naval base in a Channel that British naval experts considered a death-trap. Like the White Knight, Italy felt it necessary to protect the legs of her war-horse against sharks.

The Greeks accordingly withdrew to the south of the new frontier, but immediately the highly self-conscious and prosperous Greek communities of the district proclaimed a Provisional Government and finally, by an agreement signed at Corfu, 17th May 1914, with the Albanian Government, obtained certain rights of self-government.

In October 1914, after the departure of Prince William of Wied, Albania relapsed into its native disorder. In these circumstances, Venizelos secured the consent of the Entente

[1] Florence, March 1914.

and Italy to the re-occupation of the province, on the understanding that the whole question was to be decided at the future Peace Conference. In 1916, Italy, on the ground that Constantine was a menace to the flank and rear of the Allies, occupied the province. On the return of Venizelos to power in June 1917 this excuse disappeared. Immediately after the Armistice, Venizelos again secured permission to occupy the province with Greek troops. In April and May 1920 the French and Italian forces were withdrawn, and at the time of the Treaty of Sèvres, the formal recognition of Greek sovereignty was certain in the near future.

In the course of the Turco-Italian war an Italian squadron, during April 1912, occupied the twelve islands of the Southern Sporades, known as the Dodecanese. The Italians were received with great enthusiasm by the Greek islanders and issued proclamations announcing the end of Turkish domination and promising complete autonomy. The Dodecanese had been treated as a unit and enjoyed certain privileges under Ottoman rule, and the islanders were used to acting together. An insular congress accordingly assembled in the monastery of the Apocalypse of St John the Divine on Patmos, and after expressing infinite gratitude to Italy, proclaimed the national wish of all the islanders for union with their motherland, Greece.

The attitude of the liberators at once underwent a complete change. The Congress of Patmos was dispersed by force at the orders of the Italian authorities in June 1912; meetings were prohibited; communications between the islands stopped, and the importation of Greek newspapers forbidden. The Italian Press began an inspired campaign in favour of retaining the Twelve Islands. By the Treaty of Lausanne, 15th October 1912, which concluded the Turco-Italian War, Italy promised to return the islands to Turkey so soon as the last Turkish soldier was withdrawn from Tripoli. From that date till her entry into the war on the side of the Allies, Italy kept a tight hold on the islands.

By the secret treaty of London, 26th April 1915, Italy secured from her new Allies recognition that she "should obtain full possession of the twelve islands now occupied by her." Throughout the war the repressive measures continued. Italian, for instance, was made obligatory in all the schools of a population which, with the exception of a few Jews and Turks, is wholly Greek. As a result, doubtless intended, a large emigration began. In 1912 the population is said to have been about 140,000—the Italian census of 1917 gave it as 100,000. At the present day the population probably does not exceed 80,000. To give a single example, the population of the island of Symi, between 1912 and 1919, fell from 20,000 to 6,780.[1]

With the Armistice a vigorous campaign for emancipation sprang up among the islanders. A delegation was sent to Paris. Meetings were held in the islands in spite of Italian efforts to disperse them, and in Venizelos the islanders had a champion of marvellous pertinacity and skill. As a result of this pressure, Signor Nitti, in pursuance of the much denounced " policy of renunciation," decided on a general settlement with Greece. His Foreign Minister, Tittoni, concluded an agreement with Venizelos in Rome on 29th July 1919. Italy recognized Greek claims in Thrace and N. Epirus. Greece was to grant Italy certain economic facilities in the Smyrna enclave, and Italy agreed to transfer eleven of the twelve islands to Greece on the ratification of the yet undrafted peace with Turkey. The remaining, and by far the most important island, Rhodes, was to be held by Italy so long as Great Britain held Cyprus. Italy agreed to hold a plebiscite in Rhodes within fifteen years of the cession of Cyprus, to determine the final destiny of the famous island.

Count Sforza, Giolitti's Foreign Minister, declined at first to recognize this settlement of the Dodecanese question. Venizelos therefore firmly, but temperately, refused to sign the Treaty of Sèvres until a settlement had been again reached. Since he held East and West Thrace, N. Epirus and the Smyrna enclave, and Greek forces were the only screen between the Nationalist Turks and the Allies in Constantinople, he held the whole Near Eastern settlement in his hands. His slow, patient, yet brilliant diplomacy had by the summer of 1920 made him master of the diplomatic situation. As a result, a further agreement along the lines of the Venizelos-Tittoni settlement was drawn up, and signed on the same day as the Treaty of Sèvres—10th August 1920.

On 12th August 1920, as he was about to leave Paris for Greece, an attempt was made to assassinate him on the

[1] Polybius, " Greece before the Conference," p. 71. M. D. Volonakis, " The National Claims of the Dodecanese " (Anglo-Hellenic League Publication, No. 46).

platform by two ex-officers of the Greek Navy. The news was hailed as a glorious tyrannicide by the Royalist press—a sufficient indication of the desperate nature of the feud between Royalist and Venizelist. On 13th August the mob in Athens broke loose and, under the eyes of the police, sacked Royalist clubs and newspaper offices, and the homes of four leading members of the Opposition. The Premier's Cretan Guards murdered M. Jon Dragoumes, a well-known anti-Venizelist and the son of a former Premier. From his bed Venizelos telegraphed a strongly-worded rebuke to the Government, but on his return to Greece he failed to take any action and publicly embraced M. Repoulis, the acting Prime Minister, who had explained to the Chamber and his chief that the Government had been overborne by the violence of extreme elements in the populace.[1] Once again Venizelos had committed a grave psychological blunder—this time prompted by a natural generosity to one of the most devoted of his supporters.

On 7th September 1920 he formally presented the fruits of his two years' work in Western Europe to the Chamber—the Treaty of Neuilly with Bulgaria, the Treaty of Sèvres with Turkey, and the Treaty with Italy. Although obviously suffering from the effects of the wounds inflicted by his would-be assassins and speaking in a weak voice, he introduced the Treaties in a long speech reviewing the international position and the prospects of Greece. He was unanimously voted the saviour of his country.

It was indeed a prodigious achievement. His bitter enemy, the aged ex-Premier Rhalles, exclaimed, after studying the Treaty of Sèvres: "It is a masterpiece!"[2] Yet critics were not wanting, especially abroad, who emphasized, for the most part at a later date, the undoubted dangers of the policy of cutting off Bulgaria from the sea and expanding into Asia Minor. Did not the disturbances that marked the Greek landing at Smyrna in 1919 justify the assertion that the Greeks could not rule mixed populations? The keenest of those later critics of Venizelos has been Mr A. J. Toynbee. It will be right to quote here his analysis of the motives of Greek policy at Paris: "What had happened to M. Venizelos? . . . Had he simply been infected by the hysteri-

[1] Abbott, "Greece and the Allies," pp. 221-2.

[2] Testimony of George D. Rhalles (son of ex-Premier) before the Revolutionary Tribunal for Trial of Ministers, *Empros* 4/17th November 1922.

cal atmosphere of the Peace Conference? Had the sudden passage from the verge of defeat to apparently absolute victory blinded him to the fact that the momentarily prostrate enemy nations would sometime become powers again? Had his head been turned by his Western colleagues' recognition of his personal qualities? All these things happened to other prominent members of the Conference, but it is difficult to believe that a statesman with such a long experience, such a record of liberalism and moderation, and so much intellectual originality and strength of will, can have based an elaborate programme on passing impulses and emotions. These may have weakened his judgment, they can hardly have overthrown it. The less improbable explanation is that his optimism was largely feigned, that he was taking the risks with his eyes open, and that his policy was decided partly by some *force majeure* and partly by the expectation that the dangers, while real, could be discounted by some effective means of insurance. . . .

"The *force majeure* is not far to seek. It lay in the necessities of Greek internal politics." [1]

This analysis fails to explain the motives of Venizelos simply because it ignores the patent fact that it was in order to carry out the policy which he did carry out at Paris, that he dared to run the tremendous risk of dividing the nation by rebellion. His optimism was not feigned simply because his whole life reveals it as of the very stuff of his character, for optimism always is the motive of any great achievement. He believed that he was interpreting the dearest dream of the Hellenic race, and he was right; for at no time have the Greeks shown that they repudiated the principles or the objects of his marvellous diplomacy.

In the introduction to the second edition of his work, from which the above extract was taken, Mr Toynbee observes: "I have not yet come across any denial of the motives which I conjecturally attributed to him." [2] That Venizelos, who had discussed Greek aspirations in Asia Minor with King Constantine in 1914, occupied Smyrna in 1919 and Eastern and Western Thrace in 1920 because of "necessities of Greek internal politics," or, in clearer terms, for electioneering reasons, surely requires no denial. M. Venizelos would be unlikely to deviate

[1] A. J. Toynbee, "The Western Question in Greece and Turkey," pp. 71-2.

[2] *Ibid.*, 2nd ed., Introduction, p. xix.

from good taste by protesting that he was an honourable man.

At the cost of setting his face against national sentiment, and in terms of that ideal of a permanent Balkan Confederation, which has been the twin-motive of most of his statesmanship, he was prepared in 1913, and again in 1915, to pay a high price to win Bulgaria to the idea of that Confederation. On both occasions, Bulgaria refused everything short of her own unquestioned supremacy. No sacrifices could win her in the days of her triumph or in the days of her defeat, and by 1919 Venizelos had neither the inclination nor the power to go on postulating a change of spirit. Serbia, by realizing her full national unity as Jugo-Slavia, had escaped from the Balkan cockpit. Greece must do the same and escape on the flood-tide of an unique victory. Repeated assertions have been made that the Greeks could not administer a territory with a mixed population. The riots at Smyrna on the Greek landing, and those military outrages along the south coast of the Sea of Marmora that wrought so radical a change in the opinions of Mr Toynbee, have again and again been adduced as proof. What is forgotten or neglected is that Asia Minor was the theatre of a war, and in a war area anything may happen. It is significant that no such charges have been made against Greek administration in Eastern Thrace, where the population is certainly mixed.

Perhaps at the risk of divagation, it would be as well here to discuss some aspects of the famous landing at Smyrna on 15th May 1919.

On receiving news of the disturbances that followed the landing, Venizelos immediately asked the Allies to appoint a Commission of Inquiry. This request was refused. When, however, the Sheik-ul-Islam made a similar request on 18th July 1919, it was granted. On receiving particulars of the procedure to be adopted, Venizelos rightly pointed out that Greece was placed in the position of a defendant, and that she should be represented on the Inquiry.[1] He was informed that a Greek representative could attend the meetings of the Commission, but should not have a vote or take part in drawing up the final Report.[2] These conditions Venizelos accepted, and he then nominated Colonel Mazarakis to watch the procedure of the Commission.[3]

[1] Venizelos to Clemenceau, 19th July 1919.
[2] 21st July 1919.
[3] Venizelos to Clemenceau, 31st July 1919.

The Commission began its labours at Constantinople, but the Greek delegate was not allowed to attend its meetings.[1] He was then informed that the depositions of the Commission, which had gone to Smyrna, would be given to Colonel Mazarakis, who would be kept "au courant des travaux de la Commission." The work of the Inquiry went on, but the promised depositions were not made, and, more important, the Commission refused to hear many of the witnesses suggested by Colonel Mazarakis.[2]

Clemenceau replied to the protests of Venizelos by assuring him that the Supreme Council had decided that the *procès-verbaux* of the Commission would be communicated to Colonel Mazarakis, who would then be heard after he had studied the documents.[3] On 30th September 1919, Venizelos accepted this further attenuation of Allied promises, and authorized the Greek delegate to act on the lines now suggested by the Supreme Council. The Commission now found itself in a hopeless quandary. It had promised to communicate the evidence before it to the Greek representative; it had also promised the witnesses who appeared before it that their testimony and their identity should be kept secret. Both promises could not be kept in the spirit, but perhaps they might be reconciled in the letter. Accordingly, the Commission interpreted the instructions of the Supreme Council of 30th September 1919 as meaning that evidence heard *after* that date should be communicated to Colonel Mazarakis. The convenience of this interpretation lay in the fact that the Commission had already finished its work.[4] In these circumstances, Venizelos declared that he refused to accept the conclusions or evidence of the Commission, but remained perfectly ready to co-operate in a further Inquiry conducted on lines of elementary justice and good faith.

Mr Lloyd George, who now heard for the first time of the extraordinary procedure of the Commission, decided at once that its findings were worthless, and ordered the Report to be quashed. This Report, drawn up by the Commission, under the presidency of Admiral Bristol, U.S. High Commissioner in Constantinople, has since been the King Charles's head of all Turcophils. It would, they imagine, constitute

[1] Venizelos to Clemenceau, 22nd August 1919.
[2] *Ibid.*, 14th and 28th September 1919.
[3] Clemenceau to Venizelos, 30th September 1919.
[4] Venizelos to Clemenceau and Lloyd George, 23rd October 1919.

a mine of information likely to prove the unfitness of Greece to govern a mixed population. It would probably demonstrate, on the other hand, the unfitness of Levantines in giving evidence if not strictly cross-examined. That the "Bryce Reports" on "Alleged German Atrocities in Belgium" and on the "Treatment of Armenians in the Ottoman Empire" labour under the same disability of leaving the accused unrepresented and unheard is true.[1] But in the circumstances of the Bryce Reports, this was inevitable, while the procedure of the Bristol Commission was not only unnecessary, but also vitiated by bad faith. In any case, the promulgation of *ex parte* statements in the midst of a world war is scarcely an adequate reason for continuing the practice when an opportunity of doing better in finding the way of truth has at last presented itself.

There is a strong moral case for going over the question of Belgian and Armenian atrocities again—whether it is yet expedient is another matter; there is no case for following the lines of the Bristol Commission, which actually refused to hear witnesses presented by the accused. To do so would perhaps have spoilt the "entire and perfect chrysolite" of indignation, presumably still locked in the buried Pandora's box of the suppressed Report. In the result, what happened at Smyrna in those first days remains obscure. What is certain, however, is that M. Sterghiadhis arrived as High Commissioner on 21st May 1919, and speedily restored complete order; and that the court-martial set up by Venizelos to inquire into the riots, executed 3 Greeks and sentenced 45 Greeks, 13 Turks, 12 Armenians, and 1 Jew to severe terms of imprisonment.

For the consolidation of the great political structure he had built Venizelos required one thing, not always to be had for the asking—time. That the industrious Greek population of the Smyrna zone would expand rapidly and convert the area into a wholly Greek enclave was certain.[2] He counted on the extraordinary vitality of the race that had survived so many storms. If he could win it, time was on his side.

The story that culminates in the November election of 1920 is not long in telling. On the signature of the Treaty

[1] A. J. Toynbee, "The Western Question in Greece and Turkey," p. 80.

[2] "A History of the Peace Conference of Paris," edited, H. W. V. Temperley, vol. vi., p. 46.

of Sèvres, Venizelos returned to Greece after an absence of nearly two years (broken only by flying visits), to hold the long-deferred elections. The ultimate success of his policy depended upon a further period of office, during which the dangers he had foreseen in creating the Greater Greece could be faced and averted.

It is these ultimate decisions that, under all systems of government, lie finally in the hands of the people; again and again the elections had been postponed in order that the Prime Minister might present to the world of doubtful diplomats the spectacle of a united nation and a stable State. He had received his mandate, and he would execute it at all costs before he put all to the touch. Yet, during those two years of unremitting labour, he had lost contact with the people over whom he had once exercised so magical a sway. The strain of the sacrifices he demanded of them; the silence that he could not break; the blunders of nervous and tactless subordinates; the activities of the Royalist party, pursuing what was now a vendetta—all this had fatally undermined his position. On the very eve of the elections, the dynastic issue was raised in an acute form by the tragic death of King Alexander on 25th October 1920.

A Regency under Admiral Kountouriotis was set up, and the throne formally offered to Prince Paul, Constantine's third son, a youth in his teens and at the moment with his father in Switzerland. The Prince replied in a formal document calculated by the advisers of the King to state the issues for the benefit of the Greek people: "The throne does not belong to me; it belongs to my august father, King Constantine, and constitutionally my eldest brother is his successor. Neither of them has ever renounced his rights. . . . I would only ascend the throne if the Hellenic people were to decide that it did not want the return of my august father, and were to exclude the Crown Prince George from his right of succession."

Venizelos, after first taking the line that the Government would change the dynasty rather than permit the reopening of the question, suddenly swung round and recognized the inevitable by making the restoration of King Constantine the main issue of the election. He challenged the Opposition on this sole question. The Greek people should choose between himself and Constantine.[1] The Opposition, which

[1] Abbott, "Greece and the Allies," p. 225.

consisted of sixteen distinct groups, united only by a common hatred of the great Cretan, jumped at the superb election cry of "King Constantine and peace."

On 14th November 1920—three months after Venizelos had set his signature to the greatest diplomatic achievement of our time, the Venizelist party was swept from power. Venizelos himself was defeated at the polls—the liberated provinces alone returned the supporters of their deliverer. The Royalist party rose from the grave in a day—masters of Greece. The united Opposition won 246 seats, and though the Liberals with 120 were still the largest single party in the House, the disaster was overwhelming. The splendid dignity of the man was never greater than in those last days. His friends urged him to avert the disaster by a *coup d'état*—he had the means. He repulsed the suggestion as a monstrous travesty of his life. All his revolutions had been undertaken in order to give the people a voice—now they had spoken. His Liberalism did not desert him.

On 17th November he embarked on a British destroyer and left the land that he had raised from utter humiliation to dizzy heights of success, and where his life was no longer safe. That night the returning Royalist ministers received the wild ovations of the mob, tired of a discipline that had lost its novelty. For hours the triumphant supporters of King Constantine gyrated through the streets of Athens with trumpets and torches, amid the glare of searchlights and the shimmer of fireworks.

Out to sea the vessel that was bearing away the fortunes and the future of the Greeks was ploughing its solitary path among the Cyclades under the stars, and soon was rounding the last dim headlands of Hellas. . . . .

The new Premier, Rhalles, invited the dowager Queen Olga, who had returned to Greece to attend the funeral of her grandson, King Alexander, to assume the office of Regent, and on 5th December 1920, the question of the return of Constantine was submitted to popular decision by plebiscite. The Venizelists abstained, but the results were sufficiently striking, at least at the first blush. Out of 1,013,724 votes cast, 999,954 were for the exiled King. On 19th December 1920, Constantine returned to Greece. Rarely has any man been given so great a second chance or so great a second opportunity.

Blake, in one of his profound aphorisms, declares that "if a fool would persist in his folly he would become wise." Between 1915 and 1917 Constantine had devoted the whole influence of the throne and his own personal popularity to the task of defeating the policy of Venizelos and of keeping Greece out of the war. His pacificism, though not based on principle, was at any rate thorough. Any personal or national humiliation seemed to him better than intervention in the war. He returned ostensibly to give the Greek people peace after the adventures of the "tyrant" they had just voted out of political life. Had Constantine devoted the same energy he had shown in keeping Greece out of the war—even at the cost of dividing the nation and precipitating a revolution—to the task of securing the peace he had promised, the fool would have indeed been transformed into a wise man. It is safe to say that not once did he attempt to secure peace by the unwarlike methods of diplomacy, to which he had already once sacrificed his crown. Instead, he embarked on a policy of military adventure at a moment when the odds were as desperately against it as they had been against his policy of peace at any price. That simply is the whole story. But we must elaborate a little on the tragic sequence of events.

The fall of Venizelos precipitated a diplomatic revolution. It quite clearly involved the rupture of the alliance with France and Great Britain. Public opinion in those countries would not hear of continued co-operation with a monarch regarded as a declared enemy of the Entente. In France, there was a strong movement in favour of forcibly preventing the return of the King, and this was the view upheld by the French Premier, Leygues, who attended a Conference in London at which the Allies formulated a new policy. The British Government took the view that to prevent the Greek people from recalling the sovereign of their choice was an unjustifiable interference in the internal affairs of another country. On the other hand, it was agreed that a clear statement of the consequences of the probable return of Constantine must be made to the Greek Government.

Accordingly, on 2nd December 1920, the Allies presented a Note to M. Rhalles, declaring that "they had no wish to interfere in the internal affairs of Greece, but they felt bound to declare publicly that the restoration of the throne to a King whose disloyal attitude and conduct towards the Allies during the war caused them great embarrassment and loss could only be regarded by them as a ratification by Greece of his hostile acts"; accordingly they reserved to themselves "complete liberty in dealing with the situation," if he were recalled. On 8th December 1920 they followed up their first note by declaring that in the event of a restoration of Constantine they would withdraw the financial assistance they had, up to the elections of 14th November, been giving to Greece. This declaration was sufficiently definite to alarm the moderate Royalists, but it was not allowed to influence the decision of the Greek people, and was suppressed by the censorship.[1]

The news of the notes from the Powers convinced the great exile that his worst forebodings as to the consequences of the election had been fulfilled. The foundation of his diplomacy, the alliance with Great Britain and France, had already been torn up. Convinced that, in spite of all that had happened, he could still be of use to his country, Venizelos had a conversation at Cannes with Mr Philip Kerr, the Secretary of Mr Lloyd George. Mr Kerr was convinced that the restoration of Constantine was an insuperable handicap to co-operation with Greece in enforcing the Treaty of Sèvres. If the treaty could not be enforced against the Nationalists of Angora, it would have to be revised. As a result of this conversation, Venizelos, on 1st January 1921, addressed a letter to his triumphant rival, Rhalles, through the Greek minister in Paris, M. Metaxas. He reported his conversation with Mr Kerr, and suggested to Rhalles that, in view of the unquestionable hostility of the Powers to King Constantine, Greece should make ready to cut her losses in Anatolia and should at once withdraw all her forces to the Sèvres zone. This would relieve Greece of a considerable military expenditure, enable her to keep her grasp on the city of Smyrna as firmly as before, and, at the same time, indirectly bring moral pressure to bear on France and Italy, whose tasks in Syria and Adalia would be rendered far heavier in the event of a Greek evacuation, for which at the moment they were not prepared. Faced by the prospect of losing the benefit of Greek co-operation, they would have to consider seriously exactly to what extent they would be prepared to continue their support. Venizelos saw clearly that the one absolutely

[1] Not published in Greece until 19th March 1922.

fatal policy was that of the "lone hand." If Greece retreated to the Sèvres zone at once, she would already have brought pressure to bear on the forthcoming Conference to which the Allies proposed to invite both Turks and Greeks.

The aged Demetrios Rhalles, now for the fifth time Premier of Greece, was one of the least Royalist and most moderate members of the Opposition. He seems indeed to have regarded King Constantine and the whole Danish dynasty, including its founder, King George, with considerable contempt and distrust. In 1917, he said that the whole secret of Greek neutrality in the war up till then was the cowardice of Constantine: "Constantine is a coward. He is afraid of Germany. . . . All autocrats are cowards, and Constantine is an autocrat of the worst type."[1] His hatred of Venizelos was deep but purely personal: "I have a right to hate him," he told Mrs Kenneth Brown. "For over forty years I have never once missed being elected deputy—and Venizelos defeated me. . . . I wish to punish that man. You know he is from a low origin. He is not any relation to the great family of Venizelos."[2] But Rhalles knew how to make distinctions between his personal and political feelings, and he was always a patriot. The letter from Venizelos impressed him greatly. He saw that the diplomatic situation had been revolutionized by the elections, and realized clearly that for Greece to attempt to stand alone would be to court disaster.

On 14th January 1921 Greece received a formal invitation to a Conference in London to which the Allies were also inviting the Turks of Constantinople and Angora. Immediately, a struggle broke out in the Greek Cabinet between Rhalles, who proposed to head the Greek delegation to London, and Gounaris, who considered that, in view of the importance of his party, he, rather than Rhalles, should represent Greece. Rhalles was strongly opposed to the whole idea of Gounaris visiting London in any capacity. The political importance in Greece of Gounaris was an irrelevant detail beside the glaring fact that of all Royalist leaders he was the most obnoxious to the Allies, and had actually been interned in Corsica by France during the later stages of the war. A further cause of friction supervened when Gounaris realized

[1] Demetra Vaka (Mrs Kenneth Brown), "Constantine, King and Traitor," pp. 162-3. Conversation with M. Rhalles.

[2] *Ibid.*, p. 166.

that Rhalles was considering the possibility of utilizing the diplomatic services of Venizelos, and actually proposed to show the letter from Venizelos of 1st January 1921 to the King.[1] Presumably, Constantine's feelings must not be harrowed by perusing the gratuitous advice of his arch-enemy.

The result of the conflict was the resignation of Rhalles on 9th February 1921. He was succeeded (as a compromise) by Kalogeropoulos, who proceeded to London as the head of the Greek delegation to the Conference that opened on 21st February.

Both Constantinople and Angora were represented. The difficulty of their mutual relationship, that of a legitimate Government and a rebellion, was solved with grace and dignity. The Turks realized that, so far as the victorious Allies and the Treaty of Sèvres were concerned, they were at one. The representative of the Sultan's Government at Constantinople accordingly retired to his bed, and in view of his indisposition, handed over the task of representing both Turkish Governments to the delegate from Angora, Bekir Samy Bey.

At the opening of the Conference, Venizelos had come to England at the unofficial invitation of the British Government, and hoping to be able to co-operate with the Royalists in defending his great creation, the Treaty of Sèvres. He did not disguise the dangers that were already overhanging the whole settlement of the Near East. "I hope," he said to an English friend, "that there is nothing ill-omened in a name, and that the Treaty of Sèvres will not prove as brittle as its china!"[2] He came to London, and unofficial efforts were made to induce Kalogeropoulos to admit Venizelos into the Greek delegation as the representative of the "unredeemed Greeks." The head of the Greek delegation, who was the mere nominee and tool of Gounaris, violently repudiated any idea of co-operation with "the Cretan."

On 12th March 1921, after various proposals had been considered and rejected, the Allies produced a detailed scheme. Smyrna was to remain under Turkish sovereignty, but a Greek force was to be stationed in the city itself, while

[1] Testimony of George D. Rhalles (son of Premier) before the Revolutionary Tribunal for the trial of the Constantinist ministers and others. *Empros*, 4/17th November 1922.

[2] V. J. Seligman, "M. Venizelos on the Greek Situation," art. *The Fortnightly Review*, April 1921, vol. 109, p. 619.

in the rest of the enclave order was to be maintained by a gendarmerie under Allied officers, and recruited in proportion to the numbers and distribution of the population in given districts. A Christian governor appointed by the League, and assisted by an elective Assembly and Council, would administer the autonomous area, and the Governor would be responsible for collection and payment to Turkey of a yearly tribute, which would increase with the expansion of the trade of the new region. At the end of five years, the whole arrangement might be reviewed by the League at the request of either the Greek or Turkish Government.[1]

The Turks, remembering how similar arrangements in Eastern Roumelia and Bulgaria had paved the way to complete separation, rejected the proposal. The Greeks were unenthusiastic about it. On 24th March Gounaris, who had come to London after the Conference started, brought it to an abrupt end by ordering a general offensive. In a few days, the Greek forces had occupied the two vital railway junctions of Afion Kara Hissar and Eskishehr.

Gounaris was not only over-confident in the equipment and ability of the Greek army to enforce a decision, but he believed that in taking the offensive he was really interpreting British wishes on the Turkish Question.[2] The fact that the French Premier, Leygues, had advocated the use of force to prevent the return of Constantine, and that Great Britain had opposed this extreme measure as an unjustifiable interference, persuaded him that there was a fundamental difference between Britain and France at this period over the whole Near Eastern Question, and that the terms presented to the Greeks and Turks in the name of the Allies represented a hollow compromise between the British and French views. In breaking up the Conference and resuming the war, Gounaris not only hoped to win British support, but, in the event of victory, which he believed certain, to secure the recognition of King Constantine, with whom the Allies had refused to renew relations—a recognition to obtaining which his whole policy was directed.

Yet, in counting on the divisions of the Western Powers (who certainly did not see eye to eye), Gounaris was making a fatal breach in the policy of Venizelos, which had been

[1] A. J. Toynbee, " The Western Question in Greece and Turkey," p. 95.
[2] Testimony of George D. Rhalles (son of Premier) before the Revolutionary Tribunal. *Empros*, 4/17th November 1922.

throughout based on the alliance of France and Great Britain. It need not have required the genius of a great statesman to realize that if a small Power like Greece fell between the stools of two Great Powers, it was courting destruction. The Allies had presented a definite and united programme. Gounaris had incurred the fatal responsibility of rejecting it.

But even the military gamble did not succeed. On 2nd April 1921, the Greeks were severely defeated, forced to abandon Afion Kara Hissar and Eskishehr, and driven by the Turks back upon their old positions. Gounaris now considered the prestige of the Restoration at stake. On 7th April he became Premier, and subordinated everything to a policy of military adventure in terms of the same over-subtle calculations.

In the meantime the new Chamber had met on 1st February 1921, and declared itself a National Constituent Assembly. It was marvellously representative of all those political elements in Greece that Venizelos had apparently annihilated in 1910. It was even more representative of a corrupt and incompetent past, for some of its most prominent figures had not been heard of since 1897 and the disastrous Turkish war of that year. Most of its time was spent in denouncing the Venizelist "tyranny," and voting compensations to its victims. One of the despotic acts complained of was the introduction of the teaching of the "demotic," or popular language of the people, into the National schools. Here it will not be out of place to mention that many votes were cast against Venizelos at the elections in Athens itself because of his "oppressive" regulations against the over-driving of donkeys and cruelty to animals in general.[1]

Gounaris was not sorry to see the National Assembly occupied with the one subject on which it could remain united —the wickedness of Venizelos. He also submitted an elaborate scheme for constitutional reform, providing for non-political governments of permanent civil servants; women's suffrage; an industrial council of legally organized trades to advise on social and economic questions; for plebiscites to be held on the demand of the King, the Chamber, or a fixed number of citizens. D'Annunzio and his "Constitution of the Regency of the Carnaro" may have provided the bold and stimulating outlines. In any case the Chamber was well occupied, and on 23rd May 1921 it voted monuments to 140 military

[1] A. J. Toynbee, "The Western Question in Greece and Turkey."

mutineers shot by Venizelist courts-martial during the war, and compensation to their relatives.[1]

Meanwhile unheard-of efforts were being made to equip the army in Asia for a further offensive. Public opinion was assured that it would prove decisive, and in order to calm the anxiety caused by the fall of the exchange and the rise in the cost of living that was already manifesting itself, a deliberately concocted fable was assiduously circulated that Great Britain was secretly assisting Greece, not only with money and munitions, but with an army and fleet.

On 20th May 1921 the British, French, and Italian High Commissioners proclaimed the neutrality of the Zone of the Straits under their military occupation, during the Græco-Turkish War. But nothing could deflect Gounaris and the King from their gamble, and on 11th June (the anniversary of the fall of Constantinople in 1453, and the death of the last Greek Emperor, Constantine Palæologos) Constantine left Athens for the front. In the Government press he was hailed as the Commander-in-Chief of the Anglo-Greek armies of the East.[2]

The Allies had now lost control of the situation, but they made another effort to induce both parties to accept a settlement. On 21st June 1921 they informed the Greek Government that they were "prepared to attempt the task of conciliation, if the Hellenic Government were disposed to place its interests in their hands." If it refused, the Allies declared they could accept no responsibility for the consequences, but "should it accept the intervention of the Powers, they would be prepared to state the terms upon which their assistance would be proffered, and, in the event of their being accepted, to approach the Turkish Government with a view to the immediate suspension of hostilities and to negotiations for the conclusion of peace."[3] At the same time, another letter from Venizelos, communicated through the Paris Legation, was received by Gounaris. In it he informed the Greek Government of the conditions which the Powers contemplated

[1] Speech for the prosecution (Advocate Gregoriades) before the Revolutionary Tribunal for trial of ministers and others. *Empros*, 11/24 November 1922.

[2] "Notes on Greek History, 1910-23," communicated by Mr John Mavrogordato.

[3] Quoted Toynbee, "The Western Question in Greece and Turkey," p. 97.

proposing, and of which he had been informed.[1] Once again he urged his enemies to retrieve their position of hopeless isolation by taking the Powers at their word. The conditions the Powers had in mind were the preservation of Thrace up to the Chatalja Lines under Greek sovereignty, and the autonomy of the Smyrna district under a governor-general appointed by the League of Nations, who would organize the administration and military forces. When these were considered sufficiently strong all Greek troops would be withdrawn.[2]

On 25th June, after the adventurers had held a Council at Smyrna under the presidency of the King, the Government replied that Greece thanked "her great *Allies*" for their offer, but could not postpone an offensive designed to enforce the Treaty of Sèvres. In this she was only continuing the task undertaken by her in conjunction with "her great Allies," since experience had demonstrated that the Turkish Question could only be solved by force of arms.[3] The reference to "her great Allies," in view of all that had happened since the return of Constantine, was merely impudent, but there was enough in the reply to make it uncomfortable reading to the Allies. What had been their own policy, embodied in the Treaty of Sèvres, was being exploited. Gounaris had sacrificed the real interests of Greece, but he had scored a verbal victory over the Powers. On 19th July 1921, the Greek army again took the offensive, and in a few days had again seized Afion Kara Hissar and Eskishehr. The wine of victory intoxicated the nation, and many Venizelists rallied to the Government, which they believed was carrying on the national policy of their leader.

On 3rd July 1921, on the eve of the offensive, when the war fever was raging in Athens, Venizelos wrote from Aix-les-Bains to General Danglis, the Chairman of the Executive Committee of the Greek Liberal Party in Athens, perhaps the greatest letter of his life:—

"The refusal of the Government to accept even in principle the intervention of the Powers is its last crime against Greece. How can there be a question of the continuance of our national policy under the present Government, when, by the vote of

[1] Testimony of K. Rentes (formerly Director of Greek Foreign Office) before the Revolutionary Tribunal. *Empros*, 5/18 November 1922.

[2] Venizelos to General Danglis, 3rd July 1921. *Times*, 5th October 1922.

[3] "Notes on Greek History, 1910-23," communicated by Mr John Mavrogordato.

14th November and the rupture of our alliance with the Great Powers consequent upon this, the whole foundations of that policy were torn up?

"Was it possible that I should contemplate carrying on a single-handed war against Turkey, without the alliance with our Allies, and indeed against them? The unfortunate thing is that even the Liberals have failed from the beginning to understand the true state of affairs, and continue to believe that the present Government is carrying out our national policy, and to give an over-enthusiastic support to this, while in reality the continuance of this policy has become an impossiblity since the elimination of its first postulate, namely, our alliance with the Western Powers. Consequently, no alternative could remain to the present Government other than to attempt to arrive at a compromise, with a view to bring the state of war to an end, and to preserve whatever still could be saved out of the fruits of our policy. . . . It must be noted that, when I maintain that the Government committed a crime in not accepting the intervention of the Powers, I did not maintain with certainty that the Turks would have accepted a solution in accordance with the British point of view. But, in the event of a refusal of the Turks to accept this solution, Great Britain would have been able to support us, with public opinion behind her action, in the enforcement of the Treaty of Sèvres, while, now that the refusal has come from us, public opinion in England will in no event allow the Government to assist us, and, therefore, such assistance is completely out of the question.

"Thus, having broken the last moral bond with the Powers, formerly our Allies, by the rejection of their intervention and the resumption of war, the Government are leading Greece into danger of complete disaster, because a military victory so great as to subject the enemy to our will and to oblige them to sign and execute a treaty dictated by us must be regarded as an absolute impossibility by anyone still retaining his senses. . . .

"But since such a complete military victory is out of the question so long as the enemy knows that we are diplomatically isolated, and his capital[1] is completely protected against any attack by us by those very Powers who were until recently our Allies, to what other result can resumption of hostilities lead than to complete economical and military exhaustion,

[1] Constantinople, occupied by the Allies.

which will compel us, after a few months, to go down on our knees and beg for intervention under incomparably more unfavourable conditions than those offered before? That is the sombre picture presented to my eyes by the state of things now brought about."[1]

This letter, marvellous in its prescience, and the clearest proof of the wisdom and statesmanship of Venizelos, was published in the Athenian press a few weeks later. Gounaris considered it worthy of an open letter in reply, in which he asserted that there had been no change in Greek relations with the Powers — on the contrary they had improved. Throughout this period, the proclamations of Constantine were full of such deliberately misleading statements as the following: "By our military action we aim at the tranquillization of the East in common with the Allied Powers." Whereas the plain truth is that the Allies, directly and indirectly, had given the Greek Government to understand that Constantine should abdicate.

A final effort at mediation was made after the resumption of the offensive operations on 19th July, when Lord Granville, the British minister, brought to the notice of the Greek Foreign Minister, Baltazzi, in an unofficial way, that Great Britain was still ready to offer her mediation. This step was left unanswered, and was not even brought to the notice of the Cabinet.[2]

The advance into the heart of Anatolia continued until after the middle of August, when the line of the River Sakkaria was reached. It was a remarkable military feat, of which any country might be proud, but the enemy had not been destroyed. The resounding military victory for which Gounaris was playing had not been achieved. The Greek armies had reached the site of the ancient city of Gordium, in the temple of which Alexander the Great had cut the Gordian knot. Would not the occupation of Angora cut the Gordian knot of the political situation, force the Turks to conclude peace, and win for Constantine his long-sought recognition? A Council assembled at G.H.Q., in Kutaya, to decide the momentous question.

The King presided, and the meeting was attended by Gounaris and Theotokis, General Papoulas, the Commander-

[1] *The Times*, 5th October 1922.

[2] Testimony of K. Rentes (formerly Director of the Foreign Office) before the Revolutionary Tribunal; *Empros*, 5/18 November 1922. Also of George D. Rhalles; *Empros*, 4/17 November 1922.

in-Chief, Major-General Pallis, the Chief of the General Staff, Colonel Sarigiannes, and one or two others. The responsible military authorities were against the expedition, since the only chance of crushing the enemy had passed when the Turks escaped to the other side of the Sakkaria.[1] The two civilians, Gounaris and Theotokis, insisted that the occupation of Angora was politically necessary, and the King, apparently, supported them.[2] They prevailed, and the attack across the Sakkaria was launched, which culminated, on 26th August 1921, in a grave defeat. A general retreat to the line Afion Kara Hissar-Eskishehr became necessary, which occupied the most of September. When, on 29th September 1921, Constantine returned to Athens, the battle-line had been stabilized, but Greece had lost 6200 dead and 23,000 wounded. In all there had been 31,000 casualties.[3] The Turks, assailed in their last strongholds, had fought with all their old genius for defensive warfare, Greek *moral* was seriously shaken, and France and Italy, already weary of the burden of their Turkish commitments and only too anxious to find a short cut out of them, became convinced that the ultimate victory of the Turks was certain.

In October 1921, the National Assembly was informed that the campaign had been successful, but that the enemy had not been destroyed. On 16th October Gounaris and Baltazzi left for Paris and London. For five months they wandered about Western Europe, interviewing statesmen, and, absolutely unable to think of anything to retrieve the situation, after repeated interviews with Lord Curzon, during which they gradually told him the complete truth, they ended by accepting his advice and placing the interests of Greece unconditionally in the hands of the Allies. They had rejected mediation on terms thoroughly favourable in March, in June, in July; now in November they abandon all control of the fortunes of their country into the hands of the minister of a foreign Power. However benevolent that minister was —and Lord Curzon devoted all his energies to extricating Greece from the slough in which she was sinking—such a decision on the part of responsible ministers was a shocking

[1] Testimony of General Papoulas before the Revolutionary Tribunal; *Empros*, 2/15 November 1922. Testimony of Major-General Pallis; *Empros*, 6/19 November 1922.

[2] Deposition on oath of Colonel Sarigiannes, read before Revolutionary Tribunal; *Empros*, 6/19 November 1922.

[3] Official figures.

dereliction from duty at a moment when they were assuring the National Assembly that the war in Asia Minor had been victorious.

They followed up this negative achievement by signing, on 21st December 1921, a financial agreement with Sir Robert Horne, by which they gave up all claims on the credits guaranteed to the Venizelist Government, but cut off on the restoration of Constantine, and in return received permission to raise a loan under the Trade Facilities Act or on the open market, if they could. If they could satisfy the bankers, the British Government had no objection to the raising of a loan up to £15,000,000. That was all. In the financial condition in which Greece then was, there was not the slightest chance of such a loan materializing.

In the meantime, three successive blows had fallen on the cause of Constantine. On 20th October 1921, as soon as it became evident that the Greeks had shot their bolt in Asia Minor, the French cut their losses by concluding the notorious pact known as the Franklin-Bouillon Agreement with the Angora Nationalists. By this agreement, reached without the knowledge and behind the back of Great Britain, France secured her hold on Syria, and bought peace with the Turkey of Mustapha Kemal by surrendering the whole stretch of the Bagdad Railway between French Syria and Mesopotamia. In return, she received economic concessions that events were to render valueless. A separate peace between France and the Nationalists had been concluded, the Treaty of Sèvres had been ignored, and the Anglo-French Entente strained to the breaking-point.[1] M. Poincaré was clearing the stage for his Reparations Drama further to the West. An acrimonious correspondence between France and Great Britain revealed to the Turks the breach between the two Great Powers, and strengthened their resolve to play for time and their full programme of restoration both in Smyrna and Eastern Thrace.

On 18th November 1921, the Ambassadors' Conference, under the inspiration of Italy, finally awarded Northern Epirus to Albania. No final arrangement had been made at the time of the Greek elections of November 1920, but, as has been said above, the reversion of the province to Greece seemed certain, and Greek troops were in occupation. Albania appealed against the frontier claimed by Greece

[1] Diplomatic Correspondence, Parliamentary Paper, Cond. 1570.

to the League of Nations, and on 23rd June 1921, the Council, relying on the declaration of the Powers in *1914*, that the question must be decided at the Peace Conference, declared that only the supreme organ of the Great Powers, the Ambassadors' Conference, was competent to deal with the matter. That organ was now, as we have seen, in the mood to listen to the usual Italian suggestions for the truncation of Greece. It is quite certain that if the League of Nations continues to regard itself as bound by decisions made before it came into existence, it will finally stultify the hopes built on it as the possible organ of impartial judgments.

Finally, on 7th December 1921, the Synod of Constantinople elected as the Œcumenical Patriarch, Meletios Metaxakes, formerly Venizelist Archbishop of Athens, living at the moment in exile in the United States. On 18th January 1922, the Patriarch-elect, passing through London on his way to Constantinople, had a long interview with Mr Lloyd George, who told him again and again that, with Constantine on the throne, it would be impossible for Greece to retain Smyrna much longer. The most stringent precautions were taken by Gounaris to prevent a report of this vitally important interview from appearing in the Greek press. He denied all knowledge of it, though a report of it was found among his papers after his arrest. Further, when M. Kabafakes, the editor of the Venizelist *Eleutheros Typos*, did venture to publish news of the interview, he was immediately murdered.[1] One of the formal charges later made against Gounaris and his colleagues was that they "tolerated the formation of an organization which supported them in office by terrorism and assassination." [2] That such extremist Royalist organizations existed admits of no doubt; what relations Gounaris had with them, however, is a difficult problem. The man who did not scruple to show obviously forged documents to those whom he hoped to convert to his own extraordinary hatred of his great rival,[3] the man who was obviously chagrined at the discovery of a plot against the life of Venizelos in the summer of 1915 [4]—it is unlikely that such a man would scruple to employ the services of the Royalist secret societies.

[1] Speech of the Advocate for the prosecution—Zourides—before the Revolutionary Tribunal; *Empros*, 13/26 November 1922.

[2] Article 14 of the Indictment before the Revolutionary Tribunal.

[3] Demetra Vaka, "Constantine, King and Traitor," p. 104.

[4] Mélas, "Ex-King Constantine and the War," pp. 189-91.

On his return to Athens in March, he represented his financial arrangements in London as triumphantly successful, and the £15,000,000 as practically in the empty treasury; but certain leaders among the Royalist bloc were not deceived. As the result of attacks by Stratos on the Government, it was defeated in the Chamber. Gounaris resigned on 10th March 1922, but re-formed his Government on the failure of his rivals. No attempt was made to ask the leader of the Liberal Opposition (General Danglis), 90 strong, to form a Government.

Between 22nd and 26th March 1922, as the result of Lord Curzon's efforts, an Allied Conference assembled at Paris. The fact that the position of Greece was rapidly becoming desperate naturally meant that the terms the re-united Allies drew up were more favourable to the Turks than their previous proposals. They proposed an immediate armistice; granted Turkey the right to have an army of 85,000, as compared with the 50,000 limit of the Treaty of Sèvres; conceded the complete restoration of Turkish sovereignty over Smyrna, and advanced the Turkish boundary in Eastern Thrace from the Chatalja Lines to Rodosto. The Turks had placed the retrocession of Eastern Thrace in the forefront of their programme, and already the Allies had granted partition.[1]

The Greek Government and the Constantinople Turks accepted, but the Kemalists replied that though they accepted the terms in principle, they would only grant an armistice provided the Greek evacuation of Asia Minor began at once, and was completed within four months. The Allies replied, on 15th April 1922, that they could not accept immediate evacuation, and, as a result, once again the negotiations languished, and Greeks and Turks continued to face each other while the campaigning season rapidly approached. Once again Gounaris went abroad and interviewed Mr Lloyd George at Genoa. He returned to Athens in a mood akin to despair, and, on 12th May 1922, resigned. Stratos formed a Government, and was immediately defeated through the manœuvres of Gounaris, and finally, as a compromise, both Royalist leaders formed a coalition, under the premiership of Protopapadakis, who had recently created a sensation as Finance Minister by his famous device for raising a forced internal loan by

[1] "A History of the Peace Conference of Paris," ed. Temperley, vol. vi., pp. 35-6.

cutting in half all the bank notes in circulation. With the aid of the 1500 million drachmæ thus raised the Treasury gained a respite in its descent towards bankruptcy.

The first act of the new Government was to get rid of the Commander-in-Chief, General Papoulas. He resigned, as he was convinced he was no longer trusted by the Athens Government when he heard that his unlucky successor, Hadjianestes, had been sounded.[1] Apparently, the Royalists had heard that General Papoulas was in communication with the Patriarch Meletios and a London Committee on the possibility of giving commands to some of the Venizelist officers in Constantinople, and admitting Venizelist volunteers to the fighting line. Throughout the summer the Government vainly tried to force the Turks, now convinced that the longer they waited the greater the chances of a Greek collapse, to a compromise. On 7th June the Greek fleet bombarded Samsun on the Black Sea coast of Anatolia, the centre of some of the most horrible of the Turkish outrages against Greeks and Armenians. On 30th July, the High Commissioner, Sterghiadhis, proclaimed the independence of Ionia at Smyrna. The Powers, who in March had postulated the retrocession of Smyrna to the Turks, were not impressed by this demonstration, mainly intended for home consumption. Stratos proposed that the new State should request the Greek Government to keep the army in Asia Minor.[2]

Simultaneously occurred the obscure and extraordinary episode of the Greek threat to Constantinople. Troops were transferred from Asia Minor to Thrace, with the approval of the new Commander-in-Chief, General Hadjianestes, who found that the idea of activity in Thrace "inspired him."[3] When all was ready, a note was forwarded to the Allies and to the High Commissioners in Constantinople on 29th July 1922, in which the Greek Government announced that it was about to occupy the city in order to force the Turks to conclude peace. The note was followed by the landing of 25,000 Greek troops at Rodosto; but the whole adventure was brought to an abrupt end by the warning of the British Government that it would oppose by force any such attempt.[4]

[1] Evidence of General Papoulas before the Revolutionary Tribunal; *Empros*, 2/15 November 1922.

[2] Testimony of Stratos before the Revolutionary Tribunal; *Empros*, 10/23 November 1922.

[3] Testimony of General Hadjianestes before the Revolutionary Tribunal; *Empros*, 8/21 November 1922.

[4] Annual Register (1922), p. 211.

It was a gambler's last throw. Undoubtedly, the occupation of Constantinople by the Greeks would have forced the hands of the Nationalists and inclined them to a compromise. What is so astonishing is that Gounaris can have possibly imagined that the Allies would permit the occupation. It is not necessary to accept the view that the politicians at Athens, contemplating the evacuation of Asia Minor and unable to face public opinion, deliberately weakened the front in order to bring about a military defeat which would justify the abandonment of the great city, Smyrna. It is more probable that Gounaris, with characteristic hyper-subtlety, misunderstood some remarks of Mr Lloyd George. Defending himself against the charge of favouring the Greeks, the British Premier pointed out that by their occupation of Constantinople the Allies were actually preventing the Greeks from bringing the war to a victorious conclusion by the seizure of the Turkish capital. Such a statement may well have been taken as a hint that the occupation of Constantinople by Greece would be welcomed by Great Britain as a means of forcing the hands of her Allies.[1]

The discovery that the Greek front had been weakened, and that there was no sign that the troops were being brought back to the front, determined Mustapha Kemal to risk an offensive movement. Though he was well provided with ammunition from Bolshevik Russia, and with military aeroplanes from France, apparently he did not expect a decisive success. Almost a year of stagnation had fatally sapped the *moral* of the Greek army that had so impressed foreign military attachés during the 1921 campaign. The men were badly paid, badly clothed, badly fed. Hadjianestes had lost no opportunity of telling them they were shortly to abandon Asia Minor. In spite of their homesickness, up to 1922 they had fought magnificently and done wonders, solely out of a deep sense of responsibility for the Greeks of Anatolia. Now they were told that these people were to be left to their fate.

The resulting demoralization was hastened by the progressive paralysis of the higher command. Dry rot had set in after the general post of Venizelist officers in 1921; the purely political appointment of the eccentric Hadjianestes completed the process. He proceeded to make Valettas, notorious as the Chief of Staff of the 4th Army Corps when it surrendered

[1] Gounaris may have been attempting to evacuate Asia Minor while trying to disguise the fact.

to the Bulgarians at Kavalla in 1916 and was interned in Germany, his Chief of the General Staff. The fatal weakening of the front for the futile Constantinople demonstration followed.

On 26th August 1922, the Turkish offensive opened with an attack on the key position of Afion Kara Hissar, which was captured the next day. From this moment all was lost. The Greek Army was cut in two—the northern half evacuated Eski-Shehir on 1st-2nd September, and, well led, fought a successful rearguard action to the Sea of Marmora, where it embarked. The southern body in a few days was a horde of fugitives flying wildly towards Smyrna and the sea. The Greek population, knowing the vengeance that was following hard after, fled with the broken army; the roads were blocked with wailing refugees. A few able officers, by a supreme effort, managed to evacuate the bulk of the army by transporting the troops to the neighbouring islands. As for the politicians at Athens, they were paralysed before the spectacle of their handiwork. On 9th September, Turkish cavalry, amid a dead silence, rode triumphantly into "Infidel Smyrna." [1]

On 8th September, the Protopapadakis Cabinet resigned after it had issued a general demobilization order of 3rd September, designed to disperse the insubordinate troops as soon as possible.[2] Once again, the object of the Government was not to re-form and reorganize the shattered forces of the country as quickly as possible, but to preserve the throne, already shaken to the foundations. The full magnitude of the disaster dawned on the Athenian populace when the transports, loaded with destitute, half-starved, and panic-stricken refugees, began to arrive in the Piræus. Stratos, beside himself with anxiety, went down in person to the transports which were hourly steaming in, packed with troops firing in the air, and disarmed the men with his own hands.[3] The new Kalogero-

[1] Some time before his fall Venizelos had appointed a committee to study the question of the fortification of Smyrna and the Tchesmé Peninsula (a glance at the map will indicate the natural strength of the latter land formation), but after the elections of November 1920 the committee was dissolved. We shall never know the possibilities of these potential lines of Torres Vedras. Evidence of Colonel Spyridonos before the Revolutionary Tribunal; *Empros*, 3/16 November 1923.

[2] Testimony of Theotokis before the Revolutionary Tribunal; *Empros*, 9/22 November 1922.

[3] N. Stratos before the Revolutionary Tribunal; *Empros*, 10/23 November 1922.

poulos Cabinet forbade any criticism of past and present administrations, and proceeded to arrest leading Liberals. A *coup d'état* was expected at any moment.

In the meantime, Colonel Plastiras, an officer who had served with distinction both under the Venizelist and Royalist administrations, had fought his way back from Ushak through Philadelphia to the Tchesmé Peninsula. From there he had succeeded in extricating his little force, and on 7th September he arrived in the island of Chios. At the same moment, Colonel Gonatas was rallying his troops on Mitylene.[1] The two Colonels got into touch and were shortly joined by Captain Phocas of the battleship "Lemnos." In profound secrecy preparations were made for the overthrow of a Government that had ruined Greece, and was now more concerned with maintaining itself and the dynasty on which it depended than on saving Greece.

On 26th September manifestoes from the Revolutionary Committee, calling for the abdication of the King, were showered over Athens from aeroplanes. The new Triantaphyllakos Cabinet, which had succeeded the ephemeral Government of Kalogeropoulos, was suddenly faced with revolution in earnest. On 27th September, 20,000 Revolutionary troops landed at Lavrion, and at the same time the battleship "Lemnos" arrived off the Piræus with the Revolutionary Committee. After some hours of hesitation, the King gave way and abdicated in favour of the Crown Prince. The same day the army of the Revolution entered Athens, and Colonel Plastiras rode into the capital that had been his for the taking. Delirious crowds greeted him. Even in that darkest hour of despair and prostration, all the bells of the city rang. People hurled themselves weeping before him and kissed his feet. In the mighty shouting could be heard the cries: "Christ is risen! Hail! Our Saviour! Long live the Army! Long live Venizelos!"[2] The same day also the Revolutionary Committee dispatched a telegram to the great exile, placing in his hands the foreign policy of his unhappy country.

He had watched with agonized anxiety the steady drift towards disaster. Those who saw much of him in those days tell of his stoical calm and silence, while month by month he seemed literally to shrink and become physically smaller under

[1] B. Bareilles, "Le drame oriental—d'Athènes à Angora," p. 244.
[2] *Ibid.*, p. 246.

the burden of a prescience compelled to await the fulfilment of its darkest divinings without the power to raise a finger to avert the tragedy. Now once more he was caught up upon the crest of great events—once more he was called to ride on the wings of the storm.

He replied to the Revolutionary Committee that he would investigate the position, and, if he thought he could be of use, he would make certain recommendations; if the Committee accepted these suggestions he would represent them.

The diplomatic situation had again been revolutionized. After the occupation of Smyrna, the Turkish army had rolled northwards and advanced into the zone of the Straits proclaimed neutral by the Allies. Immediately the French Government, on 18th September, had ordered all French troops to abandon the Asiatic side of the Straits and cross over to Gallipoli. M. Poincaré, strong in the separate Franklin-Bouillon agreement, had resolved that under no circumstances would he fight the Turks. The small British forces at Chanak found themselves isolated in the face of the advancing Turks. For a short time it appeared as though the Entente had come to a final end, but as the result of a hurried visit to Paris, Lord Curzon re-established it by agreeing to the French programme for the future peace. The restoration of Turkish authority in Eastern Thrace up to the Maritza was accepted, and offered in a joint-note of 23rd September 1922, to the Nationalist Turks, who were at the same time summoned to respect the neutral zones and to refrain from attempting to dispatch troops to Eastern Thrace. On 29th September the Angora Government accepted the Allied terms, and suggested a conference to arrange the preliminary armistice. On 3rd October General Harrington, with his French and Italian colleagues, met Ismet Pasha at Mudania, and the famous negotiations for an armistice began.

In the meantime Venizelos had ascertained at Paris and London that the two Allied Powers were resolved on cutting their losses by eventually evacuating Constantinople and restoring Eastern Thrace, including Adrianople, to Turkey. It became clear to him that Greece could only secure peace by nerving herself to another sacrifice. He was aware that one of the motives of the Revolution in Greece was the preservation of Eastern Thrace. Colonel Plastiras had begun despatching reinforcements to the province, and every effort was being made to re-equip the shattered army. In several speeches the Revolutionary leaders declared their resolution to defend to the end the Greeks of Thrace. Had Venizelos refused to consider the evacuation of Eastern Thrace nothing could have been more likely than the outbreak of an Anglo-Turkish war—every day the position at Chanak was becoming more strained. But if he was to use the whole of his great authority in persuading the Revolutionary Committee to resign themselves to the sacrifice of Eastern Thrace, it became essential to find out when and how the Allies proposed to restore Turkish authority. Unless the Christian population were adequately secured against the horrors of Smyrna, no Greek Government could possibly consent to surrender the province. In these critical circumstances, Venizelos arrived in London in the first days of October.

He found the public opinion of a great Power hag-ridden by a press campaign of unexampled violence and stupidity. Each party vied with the other in magnifying a panic exploited by the sinister and the interested. Great Britain was represented as on the eve of a great war. The levies of Mustapha Kemal were painted as more than Germanic in their efficiency. Apparently, they were not only efficient but amphibious, as at any moment Europe might be invaded by armies swimming across the Marmora and the Bosphorus to their objectives on undreamed-of shores. The crisis in fact presented an unique opportunity for attacking and vilifying the divided Coalition and its leader. The news that Venizelos was in London was the signal for those ignorant of the heroic resolution he had reached to redouble their outcries. He was hailed as "a fiend and a warmonger," the Government was ordered to expel him from the country, etc.; in a word, the journalistic exhibition was both pitiable and disgraceful.

The diplomatic situation was even worse. In deference to M. Poincaré's passionate eagerness to placate the Turks by restoring them at once to Eastern Thrace, the Allies were contemplating the immediate transference of Eastern Thrace to Turkish administration, and the establishment of a force of Turkish gendarmerie in the province, under the supervision of a few Allied officers. Venizelos pointed out that this was equivalent to sentencing the Christian population to death—a few officers could not control enraged Turks certain to continue in Thrace the infamies they had already perpetrated in Asia Minor. His advice was ignored, but the "resources of civilization" were not yet exhausted.

On 4th October 1922 the diplomatic world was startled by a long letter from Venizelos, published in the *Times*. He enumerated the arguments against the immediate restoration of Turkish sovereignty. ". . . Is it possible for public opinion in Great Britain indifferently to envisage the further destruction of so many homes and lives, and of fortunes amounting to many hundreds of millions? Surely public opinion will not allow the Government of this country to share the responsibility of such destruction in imposing on Greece the immediate evacuation of Eastern Thrace and its transference to Turkish administration and Turkish police. . . . The Turkish Empire is being reconstituted. Turkey is again becoming a European Power, and the Balkan Peninsula is again exposed to new dangers, or rather to the old ones. Since the beginning of the war, Turkey has destroyed in Asia Minor between a million and a half and two millions of Greeks and Armenians. Surely our former Allies are in duty bound to help in averting the extermination of yet another million upon the soil of Europe itself. If it is necessary to give further guarantees to Kemal that the promise concerning the return of Eastern Thrace will meet with no obstacle in its execution, this Province could, as a last resource, be occupied by Allied troops until the execution of the Treaty. . . . In this manner, either the Christian population would be guaranteed by the Treaty of Peace, or should Turkey insist on the evacuation, the Powers would be able to assure the orderly evacuation of this before the Turkish occupation began.

"Can it really be said with honesty that I am asking too much, or that I came here as a fiend and warmonger?"

It was a master stroke. By coming into the open he turned the flank of those who work best in darkness, strengthened the hands of those already contending for justice, and galvanized into action that great body of Liberal public opinion whose voice had been drowned in the uproar and panic of the previous weeks. He followed it up the next day by calling on the American Ambassador. It became evident that the great Greek had appealed for American diplomatic intervention on grounds of common humanity and would leave no stone unturned to secure the safety of the Christian populations of Thrace. The results of his efforts can be read in the provisions of the Mudania armistice signed on 11th October

1922. The withdrawal of the Greek forces was to take place under the supervision of Allied missions and "in addition to these missions Allied contingents shall occupy Eastern Thrace."[1] They were to remain in occupation thirty days after the withdrawal of the Greek forces. In this way the newly installed Turkish administration would be under surveillance long enough—though barely long enough—to allow those of the population who desired to escape its clutches to follow the retreating army. The haste in restoring Turkish administration and authority, even after elementary precautions had been taken, reflects no credit on the wisdom or humanity of the Allied Governments. In the result, a great mass migration denuded Eastern Thrace of its Christian inhabitants, who were allowed, largely by the efforts of Venizelos, to escape with their lives and some of their goods to Greece.

The letter of Venizelos did not at once quell the storm. The next day in a leading article headed, "No Holy War!" a leading London paper accused him of endeavouring "to get up a Holy War" against Mohammedans. "M. Venizelos now speaks unctuously of the Greeks as Christians—as though they had suddenly become Christians—and apparently wants to raise the Cross against the Crescent. This is a mere politician's device which will not help him this time. . . . The war makers have not been stopped. So we said yesterday, and it is true to-day. M. Venizelos proves it by his artful attempt to inveigle Great Britain into his 'Holy War,' in support of a feeble people against a more virile race."[2] The campaign against him was, however, abruptly discredited when on 5th October he published in *The Times* the letter to General Danglis of 3rd July 1921, which was quoted above.

On 6th October the Greek Revolutionary Committee and the new Government, "with death in their hearts," accepted the insistent advice of Venizelos that Eastern Thrace must be given up. It cannot be too often reiterated that it was this exercise of his gigantic moral authority over the new Greek Government that alone made possible the Armistice of Mudania and paved the way for the ultimate settlement.

On 20th November 1922 the Lausanne Conference assembled to begin those protracted negotiations that cul-

[1] Article 9 of Armistice of Mudania, 11th October 1922.
[2] *Daily Mail*, 5th October 1922.

minated in the Treaty of 24th July 1923. Venizelos and Caclamanos, the newly appointed minister in London, represented Greece. The Conference had scarcely sat eight days when it experienced its first crisis on the news of the famous Greek executions.

On the Revolution of 27th September, various members of the Royalist Governments had been arrested as well as the last Commander-in-Chief, Hadjianestes. The Revolutionary Committee appointed a Special Commission of Inquiry into the responsibility for the disasters. It reported on 6th November, and on its report were founded the fifteen indictments on which five Ministers, Demetrios Gounaris, Nicolas Stratos, Peter Protopapadakis, Nicolas Theotokis, and George Baltazzi, were charged before a specially instituted Revolutionary Tribunal of eleven officers. In addition, the former Commander-in-Chief, George Hadjianestes, Michael Goudas, a retired rear-admiral who had taken to politics, and Xenophon Strategos, a retired officer and an intimate of the Ministers, were also indicted. The Court consisted of nine Royalists and two Venizelists,[1] and the right to challenge the composition of the extraordinary court martial was granted to the accused. They exercised their option and challenged four of the judges, who were replaced.[2] The accused were charged with restoring the King in spite of the declaration of the Powers, and concealing the note of 8th December 1920 concerning the "economic blockade" of Greece and the cutting off of credits; removing efficient officers from the army and appointing for political reasons men without war experience; ordering the advance on Angora in spite of the declared opposition of the competent Commander-in-Chief; refusing the favourable proposals for mediation by the Powers in June 1921; leading the National Assembly to vote compensation to rebels, mutineers, and deserters as well as to members of their own party, thus "dilapidating the public Treasury at a time when the economic exhaustion of the country was already depriving the army of necessary supplies of money, food, and clothing"; "withdrawing troops from the fighting-line in Asia Minor in order to stage a make-believe demonstration in Thrace"; allowing the formation of organizations to support the Government

[1] George Glasgow in article "Foreign Affairs," *Contemporary Review*, January 1923, vol. 123, pp. 110-11.

[2] Report of first day of trial, 13th November 1922; *Empros*, Tuesday, 1/14 November 1922.

by terrorism and assassination; and appointing as Commander-in-Chief Hadjianestes, known to be an incompetent officer.

It is evident that these charges are of very various degrees of seriousness, all except the charge of terrorism are offences outside the scope of common law. That does not mean that these actions may not constitute cumulatively an offence against the nation for which a reckoning may be demanded.

The trial opened on 13th November and concluded with the promulgation of the verdict at 6 a.m. on the morning of Tuesday, 28th November 1922. The judges by a unanimous vote found all the accused guilty, with extenuating circumstances in the case of Strategos and Goudas. Accordingly, the Court sentenced the five ministers and the Commander-in-Chief to death and Goudas and Strategos to imprisonment for life. In addition, the military prisoners were sentenced to degradation and the ministers and Goudas were fined enormous sums "in compensation to the Treasury."[1] Within a few hours of the promulgation of the sentences the five ministers (Gounaris, Stratos, and Protopapadakis were all ex-Premiers) and the Commander-in-Chief were executed.

For some weeks Lord Curzon and the British Government had been disquieted at the proceedings of the Revolutionary Tribunal, and on several occasions endeavoured to persuade Venizelos to intervene; but he had steadfastly refused to take any action either for or against the ministers. When it became likely that some of the accused men would be sentenced to death, the British Government began its diplomatic intervention on 24th November. On that day the British minister in Athens, Lindley, called on the Greek Foreign Minister, Polites, and in a long conversation threatened the rupture of diplomatic relations in the event of the execution of the ministers. He suggested, wrongly, that France would associate herself with this step. Polites asked if Great Britain would give a formal guarantee that if these men were banished, they should never again take part in Greek politics. Lindley replied that he had asked his Government this question, and had received a definite refusal to give any such guarantee.

Immediately after this, a Cabinet crisis was precipitated by the resignation of the Prime Minister, Krokidas, unwilling to run the risk of again incurring the displeasure of Great

[1] *Empros*, 16/29 November 1922.

Britain. Unable to secure a civilian Prime Minister, the Revolutionary Committee proceeded to take over the government, and Colonel Gonatas became Premier. Greece was now completely under a dictatorship, as the Constantinian National Assembly had been dispersed on the Revolution.

On 27th November 1922 the minister, Lindley, called on the new Foreign Minister, Rentes, and this time adopted a definitely threatening attitude. Finally, he asked to see the real master of Greece, Colonel Plastiras. He had an interview with him in the presence of Rentes. The dictator again put the question to Lindley whether Great Britain, who seemed to be claiming the right of interference in the internal affairs of Greece, would give a formal undertaking that the accused ministers should never again take part in Greek politics. Lindley had to declare that the English Constitution made it impossible for his Government to undertake such an obligation.[1]

The next day, 28th November, Venizelos despatched a telegram from Lausanne to the Revolutionary Committee, pointing out that the political consequences of the execution of the ministers might be serious. But the same day, as we have seen, the ministers were executed, and that evening Lindley broke off diplomatic relations with Greece and left Athens.

Venizelos, who had refused to intervene on behalf of the fallen ministers, now indignantly spurned the suggestion that he should resign as a protest. He made perfectly clear to Lord Curzon, who openly reproached him at the Conference, that his resignation, if he tendered it, would be the result not of the execution of the ministers, but because he found it no longer possible to co-operate with the British delegation. For a short time this seemed likely, and on 29th November he telegraphed to the Committee to select his successor. But the first wave of indignation which was voiced in the exclamation of one of the Allied delegates, "Venizelos has had his revenge!" soon passed. Lord Curzon was bent on peace with the Turks, and it was not long before he realized that to drive from the Conference the only man who could control the Revolutionary Committee was not likely to conduce to a peaceful dénouement, at a moment when Greeks and Turks were facing each other along the line of the River Maritza.

[1] "Notes on Greek History, 1910-23," communicated by Mr John Mavrogordato.

Within two days the matter had been forgotten—in the diplomatic sense.

Venizelos has never disguised his opinion that the evidence produced before the Revolutionary Tribunal was overwhelming and more than sufficient from the point of view of a Court Martial. Very rarely are "les grands coupables," Tsars and ministers and other eminences, brought to a justice, however poetic and irregular—often enough in time of war common soldiers, far more worthy as men, are shot for sleeping at their posts.[1] But Colonel Plastiras put the real issues quite clearly. These men, beyond all question, had already ruined Greece twice—for that alone they deserved death, if no other way could be found of ridding Greece of their noisome influence. If Great Britain wanted to save them she could, but on the inexorable condition that never again should unhappy Greece be troubled with the intrigues of a Gounaris. The cold and upright dictator could not be intimidated once he had defined the issues.

So far as Greece was concerned, the main settlement at Lausanne was not long in constructing. The territorial question had been settled by the decision to surrender Eastern Thrace, and on 30th January 1923 the famous Greco-Turkish Convention for the exchange of populations was signed. It was but the formal recognition of the inexorable decision to expel every Greek in Asia Minor. In pursuit of this policy, first begun in 1909, the rulers of Turkey were willing to inflict unnecessary misery on their own countrymen in Macedonia, who were to be expelled from Greece to make room for those Greeks of Pontus who had not yet fled the country. To this day, Salonika is a vast clearing house where two tides of human suffering are constantly passing each other.[2] When the terrible process is completed, it is estimated that the total number of Greek refugees from Asia Minor and Eastern Thrace will be not far short of one million and a half persons. The problem of absorbing this vast mass of humanity into the settled population has been a stupendous work. The innate vitality of the Greek race has never been so brilliantly demonstrated than in the marvellous and successful efforts of the little country, nobly aided by

[1] See Glasgow, article "Foreign Affairs," in *Contemporary Review*, January 1923, vol. 123, pp. 109-11.

[2] See article, *The Times*—"Greek Refugees"—21st August 1924, and address by Dr Harold Spender to the Annual General Meeting of the Anglo-Hellenic League, 25th June 1924 (Anglo-Hellenic Publication, No. 54).

international organizations, to grapple with the problem. The fine stock of the Pontic Greeks cannot but be a splendid asset to the nation; Macedonia is a land of promise, and already, with the unconquerable optimism of their character, the Greeks are looking forward to a bright future. With the utmost difficulty, the Turks were persuaded to leave the Greeks of Constantinople untouched.

After several times appearing to be on the verge of a complete breakdown, the Conference culminated in the signing of the Lausanne Treaty on 24th July 1923. The Turks had early discovered that they had nothing to fear from the divided Allies. The one tangible force with which they had to reckon was the reorganized and re-equipped Greek army massed along the Maritza. Not until Venizelos had threatened the resumption of war did the comedy end. So eternally true does it remain that the Turk brings to diplomacy the methods of the oriental bazaar, nor will he make up his mind until he sees that you have made up yours. Ismet Pasha's success in huckstering the Allies out of practically all their positions reflects great credit on the deaf but diplomatic soldier, but serves to illuminate the depths of impotence to which the "peacemakers" had sunk.

The Allies had not much to show for their efforts. They had abandoned Armenia. By restoring Turkish sovereignty on both sides of the Dardanelles, that is, by surrendering the Peninsula of Gallipoli, they had rendered the nominal "Freedom of the Straits" a farce, since the Turks can close them in a few days as effectively as they closed them in 1914. By allowing Turkey and Bulgaria once more to share a common frontier, they have laid the foundations of a new and predatory Balkan Alliance. It is vain to imagine that the bourgeois Bulgarian parties who ruined their country by the gambles of 1913 and 1915, and recovered their power in 1923 by murdering the great peasant leader Stambulisky who had begun to win confidence by his moderate policy, have either learnt anything or forgotten anything. The dictatorship of a self-conscious bourgeoisie is more selfish, more oppressive, more odious in every way, as being the rule of an oligarchy, than the much-denounced "dictatorship of the proletariat." Of the two extreme evils, the latter is probably preferable, for some new thing may evolve from a mass whereas nothing can be expected from the arid rule of a clique cut off from the sources of their existence. We need expect nothing but mischief from a Turkey anxious to repass the Maritza and a Bulgaria controlled by the former lackeys of King Ferdinand.

The Eastern Question, which might have been solved in 1920 by the final expulsion of Turkish political authority from Europe, and the organization of Constantinople as a Free City under the control of the League of Nations, has once more been posed with all its menacing possibilities by the settlements of Lausanne. Sooner or later, Russia, in all human probability, will resume her advance on the golden city of her dreams, since her dreams correspond in this matter with the inflexible facts of geography. It is all to the interest of Russia that the keys of the Black Sea remain in the hands of a Power that has already committed economic *hari-kari* by the expulsion of practically every industrious and enterprising element in its national life. The economic decay of Spain began with the expulsion of the Moriscoes. As for the "political regeneration" of Turkey by the latest metamorphosis of the C.U.P., these profound words of Cavour are not without significance: "The political regeneration of a country is never separate from its economic regeneration. The conditions of the two forms of progress are identical."

During the Lausanne Conference, Greece had been in the tight grip of the Revolutionary Dictatorship. The desperate feuds of Royalists and Venizelists, checked for a time by Constantine's sudden death at Palermo, on 11th January 1923, revived as the faction fights of Monarchists and Republicans. Throughout the year, the Republican party, hitherto negligible, grew steadily in strength. Party passion reached unheard-of heights. There were Monarchist and Venizelist concerts, Monarchist and Venizelist pork butchers, —Greek life was in two sections, held together by the iron hand of the military dictatorship. The Revolutionary Committee in the midst of its struggle with the refugee problem made earnest attempts to construct a Constitutional party, representative of the moderate elements in all parties, into whose hands it could safely surrender its powers. But the attempts of M. Zaimis in September 1923 to form such a political "bloc" broke down completely.

At the conclusion of the Treaty of Lausanne, Venizelos issued an address to the Greek people explaining his reasons for refusing the persistent invitations to return to Greece with which he was bombarded. Greece needed internal peace, and his personality was far too controversial for him to be of any service to Greece in her internal political life. He was ready as ever to serve her abroad. The elections of November 1920 had put an end to his political career simply because he realized that no honest politician who had taken measures on his own authority and in the exercise of his mandate—measures that required as their justification national consent, could fail to regard his career as at an end when that national consent was withheld by the people from whom he derived his authority. For the rest, unless Greeks of all parties could forget the past and concentrate on rebuilding the future, they would drift to destruction, knowing, like Medea, the evil that they did, but helpless to escape it because passion overswayed their reason.

The elections which the Government had hoped to hold soon after the definite conclusion of peace were postponed as the result of the sudden bursting of the Italian crisis, when Mussolini, holding Greece guilty of a crime whose authorship has never been proved, first served a series of impossible demands on the Greek Government, and then, when some of them were refused, proceeded to occupy Corfu "as a pledge." The obvious imitation of M. Poincaré's Ruhr policy was flattering to that statesman, but can scarcely have been convenient. The situation became serious when Italy defied the mediation of the League of Nations, to which Greece had appealed. Public opinion, and the fact that France and England found themselves at one in disliking the prospect of Italy permanently established at Corfu, combined to freeze Signor Mussolini out of an island which his inspired press has not failed to point out once belonged to the Venetian Republic. Greece was fined £500,000 at a moment when she was struggling with depleted resources to make headway against the greatest refugee problem of modern times. With this *solatium* to her honour Italy ended one of the most disgraceful chapters in the recent history of the "Great Powers."

Scarcely had Greece weathered this diplomatic crisis when a Royalist insurrection broke out at the end of October 1923. It was crushed in a few days, but once again the elections had to be postponed.

The Republican movement continued to grow, and at the same time the Liberal Venizelist party continued its efforts to persuade its great leader to return. On 2nd

December 1923, a mass meeting of Venizelists attended by 90,000 people was held in Athens and passed a resolution urging him to return to Greece and undertake the work of reconciling the contending parties and giving back to Greece her Constitutional liberties. On 5th December, Venizelos once more declined this impressive invitation: "So pronounced a manifestation on the part of a large section of public opinion, and more especially my appreciation of the dangers looming ahead, have obliged me to take serious thought whether I ought not to reconsider my decision. I regret to announce that the result of my deliberations is negative. The country stands in absolute need of a definite cessation of civil strife and of the restoration of internal peace under conditions guaranteeing the normal operation of free institutions. Unfortunately, a large political section of the nation entertain towards me a feeling of deep repulsion, and many do not forgive, not so much the faults I may have committed as the great achievements realized by the nation under my guidance. Under these circumstances, my return to political life would exacerbate rather than appease the existing differences.

"I also considered whether I could not return temporarily only in order to bring about an understanding between conflicting parties, so that the participation of all in the coming elections might be possible. And for a moment I inclined towards this solution. But I was obliged with great regret to reject this also. For the deep distrust which I inspire in the minds of the opposite political party makes me least of all suitable to act as a peacemaker and conciliator. In such conditions, I am compelled to refuse the invitation addressed to me.

"But it would be unjust to suppose that this refusal is due to resentment on my part at the vote of the Greek people three years ago. That vote simply put an end to my political career, for reasons which I have already explained to the Greek people. But it has not freed me from the obligation, or lessened my desire, to serve the country, whenever I can be of use. . . ." [1]

The refusal seemed absolute.

But once again the situation was revolutionized. On 16th December 1923 the elections were at last held, and took place, to the surprise of many, in an atmosphere of general

[1] *The Times*, 6th December 1923.

tranquillity. The Venizelists and Republicans swept the country, winning 370 seats out of the total of 401. The result stimulated the extreme Republicans, whose effort to proclaim a Republic in November had been scotched by a letter from Venizelos. The Government felt unable to resist the pressure of the army, which accused the King of having entered into relations with the Royalist Revolutionaries of the previous October. On 18th December the King and Queen, at the request of the Government, left the country on a prolonged "leave of absence." Once again Admiral Kountouriotis became Regent. The pressure on Venizelos to return to Greece now became overwhelming; fresh appeals poured in from the Revolutionary Government, from political organizations, and from King George II. himself. His every comment created a crisis, and it was evident that he could not continue "to govern Greece from a hotel in Paris."

On 25th December he informed Colonel Plastiras that he had resolved to return to Greece provisionally, to help his countrymen to solve the political crisis, and on 30th December the great exile embarked at Marseilles on the "Andros." At the opening of the National Assembly three days later, Colonel Plastiras announced that the Revolutionary Committee considered that it had fulfilled its mission: shortly "the greatest of the Hellenes" would again be in Greece, and his advice would be at the service of the National Assembly.

At 3 a.m. in the morning of 4th January 1924, Colonel Plastiras met Venizelos off the island of Ægina. During the voyage of the "Andros," he had already, by a wireless message, defined his programme. The dynastic question could only be settled by a free vote of the Greek people, and he proposed a plebiscite at which two questions would be asked: (1) Do you desire Greece to become a Republic or remain a Monarchy? (2) If you wish her to remain a Monarchy, do you desire the present dynasty to remain on the throne, or the election of another? He added that, in his opinion, at least 70 per cent. of the electorate must vote for a Republic before so radical a change would be justified. Nothing could be more democratic than these proposals, which he hoped would win the approval of the Royalists. The Royalist newspapers, on the day of his arrival in Athens, published photographs of the ministers executed in November 1922. Simultaneously, the extreme Republican party began an intensive campaign in favour of an immediate proclamation of a Greek Republic.

On 6th January Venizelos appeared before the National Assembly, amid scenes of tremendous enthusiasm, and was elected its President by 345 votes to 9. During the following week an acute political crisis developed, owing to the fact that neither the Right nor Left wing leaders of the Liberal party would serve under the other. The crisis was only ended by Venizelos at last consenting to form a Ministry, in which all sections of the Liberal party served under him himself. On 11th January 1924 he became Premier for the fourth time.

The news of his acceptance of office was immediately followed by the resumption of diplomatic relations with Greece by the British Government. On 19th January he defined the policy of his Government and, amid tempestuous applause, announced that he himself favoured the establishment of a Republic, but desired above everything that the Greek people should have a free and unprejudiced choice on this great issue.

But the embittered opposition of the Royalists and the fanaticism of the Republicans did not abate. In a few days it became evident that the health of Venizelos would not stand the strain. Twice he collapsed in the Chamber, and finally, on 4th February, acting on medical advice, he resigned. The policy which he had defended, however, was continued by his successor, Kaphandaris, and received a large majority in the Chamber. On 26th and 28th February 1924 the National Assembly rejected the extremist Republican motions for the immediate dethronement of the dynasty, on the latter occasion by 192 votes to 18. The extremists thereupon withdrew from the Chamber.

But this withdrawal did not mean that they had been defeated, but merely that they were about to find other means of persuasion for a Chamber too much under the influence of the intolerably moderate and liberal Venizelos. On 7th March a Committee of five officers of high rank, representing the recently reconstituted Officers' League, waited upon the Regent, and demanded the immediate deposition of the dynasty. M. Kaphandaris, indignant at this attempt at military interference, summoned a Cabinet meeting, which resolved to ignore the representatives of the League, the dissolution of which had been one of the conditions of M. Venizelos's return.

On 9th March the Committee of Officers waited on M. Kaphandaris. The nature of their arguments may be surmised by the fact that the Government at once resigned, and the Regent sent for the Republican leader, M. Papanastasiou. By 4th March 1924 Venizelos had realized that his attempts to secure an agreed policy had been shipwrecked on the intransigence of the Royalists, who demanded the recall of the King before the plebiscite, and of the Republicans, who insisted on the deposition of the dynasty and the proclamation of a Republic by the National Assembly, to be followed by a plebiscite to ratify or reject the decision. With extraordinary frankness, the Republicans told Venizelos that if the people, in the free plebiscite he was trying to secure, decided for the maintenance of the existing Glücksburg dynasty, they would resort to civil war rather than permit the return of the King. In a letter to the Premier, Venizelos confessed his profound disillusionment and the mistake he had made in hoping that he could be of any use in Greece. He could see that the large majorities in the National Assembly for his policy represented nothing so long as the ultimate appeal was to the power of the sword. His health would not permit him to fight for the liberties of Greece. Since he would not acquiesce in the destruction of his policy, nothing remained but once more to leave Greece with the hope that she might not founder on the rocks to which he saw she was drifting. On 10th March he passed once more from the stage of Greek politics into voluntary exile. On the evening before he left, he entertained the members of the British Legation and some friends at a farewell dinner. Those who saw him were astonished at his tranquil dignity.

After all, he had been a *revenant* from that heroic past in which he had created the Greece which seemed to have outgrown the venerable statesman. "The past belongs to our ancestors," he had once said many years before, and for the mass of the Greeks Venizelos has already passed to the Olympian heights. His cold wisdom they have never understood, unless his tireless energy and imperious will drove them to great achievement. When he had become merely a voice, and the iron hand of the great leader was no longer felt, a tiny minority, interpreting the inclinations of the majority in the National Assembly, urged them to take a short cut to their goal. On 25th March the Glücksburg dynasty was deposed, and the Greek Republic proclaimed amid triumphant enthusiasm and salvoes of artillery. The resolutions of M. Papanastasiou were passed by a unanimous vote of 284; only the followers of M. Kaphandaris, who stood for the programme of Venizelos, abstained.[1]

In such inauspicious circumstances, the Greek Republic—a name so satisfactory to lovers of the past glory of Hellas—came into being and was subsequently approved by the nation at the plebiscite, doubtless more for the sake of peace than because the dethroned dynasty had lost the affections of the people.

And what of Venizelos? Few men have had a career so shot through with colour, adventure and vicissitude, and few have passed through life so consistently faithful to guiding principles. In the life of Venizelos we can detect three great beliefs: belief in liberty, self-government, progress, in a word, liberalism; belief in the future of Greece and her duty to reunite in one national State the unredeemed Hellenism that could be delivered from that yoke under which he was born; belief in international co-operation rather than rivalry, an idea that took form in the Balkan League, a League that Venizelos dreamed might eventually be changed into a perpetual Confederation.

Like all great ideas, these conceptions are simple, but Venizelos brought to their service a mind as swift and subtle and ever-changing as Cavour's. His prescience, ever unclouded by passion or prejudice, has in its cold intellectual clarity an element almost of the uncanny. It is not necessary to cite the great letter to General Danglis of 3rd July 1921. Truth, when she appears, is always obvious, but it requires genius to divine her before she appears. It needed not only great wisdom but also high courage to conclude the alliance with Bulgaria on the terms in which he did conclude it. A merely subtle mind like that of the unhappy Gounaris was at once lost in the reverberating labyrinth of the Great War. A certain simplicity of faith in a few great ideas that shine with the calm certitude of fixed stars enabled Venizelos to steer a triumphant course through the tempest. "Greece, like a midwife, will assist the birth of great events"—the saying is worthy of any one of the great leaders of men who have shown their greatness in nothing more than in this, that they have never been wholly the toy and sport of circumstance. They have known how to see facts, to accept them,

[1] *The Times*, 26th March 1924.

and yet to transform and mould them to something "nearer to the heart's desire." Yet this quality is simply what an Authority—higher even than that of great statesmen, has declared requisite for the moving of mountains.

Venizelos has been hated as few men in our day have been hated, and it is not difficult to find the reason. To read one of his debates on great occasions with his enemies in the Greek Chamber is sufficient. To confound a clever sophist by force of an immeasurable intellectual superiority does not convert the sophist or win his love—it merely convinces him that his opponent is the greatest sophist of all. Venizelos has known how to impale lies with an epigram, as when, in reply to the suggestion that since Serbia was bound to be beaten, the best thing for Greece would be to share in the spoils, he made the famous reply, "Greece is too small a country to commit so great an infamy."

His struggle with King Constantine is the tragedy of Greece, but to assert that the reason for it was that the King was a pro-German, willing to sacrifice his country to the convenience of his Imperial brother-in-law, is to fall into the error of distorting issues in the effort to find a simple, clear-cut explanation. That the King favoured Germany was neither surprising nor a crime; that he consciously sacrificed Greek interests has yet to be proved. He seems to have been convinced that Germany would win the war, and he gambled on that conviction to justify him in the end for breaking the spirit of the Greek Liberal Constitution. He was equally convinced that Greece needed strong government, and that his father's political tight-rope walking, which lasted fifty years, was neither good for the volatile Greeks nor worthy of a king. For these reasons, he did not intend to abide by the spirit of his father's political testament: ". . . never forget that thou art King of a southern people, whose wrath and excitement are kindled in a moment, and which at such a moment is capable of saying and doing many things which a moment later it will perhaps forget; and remember that it is often better for the King himself to suffer, even morally, rather than the people, whose interests should take precedence of all others."[1] Yet, perhaps, in 1916-17 he persuaded himself that he was suffering through his care of the interests of the people whose love he had

[1] Quoted Miller, "The Ottoman Empire and its Successors, 1801-1922," p. 506.

certainly won. This resolute determination to have his own way did not spring from the will of a strong man. His weak obstinacy forced him back on councillors like Gounaris and Streit, whom he acknowledged to be the political and intellectual inferiors of his great Prime Minister. He was incapable of making the sacrifice of Louis XIII., who could support Cardinal Richelieu, whom he disliked, against every attack. Constantine began by admiring Venizelos and ended by fearing him. He did not feel himself his own master in the presence of "the Cretan." Shortly after his accession, he seems to have felt himself as much muffled and overshadowed by Venizelos as the young Emperor William II. by the Iron Chancellor before he nerved himself "to drop the pilot."

The issue of peace or war—intervention or neutrality—gave the King at last a cause on which he could break with Venizelos in the conviction that he was the true interpreter of Greek interests. Only with the aid of the King could the sinister politicians, whose political fortunes Venizelos had shattered in 1910, creep back into power; only with their aid could the King, convinced of his own good intentions, withstand the overwhelming influence of Venizelos. In this way, insensibly perhaps, the King found himself at the head of a party. The further he advanced the more impossible it became to retreat. His dislike of Venizelos became a consuming hatred—in this fact he again reveals the essential weakness of his character. "Naturally I was looking ill that day," he answered his Secretary's enquiries, "you know whom I had seen in the morning." It was the August day in 1915, on which, as the result of the June elections, he had been compelled to send again for M. Venizelos.[1] Not all the supporters of the King were pro-Germans. There were many people in Greece to whom if M. Venizelos were worse than the devil, Germany was less inviting than the deep sea.[2]

Venizelos had no more bitter enemy than Prince George, the King's brother, for reasons which have been related above. Yet he was the true friend of the Allies, as his despairing telegram to Constantine from Paris, in April 1915, proves: ". . . by now refusing our co-operation or proposing it only subject to conditions that we know cannot be accepted, we

[1] G. H. Mélas, "Ex-King Constantine and the War," p. 109.

[2] John Mavrogordato, "England and the Balkans," p. 14. (Anglo-Hellenic League Publication, No. 24.)

expose ourselves to the certain danger of seeing England and France even hostile in the future, which would mean the ruin of Greece. Our interests in the Mediterranean and in Asia Minor will be sacrificed to the interests of Italy and others, and nothing will be able to save us. . . . March in the name of God. Not to do so is certain suicide for you and for the nation."[1] But the King was unconvinced, and perhaps, even without formulating it to himself, he knew that intervention must spell, sooner or later, the return of its chief exponent—Venizelos.

In the result, the nation was hopelessly split into two contending camps. To avert the possibility of such a *dénouement* was exactly the purpose of his father's political testament. Had Constantine sacrificed his convictions—or expressed them within the spirit of the Constitution as well as according to its letter—Greece would not have been ruined. Those who naïvely ask why Venizelos should not have given way rather than the King, are evidently incapable of grasping the idea of a constitutional monarch or a Liberal constitution. And just because of the dilemma in which they were placed in having the King as their party leader, the Royalists were driven to adopt those absolutist and semi-absolutist ideas to which Constantine naturally inclined. The Royalist ministers and the King became more closely interdependent, and at the same time, the earlier question of intervention or neutrality became fatally complicated by a new issue of Liberalism against Absolutism, Democracy against "the idea of a patriot King." From such an impasse revolution is the only way out, and it was as a Liberal that Venizelos raised the standard of revolt.

His Liberalism has been disputed: "By nature," writes one of his most mordant critics, "he was more fitted to rule in a despotic than to lead in a constitutional State. Had he been born an Emperor, his fertile genius might, unless betrayed by his restless ambition, have rendered his reign prosperous and his memory precious. As it is, in his career, with all its brilliance, posterity will find not so much a pattern to imitate, as an example to deter."[2]

Yet the fact remains that it was as the exponent of Constitutional Government that he fought Prince George in

[1] "Prince George to King Constantine," 27th April 1915. Quoted in full, Mélas, "Ex-King Constantine and the War," pp. 250-1.

[2] Abbott, "Greece and the Allies, 1914-22," p. 229.

Crete. In 1910 he renovated and defended the Greek Constitution, and proved by his triumphant success at the polls that a democracy can recognize and follow a strong and courageous leader. Despotism at all stages of his career he has denounced as "an iniquity," and "the democratic ideal" as the ultimate goal of political evolution.

Like all great Liberals—Lincoln, Gladstone, Cavour—he has not hesitated, in the furtherance of a policy once approved by the people, to use strong, even despotic, measures. His return to Athens in 1917 was the direct result of a revolution, and revolutions do not create the best atmosphere for constitutional procedure. But he recognized that all those measures, martial law, D.O.R.A., etc., on which his enemies wholly concentrate and which he was driven to adopt as the result of a political convulsion, must be approved and ratified by the people. He realized that the failure to win that approval had put an end to his political career, and he did not regard his return in January 1924 as other than temporary. The proposals he made on that occasion are sufficient to prove—if the study of his career were not sufficient—that his outlook is fundamentally Liberal.

His enemies have failed to construct an adverse sketch of his character sufficiently self-consistent to bear examination. Mr Paxton Hibben seems to find it enough to indicate that Venizelos came from Crete a poor man, but that in 1916 he was able to buy a house in the fashionable quarter of Athens, for this to constitute a proof that he was in the pay of the Allies. Presumably, the Salonika Revolution was initiated in order to maintain the new establishment.

Mr Abbott writes in an interesting character sketch of Venizelos early in his book: "His initiative was indefatigable; his decision quick. Unlike most of his countrymen, he did not content himself with ideas without works. His subtlety in thinking did not serve him as a substitute for action. . . ."[1] Later on, when his narrative of the ill deeds of "the Cretan" has waxed fast and furious, he writes of the pause before Venizelos finally left Athens and proclaimed the rebellion in September, 1916: "It is possible that he suffered . . . from one of those attacks of timidity to which he was subject in a crisis."[2]

It is safe to say that Mr Abbott's picture of the "needy and ambitious child of fortune," is as unreal as Mr Hibben's dealer in second-hand shrouds. The final impression given

[1] Abbott, "Greece and the Allies," p. 4.

[2] *Ibid.*, p. 129.

by Mr Abbott is that King Constantine was not unlike St George, and that M. Venizelos was a more than usually potent dragon. If his picture of the great statesman were true, then Venizelos for the whole of his political career has been animated solely by greed and ambition forever masked by a cloud of hypocrisy that rendered for a time his self-seeking invisible to the eyes of an infatuated electorate. Since the beginning of history such a character has never existed. It is as much of a chimera as the "economic" or the "political" man. An attempt to simplify has ended, as usual, in a horrible distortion.

Mr Toynbee, on the other hand, regards M. Venizelos as "a great statesman and a great man." He concentrates on his record in Paris and seeks the key to the foreign policy of Venizelos, as we have seen, in the exigencies of the electoral situation at home. The Smyrna policy was the root of all the later troubles of Greece, and King Constantine was only a cypher. "A statesman of distinction," he writes, "who makes a capital mistake, admits it, and then does his best to retrieve it, is a much more human figure than that incongruous object, the statesman in a halo." [1] But the dilemma is not complete—a statesman without a halo may inaugurate a policy full of promise, and, so long as he conducts it, crowned with success, but later, in other hands, his work may be wrecked in a great catastrophe.

He took to Paris, not fears for a general election, but hopes for a Hellas reunited, great and powerful. Such had always been the goal of his sleepless activities.[2] That his was the great personal triumph of the Conference was admitted by friends and enemies alike. It was the triumph of supreme ability subordinated to and absorbed by a great idea.

It is this dominant idea of a reunited and liberated Hellenism that gives unity to the infinite combinations of his political career and raises it far above the inspired opportunism of the successful *arriviste*. The simple narrative of his life reveals more than elaborate disquisitions on individual aspects of his policy, for the greatness of Venizelos does not consist in any individual quality or characteristic, foresight, audacity, imagination, width of knowledge, so much as in the combination of all these in a personality utterly single-

[1] Toynbee, "The Western Question in Greece and Turkey," preface to 2nd edition, p. xxii.

[2] See "La Politique de la Grèce," Speeches, October-November 1915.

minded and single-hearted in its devotion to the great idea that unifies and inspires its every activity. When to these qualities one adds personal charm and the industry without which political genius has so often failed, the result is a combination almost irresistible—the perfect instrument of a will that may be compared to a tempered Toledo blade, that bends but pierces.

Much of his work remains—the settlement of 1913 stands unshaken. He taught the Greeks to rise above the levels of a tolerated existence and to vindicate the proudest claims of the Hellenic race. The story of his life, as the years pass, will become the heritage of every Greek, for it holds the inspiration and the challenge of all high achievement.

At the moment, when the voices of his critics are raised in loudest dissent, Venizelos suddenly eludes them by an ultimate appeal and passes at once into a purer air: "Even if we fail, we shall know that we have done our duty."

A LIST OF AUTHORITIES

Abbott, G. F. "Greece and the Allies, 1914-22." (Methuen, 1922.)

Baker, R. S. "Woodrow Wilson and World Settlement." 3 vols. (Heinemann, 1923.)

"Balkanicus" (Stojan Protich). "The Aspirations of Bulgaria." (Simpkin, 1915.)

Bareilles. "Le Drame Oriental, D'Athènes à Angora." (Paris, 1923.)

Cassavetti. "Hellas and the Balkan Wars." (T. Fisher Unwin, 1914.)

Chester, S. B. "Life of Venizelos." (Constable, 1921.)

Churchill. "The World Crisis." 2 vols. (Butterworth, 1923.)

Cosmin, S. "Diplomatie et Presse dans l'affaire Grecque, 1914-16." (Paris, 1921.)

Fournet, D. du. "Souvenirs de guerre d'un Amiral, 1914-16." (Paris, 1920.)

Gauvain. "The Greek Question." (Translated from French for American-Hellenic Society, 1918.)

Gibbons, H. A. "Venizelos." (T. Fisher Unwin, 1921.)

*Glasgow, G. "Ronald Burrows—A Memoir." (Nisbet & Co., 1924.)

Gueshoff, J. E. "The Balkan League." (John Murray, 1915.)

Hibben, Paxton. "Constantine I. and the Greek People." (New York: Century Company, 1920.)

Kerofilas, C. "Eleftherios Venizelos: His Life and Work." (John Murray, 1915.)

* Inserted for reference. I regret this was published too late to influence the foregoing essay.

LAWSON, J. C. "Tales of Ægean Intrigue." (Chatto & Windus, 1920.)
MÉLAS, G. H. "Ex-King Constantine and the War." (Hutchinson, 1920.)
MILLER, W. "A History of the Greek People, 1821-1921." (Methuen, 1922.)
—— "The Ottoman Empire and its Successors, 1801-1922." (Cambridge University Press, 1923.)
NEKLUDOFF, A. V. "Diplomatic Reminiscences, 1911-17." (John Murray, 1920.)
"POLYBIUS." "Greece before the Conference." (Methuen, N.D.)
RECOULY. "M. Jonnart en Grèce et l'Abdication de Constantin." (Paris, 1918.)
REGNAULT. "La Conquête d'Athènes Juin-Juillet, 1917." (Paris, 1920.)
SARRAIL. "Mon Commandement en Orient, 1916-18." (Paris, 1920.)
SELIGMAN, V. J. "The Victory of Venizelos: a Study of Greek Politics, 1910-18." (G. Allen & Unwin, 1920.)
TOYNBEE, A. J. "The Western Question in Greece and Turkey." (2nd ed. Constable, 1922.)
TEMPERLEY, H. W. V. (Editor). "A History of the Peace Conference of Paris." Vol. VI. (Henry Frowde and Hodder & Stoughton, 1924.)
VAKA, D. "Constantine, King and Traitor." (John Lane, The Bodley Head, 1918.)
VENIZELOS. "Greece before the Peace Conference of 1919: a Statement of Greek Claims." (Trans. American-Hellenic Society, New York, 1919.)
—— "Grand discours de, sur la crise Balkanique." (Dent, 1913.)
—— "Vindication of Greek National Policy, 1912-17: a Report of Speeches in the Greek Chamber, August 24-26, 1917." (G. Allen & Unwin, 1918.)
—— "La politique de la Grèce—ouvrage contenant les discours prononcés par l'homme d'État aux séances historiques du Parlement Hellénique" (Octobre et Novembre, 1915). (Paris, 1916.)
—— "Speech at Athens, 27th August 1916." (Anglo-Hellenic League Publication, No. 28, 1916.)
—— "The Internal Situation in Greece and the Amnesty of Political Offenders. Speech in Greek Chamber, 23rd April/6th May 1920." (The Greek Bureau of Foreign Information, 1920.)

THE GREEK WHITE BOOK. "Supplementary Diplomatic Documents, 1913-17." (Trans. American-Hellenic Society, 1919.)
—— "Diplomatic Documents, 1913-17." (Trans. American-Hellenic Society, 1919.)
DOCUMENTS DIPLOMATIQUES. "Les Affaires Balkaniques, 1912-14." (Ministère des Affaires étrangères. Paris, 1922. 3 vols.)

WOODROW WILSON

" What is needed is an inner renovation without which there is no meaning in political liberty. What is needed is an active love for one's neighbour, without which there is no true patriotism. What is needed is to love, to seek and to defend the truth. What is needed is to establish public life upon the basis of morality and truth."

THOMAS GARRIGUE MASARYK,
President of the Czecho-Slovak Republic.

" Rightly to be great
Is not to stir without great argument . . ."

SHAKESPEARE, *Hamlet.*

WOODROW WILSON.

WOODROW WILSON

AMONG the great political figures of our day, none has occupied so unique and spectacular a position as did President Wilson at the moment when the Allies, almost against hope, found themselves masters of the world on 11th November 1918. He was the chief magistrate of a nation whose decisive intervention had turned the tide of war, and made victory over the German alliance possible if only the strength and endurance of the nations whose sons had borne the burden and heat of the day, would rise to the height of a great opportunity.

Not only was the President the chief magistrate of the great Republic that stood not yet as a fighter upon whose heart has fallen the chill of war-weariness, that was still mobilizing with marvellous enthusiasm its vast resources; but, throughout 1918, he had won for himself the fascinated attention of all who demanded an articulate voice, some formulation of the desire to escape from the nightmare that raged around them. In the great pronouncements of the President on the objects of the war, they found the formulation, the rationalization that made him the veritable prophet of a new and better world. Yet, because of the half-hysterical hopes he inspired, more was demanded of him in those days than flesh and blood could compass. Judged by such grandiose standards, his greatest achievements have shrunk to the dimensions of failure, and one who seemed to be the unchallenged master of events in those days of fevered hope, has been represented since as the mere toy and sport of circumstance and of his own idiosyncracies and vanity.

It is safe to say that no man who has ever held the destinies of men for any time in his hands has escaped, or ever can escape, such charges. This song of the permanent Greek chorus of scoffers is sometimes true, sometimes justified, more often mere noise; in the case of President Wilson the chorus has been corybantic as well as vociferous. But the chorus has recruited not alone the irresponsible idealists who live by exploiting their disappointments, but many sober onlookers who lay to the charge of President Wilson the evils of the "Carthaginian Peace." The best way of testing, and perhaps correcting, such a judgment, is not to discuss directly and polemically this or that charge directed against this or that policy, but to try to reconstruct, however summarily, the life in time and, as it developed, of the historical figure round whose acts and days controversy has circled. So policies and programmes come to have a background, and cease to lie about as mere *disjecta membra*.

Thomas Woodrow Wilson was born at Staunton, Virginia, on 28th December 1856. He came of a Scottish-Irish stock, and both his father's and his mother's family had settled in the United States as emigrants from the United Kingdom during the first half of the century.

His paternal grandfather, James Wilson, a young emigrant from County Down, had come to Philadelphia, then the capital of the States, in 1807, and there had obtained employment in the office of William Duane, the famous editor of the *Aurora*. After the Peace of Ghent in 1812, which ended the second war of the States and Great Britain, James Wilson went to Pittsburg, and from there to Steubenville, in the newly founded State of Ohio. At Steubenville he founded *The Western Herald*, and in 1832 followed up this successful journalistic effort by starting *The Pennsylvania Advocate* in Pittsburg. He continued to direct both papers to his death in 1857.[1] Altogether, this active and influential journalist, who was also a J.P.—from which office he was usually known as Judge Wilson—" must be held responsible for a goodly portion of the printed wisdom and folly of the early nineteenth century in the States." [2]

Judge James Wilson brought up every one of his seven sons at Steubenville to be an expert compositor, which suggests that this vigorous personality, far-famed for the definiteness of his opinions, had practical views on the education of children and the desirability of fitting them into pre-arranged grooves. At Steubenville his youngest son, Joseph Ruggles Wilson, the father of the President, was born on 28th February 1822.

Joseph Ruggles was the scholar of the family. After graduating he taught for some time at a school; later he was ordained a minister of the Presbyterian Church in which he had been brought up. Throughout his distinguished career he oscillated curiously between an academic and a pastoral calling. From 1851-5 he was Professor of Chemistry and Natural Science in Hampden Sydney College, Virginia; from 1858-70 he was pastor of the First Presbyterian Church of Augusta, Georgia; 1870-4 Professor of Pastoral and Evan-

[1] Ford, " Woodrow Wilson: The Man and his Work," p. 2.
[2] Hale, " Woodrow Wilson: The Story of his Life," p. 9.

gelistic Theology, Columbia, South Carolina Theological Seminary; 1874-85 Pastor of the First Presbyterian Church, Wilmington, North Carolina; 1885-93 Professor of Theology in the South-West Presbyterian University, Clarksville, Tennessee. He was Permanent Clerk of the General Assembly of the Presbyterian Church of the South, 1865-99, and served as Moderator in 1879.[1]

In 1849, just before his ordination, Joseph Ruggles Wilson married Janet Woodrow, the daughter of Dr Thomas Woodrow, and as we have seen, their third child and first son, Thomas Woodrow Wilson, was born in 1856.

Dr Thomas Woodrow, the maternal grandfather of the President, had been born at Paisley in Scotland in 1793. After graduating at Glasgow he was ordained a minister of the Presbyterian Church, thereby conforming to the tradition of his family, which numbered many ministers and more than one martyr in the "killing times."[2] Not long after his ordination he crossed the Tweed to accept the call to be pastor of the Independent Congregation at Carlisle, where he served from 1819-35. In the latter year he decided to emigrate with his family and embark on missionary work in Canada, where he worked for a year or so, before accepting the call to the pastorate of the First Presbyterian Church of Chillicothe, Ohio. He served at Chillicothe from 1837-49, when he went to Columbus, where he was a minister to his death in 1877.

The history of the Presbytery of Chillicothe describes Dr Woodrow as "a fine scholar, a good preacher, and especially powerful in prayer. He was conservative in his views and thoroughly Presbyterian in his belief. His sermons were always instructive and pointed. He loved to dwell on the great cardinal doctrines of the Gospel and to proclaim them in their simplicity and fulness."[3]

Thomas Woodrow Wilson was then a "son of the manse." He came of a race of scholars, ministers, editors, and men of enterprise. He was born into a strongly Presbyterian tradition. His father was a pastor, his mother's father—who seems to have won the affections and captured the imagination of the boy—was also a pastor. If we are to believe the testimony of the "Dictionary of National Biography," the sons

[1] Ford, "Woodrow Wilson: The Man and his Work," pp. 4-5.
[2] Hale, "Woodrow Wilson: The Story of his Life," p. 16.
[3] Quoted Hale, "Woodrow Wilson: The Story of his Life," p. 19.

of the clergy, taken as a whole, have proved themselves a body with considerable possibilities.

Woodrow Wilson was a little over four years old when the Civil War between North and South broke out. The war made little impression on his mind, and though he grew up in an atmosphere of Southern patriotism, he carried with him no such vivid memories as did his friend of later years, Walter Page. Dr Wilson, his father, espoused the cause of the South with passionate fervour, and on the division of the Presbyterian Church into Northern and Southern branches, he became Permanent Clerk to the General Assembly.

But Augusta lay outside the main tracks of the war, and was not occupied by a Federal force until after the war and the period of "Reconstruction," at the time when the young Wilson thought "all good people were Presbyterians and all wicked ones Yankees."[1] The war probably delayed the beginning of his education, though the fact that he was not taught the alphabet until he was nine, may have been due to his father's independent views on the education of children as on most other subjects.

His father was a decisive influence in the development of the boy. He was a man of cheerful disposition, at the same time deeply studious. He made a point of talking a great deal with his son, reading to him and taking him about with him on his journeys, on which he never missed pointing out things of interest, especially delighting in explaining the working of machinery. Above all he trained him in the careful use of English, with the result that even before he could read the boy could express himself with remarkable ease and clarity. His father was never tired of impressing on him that "nobody had a thought until he could put it quickly and definitely into words."[2] He had at one time been a teacher of rhetoric and all his life remained a lover of the *mot juste,* and of striking clear-cut and harmonious composition. He inculcated in his son a love of the restrained and sober in expression and a hatred of all verbal extravagance —he had, on the other hand, an amiable weakness for an occasional preciosity, and the unusual use of words, which was certainly not without influence in forming the striking and scholarly style of the later famous pronouncements of his son.

[1] Hale, "Woodrow Wilson: The Story of his Life," p. 36.
[2] *Ibid.*, p. 41.

After attending small schools at Augusta and Columbia, the young Wilson was sent in 1873 to Davidson College, North Carolina, where he spent a year until compelled to return home for a year's rest after a breakdown in his health. He spent his leisure in general reading and getting up Greek for Princeton, which he entered in September 1875.

During his four years at Princeton he gradually drew increasing attention to himself by the slow but impressive unfolding of his intellectual powers, though there was nothing startling about his career. Princeton grouped as "honours" graduates all who at the end of their four years' course maintained an average of 90 per cent. of possible marks.[1] In 1879 Woodrow Wilson was 38th in a graduating class of 106,[2] of whom 42 were "honours" men. In a word, "his record for scholarship was sound without being brilliant."

What personal glimpses we have of him in those years reveal him as generally popular and notable for his charm and openness of manner, but at the same time fastidious in the choice both of his clubs and of his friends. His interest in politics and public life was first stimulated by his finding *The Gentleman's Magazine* in the Chancellor Green Library at Princeton, and reading the famous articles on "Men and Manners in Parliament" by "The Member for the Chiltern Hundreds." The Editor had planned them as the modern counterpart of those famous "Parliamentary Reports" Dr Johnson had written for the same magazine some hundred and thirty years before.[3] He committed the execution of the plan to one who was later to become equally famous as the "Toby M.P. of *Punch*—Henry Lucy, who, years afterwards, was knighted by King Edward. Through his superb descriptions, that brought vividly before the mind's eye the great stage of Westminister, Wilson fell under the spell of the great English masters of that day—Gladstone, Bright, Disraeli. He became deeply interested in English history and English political institutions, and read widely and thoughtfully in political science and history.

Already resolved to embark on public life, he took an active part in debating. On entering Princeton he joined the "Whig Society," one of the two rival debating clubs, and though he was slow in coming to the front, by his fourth

[1] Hale, "Woodrow Wilson: The Story of his Life," p. 58.
[2] Ford, "Woodrow Wilson: The Man and his Work," p. 9.
[3] Hale, "Woodrow Wilson: The Story of his Life," pp. 61-3.

year he was recognized as the club's best speaker. In the annual debate for the Lynde Prize between the Whig Society and its rival the Cliosophic Society in 1879, Wilson was chosen to represent his club. The subjects were not arranged beforehand, the speakers being required to speak extempore on a subject found inscribed on a paper drawn from a hat. The theme for 1879 was Tariffs, and chance decided that Wilson should speak in favour of Protection. He tore up the slip and retired from the debate, refusing absolutely as a passionate Free-Trader to speak against his convictions.[1] As a result the Cliosophic man carried off the prize from Wilson's substitute.

"The interest of an episode trifling in itself lies in the evidence it affords of the depth of Wilson's political convictions at the time."[2] In his fourth year, 1879, he won a prize for an essay on William Pitt the Elder, and followed it up with two others on Gladstone and John Bright, printed in 1880 in the Magazine of the University of Virginia. More important still he was successful in getting an elaborate essay on "Cabinet Government in the United States" accepted and published in August 1879 by *The International Review*—a serious magazine with a national reputation. The essay occupies nearly eighteen pages and is certainly a remarkable literary achievement and a striking piece of political writing. The essayist sets himself to answer the question why "anxiety about the future of our institutions seems to be daily becoming stronger in the minds of thoughtful Americans." He finds it in the irresponsibility of Congress, divorced by the Constitution from the Executive which has no means of proposing or defending measures before the legislature. All free and open debate had withered because "there is no one in Congress to speak for the nation. Congress is a conglomeration of inharmonious elements." As a result legislation has been parcelled out among a number of Standing Committees behind whose closed doors private interests conceal themselves. "The Executive is in constant need of legislative co-operation; the legislative must be aided by an Executive who is in a position intelligently and vigorously to execute its acts. There must needs be, therefore, as a binding link between them, some body which has no power to coerce the one, and

[1] Hale, "Woodrow Wilson: The Story of his Life," p. 70.

[2] H. Wilson Harris, "President Wilson: His Problems and his Policy," p. 22.

is interested in maintaining the independent effectiveness of the other. Such a link is the responsible cabinet."[1]

The essay is remarkable as containing in embryo much of Wilson's later political thought. But early as it was, there were still some years to pass before he wholly left the preparatory stage of scholastic life. Still bent on entering public life, he decided that legal qualifications were the best introduction since many Southern politicians had been lawyers. Accordingly, after taking his Princeton degree, he entered the law department of the University of Virgina, Charlottesville. At the end of a year his health broke down owing to overwork and he was compelled to spend a year at home recuperating.

In 1882, being duly qualified, he embarked on legal practice at Atlanta, working in partnership with another young lawyer named Renwick. Atlanta seemed a promising place for a start as it was rapidly growing, but the notice Renwick and Wilson hung from a second-floor window in a side street did not attract clients; for eighteen months the partners waited, Wilson well occupied in intensive reading in politics and economics.[2] At last it became obvious that there was very little prospect for a man without private means and not content to wait for the slow arrival of shy clients. If he could not practise law Wilson could at least teach it and other subjects. So the partnership was dissolved and Wilson entered on a post-graduate two years' course in history and political economy at Johns Hopkins University, in the autumn of 1883. In the second year he was the holder of an historical fellowship.[3]

Wilson's career at Johns Hopkins was brilliantly successful. Now at last, after a curiously slow development, began the flowering-time of that powerful, carefully-trained and disciplined intellect. In 1885 he completed a book which was published the same year, the first-fruits of those studies stimulated at Princeton by his casual readings in *The Gentleman's Magazine.* "Congressional Government: a Study in American Politics," is a close examination and description of the actual working of the American Constitution, not in terms of its theory, but of its fact. The book did for the American student of politics what Bagehot's "English Con-

[1] Quoted Ford, "Woodrow Wilson: The Man and his Work," pp. 17-18.
[2] Hale, "Woodrow Wilson: The Story of his Life," pp. 86-7.
[3] *Ibid.*, p. 91.

stitution" did for the English. For the first time the machinery of Congress and the real though unrecognized power of its Standing Committees were discussed. The book, which in 1886 he submitted for the Ph.D. of Johns Hopkins, met with instant success, "comparable among university theses only with Bryce's "Holy Roman Empire," first written as an Oxford prize exercise."[1] Since its publication it has passed through close on thirty editions. It was at Johns Hopkins that he rapidly acquired the kind of academic reputation that marks a man out for preferment. Invitations to occupy several academic posts immediately followed the publication of the book.

In 1885 he accepted a lectureship at Bryn Mawr, a women's college not far from Philadelphia. At the same time he held a visiting lectureship at Johns Hopkins. At twenty-nine he had fairly begun his career and in the year that he went to Bryn Mawr he married his first wife, Ellen Louise Axson, an old acquaintance of the Augusta days[2] and the daughter of a distinguished Presbyterian minister of Savannah.

In 1888 he was elected to the Chair of History and Political Economy at Wesleyan University, Middletown, Connecticut. While at Wesleyan University he published in 1889 an extensive textbook on the actual form and organization of ancient and modern government under the title "The State: Elements of Historical and Practical Politics." The preparation of the book involved an enormous expenditure of labour, as it contains a detailed description of the mechanism of government in the chief modern states. The book was a pioneer in a vitally important department of political science and won an enthusiastic reception. Since its publication a new edition has been called for practically every year. In four years he had won wide recognition and a definite position in the intellectual life of America, and this fact was demonstrated when, in 1890, he was offered and accepted, the Chair of Jurisprudence and Politics at his old college,[3] Princeton, where he was to spend the next twenty years of his life.

The period in his life between the publication of "Congressional Government" in 1885 and his appointment as

[1] H. Wilson Harris, "President Wilson: His Problems and his Policy," p. 28.

[2] Hale, "Woodrow Wilson: The Story of his Life," p. 88.

[3] Princeton became a University in 1896.

President of Princeton in 1902 was one of marvellous literary activity. In Princeton Library there is a bibliography of his published writings which, though not complete, runs to seventy-five entries. All, with one exception, belong to this period.[1] "It was as if the preparatory stage had been employed in assembling materials and in setting up apparatus whose products now came forth in remarkable variety."[2] In 1893 he wrote the concluding volume of a series of three studies in "Epochs of American History." Under the title "Division and Reunion," the Professor dealt with the vital period of American History, 1829-89. A second edition was called for within two months of its publication, and up to 1912 the book passed through twenty-five editions. A "Life of George Washington" followed in 1897, and in 1902 his most ambitious work, a "History of the American People," in five volumes. For the volume on America in the "Cambridge Modern History" he contributed a valuable chapter on "State Rights," covering the decade of crisis in the history of the United States, 1850-60.

Throughout these twelve years as a Professor at Princeton, before his election as President of the University in 1902, he became widely known for his many articles on political and educational subjects. In the March number of *The Atlantic Monthly* in 1897 appeared an article on "Mr Cleveland as President," which, at a moment of great party passion, attracted widespread attention for its detachment, followed in July by an essay on "The Making of the Nation," in which he presents again and elaborates those ideas of the Constitution which had informed his undergraduate article in the *International Review*: "Congress . . . has no responsible leaders known to the system of government, and the leaders recognized by its rules are one set of individuals for one sort of legislation, another for another. The Secretaries cannot address or approach either House as a whole; in dealing with committees they are dealing only with groups of individuals; neither party has its leader—there are only influential men here and there who know how to manage its caucuses and take advantage of parliamentary openings on the floor. . . . It is with such machinery that we are to face the future, find a wise and moderate policy, bring the nation to a common,

[1] Ford, "Woodrow Wilson: The Man and his Work," p. 53.
[2] *Ibid.*, p. 22.

a cordial understanding, a real unity of life. . . . Once more is our problem of nation-making the problem of a form of government." [1]

Many were his addresses and articles on ideals in education, and they invariably excited widespread discussion. He set his face like a rock against the superficial enthusiasm of the day for a "scientific" rather than "literary" education. The newest thought held that the cultural ideas of the past were outworn: science would provide the chief intellectual discipline of the future. In his address on "Princeton in the Nation's Service," on 21st October 1896, published in the *Forum* for December 1896, and widely quoted in other magazines and journals, he said: "Science has bred in us a spirit of experiment and a contempt for the past. It has made us credulous of quick improvement, hopeful of discovering panaceas, confident of success in every new thing. . . . It has given us agnosticism in the realm of philosophy, scientific anarchism in the field of politics. . . . This is not the fault of the scientist: he has done his work with an intelligence and success which cannot be too much admired. It is the work of the noxious, intoxicating gas which has somehow got into the lungs of the rest of us from out the crevices of his workshop—a gas, it would seem, which forms only in the outer air. . . . Science has not changed the laws of social growth and betterment. Science has not changed the nature of society, has not made history a whit easier to understand, human nature a whit easier to reform. It has won for us a great liberty in the physical world, . . . but it has not freed us from ourselves. It has not purged us of passion or disposed us to virtue. It has not made us less covetous or less ambitious or less self-indulgent. . . . It has wrought such instant, incredible improvement in all the physical setting of our life, that we have grown the more impatient of the unreformed condition of the part it has not touched or bettered. . . . Can anyone wonder, then, that I ask for the old drill, the old memory of times gone by, the old schooling in precedent and tradition, the old keeping of faith with the past, as a preparation for leadership in days of social change?" [2]

The theme is that the true function of education is to make men and women good citizens with steady nerves and calm

[1] Quoted Ford, "Woodrow Wilson: The Man and his Work," pp. 71-2.
[2] *Ibid.*, pp. 31-3.

and critical judgments. "The world in which we live," he wrote in an article in the *Forum* for September 1894, "is troubled by many voices, seeking to proclaim righteousness and judgment to come; but they disturb without instructing us." An acquaintance with great literature, a sound and wide knowledge of history, will teach us that these glittering dreams have beguiled men before. "Here is like wild talk and headlong passion for reform in the past—here in the books—with all the motives that underlay the perilous utterance now laid bare: these are not new terrors and excitements. . . . It is no new thing to have economic problems and dream dreams of romantic and adventurous social reconstruction. And so it is out of books that we can get our means and our self-possession for a sane and systematic criticism of life."[1] Here is doctrine that "comes home to the business and bosoms" of us living in the world as we see and know it, the prey of frenzied gospels and armed apostolates, with even greater force and pungency than to the Americans of the '90's.

In June 1902 the President of Princeton, Dr Francis Landey Patton, resigned, and in September Dr Woodrow Wilson—the first layman to hold the office—succeeded him, "the appointment falling by universal consent to the member of the faculty whose writings and occasional addresses, principally on educational subjects, outside Princeton, had won him distinction such as none of his colleagues could claim."[2]

The President of an American university is a person who bulks far larger in the public eye than the holder of the corresponding office at an English or Scottish university. His importance has been clearly sketched by Lord Bryce.[3] "His powers in the management of the institution and the selection of professors are much greater than those of the head of an English or Scottish university. But he is often also a leading figure in the State, perhaps even in the nation. No persons in the country, hardly even the greatest railway magnates, are better known, and certainly none are more respected than the Presidents of the leading universities." For this reason Mr Wilson Harris considers that the public career of President Wilson "may more properly be fixed in

[1] Quoted Ford, "Woodrow Wilson: The Man and his Work," pp. 28-9.
[2] Harris, "President Wilson: His Problems and his Policy," p. 29.
[3] Bryce, "American Commonwealth," ii., cap. cix.

1902, when he became President of Princeton, than in 1910, when he was elected Governor of New Jersey." [1]

As Professor for twelve years at the University he was now called upon to rule, he had formed clear and often expressed ideas of the things that required to be done before Princeton could be roused from the slumber into which it was fast falling and made a centre of light and leading. The popularity of his lectures, the open house he kept for students at his home in Library Place, had enabled him to establish that personal relationship between pupil and teacher which he held to be essential if education is to be true to its name and in any way different from the instruction to be found in text-books and encyclopædias.

His Presidency falls into two periods—five years up to 1907, of peaceful and generally accepted reforms, and three years, ending in 1910, of struggle with a steadily strengthening opposition. His predecessor, Dr Patton, had acknowledged that in his opinion it was impossible for Princeton to be other than a university for rich men's sons.[2] Such it was fast becoming, and as a result the standard of scholarship was deplorably low. Dr Wilson immediately appointed a committee to consider ways and means of enforcing what had become the nominal standards of achievement. A scheme came into force by which men either passed their examinations or went. There was a certain outcry against this startling decision, but when the most vocal protesters had been duly weeded out, a fresh generation was not long in arriving, which accepted the new standards. But this was only a beginning. Another committee was appointed to overhaul and recast the entire curriculum of the University. The revolt against the old discipline of the classical languages and mathematics, which has been mentioned above, had led on to the multiplication of "subjects" and a freedom of choice as to his course thoroughly dangerous to the callow youth entering the University at nineteen, and called on to map out his course for the next four years. That there must be a freedom of choice was obvious, but it must be a choice within limits, and the subjects must be so grouped that, however he chose, the undergraduate could not by any ingenuity escape a liberal education. In his inaugural address on his election as President, Dr Wilson declared his principles. Out of the

[1] Harris, "President Wilson: His Problems and his Policy," p. 30.
[2] Hale, "Woodrow Wilson: The Story of his Life," p. 112.

legion of studies "we must make a choice, and suffer the pupil himself to make choice. But the choice we make must be the chief choice, the choice that the pupil makes the subordinate choice. We must supply the synthesis, and must see to it that, whatever group of studies the student selects, it shall at least represent the round whole, contain all the elements of modern knowledge, and be itself a complete circle of general subjects."[1] As a result, the group system of studies was formulated, sometimes called "group electives," because the student is limited to a choice among groups of co-ordinated subjects.[2] The system—not wholly of Dr Wilson's devising—has, however, spread widely among American universities, largely owing to his pioneer work at Princeton.

The President's experience as a Professor, and observation as President, convinced him that teaching at Princeton was arid because it was wholly instructional. The undergraduates appeared two or three times a day at lectures more or less interesting, according to the lecturer, who tended inevitably to attempt—for lack of other contacts with the students—to do their work and their thinking for them, that is to digest books which the undergraduates should have been reading for themselves, and deliver the chapter of a potential text-book instead of a guide to research and discussion of outstanding problems. Of course there was room for the instructional lecture, but it was not enough and it was not educative. Dr Wilson met the problem by proposing and securing the adoption of the preceptorial system, whereby small groups of students, under the guidance of young tutors, met regularly for discussion and study. In December 1902 he outlined his scheme to a meeting of Princeton *alumni* at New York: ". . . If we could get a body of such tutors at Princeton we could transform the place from a place where there are youngsters doing tasks to a place where there are men doing thinking, men who are conversing about the things of thought, men who are eager and interested in the things of thought. . . . Wherever you have a small class and they can be intimately associated with their chief in the study of an interesting subject, they catch the infection of the subject; but where they are in big classes, and simply hear a man lecture two or three times a week, they cannot catch the infection of any-

[1] Harris, "President Wilson: His Problems and his Policy," p. 34.
[2] Hale, "Woodrow Wilson: The Story of his Life," pp. 116-7.

thing, except it may be the voice and enthusiasm of the lecturer himself. This is the way in which to transform the place." [1]

The system introduced at Princeton is more like the seminar of German universities, which inspired the idea, than the tutorial system of individual instruction as it has been developed at Oxford and Cambridge. Inevitably the introduction of the preceptorial scheme at Princeton involved considerable expense and the addition to the staff of a hundred young, though advanced, scholars, selected by the President himself, who found them for the most part in Great Britain and the United States.[2] In spite of all difficulties the system was working by 1905, and has had a marked effect since in raising the standard of scholarship and transforming the character of the lectures at Princeton. The President boldly affirmed that the college and university did not exist to teach a man how best to earn his bread and butter, "to give him the skill and special knowledge which shall make a good tool, an excellent bread-winning tool of him"—such work was excellent, but belonged to the technical schools. "The college is not for the majority, who carry forward the common labour of the world, nor even for those who work at the skilled handicrafts which multiply the conveniences and the luxuries of the complex modern life. It is for the minority who plan, who conceive, who superintend, who mediate between group and group, and who must see the wide stage as a whole. Democratic nations must be served in this wise, no less than those whose leaders are chosen by birth and privilege; and the college is no less democratic because it is for those who play a special part. . . ." [3]

As a corollary of his preceptorial system, the reforming and indefatigable President realized that there must be a deepening of corporate spirit at Princeton, and he conceived the idea of making Princeton a wholly residential University, in which the undergraduates would live together in halls, independent, except on questions of education, which would be wholly controlled by the University. For freshmen and sophomores, second-year men, he succeeded in making hostels rather than lodging-houses the usual places of residence,[4] but

[1] Quoted Ford, "Woodrow Wilson: The Man and his Work," p. 46.
[2] Halévy, "President Wilson," pp. 73-4.
[3] Ford, "Woodrow Wilson: The Man and his Work," p. 36.
[4] Harris, "President Wilson: His Problems and his Policy," p. 36.

in the further development of his scheme he was to encounter an insuperable obstacle.

Every student on his natriculation had long been required to make a formal promise that he would not join any fraternities or semi-Masonic college societies so familiar in other American universities, and usually bearing a name formed by two or three Greek letters. President Wilson himself, after leaving Princeton in 1879, had been initiated, at the University of Virginia, into a Greek letter fraternity known as the Phi-Kappa-Psi.[1]

Owing to this prohibition, and to the fact that the College (as it then was) did not provide any eating-places for the students, various eating clubs sprang up in the '70's, one of which, the "Ivy," hit on the idea of perpetuating itself in a Club building. This is the origin in the early '80's of the famous Clubs, now twelve in number, which line Prospect Avenue. Each Club housed, at the time we are discussing, about thirty members: fifteen juniors or third-year men, and fifteen seniors or fourth-year men. They were admirably run, luxuriously furnished, and extremely exclusive. Mere considerations of space involved the exclusion of 300 or so of the two eligible classes: only about 350 juniors and seniors enjoyed the amenities of the "Ivy," the "Cap and Gown," "Tiger Inn," and others, and, as a result, the competition and intrigue in order to secure membership of a club on the part of those outside was intense. The "sophomores," early in their second year, began operations to win an entry the moment they became "juniors." Wealthy parents have even been known to visit Princeton, before their son had arrived as a freshman, in order to set the necessary forces in motion calculated to land him in a swagger club the moment he became a junior.[2] In the telling words of the President, "the side-shows had swallowed up the circus."

Without making a direct attack on what he regarded as dangerous and unhealthy centres of snobbery, in 1907 the President submitted to the Trustees his scheme for dividing Princeton into a number of residential "quads" or halls, each provided with its common-room and dining-hall. He explained to the Trustees that he aimed at "the social co-ordination of the University." Freshmen, sophomores, juniors, and seniors would be distributed promiscuously

[1] Hale, "Woodrow Wilson: The Story of his Life," p. 78.
[2] *Ibid.*, p. 128.

among the halls and inevitably thrown together. At the June meeting in 1907, 25 of the 27 Trustees, were present, and 24 accepted the President's proposals. On the Friday night before "Commencement," in October 1907, a circular was sent round to the Clubs explaining the "quad" scheme. Instantly it was grasped that the proposals involved, if not the extinction, at least the transformation of the omnipotent Clubs. A howl of indignation went up not only from the Clubs, but from the more crusted of the conservatives among old Princetonians.

The "Die Hards" among the latter wrote long letters to the *Alumni Weekly*, expressing indignation and grief that a President of Princeton should actually propose in all seriousness to "make a gentleman chum with a mucker."[1] It did not occur to these good people that organized social exclusiveness and the idea of a university are incompatible, and that if men are good enough to be at a university at all, they are good enough to share the same common-room and have their meals together. But the uproar was sufficiently disturbing to intimidate the Trustees, who, on 17th October 1907, requested the President to withdraw his proposal. It was his first defeat. His own views he did nor disguise, and one who saw him at this time reports that "he felt that in this there was too strong a tendency to glorify money merely. That with the increasing wealth of the country this tendency would be accentuated. In short, he feared that we would rapidly drift into a plutocracy."[2] The fact that many of the richer *alumni* had not confined their opposition to protests, but announced their intention of withdrawing their financial aid from the University if the reforms of the President were carried, prompted his comment: "It was then that I met Wall Street for the first time, and I saw for myself the manner in which Wall Street opposes everything that is attempted for the good of the country."[3]

He was to meet Wall Street yet again as President of Princeton, but he was still willing to fight it: "The older I become," he said at the annual banquet of the Civic League of St Louis in 1909, "the less and less fit I am to speak at banquets, for I become more and more serious. I consider some of my friends with a hopeless envy. They are so measured in tone,

[1] Hale, "Woodrow Wilson: The Story of his Life," p. 134.
[2] Hale, *Ibid.*, p. 138.
[3] Halévy, "President Wilson," p. 77.

so cold. Their judgments are always so separate from the active movements which animate them. As for myself, the older I become, the more I become ardent. . . ."[1]

Some time before Dr Wilson became President, Professor Andrew F. West had been given the title Dean of the Graduate School, together with the means for a tour in Europe for the purpose of studying post-graduate systems of study. He returned, and published an elaborate scheme for a graduate college. In December 1906 Mrs Thompson Swann left by her will $250.000 for the projected college. The Trustees revised Dr West's scheme, and plans were drawn up for a graduate college in the grounds of the University on the site of the President's House, "Prospect." By 1909 the work had not yet been undertaken, when Mr William C. Proctor of Cincinnati offered $500,000, on condition that a similar sum were raised by subscription. But at the same time, he insisted that Dr West's plans should be carried out, and Dr West's site, remote from the main body of University buildings, should be substituted for that already fixed upon.

At once it became evident that there was a serious difference between Dr West and his supporters and the President. Dr Wilson was strongly opposed to the grandiose scale of Dr West's project, and above all, his whole conception of Princeton as an organic whole and democratic in spirit was violated by the attempt to segregate the graduates in a sumptuous building altogether separate from the University, as though to emphasize the fact that those who lived there under the sway of their superior Dean had souls like stars and dwelt apart. "A university," declared the President, "does not consist of buildings or of apparatus: a university consists of students and teachers."[2] He had the support of the majority of the Trustees in indicating to Mr Proctor that, grateful as the University was for the offer, it could not allow such matters as the choice of sites to be taken out of its hands. "I cannot accede," he wrote later, "to the acceptance of gifts upon terms which take the educational policy of the University out of the hands of the Trustees and faculty, and permit it to be determined by those who give money."[3]

The news that the Proctor offer had been withdrawn at the moment when the corresponding public subscription

[1] Quoted Halévy, "President Wilson," p. 82.
[2] Quoted Hale, "Woodrow Wilson: The Story of his Life," p. 145.
[3] *Ibid.*, p. 151.

had nearly been subscribed, lashed the supporters of the West scheme into a fury of vituperation. That a university should refuse $1,000,000 on a question of principle was inconceivable were it not true. President Wilson was assailed in terms of bitterest denunciation as a self-willed tyrant, or as a Socialist who wanted to ruin " the Princeton spirit " by his sentimental ideas about a democratic university. In April 1910, the President, in a speech at Pittsburg to Princeton *alumni*, answered the open attacks of certain sections of the Press and the covert vilifications which were being circulated as handbills and privately printed pamphlets: " I have dedicated," he said, " every power that there is within me to bring the colleges that I have anything to do with to an absolutely democratic regeneration in spirit, and I shall not be satisfied—and I hope you will not be—until America shall know that the men in the colleges are saturated with the same thought, the same sympathy, that pulses through the whole great body politic. . . . Will America tolerate the seclusion of graduate students? Will America tolerate the idea of having graduate students set apart? America will tolerate nothing except unpatronized endeavour. Seclude a man, separate him from the rough and tumble of college life, from all the contacts of every sort and condition of men, and you have done a thing which America will brand with its contemptuous disapproval." [1] It seemed that the President had won a decisive victory.

Within a month of the speech died Isaac C. Wyman, who had graduated at Princeton in 1848, and had never since returned. He bequathed to the graduate college $3,000,000, appointing Dr West one of the two trustees. Simultaneously Mr Proctor renewed his offer. The Trustees could not resist the impact of so many millions. All opposition to the West scheme vanished. The Dean had triumphed. " When the country is looking to us," the President had asked in the course of the controversy, " as men who prefer ideas even to money, are we going to withdraw and say, ' After all, we find we were mistaken: we prefer money to ideas? ' " [2] It appeared that his question had now been answered. The President bowed to the inevitable, but immediately bethought him of retiring from a post he doubted whether he could conscientiously continue to hold.

[1] Quoted Hale, " Woodrow Wilson: The Story of his Life," pp. 152-3.
[2] *Ibid.*, p. 147.

In a few weeks he received an invitation to leave the academic world and embark on that political life he had all his life so closely studied. In July 1910, he was asked by the Democratic Organization of New Jersey, the State in which Princeton is situated, to stand for the office of Governor. Suddenly Democratic newspapers throughout America began to speak of the President of Princeton as the future Democratic candidate for the Presidency of the United States. What had brought about this extraordinary ascendancy?

For several years a new spirit of reform and criticism had been growing up in the United States. It had become obvious to an increasing body of thoughtful American citizens that all was not well with the politics and the political institutions of the country. In 1904 the Democratic candidate for the Presidency had challenged the party in power with being financed by corporations and trust magnates.[1] Civic Leagues began to spring up in various States, that devoted their activities to stimulating the interest of a sluggish public opinion in the cause of political purification. Yet it would perhaps be fairer to say that public opinion was overwhelmed rather than sluggish.

The fathers and founders of the Republic, "a rural aristocracy and the cream of Puritan jurists,"[2] had taken it for granted that the officials of the new State were not likely to become very numerous; they therefore arranged for the popular election of every official. The all but incredible growth of the great Republic has saddled every conscientious citizen with an overwhelming burden of selection. In March 1909, in an address to a Civic League, President Wilson discussed the results of this fearful multiplication of elections: "You have given the people of this country so many persons to select for office that they have not time to select them, and have to leave it to professionals, that is to say, the professional politicians—which, reduced to its simplest term, is the boss of the district. When you vote the Republican or Democratic ticket you either vote for the names selected by one machine or the names selected by the other machine. This is not to lay any aspersion upon those who receive the nominations. I for one do not subscribe to the opinion that *bosses* under our Government deserve our scorn and

[1] Ford, "Woodrow Wilson: The Man and his Work," p. 114.
[2] Halévy, "President Wilson," p. 102.

contempt, for we have organized a system of government which makes them just as necessary as the President of the United States. They are the natural, inevitable fruit of the tree, and if we do not like them we have got to plant another tree. The boss is just as legitimate as any member of any legislature, because by giving the people a task which they cannot perform, you have taken it away from them, and have made it necessary that those who can perform it should perform it. . . . What is the moral ? . . . Simplify your processes, and you will begin to control; complicate them, and you will get farther and farther away from their control." [1]

In 1910 the State of New Jersey was, like so many other States at the time, in the grip of financial corporations and political bosses. A glance at the map will reveal that Jersey City is really a part of New York, lying on the other side of the Hudson, but separated by the frontier of the State. New York had adopted a stringent policy of control and supervision over the activities of the Financial Corporations, which had in consequence merely shifted their headquarters across the river to Jersey City, where they were free, and where they entered into close relations with the political "bosses" of the Democratic and Republican parties.[2] This was possible simply because the original source of political authority in the Republic was not the Union but the individual States. Each State reproduces in miniature, the structure of the Federal State. The Governor takes the place of the President, and the legislature consists of a Senate and an Assembly. Since the States are the ultimate unit of the Republic they exercise all powers not expressly delegated to the National Government. Within the limits of the Federal Constitution, the individual States can conduct their affairs as they choose, and the result is inevitably a great variety of legislation within the grand unity vindicated by Lincoln. Hence such a situation as that indicated above, of financial Corporations, strictly controlled in New York, making New Jersey, just across the river, a happy hunting-ground, is by no means unusual.

In America municipal development has been slow, and much of the public services, such as gas, road-cleaning,

[1] Quoted Halévy, "President Wilson," pp. 104-5.
[2] *Ibid.*, p. 90

tram-cars, etc., are still in the hands of private companies.[1] Hence the ceaseless intrigues of the competing companies in the legislatures of the various States for the contracts and other privileges arising out of legislation. In 1910 the dominant financial influence in the State was "a combination of electric light and power companies, gas companies, and trolly lines, controlled by the Prudential Insurance Company and the malodorous United Gas Improvement Company of Philadelphia." [2] Direct and flagrant corruption of State Congress legislators by financial interests has probably been exaggerated, " but the relations between individual members of a State Senate or Assembly and a railroad apprehensive of regulative legislation, a light or power company playing for the grant of a monopoly, or a contractor angling for the supply of goods to a public institution, are notoriously equivocal." [3] Such are the forces manipulated by the " bosses " and the " machines " of the rival parties, and as for the chances of effectual control by the average conscientious citizen, it can be gauged by the fact that a New York ballot-sheet in the 1916 election was eight feet long. Decidedly control could come only through simplification.

The Republican party in 1910 had held control of the Governorship of New Jersey, and controlled the legislature for fourteen years; and though the leader of the Democratic Opposition machine, a certain Mr James Smith, had—by arrangement with his official political enemies—received some handsome pickings from the State patronage, he had come to the conclusion that it was about time for a spell of Democratic government. Smith had formerly been a Senator at Washington, but had retired from this branch of public life owing to a financial scandal. He observed that the reforming wave had reached New Jersey, and that the rise of the Radical wing of the Republicans and the activity of the Civic Leagues clearly indicated the disgust of public opinion at the present condition of the two party machines. But he saw no chance of breaking the Republican monopoly unless he could secure a popular cry and a popular candidate for the office of Governor. He conceived the inspired idea of returning to power as the exponent of reform and political purity—the machine would

[1] Harris, " President Wilson : His Problems and his Policy," p. 57.
[2] Hale, " Woodrow Wilson : The Story of his Life," p. 160.
[3] Harris, " President Wilson : His Problems and his Policy," p. 49.

do the rest if he could find a Democratic candidate uncompromised by association with either bosses or machine. His inquiries and meditations led him to the conclusion that, if he could be induced to stand, the austere President of Princeton was the very man behind whom the embattled interests of the Democratic bosses of New Jersey might return to power and the Promised Land of patronage.

As has already been indicated Dr Wilson, even after his apparently final absorption into academic life, had never lost sight of the possibility, in favourable circumstances, of his entry into active politics. As President of Princeton, his many political essays and addresses had attracted widespread attention. He was known as a fearless and convinced Radical and Democrat, both in the general and the party sense. His recent struggle against powerful interests at Princeton had brought him prominently before the eyes of the electors of New Jersey and elsewhere. Though a Democrat, he was known as a fearless and outspoken critic of the party machine. In an address before a Democratic gathering at Elizabeth, New Jersey, on 29th March 1910, he defined his conception of Democratic principles. He asserted that the policy of the Republicans had shown that " their confidence was not in the views and desires of the people as a whole, but in the promotion of the interests of the country at the hands of those who chiefly controlled its resources. It has been their first thought to safeguard property and establish enterprise." The Democratic position was that " Society must be organized so that the individual will not be crushed, will not be unnecessarily hampered. Every legal instrumentality created for his convenience, like the corporation, must be created only for his convenience, and never for his government or suppression." Corporations should be strictly controlled, but the Government should never attempt to do their work for them. The tariff legislation of the country, which has long since " ceased to be a policy of protection and become a policy of patronage, a policy of arrangement by which particular interests in the country may be sure of their profits," must be drastically overhauled. Finally, the party must undertake to restore popular control to its full influence by a thorough " simplification of electoral processes." [1] These and similar addresses had rallied most of the independent and liberal-minded citizens of the State, and Dr Wilson, as has been said above,

[1] Ford, " Woodrow Wilson : The Man and his Work," pp. 116-18.

began to be canvassed not only in New Jersey, but in the country generally, as a possible candidate for the Presidency. Then came the altogether unexpected overtures of the Democratic bosses to stand as Governor of the State in which he was so widely known. The offer came at a moment when Dr Wilson had begun to think that he had no more work to do at Princeton.

Twenty years' observation of the workings of the political machines in New Jersey had convinced the President that there was much work for a reforming and independent Governor to do in a State that, in his opinion and that of most sober-minded citizens, needed a thorough "clean up." His wider ambitions would not be hindered by a successful Governorship, rather was a Governorship to an increasing extent regarded as a stepping-stone to the White House. James Smith and his friends had thought to lure the scholar from Princeton to the Governorship, with the promise of a nomination as the party candidate for the Presidency; but Dr Wilson had considered all this before they approached him. What did surprise and puzzle him was that the controllers of the party machine should approach him of all people as their candidate in the campaign. It was evident that they wanted something in return for the largess of their favour, and he asked them bluntly what was this *quid pro quo*. Did Mr Smith desire to stand again as the Democratic nominee for the New Jersey senatorship in the event of the Democrats securing a majority? If such were Mr Smith's intentions, he would oppose Mr Smith with his full power as Governor. The deputation was quite explicit that Smith had no thought of standing again—the state of his health precluded the possibility. The "machine" was not at all disconcerted by Dr Wilson's reception of their offers—it was quite usual for a candidate to avow the perfect independence of his views; time and judicious pressure were always sufficient to bring the wild cony to heel. The President divined that the bosses intended to return to power with the aid of his popularity and prestige, but confined himself to assuring them that, though he believed in the party system and would co-operate with all party leaders, he would, if elected Governor, regard himself as the head of the Democratic party in New Jersey. On 25th July he announced that he would accept nomination as the Democratic candidate for the Governorship of New Jersey. The news, though not wholly unexpected, created a sensation. Many who had been most anxious to see the President of Princeton enter the arena of national political life, were disconcerted to find him supported by the political bosses, and found it hard to believe the simple fact that Dr Wilson presented himself to the electors of New Jersey unfettered by a single pledge or engagement to the organization that was normally the clearing-house of unsavoury bargains, and that was now exerting all its efforts to securing the election of the austere professor.

Throughout New Jersey a spontaneous feeling had been for some time growing up that Dr Wilson would make an ideal Governor. The Radical wing of the Republicans were inclined to support him, the September Convention revealed that all groups in the Democratic organization would follow him in the campaign. So swiftly did events move that Dr Wilson was accepted as the Democratic candidate at the first ballot, securing 749 votes, 709 of which were necessary for election. The President was hastily summoned from Princeton and motored to Trenton. The messengers had found him in the middle of a game of golf. Full of impatient curiosity, the Democratic Convention awaited the new leader, whom most of the delegates had never seen. How would their extraordinary experiment turn out? Was a scholar, a professor, and a publicist really likely to storm the Republican entrenchments consolidated by fourteen years of power? In any case, did his declarations of independence mean more than that Joseph Smith's collar at first rather chafed his academic neck? The Democratic candidate stood before them a striking and commanding figure, calm, gracious in manner, absolutely self-possessed. Eagerly the Convention awaited his first words. Among other things he said: "I feel the responsibility of the occasion. Responsibility is proportionate to opportunity. It is a great opportunity to serve the State and nation. I did not seek this nomination; I have made no pledge and have given no promises. If elected, I am left absolutely free to serve you with all singleness of purpose. It is a new era when these things can be said, and in connection with this I feel that the dominant idea of the moment is the responsibility of deserving. I will have to serve the State very well in order to deserve the honour of being at its head. . . . Did you ever experience the elation of a great hope, that you desire to do right because it is right, and without thought of doing it for your own interest? At that period your hopes are unselfish. . . ." He outlined his programme of reform, and proceeded: "The future is not for parties 'playing politics' but for measures conceived in the largest spirit, pushed by parties whose leaders are statesmen, not demagogues, who love not their offices but their duty and their opportunity for service. We are witnessing a renaissance of public spirit, a reawakening of sober public opinion, a revival of the power of the people, the beginning of an age of thoughtful reconstruction that makes our thoughts hark back to the age in which democracy was set up in America. With the new age we shall show a new spirit. We shall serve justice and candour and all things that make for the right. Is not our own party disciplined and made ready for this great task? Shall we not forget ourselves in making it the instrument of righteousness for the State and for the nation?" The effect was electrical, the Convention had never before heard words like these, it felt itself suddenly lifted as it were into a purer air. Many were moved to tears, all acclaimed the new leader with passionate enthusiasm. One who but a few hours before had bitterly opposed the nomination of Dr Wilson, listened to the speech as in a dream. At the end he leaped to his feet, waved his hat and cane in the air, and yelled at the top of his voice, "I am sixty-five years old, and still a damn fool!" [1]

In the campaign that followed the new man rallied to him all that was idealistic, all that was progressive in the State. He outlined a programme of constructive reform of which most thoughtful citizens had dreamed for years, the control of financial corporations, employers' liability, war on electoral corruption, reorganization and economy in administration, equalization of taxation, and conservation of national resources for the good of the State. He explained his programme in the simple, elevated and eloquent language characteristic of all his great speeches. The intense sincerity of the candidate, the burning seriousness with which he preached his gospel of reform as the beginning of a new life not only for New Jersey, but for the great Commonwealth of which New Jersey was a part—this prophetic fervour roused the electors like a trumpet. He was asked in an elaborate questionnaire whether he opposed the "boss" system, and his answer was decisive: "I have made it my business for years to observe and understand that system, and I hate it as thoroughly as I understand it. . . . I would propose to

[1] Tumulty, "Woodrow Wilson as I know Him," p. 22.

abolish it by the above reforms, by the election to office of men who will refuse to submit to it and bend all their energies to break it up, and by pitiless publicity." [1] In his final speech of the campaign he summoned his followers to a new Crusade: "We have begun a fight that, it may be, will take many a generation to complete, the fight against privilege; but you know that men are not put into this world to go the path of ease. They are put into this world to go the path of pain and struggle. No man would wish to sit idly by and lose the opportunity to take part in such a struggle. . . . Trust your guides, imperfect as they are, and some day, when we all are dead, men will come and point at the distant upland with a great shout of joy and triumph and thank God that there were men who undertook to lead in the struggle. What difference does it make if we ourselves do not reach the uplands? We have given our lives to the enterprise. The world is made happier and humankind better because we have lived." [2]

On 8th November 1910 the former President of Princeton was elected Governor of New Jersey by a plurality (that is, votes cast in excess of minimum required by the Constitution) of 49,000 and a majority over the Republicans of nearly 40,000. Two years before, Taft had carried the State for the Republicans by a plurality of 82,000 at the Presidential election.[3] At the elections for Senate and Assembly, the Democrats secured a majority of 42 to 18 in the Assembly, and though the Republicans retained a majority of 3 in the Senate, the Democrats had converted a Republican majority of 31 on a joint ballot of the two Houses for the election of a National Senator, into a Democratic majority of 21. All over the country the Democrats were amazed and delighted. "It seemed that even a 'rock-ribbed' Eastern State could be won . . . if good men could ever get nominations." [4]

Even before he formally undertook his new office the Governor-elect was called upon to fight for his principles. The election of United States Senators was at that time in the hands of the individual State legislatures, the Senate and Assembly sitting together for the purpose. The New Jersey legislature had passed a law to the effect that the electors of the State, when voting for a new legislature, might, at the same

[1] Quoted Ford, "Woodrow Wilson: The Man and his Work," p. 128.
[2] Quoted Tumulty, "Woodrow Wilson as I know Him," pp. 44-5.
[3] Hale, "Woodrow Wilson: The Story of his Life," p. 177. Harris, "President Wilson: His Problems and his Policy," p. 50.
[4] Dodd, "Woodrow Wilson and his Work," p. 89.

time, determine their party candidate for the Senatorship. The purpose of the law was that whichever party secured a majority at the joint session, should designate Senator the party candidate approved by the voters who had returned the majority. But the theoretical freedom of the Legislature to select whom it would remained unimpaired.

Though the Democratic bosses had hoped to carry the Governorship they had not expected in their wildest dreams to secure a majority at the joint session of the Houses.[1] Smith, though powerful, was unpopular, and so he had stood aside and at the election James E. Martine was approved, by those of the electorate who exercised the option, as the Democratic candidate for the Senatorship. The unexpected victory in the legislative elections transformed the situation. Smith, whose personal influence and party machine carried great weight, now came forward as a candidate for the Senatorship. The fact that President Wilson had told him before the Democratic Convention that, as Governor, he would be obliged to oppose a candidature which violated his dearest political convictions, did not weigh with one who controlled a party machine so efficient as his own. His health had marvellously improved, he told the Governor, and he proposed to stand. As for the "direct primary" election which had designated Martine, it was a joke. "It was very far from a joke," replied the Governor, "but assume that it was. Then the way to save it from being a joke hereafter is to take it seriously now. It is going to be taken seriously, and there will be no more jokes. The question who is to enjoy one term in the Senate is of small consequence compared with the question whether the people of New Jersey are to gain the right to choose their own Senators forever."[2]

After endeavouring privately by every means to induce Smith to give up his candidature, and after a characteristic period of what appeared to be vacillation, on 9th December 1910 the Governor-elect challenged the power of the political bosses by sending a statement to the press, strongly opposing Smith as the possible Senator for New Jersey: "I realize," he wrote, "the delicacy of taking any part in the discussion of the matter. As Governor of New Jersey I shall have no part in the choice of a Senator. Legally speaking, it is not my duty even to give advice with regard to the choice. But

[1] Tumulty, "Woodrow Wilson as I know Him," p. 46.
[2] Hale, "Woodrow Wilson: The Story of his Life," p. 180.

there are other duties besides legal duties. The recent campaign has put me in an unusual position. I offered, if elected, to be the political spokesman and adviser of the people. . . . It is my duty to say, with a full sense of the peculiar responsibility of my position, what I deem it to be the obligation of the Legislature to do in this gravely important matter.

"I know that the people of New Jersey do not desire Mr James Smith, Jr., to be sent again to the Senate. If he should be he will not go as their representative. The only means I have of knowing whom they do desire to represent them is the vote at the recent primaries, where 48,000 Democratic votes, a majority of the whole number who voted at the primaries, declared their preference for Mr Martine, of Union County. For me, that vote is conclusive. I think it should be for every member of the Legislature.

"Absolute good faith in dealing with the people, an unhesitating fidelity to every principle avowed, is the highest law of political morality under a constitutional government. . . ."[1] The Governor-elect did not confine himself to issuing proclamations. In order to break up the machine controlled by Smith, it was necessary to liberate the delegates dependent on it, and to do this the electors had to be roused to bring pressure to bear on their representatives. For this purpose the Governor-elect summoned the members of both Houses to a series of conferences, and again swept through New Jersey summoning the electorate to see that they secured as Senator the man they had designated by their votes. He told electors and deputies not to be afraid of the bosses, their castles were of pasteboard and would fall at the first touch. Political bosses were "warts upon the body politic. It is not a capital process to cut off a wart. You don't have to go to the hospital and take an anæsthetic. The thing can be done while you wait, and it is being done."[2] Slowly the forces of the "Old Guard" crumbled. Immediately after the inauguration the joint session for the election of a Senator began, amid tense excitement. After several days of balloting Martine was elected Senator for New Jersey by 40 votes to 4. Governor Wilson had smashed the once all-powerful party machine, and the "bosses" had been driven into the wilderness.[3]

[1] Quoted Tumulty, "Woodrow Wilson as I know Him," p. 60.
[2] *Ibid.*, p. 62.
[3] Hale, "Woodrow Wilson: The Story of his Life," p. 184.

The victory was of extraordinary importance. The Governor had taken upon him to advise and direct the Legislature. This was not a specimen of the "horrid arbitrariness" of Woodrow Wilson, but the putting into force of a political principle developed by him in several books and innumerable addresses and political writings. The fundamental vice of the American Constitution, first analysed by him in his youthful essay "Congressional Government," in 1879, is the isolation of Executive and Legislative. Only Cabinet Government, which allows the Executive to explain its policy in the Assembly and guide the resulting debates, could, in his opinion, restore that sense of responsibility to the Legislature without which it is but a leaderless mob of deputies organized in groups and preparing the laws of the country in terms of lobby intrigues. The Constitution gives the President the right to communicate to Congress, from time to time, his views on the affairs of the Union. For lack of a radical reform of the Constitution, President Wilson was later to seek to give Executive guidance and leadership to Congress by means of messages delivered in person. This procedure, which may have been the prelude to far-reaching constitutional developments, he at once adopted at New Jersey, not only in this opening crisis over the Smith candidature, but throughout his term of office.

Once he had shattered the power of the political "bosses" by the surprising triumph we have just followed, he further developed his constitutional ideas (which his enemies might easily have discovered by reading his books on the Constitution), and the influence of the Governor on the Legislature, by constituting himself the veritable leader of the Democratic party in New Jersey. As Governor he was not invited to attend the party meetings where policy was discussed, but he invited himself, and steadily secured an ascendancy over all representatives of local interests.[1]

At once the redemption of the promises made at the election and the inauguration of a radical reform programme were undertaken. The hardest measure came first. A Bill was introduced making the nomination of party candidates for every public office dependent on the direct popular vote. "The whole machinery of party nomination would, under the terms of the Bill . . . be as much under the control and direction of the State as the actual election itself."[2] Since

[1] Halévy, "President Wilson," pp. 100-1.
[2] Harris, "President Wilson: His Problems and his Policy," p. 56.

the Bill was obviously yet another nail in the coffin of the bosses, it met with a desperate resistance. A break-away in the Democratic ranks was threatened, and conferences with the Republican opposition took place. The whole legislative programme of the Governor was threatened. He invited himself to the dissentient Convention, and after a speech lasting four hours, silenced all opposition. The Conference called to refuse the Bill ended by making it part of the party programme.[1] Knowing that the subtle hostility of the defeated Smith faction was at work to destroy his legislative programme, the Governor vindicated it point by point. It was a magnificent gesture that secured him the unquestioned leadership of the Party at a meeting where his very presence had been challenged as unconstitutional. "You can decline to follow me," he declared, "you can deprive me of office and turn away from me, but you cannot deprive me of power so long as I stedfastly stand for what I believe to be the interests and legitimate demands of the people themselves. I beg you to remember, in this which promises to be an historic conference, you are settling the question of the power or impotence, the distinction or ignominy of the party to which the people, with singular generosity, have offered the conduct of their affairs."[2]

His reform Bills were introduced—Regulation of Public Utilities, Corrupt Practices, Direct Primaries, Employers' Liability—and rapidly passed the Assembly. The Republican Senate remained a dragon in the path. In a series of conferences the Governor converted his political opponents, his frankness and willingness to discuss his measures, the personal geniality that won all who came into contact with him, his eagerness to co-operate with every liberal element in the State, whether calling itself Republican or Democrat, had removed all opposition. "The Legislature had convened in January [1911] and by the middle of April every campaign pledge that the Governor had made had been kept."[3] Though in 1912 the activities of the indefatigable Governor were hampered by the return of a Republican Legislature, his practice of co-operating and consulting freely, so far as possible, with Republicans as well as Democrats, still left him with considerable influence. His main work was done in conjunction

[1] Hale, "Woodrow Wilson: The Story of his Life," p. 197.
[2] Tumulty, "Woodrow Wilson as I know Him," p. 73.
[3] *Ibid.*, p. 77.

with the Democratic Legislature, but "within two years from the day the new 'academic' Governor took office at Trenton, the laws of the community were so re-made that reformers everywhere studied them as models for other states."[1] It was evident that a new political personal force had arisen in the United States—the speeches and policy of the Governor of New Jersey were widely studied. His career at Princeton as the exponent of a more democratic University life was recalled and studied; his triumphant battle with the "bosses" thrilled those hard-working, patient, often disappointed, citizens, whose activity in Civic Leagues on behalf of pure government had begun to create at last a ferment in the national life that coincided in point of time with the rise of the new political star. Though the Democratic party in 1912 was by no means united, the split in the opposing organization, brought about by the Republican *enfant terrible*, Theodore Roosevelt, opened up a fair prospect of sending to the White House the second Democratic President since the Civil War.[2]

The issues that divide the two great American parties, Republican and Democrat, are sometimes like those that distinguish an English Liberal from an English Conservative, evanescent to the point of non-existence. But the two great machines carry on during these times of political slump, by virtue of their own inertia. Broadly speaking, the historical origin of the two parties makes the Republicans advocates of the Federal authority and national aspect of the American Union, while the Democrats tend to emphasize and defend the rights of the individual States. That distinction has during the last twenty years become more or less academic. Again, the Republicans are generally the advocates of a protective tariff, while the Democrats stand for a low tariff for revenue purposes only. Since the Spanish-American War the Republicans have leaned to colonial imperialism. But the two parties construct their programmes for each Presidential election in terms of the existing situation; so the nation always has a choice of two platforms, the Republican tending to appeal to the Conservative and the Democratic to the Liberal instincts of the average citizen. The system has many advantages, though, as in Great Britain, it sometimes produces a position of great political unreality.

[1] Dodd, "Woodrow Wilson and His Work," p. 92.
[2] Harris, "President Wilson: His Problems and his Policy," p. 66.

In 1912 the Democratic party, though not split on a great personal issue, was yet gravely divided into Conservative and Radical wings, the Radicals led by William Jennings Bryan, who had been the Democratic candidate in 1896, 1900, and 1908. In 1912, though he was not standing, Bryan naturally controlled a great body of votes at the Democratic Convention at Baltimore in the summer. The party programme adopted on 2nd July was constructed to meet the widespread movement for reform that was sweeping over the nation. It called for the reduction and revision of the tariff; anti-trust legislation; a federal income-tax; rural credits; publicity of campaign contributions; presidential primaries, that is, the same system as that in force in New Jersey for the popular designation of a Senator, whereby a popular vote and not a party Convention would indicate the party choice for a Presidential candidate; the ultimate independence of the Philippine Islands.[1]

The New Jersey delegates now proposed Governor Wilson as the Democratic candidate. The proposal was widely anticipated. The policies and principles of the reforming Governor of New Jersey had attracted, as we have seen, widespread attention. Without attempting to build up a party machine to press his candidature, Governor Wilson had during 1911 accepted invitations to address Democratic party meetings throughout the States, which carried him as far as San Francisco and the Pacific Coast. Everywhere his speeches, devoted to the great constructive opportunity before the party of cleansing American public life by a programme of radical reform, had created a deep impression. He proclaimed the necessity for war on the Trusts which were strangling the political life of the nation, a war which, by a drastic revision of the tariff in the direction of free trade, would cut at the roots of their evil monopolies. Government must, he said, be made more representative, and he advocated a revision of the Constitution by the introduction of the Referendum, the Initiative, and the Recall. These last proposals were not embodied in the party platform and were certainly too radical to please Conservative Democrats, but they only strengthened the popular hold of the Governor.

The most prominent rival candidates were Governors Harmon of Ohio, and Champ Clark of Missouri, Speaker of

[1] Harris, " President Wilson: His Problems and his Policy," p. 70.

the House of Representatives. On eight separate ballots Champ Clark secured a clear majority, which in a Republican Convention is sufficient to secure adoption, but by the rules of a Democratic party Convention a two-thirds majority is necessary.

Everything ultimately depended on the attitude of Mr Bryan. The first crisis came when Mr Bryan wired to Wilson for his support in opposing the efforts of the reactionary group in the Convention to secure the election of one of their own men as Chairman. Bryan's query was directed, to finding out which of the leading candidates really favoured the Progressive wing of the party. Governor Wilson was not a member of the Convention; the temptation to follow the cautious advice of his manager on the spot, not to commit himself, would have been great to most politicians: caution might win him the votes of the Conservatives. Disregarding this advice, he wired to Mr Bryan, " You are right. . . . The Baltimore Convention is to be a Convention of Progressives, of men who are progressive in principle and by conviction." [1]

So obsessed was his manager with the necessity of winning the Conservative New York delegation, that on reading Wilson's telegram to Bryan he retired to a friend's house and was found weeping miserably on a bed, convinced that Governor Wilson had ruined his chances of nomination.[2] The Governor followed this up by suggesting as Chairman one of Mr Bryan's intimate friends, who was a fervent advocate of Speaker Clark. He had no reason for fearing the partiality of the delegate, and the suggestion convinced Mr Bryan that Governor Wilson would support him in every move designed to ensure the triumph of the Progressive wing. At one moment his manager telephoned that his cause was hopeless, and Governor Wilson gave him leave to release his friends to vote for whomever of the other candidates they pleased. The superb efforts of the young Liberals in the Convention and the brilliant tactics of Mr Bryan, who at the eleventh hour mobilized all his great influence on the side of one whose undeviating adhesion to the side of the Progressives had convinced him that the Democrats at last had a leader whose principles were proof to every crisis, secured the nomination of Governor Wilson at the forty-sixth ballot.

[1] Tumulty, " Woodrow Wilson as I know Him," p. 111.
[2] *Ibid.*, p. 113.

In the Presidential campaign the speeches of Governor Wilson everywhere spread the hope that the nation had found a leader ready as Roosevelt to fight all vested interests, but with a deeper sense of responsibility and a more compelling idealism. His eloquence was a new thing in American life: restrained, lofty, trenchant, it arrested attention, and by its moral elevation thrilled his audiences sometimes even to tears. Friends were surprised. They had known him for an exact and refined master of English—academic in his love of the *mot juste*; now his learning subserved and added weight to innumerable extempore speeches not easily to be rivalled for popular appeal. The secret of the new man, who now claimed the suffrages of the American people, was the secret of one who " by long incubation of the brooding intellect " has made himself master of his thought to its last subtlety. He was triple-armed by exact knowledge, and his programme was finely conceived and arresting in its presentation. In speaking of the control of great financial corporations and economic trusts, this is what he said: " I take it to be a necessity of the hour to open up all the processes of politics and of public business—open them wide to public view; to make them accessible to every force that moves, every opinion that prevails in the thought of the people; to give society command of its own economic life again. . . . Wherever any public business is transacted, wherever plans affecting the public are laid, or enterprises touching the public welfare, comfort, and convenience go forward, wherever political programmes are formulated, or candidates agreed on—over that place a voice must speak, with the divine prerogative of a people's will, the words: " Let there be light! " [1]

Perhaps the true surprise of the 1912 election was the prodigious success of the old lion, Theodore Roosevelt, who, after splitting the Republican vote, yet managed to secure 88 votes in the Electoral College and 4,125,804 popular votes, as against the 8 Electoral votes of Taft, the Republican President, and the official Republican candidate, who received 3,475,813 popular votes. Governor Wilson was elected President with 435 electoral votes and a popular vote of 6,286,087. As a result of the Republican split and the polls of three other candidates who did not secure any Electoral votes, the new President was in a minority of some 2,450,000

[1] Quoted Halévy, " President Wilson," pp. 129-30.

of all votes cast, and also in a minority of the total Republican vote. His election, though a prodigious triumph for the reviving Democratic party, was largely due to the Republican split, though it by no means follows that those who voted for Roosevelt would necessarily have voted for Taft, a peculiarly uninspiring figure when confronted with a man of Wilson's calibre.

The above paragraph may need a little elucidating. The wisdom of the fathers of the Republic had devised a system of indirect election for the Presidency. Elections were to be held in each State, not for the President but for a number of "best men" who would meet together in an Electoral College with the delegates of other States, and then, undisturbed by the rumours of the popular voice, select positively the best man in the United States for the post of President. Had the makers of the Constitution vested this selection in the two Houses of the Legislature (which, however, would have violated their theory of the division of powers) they would have secured a form of indirect election which, as in contemporary France, would have remained indirect. But the special constitution of an *ad hoc* Electoral College opened the way for the substitution of direct for indirect election. What more easy than for rival parties to select their candidate for the Presidency and then in every State propose a list of electors pledged to the election of that one man? The Electoral College was constituted on the basis of the representation of the individual State in the national Legislature. Each State sends two Senators and a number of deputies, according to population. Thus New York returns 43 members to the House of Representatives, and New Mexico 1. Therefore the relative weights of New York and New Mexico in the Electoral College is as 45 to 3. For New York the Republicans propose a list of 45 and the Democrats a list of 45—a mere plurality secures the return of one or other list, since the voters almost invariably vote for one complete list. The result is that a minute majority in New York secures 45 votes for the successful candidate. His rival might receive every vote in New Mexico, but that would only mean 3 Electoral votes. The minority in any State is wholly unrepresented, and, as a result, the popular vote of the candidate bears no recognizable relation to his votes in the now merely formal Electoral College. Thus the plans of the makers of the Constitution have been nullified and a system of direct election by States substituted, but the substitute, through its haphazard origin, is a very poor variety of direct election.

Elections for the two Houses of Congress took place simultaneously, and there also the Democrats secured a majority in both Houses. A unique opportunity presented itself to the revivified party and its leader. The President-elect felt the mighty responsibility that was resting on him to carry through the great reforms to which he and his party were pledged. His friend, Walter Page, who had played not a small part in the events leading up to his election, and whom he was shortly to send to London as ambassador (in the event one of the greatest of ambassadors), called upon him at Princeton shortly after the election.

" 'Hello, Page, come out here. I am glad to see you.' There he stood in a door at the back of the room, which led to his library and work-room. 'Come back here.'

" 'In the best of all possible worlds, the right thing does sometimes happen,' said I.

" 'Yes.'

" 'And a great opportunity.'

" He smiled, and was cordial and said some pleasant words. But he was weary. 'I have cobwebs in my head.' He was not depressed but oppressed—rather shy, I thought, and should say rather lonely. The campaign noise and the little campaigners were hushed and gone. There were no men of companionable size about him, and the Great Task lay before him. . . .

" 'I wish to find the very best men for my Cabinet, regardless of consequences. I do not forget the party as an instrument of government, and I do not wish to do violence to it. But I must have the best men in the nation,' with a very solemn tone, as he sat bolt upright, with a stern look on his face and a lonely look. . . .

" I had been with him an hour and had talked (I fear) too much. But he seemed hearty in his thanks. . . . I stepped out on the muddy street, and, as I walked to the inn, I had the feeling of the man's oppressive loneliness as he faced his great task. There is no pomp of circumstance, nor hardly dignity in this setting, except the dignity of his seriousness and his lonelineess." [1]

Long before he took up the august office to which he had been summoned, he was preparing the work, and in his inaugural address he mentioned many things that ought

[1] Hendrick, " The Life and Letters of Walter H. Page," vol. i. pp. 111-13.

to be altered—"A tariff which cuts us off from our proper part in the commerce of the world, violates the just principles of taxation, and makes the Government a facile instrument in the hands of private interests; a banking and currency system based upon the necessity of the Government to sell its bonds fifty years ago, and perfectly adapted to concentrating cash and restricting credits; an industrial system which, take it on all its sides, financial as well as administrative, holds capital in leading strings, restricts the liberties, and limits the opportunities of labour, and exploits, without renewing or conserving the natural resources of the country; a body of agricultural activities never yet given the efficiency of great business undertakings, or served as it should be through the instrumentality of science taken directly to the farm, or afforded the facilities of credit best suited to its practical needs; water-courses undeveloped, waste places unreclaimed, forests untended, fast disappearing, without plan or prospect of renewal, unregarded waste-heaps at every mine." These were material things. "There can be no equality of opportunity," he went on; "the first essential of justice in the body politic, if men and women and children be not shielded in their lives, their very vitality, from the consequences of great industrial and social processes which they cannot alter, control, or singly cope with. Society must see to it that it does not itself crush or weaken or damage its own constituent parts."

His peroration thrilled the great audience: "The feelings with which we face this new age of right and opportunity sweep across our heart-strings like some air out of God's own presence, where justice and mercy are reconciled, and the judge and the brother are one. . . . This is not a day of triumph, it is a day of dedication. Here muster, not the forces of party, but the forces of humanity. Men's hearts wait upon us; men's lives hang in the balance; men's hopes call upon us to say what we will do. Who shall live up to the great trust? Who dares fail to try? I summon all honest men, all patriotic, all forward-looking men, to my side. God helping me, I will not fail them, if they will but counsel and sustain me." [1]

In the normal course of events Congress would not have assembled until December 1913. The new President immediately convened it in special session to deal with the new tariff proposals and to inaugurate the reform platform of the

[1] Quoted Ford, "Woodrow Wilson: The Man and his Work," pp. 171-4.

Democrats. True to his conception of the President as a leader and guide to the legislature, he appeared in person to read his message to Congress, thus reviving a custom that had lapsed for more than a century. This was the outward and visible sign that he intended, in accord with the total tenour of his political thought, to make the association of the Legislative and Executive branches of the State as close as the Constitution would permit. In the course of the year that follows the President was successful in carrying the main projects of the reform programme.

The principles of the Tariff Bill were thus described by the President: "We must abolish everything that bears even the semblance of privilege or of any kind of artificial advantage, and put our business men and producers under the stimulation of a constant necessity to be efficient, economical, and enterprising masters of competitive supremacy, better workers and merchants than any in the world." The policy of the tariff was, broadly speaking, to tax luxuries and free necessities. Many commodities, such as wheat, flour, fish, potatoes, wool, coal, and leather went on the free list. Duties on clothing and textiles were reduced, and sugar was to be free after two years. To restore the balance of the revenue, the recent Constitutional amendment making possible the levying of a federal income tax was put in motion. In the Senate the vested interests were mobilized to destroy the Tariff Bill. The issue appeared doubtful, until the President again exercised his national leadership by an appeal to the people, in the form of a speech unequivocally denouncing the methods of obstruction being employed by the various business concerns alarmed for their monopolies. "Washington," he said, "has seldom seen so industrious or so insidious a lobby. . . . There is every evidence that money without limit is being spent to maintain this lobby, and to create the appearance of public opinion antagonistic to some of the chief items of the Tariff Bill."[1] The appeal had the effect of turning the light of public opinion on to the machinations in the Senate, and in a short time broke the back of the lobby. At the end of September the Senate passed the Bill, and the President signed it on 3rd October 1913.[2]

The next measure for consideration was the famous Bill to reconstruct the whole currency system of the Union. In

[1] Quoted Ford, "Woodrow Wilson: The Man and his Work," p. 186.
[2] Harris, "President Wilson: His Problems and his Policy," pp. 99-101.

June the President, in person, had commended his proposals for currency reform to Congress in another speech, in which he declared, " we must have a currency, not rigid as now, but readily, elastically responsive to sound credit, the expanding and contracting credits of everyday transactions, the normal ebb and flow of personal and corporate dealings. Our banking laws must mobilize reserves, must not permit the concentration anywhere in a few hands of the monetary resources of the country, or their use for speculative purposes in such volume as to hinder or impede or stand in the way of other more legitimate, more fruitful uses." Before his inauguration, while still fulfilling his duties as Governor of New Jersey, he had begun, in collaboration with Mr Carter Glass, the Chairman of the Banking and Currency Committee of the House of Representatives, the preparation of the Federal Reserve Banking and Currency Act, perhaps the greatest piece of constructive legislation passed in the United States for half a century. It was necessary to get the Currency Bill—designed as it was to free the credit system of the country from an incubus which dated from the crisis of the Civil War—passed as soon as possible after the Tariff legislation, which was bound at first to depress trade.

During the Civil War, Chase, the Secretary of the Treasury, had placed what amounted to a veto on the issue of notes by any bank that failed to invest one-third of its capital in Government bonds. Banks which obtained a charter from the Federal Government were allowed to issue notes up to 90 per cent. of the face value of the bonds. The result of this bond basis of the national currency was that the circulating medium had no relation to the needs of business. For instance, one peculiarity was that the greater the annual wheat harvest the more acute became the stringency in circulating medium, simply because the national assets for the moment had expanded, while the currency remained fixed. Another peculiarity was that note issues were liable at any time—usually when they were most wanted—to be withdrawn from circulation; for as the Government bonds increased in price, banks tended to surrender their right of note issue, which was based only on the face, not the current value, of the bonds, realize on the bonds held by them, and employ their capital elsewhere.[1] Every previous attempt to reform the currency

[1] Harris, " President Wilson: His Problems and his Policy," pp. 102-3; Ford, " Woodrow Wilson: The Man and his Work," pp. 195-7.

(those of the Harrison and Cleveland administrations) had been defeated, and the proposals of President Wilson, though simple, were so far-reaching that for some time it seemed certain that this attempt also would end in failure. Yet reform was urgent if the country was to be saved from recurrent financial panics and the speculations of certain great corporations addicted to manipulating a system so capricious, and therefore so easy of exploitation.

The Bill, introduced by Mr Carter Glass, and ultimately passed with some unimportant alterations, provided for the creation of twelve Federal Reserve Banks—one for each of the twelve areas into which the Union was divided for this purpose. Every bank incorporated under Federal laws, that is, every National Bank, was compelled to link itself up with the Federal Reserve Bank of its district. Every State Bank became a stockholder of the Federal Reserve Bank, and was also compelled to deposit its reserves with the Federal National Bank of its State. The Federal Banks issued notes against the reserves of the local banks—notes which could be converted into gold at any of the twelve Federal Reserve Banks, or at the U.S. Treasury. In control of the whole system, a Federal Reserve Board was established at Washington, directed by the Secretary of the Treasury and the Comptroller of the Currency. The Federal Reserve Banks are purely bankers' banks, serving as clearing-houses for their member banks, and regulating the issue of notes, against which they must maintain a minimum gold reserve of 40 per cent. of such issues. " The effect of the system is to prevent the accumulation of money-power at any single centre or in the hands of any group of financiers." [1] The Act also provided for the expansion of foreign trade by authorising National Banks to establish foreign branches,[2] and it gave the nation a currency capable of expanding according to the needs of the moment.

Once again the main opposition was located in the Senate, headed, on the Republican side, by Mr Root. All through a sweltering summer in Washington the President kept his own nose and that of every one else concerned to the grindstone of currency reform. In innumerable conferences with his opponents he met their acerbity with suavity, and their bitter prejudices with arguments. Slowly the Bill made progress, until one day Mr McAdoo, the Secretary of the Treasury,

[1] Harris, " President Wilson: his Problems and His Policy," p. 106.
[2] Brooks, " Woodrow Wilson as President," p. 119.

came to the White House to tell the President that the Opposition in the Senate was bent on securing an adjournment, leaving the Bill suspended in mid-air. The reply was swift and characteristic: "Mac, when the boys at Princeton came to me and told me that they were going to lose a football game, they always lost. We must not lose this game; too much is involved. Please say to the gentlemen on the Hill who urge a postponement of this matter, that Washington weather, especially in these days, fully agrees with me, and that unless final action is taken on this measure at this session I will immediately call Congress in extraordinary session to act upon this matter."[1] The threat that an adjournment would be met by a summons to a special session was sufficient, and the great reform was passed.

In January 1914 the President recommended, in a message to Congress, the measures for the consolidation of existing anti-trust legislation, on which he had laid such stress in his Presidential campaign. As far back as 1890 the Sherman Act had declared illegal "every contract, combination in the form of trust or otherwise, or conspiracy, in restraint of trade or commerce among the several States, or with foreign nations." Though Roosevelt had vigorously pressed the enforcement of the Sherman Act, its vagueness as to what "a combination in restraint of trade" really was led to endless legal actions and contradictory decisions in various States. The Act had also been twisted from its original purpose by the decisions of the Supreme Court in 1908 and 1911, by which Labour strikes and boycotts had been brought under the definition "combinations in restraint of trade." This decision enabled any strike to be broken by means of an injunction under the Act.

The Anti-Trust Bills initiated in 1914 set up a Federal Trade Commission with power to investigate the affairs of financial corporations, in other words, "to let in the light," and aimed at checking the evil known as "interlocking directorates," by which gigantic combines secured monopolies. In 1914, after a Congressional report on financial corporations, the members of the great house of Morgan resigned no less than thirty-three directorships, including that of the United States Steel Corporation, and various important railway companies. In his Presidential campaign Dr Wilson had emphasized the danger: "When you reflect that the twenty-four men who control the United States Steel Corporation

[1] Tumulty, "Woodrow Wilson as I know Him," p. 174.

are either presidents, or vice-presidents, or directors in 55 per cent. of the railways of the United States, you know just how close the whole thing is knitted together in our industrial system, and how great the temptation is."[1]

In connection with the anti-trust legislation embodied in the Clayton Act of 1914, it will be well to recall the President's attitude to Labour questions, defined in a letter in answer to a request from the editor of a Labour paper in 1910: "It is, in my opinion, not only perfectly legitimate, but absolutely necessary, that labour should organize if it is to secure justice from organized capital, and everything that it does to improve the condition of working men, to obtain legislation that will impose full legal responsibility upon the employer for his treatment of his employees and for their protection against accident, to secure just and adequate wages, and to put reasonable limits upon the working day and upon the exactions of those who employ labour, ought to have the hearty support of all fair-minded and public-spirited men; for there is a sense in which the condition of labour is the condition of the nation itself."[2] Accordingly the Clayton Anti-Trust Act expressly excluded Labour strikes from the prohibition of "combinations in restraint of trade," and so the Clayton Act did for the United States what the Trades Disputes Act of 1906 did for Great Britain. By this great Act the issue of injunctions during strike actions was severely limited, and "it was not without reason that Mr Wilson sent the pen with which he signed the Act as a memento to Mr Samuel Gompers, the President of the American Federation of Labour."[3]

To continue the story of the social legislation initiated or approved by the President up to 1916 and the eve of the great events that were to drag the United States into the tempest of the Great War, these are worth mentioning here: the Rural Credits Act, The Child Labour Act, and the Adamson Railway Act. The Rural Credits Act, which had formed part of the President's campaign programme, sets up a machinery very like that of the Federal Reserve Banks by the establishment of Federal Land Banks in the twelve areas into which the Union is divided for the purpose. These banks exist to advance credit for agricultural improvements, and farmers are

[1] Woodrow Wilson, "The New Freedom," cap. viii.
[2] Ford, "Woodrow Wilson: The Man and his Work," pp. 122-3.
[3] Harris, "President Wilson: His Problems and his Policy," p. 216.

given " the same facilities for raising loans . . . open to any city manufacturer and merchant with genuine assets to pledge." [1]

Such questions as the regulation of hours of work and factory conditions had been left to the individual States. Only by pressing the claims of the Constitution, which places inter-state trade and communications in the hands of the central Government, was it possible to defend the Child Labour Act —the first measure of the kind to be passed by Congress. The Act " prohibits the shipment in inter-state commerce of goods emanating from factories employing children under fourteen or under sixteen if employed at night or for more than eight hours a day." [2] After its first introduction it lapsed; at end of next session it seemed likely to be lost in the limbo of delayed bills, until the President sent for the party leaders, and urged them to save the Child Labour Bill at all costs. The Senate passed the Bill by 52 to 12, and on 1st September 1916 it was signed by the President.

The passage of the Eight Hour Law took place in dramatic circumstances. In August 1916 the United States was faced with the complete paralysis of the entire railroad system by the threatened strike of four trades unions, representing some 400,000 locomotive engineers, locomotive firemen, con-ductors, and trainmen. On the men involved depended the entire railway system. They insisted on an eight-hour day—instead of the usual nine or ten—at the same rates of pay, and extra pay for overtime. The railway companies—representing 230 systems—refused on the ground that they would have to raise their freights owing to the extra costs involved, and that they could not do so without the consent of the Inter-State Commission—a consent they had no cer-tainty of securing, so long, presumably, as it was not convinced of their oft-protested penury. On 13th August, in view of the serious threat to the nation's food supply, the President summoned both parties to meet him at the White House; day after day he met them separately in the endeavour to find some common ground; both men and managers were obdurate. In his final appeal to the representatives of the companies he used language that throws a flood of light on the vast issues that he was facing out at that time in his own mind: " I have not summoned you to Washington as Presi-

[1] Harris, " President Wilson: His Problems and his Policy," p. 219.
[2] *Ibid.*, p. 219.

dent of the United States to confer with me on this matter, for I have no power to do so. . . . What I want you to see, if you will, is the whole picture that presents itself to me, and visualize the terrible consequences to the country and its people of a nation-wide strike at this time, both as affecting our own people *and in its effect upon the Allied forces across the sea* . . . a nation-wide strike at this time would mean famine and starvation for the people of America. . . . The Allies are fighting our battle, the battle of civilization across the way. They cannot 'carry on' without supplies and means of sustenance which the railroads of America bring to them. I am probably asking you to make a sacrifice at this time, but is not the sacrifice worth while because of the things involved? Only last night I was thinking about this war and its far-reaching effects. . . . *Who knows, gentlemen, but by to-morrow a situation will arise when it shall be found necessary for us to get into the midst of this bloody thing?* . . ." [1]

All attempts to bring the two parties to an agreement having failed, the President, in these compelling circumstances, decided on drastic action. The strike was due to take place within the first few days of September, and on 29th August 1916 he appeared before Congress and, after describing the immense danger impending, demanded the immediate passage of a bill providing for the legal recognition of the eight-hour day as the basis of work and wages; the constitution of a commission to watch the working of the Act; the raising of rates by the railway companies if the Inter-State Commerce Commission were satisfied that the increased wage-change warranted a corresponding increase in rates; declaring that a strike or lock-out on the railways was illegal until a public commission had reported on the merits of the dispute, and arming the President with powers to seize the railway system in case of necessity, and work it in virtue of the powers conferred on him as Commander-in-Chief. Two days later a bill, substantially on these lines and agreed upon between the President and the leaders of the parties in both Houses, was introduced by Mr Adamson, the Chairman of the Inter-State Commerce Commission. On 1st September the Bill was passed by the House, on 2nd by the Senate, on the 3rd it was signed by the President, and the great strike due to begin on the 4th was averted. The swiftness with which the President had moved not only saved the nation from the

[1] Tumulty, "Woodrow Wilson as I know Him," pp. 199-200.

gravest possible danger, and great issues of national policy from fatal complications, but out of the opportunity of the crisis he had secured the recognition of the eight-hour day—a reform which he had long sought an occasion for carrying.

The reforming Liberalism of President Wilson was one of a ceaseless activity: "Good Heavens, man," some one had once said to him at Princeton, "why don't you leave something alone and let it stay the way it is." The reply was swift: "If you will guarantee to me that it will stay the way it is, I will let it alone; but if you knew anything, you would know that if you leave a thing alone it will not stay where it is. It will develop, and will either go in the wrong direction or decay." He concluded by reminding his Conservative friend of the saying that "if you want to keep a white post white, you cannot let it alone. It will get black. You have to keep on doing something to it." On another occasion he vividly pressed home the same view in an address: ". . . You will remember the Red Queen in 'Alice in Wonderland' . . . who takes Alice by the hand, and they rush along at a great pace, and then, when they stop, Alice looks around and says, 'But we are just where we were when we started.' 'Yes,' says the Red Queen, 'you have to run twice as fast as that to get anywhere else.' That is also true . . . of the world and of affairs." [1]

The issues which, unknown to most of the disputants, the President saw looming up behind the menace of the great railway strike, justifies a brief consideration here of the principles and ideas with which he approached the problems of foreign policy before he was confronted with the "bloody thing" that began in 1914.

Again and again, and especially with regard to his Mexican policy, President Wilson has been accused of pursuing the line of least resistance in terms of the most haphazard opportunism. It is safe to say in the light of convincing facts that the charge is wholly untrue.

In his general position he inclined to pacificism while fully admitting that on occasions the pursuit and fearless execution of a policy may involve war. He had an intense faith that given time and opportunity, clear cold thought and rationality must triumph over the folly of war. The superb, full-blooded truculence of a Palmerston or a Roosevelt, though crowned a hundred times with pacific diplomatic triumphs, was hateful

[1] Brooks, "Woodrow Wilson as President," pp 533-4.

to him. He inherited from the previous administration the arbitration policy embodied in a series of treaties between the United States and other countries providing for a "cooling-off period" of a year and the appointment of a commission of enquiry to report at the end of that time in the case of all serious disputes. Military preparations and ultimately a resort to war could only take place on the expiration of this invaluable breathing space when sweet reasonableness might have a chance. The treaties are open to quite valid objections —for instance, the offending party might consolidate himself in the possession of disputed territory during the "cooling-off" year, or continue systematically to continue the actions which had given rise to the quarrel. But the policy seemed to the President to hold much promise of that positive good, however unpretentious, which may lead on to great achievements. Accordingly, he completed and secured the ratification, between 1914 and 1916, of a series of arbitration treaties with Great Britain, France, Russia, Italy, Spain, Norway, Sweden, Denmark, China, and the majority of the South and Central American Republics.

The President did not fail to draw conclusions from Germany's absolute refusal to consider an arbitration scheme. The increasing militarism of Europe and the grave tension that the Balkan wars of 1912-13 had left behind gravely pre-occupied him. But the position did not seem wholly without hope. Great Britain appeared eager to come to some agreement for the easing off of the break-neck naval competition with Germany—a desire publicly expressed by Mr Churchill in March and again in October 1913, in speeches proposing a "naval holiday."

Germany's refusal to consider the suggestion seemed to present an opportunity to a great and influential power like the United States of gathering up the broken threads of the Anglo-German negotiations, and by her influence bringing the two great world-rivals together. Accordingly, in May 1914, with the approval of the President, Colonel House visited Berlin and London with a view to taking unofficial soundings as to the possibility of an Anglo-American-German "pact" to deal not only with "disarmament, but other matters of equal importance to themselves and to the world at large." [1] On 1st June 1914 Colonel House had a long interview with the Kaiser at Potsdam. Though cordial in tone to the President's

[1] Hendrick, "The Life and Letters of Walter H. Page," i. cap. ix.

proposals, he very emphatically rejected suggestions of disarmament and arbitration as completely Utopian and impossible. All that he saw in the course of his mission in the early days of that fatal summer convinced the emissary of President Wilson that the general European situation was wellnigh desperate. " I feel as though I had been living near a mighty electric dynamo," he told his friends. " The whole of Germany is charged with electricity. Everybody's nerves are tense. It needs only a spark to set the whole thing off." [1]

The readiness of the President to consider proposals that, at the first blush, would appear to conflict with the traditional policy of aloofness, leads naturally to the consideration of his conception of the Monroe doctrine as modified by the facts of the world-situation. Without a clear realization of the President's view of the Monroe doctrine, it is impossible, as Mr Wilson Harris has well pointed out, to understand his Mexican policy.

Long study of the problems that confronted the United States in its foreign policy had convinced him that a merely negative view of the implications of the Monroe Doctrine was no longer possible. It was not enough for the United States to announce that she was not interested in the affairs of Europe, and would permit no European intervention on the American continent. The growth of vast European interests in South and Central America—interests which at times required vindicating—would inevitably lead to European intervention, unless the United States would exercise a wise discretion as to when she should exercise her authority on behalf of Europe. President Roosevelt had recognized this when he occupied San Domingo to assert the claims of her European creditors. Similarly Dr Wilson felt compelled to occupy and administer for a time San Domingo's black but ramshackle neighbour Hayti.

Obvious difficulties are involved in this trusteeship, which is the corollary of the Monroe doctrine in an age when the world is becoming more and more close-meshed in a web of interests inconceivable at the day when President Monroe promulgated his famous message to Congress and himself entered history as the handle to his doctrine. Trusteeship slips easily into overlordship, and of such an overlordship, and of the general disinterestedness of their mighty neigh-

[1] Hendrick, " The Life and Letters of Walter H. Page," i. p. 299.

bour, the Latin Republics have been profoundly mistrustful. President Wilson considered that the only way to translate the Monroe doctrine in terms of modern facts, not the least of which were the development of vast German interests in South America and the military and naval power of Japan, was to convince the Republics of South and Central America of the disinterestedness of the United States as the first step to a Pan-American Union. A vast American alliance on terms of equality was the surest means, in an age of predatory imperialisms, of placing the Monroe doctrine on an unassailable foundation.

This idea of a Pan-American Union is the key to all his relations with the States of South and Central America. He would win the confidence of the Republics for he was building a policy which had far horizons, and he would win even distracted Mexico from the suspicious fear with which she had regarded her northern neighbour since Zachary Taylor and Winfield Scott had wrested from her feeble grasp Texas and the vast territories west of the Rocky Mountains in the '40's.

In May 1911 General Porfirio Diaz abdicated, as the result of a revolution, the Presidency of Mexico he had held since 1876. His country had prospered under the iron rule of her great Dictator, but he had not drunk of the miraculous fountain of Ponce de Leon; his rule was personal, and, sooner or later, must come to an end. His failure was that he had not trained his countrymen to self-government, for, once the strong hand of the aged statesman was removed, Mexico began to drift towards that sinister carnival of anarchy into which she had plunged two years later and from which she has but recently extricated herself. In February 1913, a fortnight before President Wilson was inaugurated, the legally elected President of Mexico, Madero, was deposed and murdered by a man who had been a member of his cabinet, General Huerta—the usurper immediately constituted himself provisional President of Mexico. On the principle that any authority in Mexico was better than anarchy, most of the Powers were not long in recognizing the impudent usurper, who telegraphed to President Taft: "I have overthrown the Government, and, therefore, peace and order will reign." President Wilson, however, at once took another line. He refused to recognize an assassin and usurper as the constituted President of Mexico, and determined, while bringing all possible moral pressure to bear upon Huerta, to refrain from active intervention in the affairs of Mexico. He was convinced that with unlimited patience and the slow percolation through Mexico of the determination of the United States to recognize none but constitutional and duly elected governments, the people of Mexico, or a sane element among them, would at last succeed in extricating themselves from anarchy and imposing themselves upon their tyrants. He was convinced that a policy of intervention to "clean up" Mexico was a stupendous undertaking of doubtful value which would hang like a millstone round the neck of the American people, and, above all, nullify itself by confirming all the dark suspicions of American intentions in Mexico which it was his far-sighted policy to allay.

The policy of "watchful waiting" did not, naturally enough, commend itself to those Americans who had great interests in Mexican oil and other enterprises. That the President should tolerate the continuance of anarchy and the jeopardizing of so much capital seemed to them to argue either cowardice or incompetence, and the Mexican policy of the Wilson administration shortly came, and continued, to be the target of envenomed attacks. Roosevelt declared that, thanks to the policy of the President, the peace he had so much at heart "continued to rage" in Mexico. Yet Dr Wilson illuminated the issues he was weighing with such anxious care when he observed: "I have to pause and remind myself that I am President of the United States and not of a small group of Americans with vested interests in Mexico." [1]

In April 1914, as a result of an outrage at Tampico, where American sailors had been arrested by a Huertist colonel, the President demanded the formal apology of a salute of the American flag and, on Huerta prevaricating, ordered the bombardment and occupation of Vera Cruz.[2] Following this, and in pursuance of his Pan-American policy, the President accepted the proposal for the mediation of the A.B.C. Republics—Argentine, Brazil, and Chile. The Conference came to nothing, and the anarchy in Mexico continued, but hurricanes of vituperation were unable to move the American Government from its policy of abstention.

Huerta was frozen out by the middle of 1914, but his

[1] Tumulty, "Woodrow Wilson as I know Him," p. 146.

[2] His hand was forced by Rear-Admiral Mayo, who demanded a salute as well as an apology. Much against his will he supported the precipitate action of Mayo. (Daniels, "The Life of Woodrow Wilson.")

elimination did not improve matters, though it was a success for the patient policy of the President. In 1915 he convened a further Conference of Latin American Republics, and in addition to the A.B.C. Group, Guatemala, Bolivia, and Uruguay were represented. The Conference served an ultimatum on Mexico, giving her three months in which to set her house in order, and threatening joint Pan-American intervention. It was not, however, necessary, as at the end of the year one of the contending parties, that of General Carranza, had obtained the upper hand, and at the end of the year, America, followed by the rest of the Entente Powers, recognized his Government. In spite of the bitter denunciations of his opponents, all advocates of a short cut and "the cutting of Gordian knots," the patience of the President had been rewarded by the establishment of a Government in Mexico that it was possible to recognize without loss of self-respect, and his care in associating the Latin American Republics in his policy had, in spite of innumerable difficulties, convinced them, and even Mexico, that the Government of the United States was not seeking a pretext for the acquirement of territory, or of economic advantages at the expense of her weaker neighbours. It was a "policy of principle," pursued with marvellous pertinacity, and crowned with remarkable success.

The lull in the Mexican storm enabled the President to take another step in the direction of a Pan-American alliance. After an exchange of views with the different American Governments, he seized the opportunity afforded by the meeting of the Pan-American Scientific Congress at Washington in January 1916, to outline his proposals. After dealing with the origin of the Monroe Doctrine, he continued: "The States of America have not been certain what the United States would do with her power. That doubt must be removed . . . if America is to come into her own, into her legitimate own, in a world of peace and order, she must establish the foundations of amity so that no one will hereafter doubt them . . . this can be accomplished . . . in the first place by the States of America uniting in guaranteeing to each other absolutely political independence and territorial integrity. In the second place, and as a necessary corollary to that, guaranteeing the agreement to settle all pending boundary disputes as soon as possible and by amicable process; by agreeing that all disputes among themselves, should they unhappily arise, will be handled by patient, impartial investigation, and settled by arbitration; and the agreement necessary to the peace of the Americas, that no State of either continent will permit revolutionary expeditions against another State to be fitted out on its territory, and that they will prohibit the exportation of the munitions of war for the purpose of supplying revolutionists against neighbouring governments." [1]

It was a practical and finely imaginative programme. The founder of the League of Nations—the man who gave that great idea "a local habitation and a name"—here advocates for the two American continents the same idea as a step towards the light out of the jealousies and darkness of the past. Negotiations were inaugurated for the conclusion of a series of treaties that may well constitute the beginning of a diplomatic revolution. The effort required was sustained, for "in Chili, in Brazil, in Colombia, Venezuela, and Mexico there had grown up a fear and a distrust of Americans that very much resembled the fear and distrust of the border peoples of the Roman Republic toward those privileged Latins who in the time of Cæsar overawed their weaker neighbours."

The negotiations of President Roosevelt for the acquisition of the Panama Canal Zone from the Republic of Colombia were, from the American point of view, opportunely interrupted by the outbreak of a revolution in Panama whose independence of Colombia the United States recognized. In the circumstances, the newly created republic offered no objection to the organization of the zone by the United States. But Colombia's claims remained, and a considerable body of American public opinion considered the attitude of Roosevelt, in spite of his vigorous defence, as somewhat shabby. President Wilson took the view that Colombia must be compensated, and in 1916 the Senate approved a treaty by which she received $25,000,000 in settlement of all claims.

The contention of the President that fair and open dealing must supersede nice interpretations of legality not only raised his prestige abroad but carried him further towards the political goal of a Pan-American alliance.

This breadth of view and imagination was displayed yet more signally in his handling of the Panama Canal Tolls controversy. The United States had secured a free hand for the construction of the long planned Panama Canal by the Hay-

[1] Scott, "President Wilson's Foreign Policy," pp. 160-1.

Pauncefote Treaty of 1901 with Great Britain, which stipulated that the Canal should be open to the vessels of all nations "on terms of entire equality." The clause was specially inserted to preclude discrimination in the matter of tolls. In 1912 an Act was passed exempting coastwise shipping from payment of the tolls, an Act which amounted to discrimination in favour of American shipping, since the coastwise trade was practically without exception in American hands. Great Britain protested, with the support of other European Powers, against the Tolls Act as a violation of the Hay-Pauncefote Treaty. Mr Taft replied by an exegesis to the effect that "all nations" meant all nations *other than* the United States. Inevitably the Irish-Americans and other anti-British interests campaigned in favour of the Act solely because they found that it annoyed Great Britain. Other more level-headed elements were pleased on seeing a horse and cart driven through what they considered a very bad bargain. But large numbers of Republicans and Democrats found Mr Taft's explanations unconvincing and felt increasingly anxious at the shocking impression created in Europe by the obvious word-splitting and quibbles of those who defended the Act. President Wilson was not long in satisfying himself from the parties to the treaty, that their plain intention had been to preclude any discrimination in the matter of tolls, and he at once resolved to recommend to Congress the immediate repeal of the Act as a plain violation of a treaty. It was represented to him that his proposal would split the Democrats, enrage the Irish and German Americans, and endanger the future progress of his reform programme. The President cut at the root of such arguments by observing: "If we begin to consider the effect upon our own political fortunes of every step we take in these delicate matters of our foreign relations, America will be set adrift and her word questioned in every court in Europe. It is important that every agreement that America subscribes her name to shall be carried out in the spirit of those who negotiated it." [1]

On 5th March 1914 the President appeared before a joint session of the two Houses of Congress, and in a brief and pregnant speech advocated the immediate repeal of the clause in the Act of 1912 relating to the exemption of coastwise shipping: "Whatever may be our own differences of opinion concerning this much debated measure, its meaning

[1] Tumulty, "Woodrow Wilson as I know Him," p. 167.

is not debated outside the United States. Everywhere else the language of the treaty is given but one interpretation, and that interpretation precludes the exemption I am asking you to repeal. We consented to the treaty; its language we accepted, if we did not originate it; and we are too big, too powerful, too self-respecting a nation to interpret with a too strained or refined meaning the words of our own promises just because we have power enough to give us leave to read them as we please. The large thing to do is the only thing we can afford to do, a voluntary withdrawal from a position everywhere questioned and misunderstood. . . . I ask this of you in support of the foreign policy of the administration. I shall not know how to deal with other matters of even greater delicacy and nearer consequence if you do not grant it to me in ungrudging measure."[1] After heated debates the repeal was carried by substantial majorities. Those "other matters," as we have seen, revolved round the preliminary soundings on the possibility of an Anglo-American-German disarmament agreement. The action of the President in the tolls question immensely raised his own and his country's prestige throughout the world. "It has not been done," said Sir Edward Grey in the House of Commoms, "to please us, or in the interest of good relations, but I believe from a much greater motive, the feeling that a government which is to use its influence among nations to make relations better must never, when the occasion arises, flinch or quail from interpreting treaty rights in a strictly fair spirit."

The consideration of the final phase of the President's Mexican policy will lead us on to an examination of his attitude in the world-crisis of 1914, and in the events preceding his great decision of 1917.

Even after his patience had been crowned in 1915 by the establishment of Carranza as ruler of Mexico—a ruler to whom the President could accord recognition—a fresh crisis broke out in 1916 with the marauding raids of the bandit Villa across the American border. Though the President himself faced the prospect of immediate war, and authorized the American forces to pursue Villa into Mexican territory, he resolutely refused to embark on a first-class "cleaning-up" campaign. Carranza's patriotic indignation at the violation of Mexican soil was mollified by the permission accorded him to pursue Villa, if necessary, into American territory.

[1] Scott, "President Wilson's Foreign Policy," p. 32.

To many Americans the attempt to regard one bandit rather than another as the rightful Government of Mexico was a hopeless farce, and in any event to flatter Carranza by treating him as an equal, a scandalous lapse of dignity. But quite apart from his resolution to pursue the difficult path of conciliating Latin-American opinion, the President's motives were far deeper than his critics imagined. He had become aware of the presence of a new and insidious factor in the Mexican imbroglio. "I came from the South," he said in the course of a private conversation in June 1916, "and I know what war is, for I have seen its wreckage and terrible ruin. It is easy for me as President to declare war. I do not have to fight, and neither do the gentlemen on the Hill who now clamour for it. . . . I will not resort to war against Mexico until I have exhausted every means to keep out of this mess. . . . The gentlemen who criticize me speak as if America were afraid to fight Mexico. Poor Mexico, with its pitiful men, women and children, fighting to gain a foothold in their own land! . . . Some day the people of America will know why I hesitated to intervene in Mexico. I cannot tell them now, for we are at peace with the great power whose poisonous propaganda is responsible for the present terrible condition of affairs in Mexico. . . . Germany is anxious to have us at war with Mexico, so that our minds and our energies will be taken off the great war across the sea. She wishes an uninterrupted opportunity to carry on her submarine warfare, and believes that war with Mexico will keep our hands off her and thus give her liberty of action to do as she pleases on the high seas. It begins to look as if war with Germany is inevitable. If it should come—I pray God it may not—I do not wish America's energies and forces divided, for we will need every ounce of reserve we have to lick Germany." [1]

These words carry us back to the problem that had been developing since August 1914. In the midst of the first stages of a programme of domestic reform that would certainly require a full term of office to carry through, the President was increasingly called upon to concentrate his attention upon the world-crisis. In August 1914 the Mexican situation was still menacing, though Huerta had been driven out. The President was not slow in seeing the terrible strain that the war was sure to put upon the cohesion and loyalty of certain

[1] Tumulty, "Woodrow Wilson as I know Him," pp. 158-9.

large elements in the vast mixed population of the United States. He was, as ever, ready to exert himself in favour of peace, and on 5th August, sitting beside the death-bed of his wife, he drafted a circular to all the belligerents offering his good offices, in accordance with the Hague Convention, in favour of peace " either now or at any other time that might be thought more suitable, as an occasion to serve you and all concerned in a way that would afford me lasting cause for gratitude and happiness." [1]

He immediately issued a declaration of neutrality, and refrained from any protest against the invasion of Belgium. His silence has been strongly condemned, but it is sufficient to note that in this matter he was supported by his great antagonist, Theodore Roosevelt, and that it was the considered opinion of Lord Bryce that to expect a different attitude on the part of a neutral power not a party to the violated treaty, was to expect something for which there was no precedent.[2] Looking back, one is inclined to agree with that great friend of the Allies, Walter Page, that the only precedent to justify such an expectation " was found in Hysteria."

The whole nation supported the President at this critical moment. He had, as we have seen, to face the possible menace to the internal peace of the State constituted by large bodies of unabsorbed aliens from many of the belligerent countries, Germans, Austrians, Russians, Poles, Finns. As the war rolled on, he had to bear in mind that national public opinion was tending to fall into two geographically determined groups —the East and the Middle and Far West. He had to remember that he was not only President of the vocal and interested East, but of the Union. And a fact to be constantly remembered is that the West was profoundly pacific. The idea of war was hateful to men absorbed in developing those vast lands. The issues of the desperate struggle in Europe were remote and half-understood. They did not for long come home to men's business and bosoms.

Since his inauguration as President, Dr Wilson had emphasized the quality of national leadership inherent in the Chief Executive of the United States. He had always been the exponent of the Lincoln school in this matter, and as the country had become accustomed to the firm expression of his views by the President, they expected a statement on

[1] Quoted Ford, " Woodrow Wilson: The Man and his Work," pp. 247-8.
[2] Hendrick, " The Life and Letters of Walter H. Page," p. 165.

the war and its issues. On 18th August 1914 he issued an appeal to the citizens of the United States to refrain from personal partisanship, to cultivate a detached and truly neutral attitude. Partisanship, however natural, would endanger the national unity: "Such divisions among us would be fatal to our peace of mind and might seriously stand in the way of the proper performance of our duty as the one great nation at peace, the one people holding itself ready to play a part of impartial mediation and speak the counsels of peace and accommodation, not as a partisan, but as a friend. . . . We must be impartial in thought as well as in action, must put a curb upon our sentiments as well as upon every transaction that might be construed as a preference of one party to the struggle before another." They must first and last be Americans, only so could they hope when opportunity offered to be of service in the restoration of peace.[1]

This endeavour to cultivate detachment was viewed in England at the time, and later, as curiously if not offensively academic. But the acute anxiety of the President to avoid the outbreak of a debate that might turn the nation into a pandemonium, is his complete justification. By succeeding he established for himself an unrivalled leadership at a moment when leadership was above all things necessary. That he did succeed is sufficiently proved by the delightfully acid comments of Walter Page on the spirit he found prevailing at Washington in the summer of 1916: "The Vice-President confessed to his neighbour at a Gridiron dinner, that he had read none of the White Papers, or Orange Books, etc., of the belligerent Governments—confessed this with pride—lest he should form an opinion and cease to be neutral! Miss X, a member of the President's household, said to Mrs Y, the day we lunched there, that she had made a remark privately to Sharp [American Ambassador in Paris], showing her admiration of the French. 'Was that a violation of neutrality?' she asked, in all seriousness.

"I can see it in no other way but this: the President suppressed free thought and free speech when he insisted upon personal neutrality. . . . The mass of the American people found themselves forbidden to think or talk, and this forbidding had a sufficient effect to make them take refuge in indifference. It's the President's job. He's our leader. He'll attend to this matter. We must not embarrass him.

[1] Scott, "President Wilson's Foreign Policy," pp. 67-8.

On this easy cushion of non-responsibility the great masses fell back at their intellectual and moral ease—softened, isolated, lulled." [1] German propaganda was very active, but the success of the President's appeal is a sufficient testimony to the ascendancy he had established. In accord with a long tradition, on 8th September 1914 he issued a proclamation designating Sunday, 4th October, as a day to be devoted to prayer for peace.[2]

It was not long before it became obvious that American interests were vitally affected by the progress of the tremendous struggle which, after the Marne, the President felt could only end in a draw of some sort. Very early the British blockade measures inaugurated a prodigious correspondence on the rights of neutrals between U.S. and Great Britain, which was followed by the graver crisis caused by the German counter-blockade of Great Britain, proclaimed in February 1915. All ships entering a certain area were liable to be sunk at sight. The American Government at once informed the German Imperial Government that it could not recognize the validity of such measures, and would hold Germany to a "strict accountability." This declaration of principle was shortly followed by news that a German submarine had torpedoed and sunk the "Lusitania" on 8th May 1915, off the South of Ireland, thereby drowning 1260 persons, among whom were 107 American citizens. A wave of horror passed over America, but the President refused to precipitate matters. In a few days he summoned Germany, in a dignified note, to make reparation, disavow the crime, and give guarantees against the repetition of such outrages. The German Government was inclined to argue, and the situation became menacing. Firmly determined to resist the outcry of the New England States for an immediate declaration of war, the President had resolved not to shrink from it if the German Government refused to yield to his patient though insistent demands. As a result the Secretary of State, W. J. Bryan, a doctrinaire pacificist, though a powerful influence in the Democratic party, resigned in June 1915, and was succeeded by Robert Lansing. The "Lusitania" crisis was complicated by the sinking of the "Arabic" on 19th August, off the coast of Ireland. For a few days war seemed inevitable, but on 1st September 1915 the German Government gave the

[1] Hendrick, "The Life and Letters of Walter H. Page," ii., p. 175.
[2] Ford, "Woodrow Wilson: The Man and his Work," pp. 248-9.

general undertaking that "liners will not be sunk by submarines without warning, and without ensuring the safety of the lives of non-combatants, provided that the liners do not try to escape or offer resistance." Such an undertaking was a serious handicap on the efficacy of the submarine, and as a result was constantly broken. Within a few days of the assurance the Allan Liner "Hesperian" was torpedoed without warning. So serious was the position, and so insistent was the able German ambassador in the United States, Count Bernstorff, that war was inevitable unless Germany retreated, that he was instructed in October to disavow the "Arabic" outrage, and to announce that the German Government declared its regret, and was ready to pay an indemnity.

His success in moderating the orgies of the Germans encouraged the President to continue his twofold policy of clearing up the submarine issue by securing respect for international law, and, if this were reconcilable with his chief endeavour, of keeping the United States out of the war. The path was beset with incredible difficulties. In September 1915 he discovered that the Austrian ambassador, Dr Dumba, was engaged in fomenting sabotage in American factories engaged in the manufacture of munitions for the Allies. He at once demanded his recall; and when the Austrian Government began to argue the case of its envoy, ordered the ambassdor to leave the country. In December he peremptorily ejected the German naval and military attachés, Captains Boy-Ed and Von Papen, for a similar abuse of their diplomatic position. It became evident that the President could not be trifled with, a discovery that was to receive further confirmation.

Early in 1916 a controversy arose as to the status of armed merchantmen. The Germans contended that an armament recognized as defensive against a cruiser was offensive against a submarine. The pro-German elements in Congress tried to meet the situation by introducing a resolution to request the President to warn all Americans against travelling on such vessels, which Germany now announced she would sink at sight on the ground that they were really auxiliary cruisers. Senator Stone, Chairman of the Senate Committee on Foreign Affairs, addressed a letter on the subject to the President, who seized the opportunity of defining his position to the new, though as yet unsubstantial, threat: "We covet peace," he wrote, "and shall preserve it at any cost but the loss of honour.

To forbid our people to exercise their rights for fear we might be called upon to vindicate them would be a deep humiliation indeed. It would be an implicit, all but an explicit, acquiescence in the violation of the rights of mankind everywhere and of whatever nation or allegiance. It would be a deliberate abdication of our hitherto proud position as spokesman even amid the turmoil of war, for the law and the right. It is important to reflect that if in this instance we allowed expediency to take the place of principle, the door would inevitably be opened to still further concessions. . . . What we are contending for in this matter is of the very essence of the things that have made America a sovereign nation. She cannot yield them without conceding her own impotency as a nation and making virtual surrender of her independent position among the nations of the world."[1] To eliminate the dangerous impression caused by the resolutions, that public opinion was not behind him in insisting on every American and human right, in a further letter he urged that the question should be brought to the vote as soon as possible. In a sense, and so far as the Constitution allowed, he had demanded a vote of confidence. The resolutions were defeated in the House by 276 to 142, and in the Senate by 64 to 14.

Within three weeks of this personal vindication the cross-Channel steamer "Sussex" was torpedoed without warning, and several Americans lost their lives, on 24th March 1916. After an investigation, which revealed no shadow of excuse for the outrage—one of many similar in these weeks—the President took decisive action. After informing the German Government that unless it abandoned its present methods and gave a pledge of such abandonment, he would immediately sever diplomatic relations, he appeared before a joint session of Congress on 19th April 1916, and reviewed the long tale of German infamies at sea: "Tragedy has followed tragedy on the seas in such fashion, with such attendant circumstances, as to make it grossly evident that warfare of such a sort, if warfare it be, cannot be carried on without the most palpable violation of the dictates alike of right and of humanity. Whatever the disposition and intention of the Imperial German Government, it has manifestly proved impossible for it to keep such methods of attack upon the commerce of its enemies within the bounds set by

[1] Scott, "President Wilson's Foreign Policy," pp. 177-8.

either the reason or the heart of mankind." [1] He informed Congress of his decision, " taken in the confidence that it will meet with your approval and support." On 4th May 1916 Germany gave way in a note wherein, embedded in a mass of verbiage, she undertook that merchant vessels should be subjected to visit, or destruction only in accordance with the clear and acknowledged principles of international law, and that " such vessels, both within and without the area declared as a naval war zone, shall not be sunk without warning, and without saving human lives, unless the ship attempt to escape and offer resistance." The note provided the German Government with a loophole by vaguely insinuating that the pledge might be withdrawn unless the United States would insist on the British blockade equally conforming to the principles of international law.

Though the President was conducting a long and sometimes acrimonious correspondence with the British Government on the enforcement of the blockade, and the procedure of British prize courts, he refused to consider the suggestion that he should play one belligerent off against the other. Acknowledging the German note, he announced that the United States would " rely upon the scrupulous execution henceforth of the now altered policy of the Imperial Government." As to the suggested *quid pro quo*, the United States " cannot for a moment entertain, much less discuss, a suggestion that respect by German naval authorities for the rights of citizens of the United States upon the high seas should in any way or in the slightest degree be made contingent upon the conduct of any other government affecting the rights of neutrals and non-combatants. Responsibility in such matters is single, not joint ; absolute, not relative."

Ambassador Page regarded the President's reply as a master-stroke. " They laid a trap for him," he wrote, " and he caught them in their own trap. The Germans had tried to ' put it up ' to the President to commit the first unfriendly act. He now ' puts it up ' to them." [2]

The question that confronted the President after the " Sussex Pledge " from Germany, as it came to be called, was simply how long would the state of affairs, stabilized for a moment by his patient diplomacy, endure. As we have seen above, during the summer of 1916 he became more and

[1] Scott, " President Wilson's Foreign Policy," p. 183.
[2] Hendrick, " The Life and Letters of Walter H. Page," ii. p. 150.

more convinced that with the indefinite prolongation of the war it was becoming increasingly probable that the United States would be drawn in. If he was to spare his country the final arbitrament, then the war must be ended. Sooner or later the Germans would play their last card and resume the unrestricted U-boat warfare that must drive America into war. From the beginning he had kept steadily before him the goal of utilizing the great influence of the United States for the restoration of peace. Already he had publicly associated himself in a speech, on 27th May 1916, with the aims and objects of the "League to enforce Peace," which was studying plans for the setting up of some international authority capable of giving the public law of nations the sanctions without which it was but a body of customs: "If it should ever be our privilege," he said, "to suggest or initiate a movement for peace among the nations now at war, I am sure that the people of the United States would wish their Government to move along these lines: First, such a settlement with regard to their own immediate interests as the belligerents may agree upon. . . . Second, an universal association of the nations to maintain the inviolate security of the highway of the seas, . . . and to prevent any war begun either contrary to treaty covenants or without warning, and full submission of the cause to the opinion of the world—a virtual guarantee of territorial integrity and political independence." Though the suggestion that the United States should join an association which guaranteed "the territorial integrity and political independence" of its members was attacked in some quarters as an abandonment of Washington's principle of avoiding "entangling alliances," there was no doubt that in his openly expressed policy of working for an opportunity of bringing about a general peace, the President had practically the whole weight of American public opinion behind him.[1]

This aspiration of the President was fully realized in Berlin from the able reports of Count Bernstorff, as well as from the hints of the American ambassador, Gerard, and of Colonel House, the President's *alter ego*, who journeyed to Europe from time to time. On 18th August 1916 the German Chancellor, Dr von Bethmann-Hollweg, telegraphed to Count Bernstorff that the German Government "would be glad to accept mediation by the President with a view to initiate

[1] Bernstorff, "My Three Years in America," p. 238.

peace negotiations between the belligerents. Kindly encourage the President in his activities along this line." [1]

As early as January 1916 General Falkenhayn had told the Minister of State Helfferich "that he could not bring the war to an end by military blows delivered on land." [2] But this realization only made the Supreme German Command more emphatic in the assertion that a decisive victory could be gained on sea by the ruthless use of the submarine. Bethmann-Hollweg and the Foreign Minister, Von Jagow, supported by Helfferich, were convinced that the resort to unrestricted U-boat warfare would be ultimately disastrous. Throughout the greater part of 1916 a concealed conflict was waged with growing bitterness between the civilian and the military authorities in Germany. If he was to be successful in his struggle with the Supreme Command, Bethmann-Hollweg realized that he must seek an early opportunity for initiating negotiations for peace on terms that would enable Germany to extricate herself from a position which, though apparently favourable, was one of increasing danger. For this reason throughout 1916 he counted on President Wilson to take some action with a view to bringing the belligerents together in negotiation. On 2nd September 1916 the Chancellor indicated to Count Bernstorff, for the benefit of the President, that Germany was ready to restore Belgium, the one detail of the future settlement in which American public opinion was profoundly interested. On all other points the President made it clear to Bernstorff that he was indifferent, his grand object being to bring the belligerents together, since, in common with well-informed governing opinion, both in the Entente and the Central Powers, once a Conference had met and an armistice been arranged, he believed no power on earth could have persuaded the men in the trenches to go on spilling each other's blood. On 25th September the Chancellor wired to Bernstorff that "a peace move by the President, which would appear spontaneous by those viewing it from without, would be given the most serious consideration by us." [3] As Bernstorff read between the lines of the dispatches and telegrams he received from Berlin, the situation was a race between unrestricted U-boat warfare on the one hand and American mediation on the other.

[1] "Official German Documents relating to the World War," vol. ii. p. 981.
[2] *Ibid.*, p. 1116.
[3] *Ibid.*, p. 986.

In the meantime the President, steadily pursuing the new line of policy he had struck out on 27th May in his address to the League to Enforce Peace, was seeking a favourable moment for launching his peace proposals. Late in 1916 he still believed the war could not end in a decisive victory for either group of powers,[1] but he feared a rebuff from the Entente. In his opinion, shared by Colonel House, the Entente powers would agree to his mediation only provided they were convinced that victory was impossible without the aid of the United States. At such a moment of depression America would speak with unrivalled authority, and such a moment depended wholly upon the ebb and flow of the far-flung battles. Watching with absorbed attention, the President seemed to see such a moment approaching at the end of August, but the intervention of Roumania dramatically tipped the scales in favour of the Entente. Inevitably this postponed his mediation, which it would be useless to offer to people elated at the prospect of victory.[2] The Presidential election was approaching, and he became convinced that the Entente would not listen to a problematical candidate. Action would have been possible earlier in the year, not on the eve of decisive elections.

But the sands were running out fast, and Von Bethmann-Hollweg was already fighting a losing battle. At a conference at Pless in September, he had been forced to agree that the Supreme Command should decide the time at which the beginning of the unrestricted U-boat war should take place. His telegrams became more urgent, and he obviously began to lose faith in the President's intentions. On 9th October he forwarded to Bernstorff a short memorandum, drafted by the Emperor for the President's notice, in which it is clearly hinted that unless American mediation materializes soon, the pressure of events may compel Germany to take advantage of the reservation in her "Sussex Pledge," and resume unrestricted U-boat warfare. On 14th October the Chancellor wired: "A spontaneous appeal for peace, toward the making of which I request that he be further encouraged, would be gladly accepted by us. It is in Wilson's power, and consequently it is his duty to sound a halt to this murder of human beings."[3]

Though the President refused to move before the election,

[1] Bernstorff, "My Three Years in America," p. 254. [2] *Ibid.*, p. 243.
[3] "Official German Documents relating to the World War," vol. ii. p. 993.

there was no reason to doubt his intentions. On 2nd September, in an address on accepting renomination as the Democratic candidate, he had said: "There must be a just and settled peace, and we here in America must contribute the full force of our enthusiasm and of our authority as a nation to the organization of that peace upon worldwide foundations that cannot easily be shaken. . . . The nations of the world must unite in joint guarantees that whatever is done to disturb the whole world's life must first be tested in the court of the whole world's opinion before it is attempted."[1]

The Presidential election of 1916 was one of the most confused on record. There would have been something Homeric in the conflict if Theodore Roosevelt, the advocate of immediate intervention on the side of the Allies, had been the Republican candidate. But the Republican "bosses" had never really forgiven him for splitting the party in 1912, and as he did not care to play another lone hand, he supported, in the interests of party unity, the colourless candidate Hughes. The supporters of the President went into the fray with the telling slogan, "He kept us out of the war." This and his great measures of domestic reform rallied the progressive elements to the Democrats, while Hughes angled for the German vote, without quite knowing how to win it. Wilson came out on a platform of "America first and last," and in a cutting telegram rejected the help of any elements who allowed their feelings to be swayed by any other motive than that of their patriotic duty as American citizens. A pro-German body, known as the American Truth Society, informed him that his "leniency to the British Empire" and approval of war loans and ammunition traffic were the issues of the campaign. He at once replied: "Your telegram received. Would feel deeply mortified to have you, or anybody like you, voting for me. Since you have access to many disloyal Americans, and I have not, I will ask you to convey this message to them.—Woodrow Wilson."[2]

Bernstorff was convinced that on the supreme issue of unrestricted U-boat warfare, neither candidate could possibly deviate from the policy, already a national one, that the resumption of such warfare would mean war between the United States and Germany.

[1] "President Wilson's Policy." F.O. Handbooks, No. 161, pp. 7-8.

[2] Quoted Harris, "President Wilson: His Problems and his Policy," p. 234.

But certain powerful German and pro-German interests began to gamble on the opportunity that the defeat of Wilson might afford them. They calculated that if Hughes were elected they could take advantage of the four months' interval between the election and the inauguration of the new President in March 1917, to rush through Congress their favourite resolutions calling on the President to prevent American travellers from sailing on Allied vessels. So grave did this possibility of a paralysis in the Government, due to the normal functioning of the constitution, appear to him, that "Wilson had firmly made up his mind, in case Mr Hughes were elected, to appoint him Secretary of State immediately, and after Hughes had informed himself on the political situation in this office, to hand over the Presidency and himself retire. Mr Wilson considered it impossible to leave the country without firm leadership at such a dangerous moment." [1]

The election itself produced an unprecedented situation. There was a Republican landslide in the Eastern States, up to then considered essential for victory, and the election of Mr Hughes was announced to the world. This victory became doubtful as other returns came in. For days the position was uncertain until the vote of the Western States returned the President by a narrow majority, known on 23rd November, sixteen days after the polling. They had voted for his peace policy, and his wisdom in refusing to be guided solely by opinion in the Eastern States was signally vindicated. In 1912 he had come in as successful in a triangular duel created by the Republican split, now he had defeated his opponents in a straight fight on a national issue. He had increased his popular majority by 2,800,000. The intensity of the national interest is revealed by the fact that Mr Hughes secured the highest vote ever recorded by a Republican and the President the highest ever recorded by a Democratic candidate.

The totals of the five candidates in the field were as follows :— [2]

Wilson (Democrat)	9,116,296
Hughes (Republican)	8,547,474
Benson (Socialist)	750,000
Hanley (Prohibitionist)	225,101
Reimer (Socialist-Labour)	10,105

[1] Bernstorff, "My Three Years in America," p. 258.
[2] Harris, "President Wilson : His Problems and his Policy," pp. 238-9.

Now at last he felt himself free to grapple with his tremendous task of wresting peace from the holocaust. The conditions for the attempt to bring the belligerents to negotiate seemed not unfavourable. The German victories over Roumania had once more inclined the fortune of war to the Central Powers. It might be assumed that the Entente would not be so hostile, even though Ambassador Page, recalled from London to report, had given the President a verbal message from the British Government that an intervention looking towards peace would not be welcomed. On 21st November Bernstorff reported that he had received a message from the President, through Colonel House, that his peace move would take place before the New Year. " In this connection he imposes as a condition that up to that time we express ourselves on the question of a peace move just as little as possible, either orally or in writing, in order to block a premature rejection on the part of our enemies, and that, further, we carry on the U-boat war in the strictest conformity with our promises and allow no new controversies to come up."[1] At the end of November the Federal Reserve Board issued a warning to American banks against taking up the unsecured bonds of foreign powers, an action which was interpreted by Bernstorff as the first sign that the American Government was disposed to exercise pressure on the Allies.[2] The note was prepared, but was again delayed owing to a further series of U-boat outrages, and the inauguration of the Belgian deportations, which roused American public opinion to passionate indignation at this latter-day slavery, and caused the President to despatch a vigorous protest. Once more Bernstorff was involved in a web of denials, explanations, and apologies.

But the Chancellor had by now lost faith in the President. The pressure of Austria-Hungary, and the consciousness that he must either win a peace or surrender to the generals, drove him to the fatal decision to anticipate the American action and issue a peace note on behalf of the Central Powers. The note had been drawn up in November, with the approval of the Supreme Command. They understood that if it failed they would have their way in the matter of U-boats. The Chancellor did not see that such action would in any event hamper the enigmatic President. He regarded it as " a

[1] " Official German Documents relating to the World War," ii. p. 993.

[2] *Ibid.*, ii. p. 997.

second iron in the fire," and was not turned from the decision to forward it to the Allies by the receipt of a message on 5th December, through the American *chargé* in Berlin, that "the President is watching the whole situation with the utmost solicitude, and has the desire and the definite purpose" to be of service in securing peace, but the Belgian deportations stood in the way. "What the President most earnestly desires is practical co-operation on the part of the German authorities in bringing about a favourable opportunity for early and affirmative action by the President looking to an early restoration of peace." [1] It was a plain hint, but it was not taken.

On 12th December the Central Powers issued their famous Peace Note. It was couched in the arrogant tones of a conqueror conscious that he is doing something magnanimous. It made no specific proposals, and was in fact an invitation to the Allies "to buy a pig in a poke." [2] The war "had been forced" upon the Central Powers, but they had vindicated "the honour and liberty of national evolution," and were ready to negotiate. Obviously the tone was for the benefit of the Supreme Command and for home consumption, but the Chancellor undoubtedly hoped and believed that the offer would be accepted. He did not know when, if ever, the President would act; his information led him to believe that there were powerful influences at work in the British Government itself in favour of a peace by negotiation.[3] He hoped to reach the people of the Entente Powers over the heads of their Governments. How he imagined that the British people could be favourably impressed by the arrogant condescension of the Note at a moment when the wisest continental observers had seen that this superbly obstinate nation had fatally set its teeth, and was concentrated, body and soul, on nothing less than the destruction of Germany; why, in a word, the Chancellor hoped to attain his ends by the methods he employed, is a psychological problem not difficult to resolve for those who have observed German diplomatic behaviour.

What had happened was that "the peace offer of the Imperial Government got involved with Mr Wilson's plans

[1] "Official German Documents relating to the World War," ii. p. 1306.
[2] Hendrick, "The Life and Letters of Walter H. Page," ii. p. 203.
[3] "Official German Documents relating to the World War," i. p. 333. Evidence of Dr von Bethmann Hollweg before the Reichstag Sub-Commission of Enquiry.

for mediation."[1] The President was profoundly disturbed and chagrined by a step which he had expressly requested should not be taken before his own peace proposals had been issued. Though he realized that his success was now problematical, he determined to continue his policy, on 18th December 1916, in a note to the belligerent Governments. In substance it was a request to each side to state their essential terms of peace. "He takes the liberty of calling attention to the fact that the objects which the statesmen of the belligerents on both sides have in mind in this war are virtually the same, as stated in general terms to their own people and to the world." If those objects were once formulated and compared, it might be found "that the terms which the belligerents on the one side and on the other would deem it necessary to insist upon are not so irreconcilable as some have feared." "In the measures to be taken to secure the future peace of the world, the people and Government of the United States are as vitally and as directly interested as the Governments now at war. . . . The terms upon which it is to be concluded they are not at liberty to suggest; but the President does feel that it is his right and his duty to point out their ultimate interest in its conclusion, lest it should presently be too late to accomplish the greater things which lie beyond its conclusion, lest the situation of neutral nations, now exceedingly hard to endure, be rendered altogether intolerable, and lest, more than all, an injury be done to civilization itself which can never be atoned for or repaired. . . . The President is not proposing peace; he is not even offering mediation. He is merely proposing that soundings be taken in order that we may learn, the neutral nations with the belligerent, how near the haven of peace may be for which all mankind longs with an intense and increasing longing."[2]

A situation had arisen, so far as Germany was concerned, that required dexterous handling, far-sightedness, and a resolute determination to make the necessary sacrifices. The moment was not unfavourable. American opinion had been offended by the unbridled language of the Entente press during the days when it believed the President had been defeated at the election. Sharp British replies to American representations on the famous "Black List" of American firms with whom British citizens were forbidden to trade, had produced acute

[1] Bernstorff, "My Three Years in America," p. 266.
[2] Scott, "President Wilson's Foreign Policy," pp. 240-4.

if passing irritation. American opinion was unconvinced by the claim of the Allies to be fighting for the liberties of small nations in view of the apparently false position into which they had been driven by the Greek tangle. Had Germany now announced her determination to effect the unconditional restoration of Belgium, the whole of public opinion would have been behind the President in bringing the utmost diplomatic pressure to bear on the Entente to agree to a conference.

But Germany could not nerve herself to fight unreservedly for peace. Her reply to the President's invitation was courteous but vague. She stated no terms, reserving them for discussion at a conference. The Entente Powers, on the other hand, seized the opportunity of the German offer to reject it with cold but stinging contempt, while on 7th January 1917 they replied, in a joint note to the President, enunciating at great length, though with a certain vagueness, the tremendous territorial programme they were afterwards to translate into the terms of the settlement of 1919.

The President's note had been received with mixed feelings in London, especially the sentence in which he pointed out the obvious fact that the purposes of the contending nations of either side, as expounded by their leaders, were virtually the same. The declaration was a deliberate and rather academic abstraction intended as a preface to the request for an explicit enunciation of war aims. But it was unfortunate, almost as unfortunate and as defensible as the much abused formula "too proud to fight." It was widely quoted and misunderstood, and by its apparent implication that there was not a pin to choose between the Entente and the Central Powers was bitterly resented. At a luncheon at Buckingham Palace on 21st December 1916, "the King, expressing his surprise and dismay that Mr Wilson should think that Englishmen were fighting for the same things in this war as the Germans, broke down." [1] The position was indeed serious. Roumania had collapsed; the news from Russia hinted at the possibility of the approaching Revolution. The sentence in the President's note in which he declared that the position of the neutral Powers was becoming intolerable seemed like a veiled threat. But the domestic situation in Great Britain had already been revolutionized by the advent to power of Mr Lloyd George,

[1] Hendrick, "The Life and Letters of Walter H. Page," ii. p. 207.

who in the previous September had nailed his flag to the mast in the famous " knock-out blow " interview. Desperately as the Allies needed American help, a hardening of temper had begun which made it almost certain that the President's effort would fail. " There is nothing that the American Government or any other human power can do," Lord Robert Cecil declared to Ambassador Page, " which will bring this war to a close before the Allies have spent their utmost force to secure a victory. A failure to secure such a victory will leave the world at the mercy of the most arrogant and the bloodiest tyranny that has ever been organized. It is far better to die in an effort to defeat that tyranny than to perish under its success." [1]

But the President pressed indefatigably on. On 22nd January 1917, in an address to the Senate, he described the results of his note to the belligerents. The fact that one group had declared their conditions was something gained. " The statesmen of both the groups of nations now arrayed against one another have said, in terms that could not be misinterpreted, that it was no part of the purpose they had in mind to crush their antagonists. But the implications of these assurances may not be equally clear to all. . . . They imply, first of all, that it must be a peace without victory." The President went on to declare that any settlement to be permanent must embody the principle that government depends upon the consent of the governed. For this reason "there should be a united, independent and autonomous Poland." It must provide for " the freedom of the seas," disarmament, the organization of peace by an association of nations. " Perhaps I am the only person in high authority amongst all the peoples of the world who is at liberty to speak and hold nothing back. . . . I would fain believe that I am speaking for the silent mass of mankind everywhere who have as yet had no place or opportunity to speak their real hearts out concerning the death and ruin they see to have come already upon the persons and the homes they hold most dear." [2] The phrase " peace without victory " was selected for violent attack, but it was evident that the President was prepared to press forward on the course he had chosen and had in effect begun to mobilize to his side all whose eyes were not yet blinded with blood. It was a prodigious effort to appeal

[1] Hendrick, " The Life and Letters of Walter H. Page," ii. p. 209.
[2] Scott, " President Wilson's Foreign Policy," pp. 245-54.

from Caesar to God, to make the still small voice of reason sound above the earthquake, the fire, and the tempest. But since truth is explosive, to have accepted his terms would have spelt destruction to the militarist autocracies of Central Europe as surely as defeat at the hands of the Allies. Already, unknown to the President, Germany had signed her own death warrant.

The wise and liberal Ambassador Bernstorff realized in December, when he heard of the resignation of von Jagow, a vehement opponent of the submarine policy, that the situation was desperate. In effect, the Chancellor's policy of keeping " two irons in the fire " had ended in his losing both. The reply of the Allies to the German overture and the terms of peace indicated in their note to the President, made it impossible for him to resist any longer the demands of the Supreme Command.[1] On 8th January, at a conference at G.H.Q. at Pless, Hindenburg and Ludendorff decided quite calmly that if, next day, the Chancellor resisted their policy of unrestricted U-boat warfare, they would remove him and compel the Emperor to appoint another Chancellor. The wavering Bethmann Hollweg appeared the next day and seems to have made no resistance. He had already lost heart, and lacked the nerve to fight the military masters of Germany. " Of course," he observed rather pathetically, " if success beckons, we must follow." [2] But he did not believe in success, and yet dared not resign, for the best of motives, for fear that he might discourage a nation that had pinned all its hopes on its submarines. It was resolved to let loose the new vessels and to proclaim unrestricted U-boat warfare at the beginning of February. The risk of war with America was faced and accepted. The rulers of Germany went to their doom with their eyes open. " If it is not trumps," said Helfferich, " Germany is lost for centuries." [3]

But meantime the President had taken another step, the prelude, perhaps, of great events that will for ever remain the embryos of time. On 27th January he informed the German Government, through Bernstorff, that he was ready to mediate on the basis of his address to the Senate, which was deliberately constructed as a reply to the " impossible terms " of the Allies. " Now we are also morally bound to

[1] Bernstorff, " My Three Years in America," p. 322.
[2] " Official German Documents relating to the World War," ii. 1321.
[3] *Ibid.*, i. p. 150.

make our peace terms known because our desire for peace would otherwise appear insincere. . . . President is of opinion that note sent to him by the Entente was a piece of bluff which need not be taken seriously."[1] He was convinced that if Germany had confidence in him he could bring about a peace conference. Bernstorff could see that the publication of moderate peace terms by Germany and whole-hearted support of the President would transform the diplomatic situation in Germany's favour. But he already had his instructions to announce, on 31st January 1917, the resumption of unrestricted submarine warfare. The Chancellor clutched at the chance like a drowning man at a straw, and on 29th January went back on his previous refusal to communicate Germany's terms by telegraphing them to Bernstorff for the President, but under the seal of confidence. The refusal to publish these terms, which still promised only the conditional restoration of Belgium, vitiated this attempt to accept the President's mediation. In any event it was now too late—or the Chancellor allowed himself to be persuaded that it was—to recall the U-boats that had already sailed for their destinations.

The die was cast, and on 31st January Bernstorff handed in the fatal memorandum announcing the abrogation of the "Sussex Pledge." The President accepted the challenge. On 3rd February he appeared before a joint meeting of both Houses of Congress, and announced the rupture of diplomatic relations with Germany. Bernstorff received his passports.

A brief period of neutrality followed during which the President ordered the arming of American merchant vessels. But it was not long before he realized that such action was in reality war in substance, if not in name. The sinkings continued, and on 2nd April 1917, in a great address to a joint session of Congress, he recommended, amid tremendous applause, a declaration of war against Germany, which was carried as a joint resolution on 6th April. The sword of the great Republic had been flung into the scales.

The President, who had fought with invincible pertinacity to keep and to secure peace, now accepted the full consequences of war. To the surprise of the world he recommended the immediate introduction of conscription throughout the vast territories of the United States. "It is a fearful thing," he said, "to lead this great peaceful people into war, into

[1] Bernstorff, "My Three Years in America," p. 319.

the most terrible and disastrous of all wars, civilization itself seeming to be in the balance. But the right is more precious than peace, and we shall fight for the things which we have always carried nearest our hearts—for democracy, for the right of those who submit to authority to have a voice in their own Governments, for the rights and liberties of small nations, for a universal dominion of right by such a concert of free peoples as shall bring peace and safety to all nations and make the world itself at last free. To such a task we can dedicate our lives and our fortunes, everything that we are and everything that we have, with the pride of those who know that the day has come when America is privileged to spend her blood and her might for the principles that gave her birth and happiness and the peace which she has treasured. God helping her, she can do no other." [1] The superb ending, when he flung in the face of "this natural foe to liberty" the immortal words of Martin Luther, was the triumph of an inspired scholarship. He passed from the White House to the Capitol to deliver his message, through wildly cheering crowds. His patience had won him the leadership of a united people, yet for a purpose that weighed like a nightmare on his spirit. "Think what it was they were applauding," he said on his return: "my message to-day was a message of death to our young men. How strange it seems to applaud that." [2] But having set his hands to the plough, he did not look back.

This is not the place to discuss the war effort of the United States. A few points may be noted. She started with the experience of the Allies to guide her, and for two years her lonely President had advocated "preparedness" and taken measures against that day that had now come. On 5th June 1917, under the operation of the Selective Service Act, 10,000,000 men were registered. No less than 32 camps, each for the accommodation of 40,000 men, were built in 90 days—an unparalleled feat of construction. A programme by which 90,000 men should be sent to Europe every month was arranged, but for some time the number was only 30,000, owing to transportation difficulties in France.

Though the President accepted the services of all, he resolutely refused to consider the proposal for a coalition. History could tell him of the troubles of Lincoln in this matter. Though he has been accused of partisanship, it is safe to assert

[1] Scott, "President Wilson's Foreign Policy," p. 287.
[2] Tumulty, "Woodrow Wilson as I know Him," p. 256.

that for over a year after the intervention of the United States he was the undisputed leader of the nation. Innumerable commissions, constructed on a non-party basis, directed the prodigious effort of America to aid the Allies, and though the usual signs—familiar to us—of waste and over-hasty improvisation, were not wanting, the enthusiasm of a great people made possible one of the most wonderful military feats of history. A few figures must suffice. By November 1917 143,918 men had been sent overseas. They were followed in the succeeding twelve months by 1,950,513, an average of 162,542 a month. In May 1918 245,951 were sent; in June, 278,760; in July, 307,182. "No such movement of troops ever took place before across 3000 miles of sea, followed by adequate equipment and supplies, and carried safely through extraordinary dangers of attack. . . . In all this movement only 758 men were lost by enemy attacks."[1] The centre of this mighty activity was the President. His interest and initiative were indefatigable. His was not the least influence that secured the unified command that finally carried the Allies to victory.

But throughout 1918 he came before the world in the series of wonderful speeches in which he sought to define the objects of the war, to rally the nations in defence of those principles he had never forgotten in peace or war. The war was to him the supreme opportunity for remoulding the world nearer to the heart's desire, and he clothed his lofty idealism in a language that lifted the cause of the Allies into a purer air. For those who could not share his vision he seemed a man advocating an unsatisfactory peace. In truth he was a man who had attained the rare balance of mind that enabled him to bend unflinchingly to the double task of beating Germany and at the same time keeping the elevated ideals, oft proclaimed by statesmen, constantly before their eyes and the eyes of the Allied nations, not only by the repetition of vague and abstract expressions, but by definitions of increasing clearness. On 8th January 1918 he delivered the famous address to a joint session of the two Houses of Congress on the conditions of peace, containing the Fourteen Points. The occasion was the revelation at Brest-Litovsk of the complete triumph, in the Central Empires, of militarism, naked and unashamed.

But the President was thinking not only of Germany and her satellites. Immediately after the American declaration

[1] Speech of President Wilson before Congress, 2nd December 1918.

of war in April 1917, Mr Balfour visited the United States at the head of a mission brilliantly successful in working out plans for the co-operation of America and her new Allies. In the course of his mission Mr Balfour revealed to the President the secret treaties into which the British Government had entered from time to time during the course of the war, with Russia, France, Italy, and other Powers. The revelation of the entanglements in which the Allies had enmeshed themselves, sometimes in pursuit of the worst and least defensible forms of economic imperialism, as in the agreements between France, Russia, and Great Britain for the partition of Anatolia, Arabia, Mesopotamia, and Palestine; sometimes compelled reluctantly to concede far-reaching claims to possible Allies whose aid was vital, as in the case of Italy and Roumania—produced a most painful effect on the President's mind. On 12th December 1917, in a conversation at the White House with ex-President Taft, he said, " there were divergences of purpose, . . . and there were features of the British policy in this war of which he heartily disapproved. The motives of the United States, the President continued, ' were unselfish, but the motives of Great Britain seemed to him to be of a less unselfish character.' Mr Wilson cited the treaty between Great Britain and Italy as a sample of British statesmanship which he regarded as proving this contention." [1]

Accordingly Point IX, in the speech of 8th January 1918, laid down as one of the requirements of a just peace that "a readjustment of the frontiers of Italy should be effected along clearly recognizable lines of nationality." To the world this seemed amiable and obvious enough, but in reality it cut, and was intended to cut, right across the secret Treaty of London of April 1915, whereby Italy not only marked out for herself a strategic frontier to the Brenner Pass, involving the annexation of non-Italian territories containing a population of 400,000 Austro-Germans, but obtained the recognition of the Allies for annexations in Dalmatia and the Adriatic islands of territories where the Italian element was not more than 3 per cent. of the population, if not less.

The speeches of 1918 were not so much the formulation *in vacuo* of the dreams of an idealist, as extraordinarily audacious attempts to break up the presuppositions of the European diplomatic world by transcending them. In his address to the joint session of the two Houses of Congress

[1] Hendrick, " The Life and Letters of Walter H. Page," ii. p. 347.

on 11th February 1918, he declared: "Peoples are not to be handed about from one sovereignty to another by an international Conference or an understanding between rivals and antagonists. National aspirations must be respected; peoples may now be dominated and governed only by their own consent. 'Self-determination' is not a mere phrase. It is an imperative principle of action which statesmen will henceforth ignore at their peril." [1] This enunciation of the principle of "self-determination" was in reality a revolutionary stroke. It foreshadowed the disruption of Austria-Hungary by forcing on a process already at work. The President had opened Pandora's box, and for better or worse had transformed the situation. If the Baron Sidney Sonnino, that fine flower of the old diplomacy, was to carry out his amputations of Austria-Hungary, it was imperative that the fabric of the Dual Monarchy should be kept in being. If the very limb he desired to amputate flew off and attached itself to another body, the task of Italian imperialism would become all but hopeless. In this way "self-determination" was indeed not "a mere phrase," it was rather one "simply loaded with dynamite." [2]

No more powerful or convincing examination of the revolutionary and destructive implications of "self-determination" has ever been penned than that by Mr Lansing, the American Secretary of State, who accompanied the President to Paris.[3] Moral ideas usually are revolutionary and destructive when put into practice. Phrases like "self-determination" and "government by the consent of the governed" indeed "traverse the world in thunders loud," but they transform and shatter the shells of outworn institutions and make possible new departures, new experiments, ultimately new conservatisms. A world case-hardened against the impact of liberal principles deserves, and will receive, no better fate than to be blown up by ideas, the limitations of which experience discovers, but which clear the ground for new assays.

At the beginning of October 1918, Germany virtually delivered herself bound into the hands of the Allies by her famous appeal to the President to secure her an Armistice. In a series of masterly dispatches he catechized the German

[1] Scott, "President Wilson's Foreign Policy," p. 368.
[2] Lansing, "The Peace Negotiations: A Personal Narrative," p. 87.
[3] Lansing, cap. vii.

Government as to their authority to represent the German people, their acceptance of the "Fourteen Points," and the terms indicated in his subsequent addresses of 1918; in a word, he made it plain that only a change of regime could save Germany from an unconditional surrender. Alone among Allied statesmen he publicly welcomed in a speech to Congress the inauguration of the German Republic, in other words he still believed in the principles he and others had ceaselessly enunciated.

In the very middle of his negotiations with Germany, Roosevelt publicly attacked the President for working for an "unsatisfactory peace." The Allies should demand unconditional surrender and march to Berlin. War fever by now was raging in the United States, and the speech was an accurate interpretation of the feelings of the nation with regard to what, diplomatically, was perhaps the President's greatest achievement, the continuous weakening and destruction of German *moral* in October 1918. Yet, throughout, he was in the closest touch with the Allies, and on behalf of the President, Colonel House, in the discussions over the terms of the Armistice, asked Marshal Foch the point-blank question: "Will you tell us, Marshal, purely from a military point of view, and without regard to any other condition, whether you would prefer the Germans to reject or sign the Armistice as outlined here?" The Marshal replied: "The only aim of war is to obtain results. If the Germans sign an Armistice now upon the general lines we have just determined, we shall have obtained the results we asked. Our aims being accomplished, no one has the right to shed another drop of blood." [1]

At the very moment when he was pressing Germany towards the Armistice and the Revolution, the President was faced by the approaching Congressional elections and the prospect of a Democratic defeat. Throughout the greater part of 1918 the Republicans had been restless under the party truce. Headed by Roosevelt, they thoroughly distrusted and disliked what they could make out of the President's speeches on war-aims. "When it comes to peace negotiations," said Roosevelt, "we should emphatically repudiate these famous Fourteen Points." [2] The unconditional surrender of the Central Powers and a march to Berlin seemed to express the views of most of them, and while ex-President Taft was a devoted

[1] Tumulty, "Woodrow Wilson as I know Him," p. 320.
[2] Creel, "The War, the World, and Wilson," p. 135.

worker for the cause of the League of Nations, constantly emphasized in President Wilson's speeches, a great body of Republican feeling were becoming increasingly anxious lest the President's policy should commit the United States in a manner against the whole tradition of her foreign policy, as embodied in the Monroe Doctrine and Washington's warning against "entangling alliances." So the Republican party, on this score alone, desired, by securing a majority in Congress, to control or check the President. But there were domestic issues. In the course of the campaign, Mr Hays, the Chairman of the Republicans, declared in a bitter speech that the President desired a Democratic Congress "to reconstruct in peace times the great industrial affairs of the nation . . . in unimpeded conformity with whatever Socialistic doctrines, whatever unlimited government ownership notions, whatever hazy whims may happen to possess him at the time, but first and above all with absolute commitment to free trade with all the world, thus giving to Germany out of hand the fruits of a victory greater than she could win by fighting a hundred years. A Republican Congress will never assent to that. Do you want a Congress that will? Germany does." [1]

As a result of his absorption in the conduct of the war, the President had inevitably neglected the fighting organization of the Democratic party. The Republican machine, on the other hand, was quite ready for an intensive campaign. In these circumstances the President issued, on 24th October 1914, his much-discussed "partisan appeal" to the nation to return a Democratic Congress at the November elections. A few quotations will indicate its nature: "My Fellow-countrymen, the Congressional elections are at hand. They occur in the most critical period our country has ever faced or is likely to face in our time. If you have approved of my leadership and wish me to continue to be your unembarrassed spokesman in affairs at home and abroad, I earnestly beg that you will express yourself unmistakably to that effect by returning a Democratic majority to both the Senate and the House of Representatives. . . . I have no thought of suggesting that any political party is paramount in matters of patriotism. I feel too deeply the sacrifices that have been made in this war by all our citizens, irrespective of party affiliations, to harbour such an idea. I mean only . . . that

[1] Quoted Creel, "The War, the World, and Wilson," p. 142.

the nation should give its undivided support to the Government under a unified leadership, and that a Republican Congress would divide the leadership. The leaders of the minority in the present Congress have unquestionably been pro-war, but they have been anti-administration. . . . This is no time either for divided counsels or for divided leadership. . . . The peoples of the Allied countries . . . would find it very difficult to believe that the voters of the United States had chosen to support their President by electing to the Congress a majority controlled by those who are not in fact in sympathy with the attitude and action of the administration. . . ." [1] In effect the President had asked for a vote of confidence in his administration. Such a request was by no means unparalleled. Lincoln, McKinley, and Roosevelt had all issued such appeals. Nor is there anything improper in such a course, since the President of the United States is not only the head of the State, but the effective head of the Government, in fact the sole executive. He is also the head of a party. Perhaps President Wilson's appeal was too blunt; at any rate, it was vociferously represented, both at home and abroad, as a deliberate attack on the patriotism of the Republican party. Mr Hays declared: "A more ungracious, more unjust, more wanton, more mendacious *accusation* was never made by the most reckless stump orator, much less by the President of the United States, for partisan purposes. It is an insult, not only to every loyal Republican in Congress, but to every loyal Republican in the land." Roosevelt declared the President had asked for a Congress made up exclusively of Democrats, and went on: "No man who is a Republican, and no man, whether a Republican or not, who puts loyalty to the people ahead of loyalty to the servants of the people, is to have a voice in determining the greatest questions ever brought before the nation." [2] The campaign was successful. The electors voted on the extraordinary question of the patriotism of the Republicans, and a Republican majority was returned both to the House of Representatives and to the Senate.

It was at this time that the President had reached the decision to go to Paris in person as the head of the American delegation to the forthcoming Peace Conference. He did so, in opposition to the considered advice of the Secretary of

[1] Tumulty, "Woodrow Wilson as I know Him," pp. 330-2.
[2] Quoted Creel, "The War, the World, and Wilson," pp. 142-3.

State, Lansing. In an interview with the President on 12th November, Lansing urged that if he remained aloof at Washington his already unrivalled authority would enable him to dominate the Conference far more completely than if he himself, in the exercise of his undoubted constitutional right, descended into the arena.[1] Six days later the President informed Lansing that it was his purpose to attend. The Secretary of State, in a note of the interview, wrote: "I am convinced that he is making one of the greatest mistakes of his career, and will imperil his reputation. I may be in error, and hope that I am, but I prophesy trouble in Paris and worse trouble here. I believe the President's place is here in America." The decision to go may have been unwise, it was certainly brave, for it is not difficult to rest on laurels already won; the things that matter are perilous, and achieved "not without dust and heat." But the recent elections and the temper of the Republican party dictated that an effort should be made to conciliate it by the inclusion of prominent Republicans on the Peace delegation. Ex-President Taft and Mr Elihu Root, both advocates of the idea of a League of Nations, seemed indicated by their sympathy with the President's ideals and their influence in the Republican party, and in the country generally.

One of the greatest mistakes of his career was made by the President when, not without careful thought, and owing probably to his lack of sympathy with Mr Root's political outlook and a slight distrust aroused in him by Mr Taft's attitude at the Congressional elections, he decided not to include these eminent Republicans on his Peace delegation.[2] Instead, he selected, in addition to Colonel House and Mr Lansing, a distinguished though not influential Republican, Mr White, a former ambassador to France and Italy, and General Tasker H. Bliss, a soldier of great ability and again without political significance. Neither of these names conveyed much to Europe, but, characteristically, the President seems to have decided that the real work of the Conference would be done by himself—with whom the ultimate responsibility lay—and the magnificent staff of experts, representative of the pick of American specialists, which he took with him.

Mr Roosevelt gave the President a magnificent send-off.

[1] Lansing, "The Peace Negotiations: a Personal Narrative," pp. 20-1.
[2] Creel, "The War, the World, and Wilson," p. 156.

On 27th November, five days before the United States delegation sailed for Europe, he sent off this message to Europe: "Our Allies and our enemies and Mr Wilson himself should all understand that Mr Wilson has no authority whatever to speak for the American people at this time. His leadership has just been emphatically repudiated by them. . . . Mr Wilson and his Fourteen Points and his four supplementary points and his five complementary points, and all his utterances every way have ceased to have any shadow of right to be accepted as expressive of the will of the American people. . . . America played in the closing months of the war a gallant part, but not in any way the leading part, and she played this part only by acting in strictest agreement with our Allies and under the joint high command . . . of the terrible sacrifice which has enabled the Allies to win the victory, America has contributed just about 2 per cent. It is our business to act with our Allies and to show an undivided front with them against any move of our late enemies. I am no Utopian. . . ."[1] Even if true, the words indicated the depth of bitterness with which the Republicans regarded the President. The spirit of faction was abroad.

The President himself, however much his own strange angularities of character and native silence and secretiveness in a land of intimate broadcasting prejudiced his success, was fully aware of the greatness of the problems that faced him at the end of his journey, and the razor's edge upon which the future seemed to balance tremulously.

"It is to America," he said in a conversation on the "George Washington" outward bound, "that the whole world turns to-day, not only with its wrongs, but with its hopes and grievances. The hungry expect us to feed them, the roofless look to us for shelter, the sick of heart and body depend upon us for cure. All of these expectations have in them the quality of terrible urgency. There must be no delay. It has been so always. People will endure their tyrants for years, but they tear their deliverers to pieces if a millennium is not created immediately. Yet you know, and I know, that these ancient wrongs, these present unhappinesses, are not to be remedied in a day or with a wave of the hand. What I seem to see—with all my heart I hope that I am wrong—is a tragedy of disappointment."[2]

[1] Quoted Creel, "The War, the World, and Wilson," p. 161.
[2] *Ibid.*, p. 163.

His reception in Europe was a veritable apotheosis. The very people who had extorted from Mr Lloyd George the pledges that were to hang like a millstone round his neck, and which he gave against his better judgment—the punishment of war criminals, the trial of the Kaiser, and the recovery from Germany of the whole cost of the war [1]—hailed the President with delirious enthusiasm. It is not necessary to postulate for those days a clear-cut contention between the passions that had dominated the British general election of 1918, or that held sway in a France bled white with war, and the idealism that looked for a new and better world; human muddle-headedness is sufficient. The victorious powers were suffering from a dangerous form of moral hysteria, "The atmosphere of the French capital and the language of the French press suggested to visitors the disquieting phenomena of shell-shock." [2] The moral hysteria consisted simply in the assumption that there could be no contradiction between the elevated moral precepts of the President and the most unblushing of predatory ambitions on the part of any of the Allies. Since the cause of the Allies was the cause of justice and truth, no sacrifices could be required in carrying out the splendid vision of the President. The attitude was sincere, and this it is that makes it almost certain that a "Wilson peace" was unrealizable in 1919. A compromise was inevitable, but the compromise seemed to imply a devastating denial of the principles which articulate European Liberalism had expected the President to vindicate.

He had come to Europe with no detailed plans for the future settlement, and with nothing worked out except the rough draft of the Covenant of the League of Nations. His lack of sympathy with Mr Lansing, due to the latter's caution with regard to the League, led him to refuse Mr Lansing's suggestion that he should prepare a draft treaty for the President's use, with the help of a committee of legal experts. Inevitably this lack of preparation forced the President to confine himself to the criticism and analysis of French and English drafts. His highly analytical and retentive mind enabled him to do so with great effect, but the very method of procedure involved a loss of initiative.

Mr Lansing has noted the President's courtesy in his dealings with his foreign colleagues, his patience and the

[1] His reservations were not noted at the time.
[2] Gooch, "History of Modern Europe, 1879-1919," p. 661.

marvellous self-control he maintained at moments when he was inwardly seething with anger at the revelations of selfishness precipitated by every crisis. The fact that there could be no question that he was working for a clean peace won him respect; his moderating influence again and again extricated the Conference from critical deadlocks, but this rôle was not what had been expected of him, and he rapidly lost the dominating position that had been his when he landed in Europe.

Long established characteristics of thought and methods of work now proved his greatest handicaps. His secretiveness and silence became more pronounced. He consulted the members of the American delegation and the experts singly and formed his own judgments alone. The peace commission often had to learn of the President's decisions from foreign delegations. There was no team-work as a consequence, and the whole burden fell on the President's shoulders. So inveterate were these habits that he seemed sometimes surprised to find that his delegation did not know his views on a given subject. To suggest that he formed his opinions *in vacuo*, however, is ridiculous. True to his methods he sought out the best possible advice, digested it and formed his own judgments. For over a year, under the direction of Colonel House, a brilliant gathering of scholars and experts had been formulating the information required for the consideration of all the major and most of the minor problems likely to confront the Conference. The President made the fullest possible use of their services. But inevitably he burdened himself with an overwhelming weight of work: "He worked longer hours, had more appointments, granted himself less recreation, than any other man high or low, at the Peace Conference." [1] These characteristics had been developed by his Presidency. Under the Constitution of the United States, the President is not a Prime Minister, a *primus inter pares* among his colleagues. His is the sole responsibility, he is the sole Executive, ministers are quite literally his clerks. No such popular magistracy exists elsewhere; the Presidency of the United States is an unique office.

The quality of reflectiveness, the desire never to act save on a clear issue, that had been his strength as President, became his weakness as negotiator. There seemed to be no clear issue at Paris. Work was done in a fog, but never-

[1] Baker, "What Wilson did at Paris."

theless swift decisions were imperative. In this way he sometimes conceded far more by way of compromise than he realized at the moment. Sometimes he chose to fight on the wrong ground, as in the famous Fiume crisis. Fiume was an Italian city, claimed by Italy on the principle of nationality, but at the same time she claimed Northern Dalmatia and the line of the Brenner Pass in direct and acknowledged defiance of that principle, and solely for strategic and sentimental reasons. Yet though he resisted her outrageous Dalmatian claims, the President did not make it the main issue of his quarrel, and he conceded the line of the Brenner Pass and the annexation of the whole of German South Tyrol. He saw that there must be exceptions to general rules, but what exceptions?

He and the Allies have been reproached for allowing the new Czecho-Slovak Republic to have the line of the Bohemian Alps, the historic frontier of the Bohemian plain, thereby involving the absorption of some 3,000,000 Germans—a population that constitutes a fringe at the foot of the mountains, or, to change the metaphor, has been spilled over from the German sea beyond the range. Deprive her of the mountain line and a glance at the map shows that the Czech Republic would become an impossibility without a single defensible frontier. As to the Tyrolese, how long had Italy been able to exist without them?

His dominating interest in the creation of the League of Nations led the President to sacrifice more than he afterwards felt was just, in his efforts to win its acceptance. The interested were not long in discovering that they might be able to secure a price for their adhesion. In the crisis over Shan-tung, Japan threatened to leave the Conference unless her claim to the succession to all German rights were conceded. The President felt that the agreement of Japan was essential to the League and he therefore gave way, contenting himself with a verbal assurance that the territory would be returned to China, and the economic privileges alone retained by Japan. But the Japanese point of view was written into the Treaty, and his critics in America did not fail to make use of this fact.

His firm stand in the crisis over the left bank of the Rhine, in the course of which he ordered the "George Washington" to Brest and made clear that he would leave the Conference if the French demand for the dismemberment of Germany were accepted, prevented the creation of another

Alsace-Lorraine. He afterwards felt he had conceded too much in granting a fifteen years' occupation by Allied forces, but the fact that British as well as French troops are in occupation seems likely to preclude the final separation of this region from Germany. Though he vigorously opposed it, he was less successful in precluding the ultimate annexation of the Saar coal region to France. Time alone can reveal whether his safeguards were adequate. Since all agreed that France was entitled to have the Saar coal until her own ruined mines were restored, the compromise provided that Saar should be governed by a special Administration of five members—three appointed by the League of Nations, one by the inhabitants and one by France. At the end of fifteen years a plebiscite will be held to decide whether the region shall be annexed to France or returned to Germany.

"President Wilson's place in history will be determined by the success or the failure of the Covenant." [1] His greatest triumph, apart from the form and structure of "the most hopeful and ambitious experiment in the story of human organization," [2] was his successful struggle to secure the inclusion of the Covenant as an integral part of the treaties which make up the settlement, and to centre the actual working out of the settlement to a great extent in the League.

On 25th January 1919, at the second plenary meeting of the Conference, on the motion of the President, it was resolved to incorporate the League in the settlement. During his absence in America on the flying visit he paid in the early days of March, a strong movement developed to draft all the main terms of the settlement in a preliminary treaty, reserving the final clearing up of details and the Covenant for later consideration. The President regarded this as an attempt to side-track the League, and, supported by Lord Robert Cecil and M. Venizelos, he made clear that he would tolerate no deviation from the terms of the resolution of 25th January 1919.[3] The danger was pressing: "So many vested interests were challenged by the League and so many new forces had been liberated in Europe which were antagonistic to it, that unless it had been made part of the peace it might have been postponed for a generation. The recognition that the problems raised at Paris can only be solved by a

[1] Gooch, "History of Modern Europe, 1878-1919," p. 677.
[2] *Ibid.*, p. 675.
[3] Baker, "Woodrow Wilson and World Settlement," i. p. 311.

permanent international organization is perhaps the greatest result of the Conference." [1]

When he returned to the United States, he had compromised on many things including Reparations. He had allowed his colleagues to avoid breaking their election promises by leaving the exact extent of the Allied claims unsettled. As Clemenceau observed: " Whatever sum the experts might name, it would still fall short of French expectation ; and Mr Lloyd George added that he too would fall if a sum were fixed." [2] The painful results of leaving undefined what was, at the same time, a first charge on the German budget have been unfolded in the years of confusion after the Treaty.[3] Again and again the President had, in the course of the Conference, been faced with the question whether he should break up the Conference or compromise. Since he believed not only in the League to which he looked to rectify the mistakes of the settlement, but also in the pressing necessity of providing Europe with some sort of bony framework before the tottering fabric collapsed, perhaps in Bolshevism, he had elected to compromise. To reproach him without facing his problems or those of his fellow-negotiators, is like reproaching a captain who has saved his vessel by jettisoning more of his cargo than it pleased his owners to lose. Perhaps if he had been more agile ; more willing to sup with the Devil by providing himself with the latest in long spoons ; given way on some points that he fought; fought some decisions that he conceded, the Treaty would have been more satisfactory. But, in any event, passion and prejudice must have left their thumb marks on its pages. The Treaty is a perfect reflection of the human spirit; where there has been failure it has been, as General Smuts has told us, not the shortcoming of a man but " the failure of the human spirit " ; it also carries within it the promise that the forces of life will ultimately triumph through the League over the forces of destruction, in the elevation of the rule of law over every human relationship.

On 11th July 1919, immediately after his return from Paris, where the Peace with Germany had been signed on 28th June, the President presented the Treaty to the Senate,

[1] Temperley, " History of the Peace Conference," i. pp. 276-7.

[2] Gooch, " History of Modern Europe, 1878-1919," p. 682.

[3] £1000 million to be paid within two years, by which time a scheme of payments extending over thirty years was to be prepared by the Reparations Commission.

and placed himself at the disposal of the Foreign Relations Committee; and the second phase of the battle for the settlement began. As early as the previous March, opposition to the President's policy showed itself in the "round robin" of thirty-seven Republican senators declaring hostility to the idea of a League of Nations in any form, Senator Borah declaring picturesquely that he would fight it, even though advocated by the "Saviour of Mankind" himself.[1] More than 160 reservations were offered to the Treaty from first to last, but ultimately the issues were narrowed to an attack on the League alone.

Senator Lodge unerringly singled out Article X. for the principal attack. The offending article ran: "The members of the League undertake to respect and preserve as against external aggression the territorial integrity and existing political independence of all members of the League. In case of any such aggression, or in case of any threat or danger of such aggression, the Council shall advise upon the means by which this obligation shall be fulfilled." The President, in his conferences with the Committee on Foreign Relations, showed no objection whatever to "interpretative reservations," declaring that Congress alone can declare war or determine the causes or occasions for war. As a result of a memorandum from Mr Taft the President, while at the Conference, had secured that the voting on the Council to be effective should be unanimous, in order to safeguard the United States from any possible combination of powers; explicit provisions for withdrawal from the League after due notice; formal reservation of domestic questions and the Monroe Doctrine. But the Lodge resolution was so worded as to amount to a repudiation of the obligation which the League had been called into being to vindicate. In its final form it ran: "The United States assumes no obligation to employ its military or naval forces, its resources, or any form of economic discrimination to preserve the territorial integrity, or political independence, of any other country, or to interfere in controversies between nations, whether members of the League or not, under the provisions of Article X., or to employ the military or naval forces of the United States under any article of the Peace Treaty for any purpose unless, in any particular case, Congress in the exercise of its full liberty of action, shall, by a joint resolution, so

[1] Creel, "The War, the World, and Wilson," p. 329.

provide."[1] The reservation amounted to the repudiation of any obligation whatever arising from the Treaty. The issues had certainly been clearly set. In his letter of 8th March 1920 the President re-stated them: "Any reservation which seeks to deprive the League of Nations of the force of Article X. cuts at the very heart and life of the Covenant itself. Any League of Nations which does not guarantee as a matter of incontestable right the political independence and integrity of each of its members might be hardly more than a futile scrap of paper. . . ."[2]

Another highly popular reservation was aimed at the inclusion in the League of the Self-Governing Dominions of the British Empire. It provided that the United States would assume no obligations until it also should be entitled to cast an equal number of votes. For the purposes of controversy with the President, the Republicans calmly assumed that the British Empire was a single member of the League, which, for some sinister reason, had been given six votes. The central control of that loose confederation was taken for granted. Apart from gratuitously offending the neighbouring State, Canada, this reservation was the product of ignorance, or else of deliberate blindness, since the Dominions sit only in the League Assembly for the purposes of discussion with all other member States. Executive action is wholly in the hands of the League Council, consisting of Great Powers equally represented, and one or more representatives of the smaller powers elected by the Assembly and approved by the Council. When it comes to action, to the carrying out of policy, in short, to deeds rather than words, the United States, if a member of the League, would find itself on a footing of perfect equality with the Great Powers who control the Council. However, the fact that the British Empire, that misleading personification, had six votes, was a useful weapon in the hands of tacticians angling for the support of those who enjoy seeing the lion's tail twisted.

The Senate gave itself up to a perfect orgy of partisanship. It constituted itself the Mecca of "oppressed nationalities," and received deputations from dissentient Arabs, Indians, Irish, and Egyptians. What it proposed to do for these plaintiffs is obscure. In the end the injustices of the Treaty passed without comment; the League was the rag of

[1] "Annual Register, 1920," p. 290.
[2] Creel, "The War, the World, and Wilson," p. 344.

Antichrist which monopolized the attention of the august body that received deputations from "oppressed nationalities," but in June 1920 formally refused the mandate for Armenia.

The cloud of reservations, the atmosphere of embittered controversy generated by the Republican campaign, convinced the Democrats in Congress that only an appeal to the people by the President himself could clear the air. He inclined to the suggestion with the more willingness that it harmonized with his conceptions of Executive leadership. At New Jersey he had, as Governor, appealed to the people against the party bosses; as President, in 1913, he had turned the flank of the vested interests in the Senate opposing the Tariff Bill by similar democratic action. He realized the vital issues at stake, and resolved to shoulder the terrible strain of a Midlothian Campaign through the States from East to West and back. Yet already he was beginning to show traces of an immense fatigue; at Paris he had been prostrated by an attack of influenza, from which he had never really recovered. Admiral Grayson, his physician, vehemently opposed the plan, and privately intimated that the President's life might be at stake. One day, after a visit from Democratic Senators urging a "swing round the circle," his Secretary urged him to give up the idea, in view of the obvious exhaustion from which he was suffering. "I know that I am at the end of my tether," he replied, "but my friends on the Hill say that the trip is necessary to save the Treaty, and I am willing to make whatever personal sacrifice is required, for if the Treaty should be defeated, God only knows what would happen to the world as a result of it. In the presence of the great tragedy which now faces the world, no decent man can count his own personal fortunes in the reckoning. Even though, in my condition, it might mean the giving up of my life, I will gladly make the sacrifice to save the Treaty." [1]

At the beginning of September 1919 he set out for the West with a speech at Columbus, Ohio. As his special train progressed farther and farther to the West, it became apparent that the President was making an impression. After he had reached San Francisco and turned east again, so encouraged was he at the progress made, that he resolved to invade the enemy's country on his return and carry his great campaign into the New England States. Day after day the train stopped at towns and cities by the way, and the President would make

[1] Tumulty, "Woodrow Wilson as I know Him," p. 435.

a long speech prepared late the night before, sometimes not prepared at all, passionately defending the Treaty and the League, and commending it to his fellow-countrymen with all his old eloquence and moral fire, with all the fine lucidity of thought that has given so many of his utterances a classic distinction. Yet throughout the whole journey he was struggling against illness and losing ground. Daily he was prostrated by terrible headaches, but he never allowed them to prevent him from keeping a single engagement. His face became lined and haggard, and he appeared to grow older by years with the passing of each day. His devoted wife, who accompanied him, has described the pilgrimage as "one long nightmare." The climax came after he had reached the coast and was returning eastward. On 25th September he delivered a great speech at Pueblo. The effect upon his audience was prodigious. "What of our pledges to the men that lie dead in France? We said that they went over there not to prove the prowess of America or her readiness for another war, but to see to it that there never was such a war again. It always seems to make it difficult for me to say anything, my fellow-citizens, when I think of my clients in this case. My clients are the children; my clients are the next generation. They do not know what promises and bonds I undertook when I ordered the armies of the United States to the soil of France, but I know, and I intend to redeem my pledges to the children: they shall not be sent upon a similar errand. . . . My friends, on last Decoration Day, I went to a beautiful hillside near Paris, where was located the cemetery of Suresnes, a cemetery given over to the burial of the American dead. Behind me on the slopes was rank upon rank of living American soldiers, and lying before me on the levels of the plain was rank upon rank of departed American soldiers. . . . I wish some men in public life who are now opposing the settlement for which these men died could visit such a spot as that. I wish the thought that comes out of those graves could penetrate their consciousness. I wish that they could feel the moral obligation that rests upon us not to go back on those boys, but to see the thing through—to see it through to the end and make good their redemption of the world. For nothing less depends upon this decision, nothing less than the liberation and salvation of the world. . . ."[1] But this was the last effort and the last speech. In the early hours

[1] Quoted Tumulty, "Woodrow Wilson as I know Him," pp. 449-51.

of the following day he was taken seriously ill. He was found sitting at his desk, pale, almost speechless. Dr Grayson ordered the immediate cancellation of the campaign. In a suffocated voice the President pleaded for a little delay: " Don't you see that if you cancel this trip, Senator Lodge and his friends will say that I am a quitter, and that the Western trip was a failure, and the Treaty will be lost ? " He tried to rise to emphasize his argument, but his left arm and leg refused to move. He was paralysed.[1] He was taken back to the White House a helpless invalid.

From that moment the tide, that for a moment his almost superhuman effort had stemmed, turned against the Treaty and the League. Three forces were contending in the Senate, the moderate Republicans who desired to ratify the Treaty with the Lodge reservations, the Democrats who refused to accept the reservation on Article 10, and the extremist Republicans who desired the defeat of the League in any shape or form. By March 1920 the Treaty was finally shelved. All this time the invalid in the White House watched the ebb and flow of the conflict with absorbed attention. Day after day he was wheeled in a chair to the offices of his secretary to hear reports on the situation. He could still write messages with all his old fire and clarity and compelling power, but nothing he could do now could avert disaster to the cause for which he had given his last ounce of strength. On the day that he knew defeat was certain, he looked better, and his secretary remarked on it. " I am very well," he replied, " for a man who awaits disaster." When he received formal intimation of the defeat of the Treaty his only comment was: " They have shamed us in the eyes of the world." The Treaty had lapsed because the Republicans failed to carry their reservations with the necessary two-thirds majority, and the attempt to carry it without reservations was defeated.

From this moment the political career of Woodrow Wilson ends, and though he remained President for another year, and continued to exercise influence far from negligible until his death in January 1924, here perhaps is the best point at which to look back for a moment over his great career.

In casting about for some historical figure the incidents of whose career would illuminate by a comparison the life of Woodrow Wilson, it is not long before the mind swings to the commanding personality of Gladstone. With all

[1] Tumulty, " Woodrow Wilson as I know Him," p. 447.

differences fully admitted, it would not be straining a resemblance too far to call Wilson the Gladstone of America—a Gladstone perhaps without that baffling subtlety of mind that confounded enemies less sincere than himself, yet retaining sufficient of the enigmatic to make his character the theme of continual speculation.

The Presidential campaign of 1912, during which Wilson delivered the fighting speeches which proclaimed the great reforms he was to carry during his first term of office, was the prelude to a legislative achievement as distinguished as that of Gladstone's first ministry. The fiery ardour of his passion for reform, the moral elevation of his speeches, the conviction he felt and induced that he was about the nation's business, called to the task of setting free the national spirit by giving it a voice and translating its dearest aspirations—these qualities are those of the great English Liberal.

The Liberalism of Wilson, though individualistic in tone, cannot be called of the nineteenth century. For Wilson freedom, at one moment, was the absence of friction in the body politic, the smooth working of the individual organs. In this he seems to incline to modern Socialism. At another moment he proclaims with emphasis the duty of the State in subserving the free development of the individual citizen by protecting him from every form of exploitation, however productive, every pressure of social organizations that cramp instead of serving him. He felt that if he could rid politics of the sinister interests, by the mere fact that he had secured a voice and political authority for the ordinary citizen, he would have secured also that a healthy public opinion would prevent the renewed development of over-mighty services. In reading his speeches a certain wideness and lack of definition is sometimes noticeable—the descrying of far horizons and cloud-capped pinnacles is the prerogative of a prophet. But in his legislative achievement, his enemies found enough that was definite of which to complain. Because he believed with a religious intensity in certain wide-embracing ideas of Liberty, Justice, Democracy, he expounded them in the exalted utterances which a French critic has called not speeches but hymns. From them one gains those abiding impressions of moral energy which can be experienced but not analysed. Those who did not respond to the impact of moral ideas felt that he was a dexterous juggler with abstractions. A political realist who believes that men can count their blessings as they count their coins is not likely to regard an aspiration as an asset. Yet because the great President gave a vision and a hope to the cause he had espoused with such matchless energy, the immortal speeches of 1918 must be regarded as not the least of the forces making for the crowning mercy. And the vision which they gave, though it faded, did not wholly pass away.

His Liberalism led him to sympathize deeply with the national movements that achieved their signal triumph at the Peace Conference and were consecrated in the treaties. Yet neither he nor the Allies did more than recognize the fact that an earthquake had altered the configuration of Europe. It is the territorial settlement of Paris that immeasurably surpasses in importance the economic simply because it embodies the clear recognition of fundamental facts. A cheap phrase, " the Balkanization of Europe," has gone the rounds of the world since the settlement. It enshrines in an epigram the discontent and the ignorance of those who cannot believe that a new thing can be good. If a railing accusation is to be brought, let it be brought not against President Wilson and the Allies for " Balkanizing " Europe, but against Mazzini, whose prophetic work they ratified because it extorted ratification. The great prophet of nationalism had asserted the brotherhood as well as the individuality of nations, the duties as well as the rights of man, and in the mere existence of the League of Nations is the promise of his completed work.

Because the President realized with an overwhelming vividness that the problem of world-government is the supreme problem of problems that confronts mankind with grim insistence, the Sphinx's riddle which must be answered if the forces of life are to defeat the forces of destruction; because he subordinated everything to the creation of the League, he has been accused of sacrificing the peace of the world, of whose problems he was ignorant and careless, to the realization of an impossible ideal.

He was not ignorant, he merely realized that in the problems of life some things are more important than others, and because of the cause for which he elected to fight and fall " he will be recognized as one of the world's great pioneers. . . ."

The successful candidate for the Presidency in 1920, Senator Harding, on accepting nomination as the Republican candidate, declared: " The resumption of the Senate's authority saved our Republic and its independent nationality when autocracy misinterpreted the dream of a world-experiment to be the vision of a world-ideal. The Republican Senate halted at the barter of independent American eminence and influence, which it was proposed to exchange for an obscure and unequal place in the merged government of the world. Our party means to hold the heritage of American nationality unimpaired and unsurrendered." [1] The lucidity of thought characteristic of the Republican opposition can best be experienced through a perusal of this and other utterances of President Harding. He was to succeed one who had always loved light, the white light of reason; one also who could pack passion and thought in epigram, and had never yet sacrificed truth to insignificant speech.

At the November election the Republicans swept the field. Senator Harding was elected President by 404 votes in the Electoral College to 127 cast for Mr Cox, the Democratic candidate. At the simultaneous elections to the House of Representatives the Republicans returned 293 strong against 138 Democrats.

March 4th, 1921, came at last, and President Wilson drove from the White House to the Capitol with the President-elect, according to the custom of that solemn ceremony of Inauguration, when the Chief Magistrate of the Great Republic appears before the people. "From the physical appearance of the two men seated beside each other in the automobile, it was plain to the casual observer who was the outgoing and who the incoming President. In the right sat President Wilson, grey, haggard, broken. He interpreted the cheering from the crowds that lined the Avenue as belonging to the President-elect, and looked straight ahead. On the left, Warren Gamaliel Harding, the rising star of the Republic, healthy, vigorous, great-chested, showing every evidence in his tanned face of that fine sturdy health so necessary a possession in order to grapple with the problems of his country." [2] There were a few documents to sign, and the President signed them. Senators and Congressmen came to the President's room to say good-bye and hasten on to meet the President-elect. The broken figure sitting at that table was still President of the United States, possessor, "for a little while longer . . . of more power than any king in

[1] "Annual Register," 1920, p. 293.
[2] Tumulty, "Woodrow Wilson as I know Him," p. 508.

Christendom." Senator Lodge, at the head of a small group of Senators, appeared. "Mr President," he said, "we have come as a Committee of the Senate to notify you that the Senate and House are about to adjourn and await your pleasure." The solitary and haggard figure at the table contemplated the most implacable of his enemies for a moment, then a faint smile flickered over his face and he replied: "Senator Lodge, I have no further communication to make. I thank you. Good morning." He sat on in silence until the clock standing in the corner of the room struck twelve. When it had finished striking he lifted himself to his feet and slowly, without aid, and leaning heavily on his stick, which tapped sharply on the stone pavement, he made his way out. A burst of cheering and a distant band announced, to the tune of "Hail our Chief," that the new President had appeared on the east front of the Capitol. He had begun his inaugural address before the lonely figure, from whose eyes yet looked a proud unconquerable spirit, had begun to climb laboriously into the waiting car.

From the address of President Harding it appeared that though a great idealist had been defeated, yet idealism had not perished from the land. "I would rejoice," he said, "to acclaim the era of the Golden Rule and crown it with the autocracy of service." [1]

A LIST OF AUTHORITIES

BAKER. "Woodrow Wilson and World Settlement," 3 vols. (Heinemann, 1923.)
BERNSTORFF. "My Three Years in America." (Skeffington, 1920.)
BROOKS. "Woodrow Wilson as President." (Chicago and New York, 1916.)
CREEL. "The War, the World, and Wilson." (Harper Bros., 1920.)
*DANIELS. "The Life of Woodrow Wilson." (Allen & Unwin, 1924.)
DODD. "Woodrow Wilson and his Work." (New York, 1920.)
EATON AND READ. "Woodrow Wilson: His Life and Work." (U.S.A., 1919.)
FORD. "Woodrow Wilson: The Man and his Work." (D. Appleton, 1916.)
GOOCH. "History of Modern Europe, 1878-1919." (Cassell, 1923.)
HALE. "Woodrow Wilson: The Story of his Life." (Grant Richards, 1912.)
HALÉVY. "President Wilson." (John Lane, 1919.)
HARRIS. "President Wilson: His Problems and his Policy." (Headley Bros., 1918.)

[1] "Annual Register," 1921, p. 302.

THREE BUILDERS AND ANOTHER

HENDRICK. "The Life and Letters of Walter H. Page," 2 vols. (Heinemann, 1922.)

LANSING. "The Peace Negotiations: a Personal Narrative." (Constable, 1921.)

LANSING. "The Big Four and others of the Peace Conference." (Hutchinson, 1922.)

*LAWRENCE. "The True Story of Woodrow Wilson." (Hurst & Blackett, 1924.)

LOW. "Woodrow Wilson: An Interpretation." (Boston, U.S.A., 1918.)

TUMULTY. "Woodrow Wilson as I know Him." (Heinemann, 1922.)

SCOTT (Editor). "President Wilson's Foreign Policy." (New York, 1918.)

SMITH (A. D. Howden Smith). "The Real Colonel House." (Hodder & Stoughton, 1918.)

YOUNG. "The Wilson Administration and the Great War." (Boston, 1922.)

"Official German Documents relating to the World War. Translated under the Supervision of the Carnegie Endowment for International Peace, Division of International Law," 2 vols. (New York: Oxford University Press, American Branch, 1923.) Containing "The Reports of the First and Second Sub-Committees of the Committee appointed by the National Constituent Assembly to enquire into the Responsibility for the War, together with the Stenographic Minutes of the Second Sub-Committee and Supplements thereto."

"President Wilson's Policy." Handbooks prepared under the Direction of the Historical Section of the Foreign Office, No. 161. (H.M. Stationery Office, 1920.)

* Inserted for reference. I regret this was published too late to influence the foregoing essay.

INDEX